PLAY

THIRD EDITION

Therapy

PLAY

THIRD EDITION

Therapy

The Art of the Relationship

Garry L. Landreth

Routledge
Taylor & Francis Group
New York   London

Routledge
Taylor & Francis Group
711 Third Avenue
New York, NY 10017

Routledge
Taylor & Francis Group
27 Church Road
Hove, East Sussex BN3 2FA

Printed in the United States of America on acid-free paper
Version Date: 20111017

International Standard Book Number: 978-0-415-88681-9 (Hardback)

Library of Congress Cataloging-in-Publication Data

Landreth, Garry L.
  Play therapy : the art of the relationship / Garry Landreth. -- 3rd ed.
    p. cm.
  Includes bibliographical references and index.
  ISBN 978-0-415-88681-9 (hardback)
  1. Play therapy. I. Title.

RJ505.P6L26 2012
618.92891653--dc23   2011038057

Visit the Taylor & Francis Web site at
http://www.taylorandfrancis.com

and the Routledge Web site at
http://www.routledgementalhealth.com

The most important task God can give
is the opportunity to be a parent.
This book is dedicated to my wife Monica
for sharing the process with me
and to Kimberly, Karla, and Craig
for the satisfaction gained from being a father.
Being a parent and the opportunity to be a grandparent
to Kara, Kristen, Travis, Julia, Ali, and Jolie
are much more important than writing a book.

Contents

Preface

My struggle in writing this book is that I cannot possibly communicate what I know, believe, and have experienced about the dynamic world of children through such an inadequate means as a few words written on a few pages of unresponsive paper. Feelings and experiences cannot be conveyed adequately through the medium of the written word, yet that is the structure I am restricted to using in this part of my effort to impact the way adults interact with children. Trying to communicate what I believe about children and have experienced to be true in my heart is an awesome task. Will I be able to make contact with the reader? Will I be understood? Will my excitement for children be felt? Will the reader see children any differently? Will the dynamics and characteristics of the child's world be better understood? Will what I write make any difference in how the reader approaches and interacts with children? At this point, it is probably obvious that I ventured forth in this process with some apprehension.

Perhaps I should state first that I have experienced play therapy to be a dynamic approach to counseling with children that allows the therapist to fully experience the child's world as the therapist ventures forth in the process of presenting the person he or she is and opening the self to receive the delicate and subtle messages communicated by the child, which declare the uniqueness of the child's personality. The process of play is viewed as the child's effort to gain control in the environment. The problems children experience do not exist apart from the persons they are. Therefore, play therapy matches the dynamic inner structure of the child with an equally dynamic approach.

The emerging growth in the number of mental health profession-als who use play therapy in their efforts to be helpful to children underscores the increased societal awareness and acceptance of the significance of the stage of development referred to as childhood. Our society may well be on the threshold of recognizing children as people, not as playthings, not as impersonal objects, not as sources of frustration to be tolerated until they mature, but as real people who possess unlimited potential and creative resources for growing, coping, and developing.

Children are quite capable of teaching adults about themselves if adults are willing, patient, and open to learning. Children are real people, not simply appendages of those adults around them. They have feelings and reactions independent of their parents' reactions. The assumption of nervous mother, nervous child does not hold true. Can we assume that if the house is blown up and mother remains calm, the child will not be affected? No. Children are personalities in their own right and experience feelings and reactions independent of significant adults in their lives.

This book is about significant learnings from children as they have taught me about themselves and their world. Children are much more than I have been able to describe in these pages. Likewise, the relationships and experiences referred to as play therapy are infi-nitely more complex than this book portrays. The process of relating to a child who is experiencing permission to be himself or herself is indescribable and can only be known in the actual shared moments of the relationship together. My intent has been to open the door to the child's world of being: experiencing, exploring, appreciating, and creating a world of wonder, excitement, joy, sadness, and the vivid colors of life.

This third edition contains numerous editorial revisions, expanded explanations of procedures, and new material. When I proofread the final copy of this third edition, I was impacted by how much more user friendly this third edition is. The chapter on child-centered play therapy has been extensively rewritten in a way to make the theory and philosophy of the approach much more understandable and personally applicable. The chapters on beginning the play therapy relationship, characteristics of facilitative relationships, and parents as partners in play therapy have been extensively rewritten and expanded.

In view of the rapidly developing interest in short-term play therapy, which has been driven largely by managed care procedures, research findings on intensive and short-term play therapy have been expanded to include the most recent research. The effectiveness of reducing the time between play therapy sessions has been researched in the Center for Play Therapy and provides impressive support for using a time-limited model that collapses the time between sessions.

Sections have been added on ethical and legal issues in play therapy, reading play themes in play therapy, the multicultural approach of child-centered play therapy, and supervision of play therapy. Current developments and trends in the field of play therapy have been included and set in place in the context of the dynamic growth process of the field. A chapter has been added to this third edition summarizing the most recent controlled-outcome research studies, including meta-analytic studies, demonstrating the effectiveness of child-centered play therapy across cultural groups and with a wide variety of problematic behaviors.

Response to the Rules of Thumb in the first two editions was enthusiastic; so I have doubled the number of Rules of Thumb clarifying the play therapy relationship in this third edition. I have retained in this third edition an exploration of topics and issues my graduate students have indicated were important in their learning about the process of play therapy and the dynamics of the relationship with children. Therefore, some of the essential topics included in this book are as follows:

- The meaning of play in children's lives and the stages of play in the therapeutic process with adjusted and maladjusted children
- Reading play themes in play therapy
- Unique aspects, key concepts, and objectives of the child-centered philosophy and theory of the play therapy therapeutic relationship
- The multicultural approach of child-centered play therapy
- What children learn in the play therapy process
- The person of the play therapist, necessary personality characteristics, and the role of the play therapist in the therapeutic experience

- Characteristics of facilitative responses, with specific guidelines on how to help children assume self-responsibility
- Detailed guidelines for organizing a playroom and recommended toys and materials
- Specific suggestions on relating to parents and how to explain play therapy
- Making contact with the reluctant/anxious child and structuring the therapeutic experience in the playroom
- How children view the play therapy experience
- When to set limits, steps in therapeutic limit setting, and what to do when limits are broken
- Typical problems that occur in the playroom and suggestions on how to respond
- An examination of issues in play therapy, such as participating in the child's play, accepting gifts, and who cleans up
- Transcripts and discussions of children in play therapy: a dying child, an acting-out child, a manipulative child, an elective mute child, and a child who had pulled all her hair out
- Short-term and intensive play therapy
- Guidelines for determining therapeutic progress in play therapy and termination procedures
- Reading themes in play therapy
- A review of controlled-outcome research studies in child-centered play therapy

Some of this book is about me, my experiences, my reactions, and my feelings. Therefore, I have tried to convey my personal reactions by using the personal pronoun I. Using the customary phrase "the author" just did not convey the personal dimensions I wanted to communicate.

Acknowledgments

The writing and completion of the first edition of this book was made possible by the loving support and encouragement of the most important people in my life, my wife and three children, who did a wonderful job of shielding me from distractions. My wife, Monica, shared a major burden by typing and having me rewrite sections that were perfectly clear to me but to no one else! A special fatherly appreciation to my three children: Kimberly, for her patient understanding when she came home for vacation and found that her bedroom had been taken over by an office computer, three tables, and stacks of books; Karla, for her exuberance about Dad writing another book; and Craig, for his expressed sensitivity by bringing me snacks late at night when I was tired.

The excitement of my graduate students in discovering the freeing and growth-promoting dimensions of the play therapy process continues to be stimulating and rewarding and was a significant factor, along with the persistent encouragement of my publisher, in initiating the process of writing a third edition of this book. I am grateful that so many people found the first two editions of this book helpful. It has been especially rewarding to hear from people who have read the international translations.

The photographs in this book are of volunteers, not of clients. I am especially grateful to the children and their parents for their cooperation. Acknowledgment and appreciation are extended to editors of journals for permission to reproduce all or parts of my articles, which initially appeared under the titles listed: "Who Is This Person They Call a Counselor Who Has a Playroom?" (1982) *The School Counselor*, *29*, 359–361 (reprinted by permission of the American Association for

Counseling and Development); "The Uniqueness of the Play Therapist in a Child's Life" (1982) *Texas Personnel and Guidance Association Journal, 10,* 77–81; and "Play Therapy: Facilitative Use of Child's Play in Elementary School Counseling" (1987) *Elementary School Guidance and Counseling Journal, 21,* 253–261 (reprinted by permission of the American Association for Counseling and Development).

Chapter 1

About Me, Garry Landreth

I have always felt that knowing the author, or at least knowing something about the author, helped me to more clearly understand what the author was trying to communicate. Therefore, I want to let you know something about me. Perhaps this will help you better understand the meaning of what I write, even though my words may not adequately convey the message. Printed words on a page are at best an inadequate method for communicating something important—and what could be more important than talking about children and their world? I experience a very real feeling of apprehension and inadequacy when I think about trying to convey through this medium what I have experienced with children, my feelings for children, my belief in children, my hopes for children, and the significance of this process we call play therapy in the lives of children. Perhaps that is why I appreciate so much the opportunities I have to be with children in play therapy relationships, for there we are not limited to words to communicate.

As a child I was scrawny and underdeveloped and attended a one-room, all eight grades, rural elementary school taught by my mother. In that setting, I developed a genuine appreciation for simple things, a propensity to strive, a love for learning, and a sensitivity for the underdog, the person who does not get noticed. Because of those experiences, I am keenly aware of children who do not get noticed.

I have not always been comfortable with children, as I suspect many of you who read this text have been, and that I regret, for I did not know experientially, emotionally the world of children. Oh, I knew intellectually from books and a university undergraduate course in child development, but I only knew *about* children. I did not *know* children with my heart in a way that touched them and their world. Children were there. I noticed them, but it simply did not occur to me to try to establish communication with them. The child in me had long before been pushed into the background out of my need to be appreciated for being mature, an adult. Being adult for me meant being serious about life, being responsible. I know now that was partially an attempt to overcome some feelings of inadequacy and the fact that, throughout my undergraduate years and my first year as a 21-year-old high school teacher, I looked much younger than my chronological age; in fact, I was often mistaken for one of the high school students.

After 4 years of teaching, a master's degree, and 2 years as a high school counselor, I gained my first glimpse into the child's world as a doctoral graduate assistant in the Children's Center on the University of New Mexico campus. There, a sensitive and perceptive professor, who saw in me qualities to which I was oblivious, encouraged me to work with children and introduced me to the exciting, multifaceted dimensions of play therapy through which I began to slowly discover and experience the unfolding of the child's world.

Is it possible to truly describe the discovery of a life-changing dimension in one's life? If so, then the experience must have been rather small or insignificant, or both, for most words are small and insignificant. At this moment, I sit here wanting to convey the genuine pleasure of making contact with children and how that added a new depth dimension to my life, and I must admit that I am unable to do so. How does one describe children's wonder, excitement in experiencing life, the fresh newness with which they approach living, and their incredible resiliency? I feel inept; my mind has suddenly come to a screeching halt. It is no longer active. All the circuits are open and searching. No words come to describe that experience, although I know the feeling well.

Life cannot be described; it can only be experienced and appreciated. Descriptions can always be evaluated, but life cannot. Life is. It unfolds and is in totality at that moment, no more and no less. We do not look at a person and judge or evaluate that person to have too little of life or too much. Indeed, one of my important discoveries was that little children seldom, if ever, evaluate the lives of other little children. They interact with each other and accept the other person as enough. In those early years of my professional development, experiencing the unconditional acceptance of children was a profound experience. They did not wish I were more or less. I experienced children accepting me for what I was at that moment. They did not try to change me or make me different in some way. They liked me the way I was. I did not have to pretend. I discovered I could just be. What a fantastically freeing experience that was and continues to be as I relate to children. As I related to children on the basis of who they were at that moment and accepted them, their personhood, this became a reciprocal experience of sharing being together and accepting each other.

My early interactions with children in play therapy awakened in me a deep appreciation for the unfolding process of life as experienced by children and in turn a new appreciation for the process of my own life, not as something to change, or undo, or overcome, or prove the worth of, but to appreciate and live out the excitement of the process of being the person God has created me to be—to be me! Being more fully me means being more fully human, accepting my strengths as well as my weaknesses, for I do have strengths as well as weaknesses—and my mistakes are only a declaration of the fact that I am indeed fallible—human. That was a significant discovery for me, and yet as I look back, it was not a discovery, for that seems to indicate an event in time. Like life, it was a process I experienced and gradually became aware of and slowly began to appreciate. What I would like to say to children is wonderfully expressed in Peccei's (1979–1980) "In the name of the children":

> If we were to allow the wonder of the life of a child to reach us fully and truly and to be our teacher, we would have to say: Thank you, child of man...for reminding me about the joy and excitement of being human. Thank you for letting me grow together

with you, that I can learn again of what I have forgotten about simplicity, intensity, totality, wonder and love and learn to respect my own life in its uniqueness. Thank you for allowing me to learn from your tears about the pain of growing up and the sufferings of the world. Thank you for showing me that to love another person and to be with people, big or small, is the most natural of gifts that grows like a flower when we live in the wonder of life. (p. 10)

As I progressed in my relationships with children in play therapy, I made a rather startling discovery about my counseling sessions with adults. The counseling process seemed to be speeding up, and I was becoming more effective. With some adult clients with whom I had experienced being stuck, little progress, therapeutic movement began to develop, and a new depth of sharing and exploring of self occurred for the client. As I examined this development, the change could be accounted for by my having become more aware of and responsive to the subtle cues in the client that had always been there. I attributed this increased sensitivity to clients' subtle cues to my increased sensitivity to children's subtle forms of communication. I discovered that as I became more effective with children in play therapy, I became much more effective with adults in counseling relationships.

I joined the Counselor Education Department at the University of North Texas in 1966 and taught my first course in play therapy in 1967. Play therapy was not very well known in Texas in those days, or anywhere else in the nation for that matter, but from that meager beginning has come tremendous growth. What an exciting adventure that has been. The Center for Play Therapy, which I founded at the University of North Texas, is now the largest play therapy training program in the world, and each year provides an Annual Play Therapy Conference and a 2-week Summer Play Therapy Institute. Graduate courses offered each year consist of five sections of Introduction to Play Therapy, Advanced Play Therapy, Filial Therapy, Group Play Therapy, master's-level practicum and internships in play therapy, a doctoral-level advanced play therapy practicum, and a doctoral-level internship in play therapy.

One thing I really enjoy about teaching play therapy is that the child part of me can emerge in the role-playing I often do, and that helps to balance my tendency to be too serious about things. I am now able to really prize the child part of the person I am and thus to more fully appreciate and be sensitive to those qualities in children. I have discovered that when I am with children, the person I am is much more important than anything I know how to do in my mind.

I am still learning about children and about myself as I experience with them the complex simplicity of their play and the unfolding of the vibrant colors of their emotional inner worlds. What I have learned and how I have come to incorporate that learning into my relationships with children is perhaps best expressed in the following principles.

Principles for Relationships With Children

I am not all knowing.
> Therefore, I will not even attempt to be.

I need to be loved.
> Therefore, I will be open to loving children.

I want to be more accepting of the child in me.
> Therefore, I will with wonder and awe allow children
> to illuminate my world.

I know so little about the complex intricacies of childhood.
> Therefore, I will allow children to teach me.

I learn best from and am impacted most by my
personal struggles.
> Therefore, I will join with children in their struggles.

I sometimes need a refuge.
> Therefore, I will provide a refuge for children.

I like it when I am fully accepted as the person I am.
> Therefore, I will strive to experience and appreciate
> the person of the child.

I make mistakes. They are a declaration of the way
I am—human and fallible.
> Therefore, I will be tolerant of the humanness of
> children.

I react with emotional internalization and expression to my world of reality.

> Therefore, I will relinquish the grasp I have on reality and try to enter the world as experienced by the child.

It feels good to be an authority, to provide answers.

> Therefore, I will need to work hard to protect children from me!

I am more fully me when I feel safe.

> Therefore, I will be consistent in my interactions with children.

I am the only person who can live my life.

> Therefore, I will not attempt to rule a child's life.

I have learned most of what I know from experiencing.

> Therefore, I will allow children to experience.

The hope I experience and the will to live come from within me.

> Therefore, I will recognize and affirm the child's will and selfhood.

I cannot make children's hurts and fears and frustrations and disappointments go away.

> Therefore, I will soften the blow.

I experience fear when I am vulnerable.

> Therefore, I will with kindness, gentleness, and tenderness touch the inner world of the vulnerable child.

Reference

Peccei, A. (1979–1980). In the name of the children. *Forum, 10,* 17–18.

Chapter 2

The Meaning of Play

Children's play is not mere sport. It is full of meaning and import.

F. Froebel

Children must be approached and understood from a developmental perspective. They are not miniature adults. Their world is one of concrete realities, and their experiences often are communicated through play. In seeking to facilitate children's expression and exploration of their emotional world, therapists must turn loose of their world of reality and verbal expression and move into the conceptual–expressive world of children. Unlike adults, whose natural medium of communication is verbalization, the natural medium of communication for children is play and activity.

Functions of Play

The universal importance of play to the natural development and wholeness of children has been underscored by the UN proclamation of play as a universal and inalienable right of childhood. Play is the singular central activity of childhood, occurring at all times and in all places. Children do not need to be taught how to play, nor must they be made to play. Play is spontaneous, usually enjoyable, voluntary, and not goal directed. In order to make children's play more acceptable, some adults have invented a meaning for play by defining it as work. In their push to be successful and to hurry up the process of growing up, many adults cannot tolerate "the waste of children's time by playing." The attitude is that children must be accomplishing something or working toward some important goal acceptable to adults.

It is regrettable that play has been identified by many writers as children's work. This seems to be an effort to somehow make play legitimate, intimating that play can be important only if it somehow fits what adults consider important in their world. Just as childhood has intrinsic value and is not merely preparation for adulthood, so play has intrinsic value and is not dependent on what may follow for importance. In contrast to work, which is goal focused and directed toward accomplishment or completion of a task by accommodating the demands of the immediate environment, play is intrinsically complete, does not depend on external reward, and assimilates the world to match the child's concepts, as in the case of a child using a spoon as a car.

Frank (1982) suggested play is the way children learn what no one can teach them. It is the way they explore and orient themselves to the actual world of space and time, of things, animals, structures, and people. By engaging in the process of play, children learn to live in our world of meanings and values, at the same time exploring and experimenting and learning in their own individual ways.

According to Woltmann (1964),

> The spontaneous and self-generated activities of the child enable him to conceptualize, to structure, and to bring to tangible levels of activity his experiences and the feelings with which he invests them. Play, in this meaning, furnishes the child with opportunities to "act out" situations which are disturbing, conflicting, and confusing to him. The small child especially lacks semantic fluency since the development of his apperceptive processes is in a state of growing...flux, various types of play materials seem to be ideally suited for the expression of his feelings and attitudes. (p. 174)

Below age 10 to 11, most children experience difficulty sitting still for sustained periods of time. A young child has to make a conscious effort to sit still, and thus creative energy is consumed in focusing on a nonproductive activity. Play therapy provides for children's need to be physically active. In play, children discharge energy, prepare for life's duties, achieve difficult goals, and relieve frustrations. They get physical contact, discharge their needs to compete, act aggressively in socially acceptable ways, and learn to get along with others. Play helps children give their imaginations free rein, learn the trappings of their culture, and develop skills (Papalia & Olds, 1986). As children play, they are expressing the individuality of their personalities and drawing upon inner resources that can become incorporated into their personalities.

Children Communicate Through Play

Children's play can be more fully appreciated when recognized as their natural medium of communication. Children express themselves more fully and more directly through self-initiated, spontaneous play than they do verbally because they are more comfortable with play. For children to "play out" their experiences and feelings is the most natural dynamic and self-healing process in which they can engage. Play is a medium of exchange, and restricting children to verbal expression automatically places a barrier to a therapeutic relationship by imposing limitations that in effect say to children, "You must come up to my level of communication and communicate with words." The therapist's responsibility is to go to a child's level and communicate with children through the medium with which they are comfortable. Why must the child accommodate the adult? The therapist is the one who is supposed to be well adjusted, to have developed coping skills, to know how to communicate effectively at all levels, and to possess a developmental understanding of children. When the therapist says, "Tell me about it," young children are placed at a disadvantage of having to accommodate the therapist.

A therapeutic working relationship with children is best established through play, and the relationship is crucial to the activity we refer to as therapy. Play provides a means through which conflicts can be resolved and feelings can be communicated. "The toys implement the process because they are definitely the child's medium of expression.... His free play is an expression of what he wants to do.... When he plays freely and without direction, he is expressing a period of independent thought and action. He is releasing the feelings and attitudes that have been pushing to get out into the open" (Axline, 1969, p. 23). Feelings and attitudes that may be too threatening for the child to express directly can be safely projected through self-chosen toys. Instead of verbalizing thoughts and feelings, a child may bury in the sand, shoot the dragon, or spank the doll representing baby brother.

Children's feelings often are inaccessible at a verbal level. Developmentally they lack the cognitive, verbal facility to express what they feel, and emotionally they are not able to focus on the intensity of what they feel in a manner that can be expressed adequately in a verbal exchange. We know from the research of individuals such as Piaget (1962) that children are not developmentally able to engage fully in abstract reasoning or thinking until approximately age 11. Words are made up of symbols and symbols are abstractions. No wonder, then, that so much of what we try to communicate verbally is of an abstract nature. The child's world is a world of concretes and must be approached as such if contact is to be made with the child. Play is the concrete expression of the child and is the child's way of coping with her world.

Children live in the world of the present; yet, many of the experiences they encounter in the adult world are future oriented and abstract. When children reenact these future-oriented and abstract experiences through play, they become here and now concrete happenings enabling them to make sense of the abstract on their terms. As children play out these experiences, the unfamiliar becomes familiar.

> The most normal and competent child encounters what seem like insurmountable problems in living. But by playing them out, in the way he chooses, he may become able to cope with them in a

step-by-step process. He often does so in symbolic ways that are hard for even him to understand, as he is reacting to inner processes whose origin may be buried deep in his unconscious. This may result in play that makes little sense to us at the moment or may even seem ill advised, since we do not know the purposes it serves or how it will end. When there is no immediate danger, it is usually best to approve of the child's play without interfering, just because he is so engrossed in it. Efforts to assist him in his struggles, while well intentioned, may divert him from seeking, and eventually finding, the solution that will serve him best. (Bettelheim, 1987, p. 40)

Play in the Therapeutic Process

Play is a voluntary, intrinsically motivated, child-directed activity involving flexibility of choice in determining how an item is used. No extrinsic goal exists. The process of play is usually enjoyed, and the end product is less important. Play involves the child's physical, mental, and emotional self in creative expression and can involve social interaction. Thus when the child plays, one can say that the *total* child is present. The term *play therapy* presupposes the presence of some possible activity that would be considered play. We do not say of a child who is reading a story, "She is playing." In keeping with this description of play, *play therapy is defined as a dynamic interpersonal relationship between a child (or person of any age) and a therapist trained in play therapy procedures who provides selected play materials and facilitates the development of a safe relationship for the child (or person of any age) to fully express and explore self (feelings, thoughts, experiences, and behaviors) through play, the child's natural medium of communication, for optimal growth and development.*

Consistent with person-centered theory and therapy (Rogers, 1951), the essential element in this definition is a focus on the relationship. The success or failure of therapy in fact rests on the development and maintenance of the therapeutic relationship. It is the relationship with the child that becomes the vehicle for sustainable change and growth by the child. Development of this relationship is facilitated by providing a developmentally appropriate modality for the child to express himself as he desires.

Although most adults are able to put their feelings, frustrations, anxieties, and personal problems into some form of verbal expression, children are not able to express themselves fully through the medium of verbalization. Play is to the child what verbalization is to the adult. Play provides a developmentally responsive means for expressing thoughts and feelings, exploring relationships, making sense of experiences, disclosing wishes, and developing coping strategies. Given the opportunity, children will play out their feelings and needs in a manner or process of expression that is similar to that for adults. The dynamics of expression and vehicle for communication are different for children, but the expressions (fear, satisfaction, anger, happiness, frustration, contentment) are similar to those of adults. When viewed from this perspective, *toys are used like words by children, and play is their language.* To restrict therapy to verbal expression is to deny the existence of the most graphic form of expression—activity (Figure 2.1).

The goal of some play therapists is to "get the child to talk." When this is the case, it usually reveals the therapist's own state of anxiety or uncomfortableness and a need to be in control by getting the child to talk. Therapy is not limited to a talking cure. If there can be a talking cure, then why not a playing cure? Play therapy offers the opportunity to respond to the total behavior of the child, not just the verbal behavior.

According to Smolen (1959), who analyzed improvement in children who exhibited very little verbal interchange with the therapist,

> We came to the rather obvious conclusion that the "talking cure" was effective only insofar as it represented an adequate substitute for an "acting cure." That words are not always adequate substitutes for actions, even in the therapy of adults, is indicated by the vast amount of literature which has grown up around the problems of the acting-out patient in therapy. Words, then, as substitutes for and abstractions of behavior can often be quite meaningful to adults who have had many years of experience. But how much less true is this of children who, by virtue of the maturational process alone, have not yet attained a capacity to utilize adequately

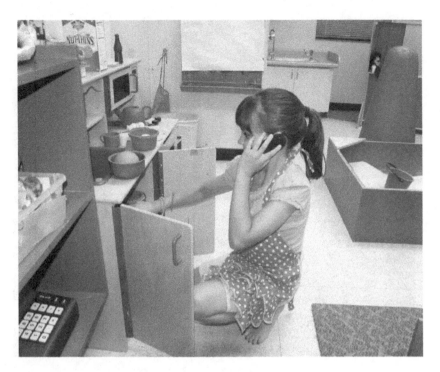

FIGURE 2.1   For children to "play out" their experiences and feelings is the most natural, dynamic, and self-healing process in which they can engage.

abstractions or symbolic forms of speech or thinking. Even though many children may have the vocabulary, they do not have the rich background of experience and associations which would render these words meaningful condensates of emotional experiences in terms of their potential usefulness in therapy. (p. 878)

Children may have considerable difficulty verbally describing what they feel or how their experiences have affected them; but, if permitted, in the presence of a caring, sensitive, and empathic adult, they will reveal inner feelings through the toys and materials they choose, what they do with and to the materials, and the stories they act out. Children's play is meaningful and significant to them, for through their play they extend themselves into areas they have difficulty entering verbally. Children are able to use toys to say what they cannot say, do things they would feel uncomfortable doing, and express feelings they might be reprimanded for

FIGURE 2.2 In play therapy, children use toys to say what they cannot say and express feelings they might be reprimanded for verbalizing.

verbalizing. Play is the child's symbolic language of self-expression and can reveal (a) *what the child has experienced*; (b) *reactions to what was experienced*; (c) *feelings about what was experienced*; (d) *what the child wishes, wants, or needs*; and (e) *the child's perception of self*. These are important messages the play therapist looks for in children's play in play therapy experiences (Figure 2.2).

Play represents the child's attempt to organize her experiences, her personal world. Through the process of play, the child experiences a feeling of being in control, even though in reality circumstances may dictate otherwise. This attempt by the child to gain control is explained by Frank (1982):

> The child in his play relates himself to his accumulating past by continually reorienting himself to the present through play. He rehearses his past experiences, assimilating them into new perceptions and patterns of relating.... In this way the child is continually discovering himself anew, revising his image of himself

as he can and must, with each alteration in his relations with the world. Likewise, in his play the child attempts to resolve his problems and conflicts, manipulating play materials and often adult materials as he tries to work through or play out his perplexities and confusions. (p. 24)

There are many experiences in childhood in which children feel they have little or no control. Play is children's way of working out balance and control in their lives, for, as children play, they are in control of the happenings in play, although it may not be possible to actually be in control of the life experience represented in the play. It is the sense or feeling of being in control in the play therapy experience, rather than actual control, that is essential to children's emotional development and positive mental health.

An understanding of children's play behavior provides cues to help the therapist enter more fully into the inner emotional life of the child. Because the child's world is a world of action and activity, play therapy provides the therapist with an opportunity to enter the child's world. The selection of a variety of appropriate toys by the therapist can facilitate a wide range of feeling-oriented expressions by children. Thus, children are not restricted to discussing what happened; rather, *they live out at the moment of the play the past experiences and associated feelings.* Therefore, the therapist is allowed to experience and participate in the emotional lives of children rather than relive situational happenings. Because children thrust their total beings into their play, expressions and feelings are experienced by children as being specific, concrete, and current, thus allowing the therapist to respond to their present activities, statements, feelings, and emotions rather than to past circumstances.

If the reason the child was referred to the therapist is aggressive behavior, the medium of play provides the therapist an opportunity not only to experience the aggressive behavior firsthand as the child bangs on the Bobo or attempts to shoot the therapist with a dart gun but also to provide the child opportunities to learn self-control by responding with appropriate therapeutic limit-setting procedures. Without the presence of play materials, the therapist could only talk with the child about the aggressive behavior the child exhibited yesterday or in the past weeks. In play therapy, whatever the reason for referral, the therapist has the opportunity to experience and actively relate to that problem in the immediacy of the child's experiencing.

Play allows children to make their internal world external. Axline (1969) viewed this process as one in which the child plays out her feelings, thus bringing them to the surface, getting them out in the open, and facing them. This process was readily evident in 4-year-old Kathy's play in her play therapy experiences. At first glance, Kathy appeared to be just a 4-year-old playing pretend. As she became agitated about the panties on the doll, placed a blanket over the doll, took the doll to the doctor for a detailed examination, and expressed the need for the doll's legs to be down, a pattern or theme began to emerge. Although she was quite young when she was abused, it appeared that she was working through some of those experiences.

Symbolic Play

According to Piaget (1962), play bridges the gap between concrete experience and abstract thought, and it is the symbolic function of play that is so important. In play, the child is dealing in a sensory–motor way with concrete objects that are symbols for something else the child has experienced directly or indirectly. Sometimes the connection is quite apparent; at other times, the connection may be rather remote. In either case, play represents the attempt of children to organize their experiences and may be one of the few times in children's lives when they feel more in control and thus more secure.

The child-centered play therapy philosophy considers play essential to children's healthy development. Play gives concrete form and expression to children's inner worlds. Emotionally significant experiences are given meaningful expression through play. *A major function of play in play therapy experiences is the changing of what may be unmanageable in reality to manageable situations through symbolic representation,* which provides children with opportunities for learning to cope by engaging in self-directed exploration. The therapist uses play with children because play is children's symbolic language of self-expression. "Through the manipulation of toys, the child can show more adequately than through words how he feels about himself and the significant persons and events in his life" (Ginott, 1994, p. 51). "A therapist who is too literal minded and who cannot tolerate a child's flight into fantasy without ordering it into adult meaningfulness might well be lost at times" (Axline, 1969, p. 127).

Symbolic play allows children to freely assimilate their experiences without environmental constraints. Assimilation, although usually outside the child's awareness, facilitates substantive change. When children are playing in the play therapy experience, they are seldom if ever aware of the symbolic representation in their play. It is this dimension of distancing from the event that makes the play experience safe for children. A child does not consciously think "I'm afraid of my father who is abusing me and this father doll too closely represents my father; so I will pretend the lion is my father and I am the lion cub, and no one will know what I am doing." In play children can safely express their experiences and feelings because they are not cognitively aware that they are symbolically playing out a threatening experience. By acting out a frightening or traumatic experience or situation symbolically, and by returning to that happening again and again through play and perhaps changing or reversing the outcome in the play activity, children experience being in control of the experience and move toward an inner resolution and then are better able to cope with or adjust to the problem.

That children unconsciously express happenings, experiences, concerns, and problems in their play can readily be seen in my play therapy sessions with 6-year-old Brenda who had to wear a catheter as a result of complications following surgery. She experienced considerable difficulty trying to empty the bag appropriately at school and make the necessary connections to put it back in place. The connections were always leaking and that caused her a great deal of frustration and embarrassment. In her play, she repeatedly played out a story using the dollhouse and depicting a problem with a leaky sink or some related plumbing problem. With great exasperation, she would grab the phone, call a plumber, and say, "The dumb sink is leaking again! Come fix this stupid thing

FIGURE 2.3 Feelings and attitudes that may be too threatening for a child to express directly can be safely projected through self-chosen toys.

again." She stopped acting out these scenes the week she learned to attach the catheter bag correctly (Figure 2.3).

There are times, though, when children are aware of the literal message in their play as in the case of showing the therapist something they have done. Seven-year-old Scott grabbed Bobo (the bop bag) around the neck in a hammer lock and yelled to me, "I'm gonna show you what I did to Roger on the playground today!"

A vivid reminder of differences in the way children and adults express their feelings and reactions occurred in the days and weeks following the terrorist attack on the World Trade Center buildings in New York on September 11, 2001. Adults told and retold their experience of shock and terror. Children who suffered through the same experience almost never talked about it. Their fearful reactions were expressed through their play. Children built towers out of blocks and crashed airplanes into them. Buildings burned and crashed to the ground, sirens wailed, people were killed and injured, and ambulances took them to the hospital. A 3-year-old child in play therapy repeatedly crashed a helicopter into the wall, watched it fall to the floor, and said vehemently, "I hate you helicopter! I hate you helicopter!"

As I write this, Japan has just experienced a devastating earthquake and resulting tsunami. My mind cannot possibly grasp what the chaos and fear are like there, especially for children. All routines have been disrupted for thousands of families; so children no longer feel secure. A 30-minute play therapy time several times a week could become the one predictable routine in their lives, a place to play out pent up fears in the safety of symbolism, a place to regain a sense of control, a place to experience tranquility as needed, an oasis in the midst of chaos.

Stages in the Play Therapy Process

Stages in the play therapy process are the result of shared interactions between the therapist and the child, experienced in the nonevaluative, freeing environment of the playroom, facilitated by the genuine caring for and prizing of the child as communicated by the total person of the therapist. In this unique living relationship, in which the unique nature and individuality of the child are accepted and appreciated, the child experiences permission to expand the horizons of her self in keeping with the degree of acceptance inwardly felt and communicated by the therapist. This experiencing and expanding of the possibilities of self often are manifested in identifiable stages of change in the developing play therapy process.

In Moustakas' (1955a) analysis of case studies of emotionally disturbed children in play therapy, he observed that children progress through five identifiable stages in the therapeutic process of moving toward self-awareness. *Initially diffuse negative feelings* are expressed everywhere in the child's play as in the case of a child who cannot tolerate any kind of mess and is overly concerned with cleanliness and neatness. Sometimes the reaction may be diffuse hostility expressed toward the room, toys, and therapist. There may also be accompanying high levels of anxiety as in the case of a child who just stands in the middle of the play-room unable to initiate any activity. Following these expressions, *in the second stage the child usually expresses ambivalent feelings that are generally anxious or hostile.* Moustakas described a child who picked up the puppets one by one, banged each puppet on the table with exclamations of disgust, threw each puppet on the floor, and said, "I don't like any of them, but I like this one" as she picked up the mouse puppet. She then quickly added, "I don't like this one either," as she squeezed the mouse's head.

The *third stage is characterized by more focused direct negative feelings expressed toward parents, siblings, and other persons in the child's life.* These feelings or attitudes are often evident in the child's symbolic play as in the case of a child who acted out strong nega-tive reactions toward her parents and new baby by lining up the mother, father, and baby family doll figures, and then announced, "They're robbers, and I'm going to shoot them," which she did, one at a time.

In the *fourth stage, ambivalent feelings are expressed again in the child's play but in the form of positive and negative feelings and attitudes expressed toward parents, siblings, and other persons in the child's life.* Six-year-old David hits and kicks the bop bag with great vigor, yelling, "I'm gonna beat you up. Nobody likes you!" Later he gets the doctor kit, doctors the bop bag, and says, "I'll bet that makes you feel better."

The *fifth stage is characterized by clear, distinct, separate, usually realistic positive and negative attitudes, with positive attitudes pre-dominating in the child's play* (Moustakas, 1955a, p. 84). This final stage is a direct result of an understanding, accepting, and caring relationship established by the therapist in which the child feels safe enough to be more fully the person the child is capable of becoming. It is this quality of being that is more important than anything the therapist does. In an accepting and safe environ-ment such as that afforded the child in play therapy, each child's uniqueness is expressed more freely and thus more completely. As this unique self is appreciated and accepted by the therapist, the child internalizes that acceptance and begins to accept and appreciate his own uniqueness, thus beginning the process of self-knowledge. This self-knowledge is then expressed through the facilitative process of play.

In one of the most comprehensive studies of the process of play therapy, Hendricks (1971) reported a descriptive analysis of the process of child-centered play therapy. She found that children followed patterns in sessions:

Sessions 1 through 4: At this stage, children expressed curiosity; engaged in exploratory, noncommittal, and creative play; made simple descriptive and informative comments; and exhibited both happiness and anxiety.

Sessions 5 through 8: Here children continued exploratory, noncommittal, and creative play. Generalized aggressive play increased, expressions of happiness and anxiety continued, and spontaneous reactions were evident.

Sessions 9 through 12: Exploratory, noncommittal, and aggressive play decreased; relationship play increased; creative play and happiness were predominant; nonverbal checking with the therapist increased; and more information about family and self was given.

Sessions 13 through 16: Creative and relationship play predominated; specific aggressive play increased; and expressions of happiness, bewilderment, disgust, and disbelief increased.

Sessions 17 through 20: Dramatic play and role-play predominated, specific aggressive statements continued, and increased relationship building with the therapist occurred. Expression of happiness was the predominant emotion, and children continued to offer information about self and family.

Sessions 21 through 24: Relationship play and dramatic and role play predominated, and incidental play increased.

A second major comprehensive study of the child-centered play therapy process was completed by Withee (1975). She found that during the first three sessions, children gave the most verbal verification of counselors' reflections of their behaviors; exhibited the highest levels of anxiety; and engaged in verbal, nonverbal, and play exploratory activities. During sessions 4 through 6, curiosity and exploration dropped off and aggressive play and verbal sound effects reached their peaks. During sessions 7 through 9, aggressive play dropped to the lowest point, and creative play, expressions of happiness, and verbal information given about home, school, and other aspects of their lives were at their highest. During sessions 10 through 12, relationship play reached its highest point, and noncommittal play sank to its lowest level. In sessions 13 through 15, noncommittal play and nonverbal expressions of anger peaked, anxiety rose over its previous level, and verbal relationship interactions and attempts to direct the therapist were at their highest levels. Differences also were found between boys and girls. Boys expressed more anger, made more aggressive statements, engaged in more aggressive play, and made more sound effects. Girls exhibited more creative and relationship play, happiness, anxiety, verbal verification of therapist responses, and verbalizations of positive and negative thoughts.

These studies illustrate that discernable patterns are evident in the process of children's play in the therapeutic relationship established in the playroom. As the play therapy process develops, children begin to express feelings more directly and realistically and with more focus and specificity. Children initially engage in exploratory, noncommittal, and creative play. In the second stage, children exhibit more aggressive play and verbalizations about family and self. In latter sessions, dramatic play and a relationship with the therapist become important. Anxiety, frustration, and anger are expressed.

Play of Adjusted and Maladjusted Children

The play of adjusted and maladjusted children, as described by Moustakas (1955b), differs in several areas.

Adjusted children are conversational and prone to discuss their world as it exists for them, whereas some maladjusted children may remain completely silent in their first few play sessions, speaking only with great difficulty to the therapist. Other maladjusted children may keep up a rapid-fire flow of questions and conversations during the first sessions. The initial reactions of maladjusted children are cautious and deliberate. Adjusted children are free and spontaneous in their play.

Adjusted children will examine the whole play setting and use a large variety of play materials, in contrast to maladjusted children, who use a few toys and play in a small area. Maladjusted children often want to be told what to do and what not to do. Adjusted children use various strategies to discover their responsibilities and limitations in the therapeutic relationship.

When bothered or annoyed, adjusted children use a concrete way to bring out their problem. Maladjusted children are more likely to express their feelings symbolically with paints, clay, sand, or water. Maladjusted children often are aggressive and want to destroy the play materials and sometimes the therapist. Aggression also is seen in adjusted children, but it is clearly expressed without massive destruction, and responsibility is accepted for the expression. Adjusted children are not so serious and intense in their feelings about themselves, the therapist, or their play as are maladjusted children.

Moustakas (1955b) concluded from his experiences with adjusted and maladjusted children in play therapy that all children, irrespective of the quality of their adjustment, express similar types of negative attitudes. The difference between well-adjusted and maladjusted children lies not primarily in the type of negative attitudes they demonstrate, but rather in the quantity and intensity of such attitudes. Adjusted children express negative attitudes less often and with more focus and direction. Maladjusted children express negative attitudes frequently and intensely, with less focus and direction.

Howe and Silvern (1981) identified differences in the play therapy behaviors of aggressive, withdrawn, and well-adjusted children. Aggressive children presented frequent play disruptions, conflicted play, self-disclosing statements, high levels of fantasy play, and aggressive behavior toward the therapist and toys. Withdrawn boys were identified by their regression in response to anxiety, bizarre play, rejection of the therapist's intervention, and dysphoric content in play. Well-adjusted children exhibited less emotional discomfort, less social inadequacy, and less fantasy play. Withdrawn girls could not be differentiated from well-adjusted girls.

Perry (1988) studied the play behaviors of adjusted and maladjusted children in play therapy and found that maladjusted children expressed significantly more dysphoric feelings, conflictual themes, play disruptions, and negative self-disclosing statements than did adjusted children. Maladjusted children also spent a larger portion of their playtime feeling angry, sad, fearful, unhappy, and anxious than did adjusted children. Maladjusted children talked and played out their problems and conflicts during more of the play session than did adjusted children. No significant differences existed between adjusted and maladjusted children in the area of social inadequacy play or the use of fantasy play.

The initial-session play therapy behaviors of maladjusted and adjusted children were compared by Oe (1989) to investigate the value of children's play for diagnostic purposes. Maladjusted children expressed significantly more nonacceptance of environment play behaviors than adjusted children. Although Oe found there were no significant differences in the frequency of initial session play behaviors of maladjusted children and adjusted children, maladjusted children expressed significantly more intensity in dramatic and role play behaviors than adjusted children in the playroom. Maladjusted girls exhibited dramatic or role behaviors more often and more intensely than maladjusted boys.

The play therapist is cautioned about unrestrained inferences as to the meaning of children's play. Neither the toys the child uses nor the manner in which the child plays with the toys is an absolute indication of an emotional problem area. Environmental factors, recent happenings, and economic depravation may be structuring factors.

References

Axline, V. (1969). *Play therapy.* Boston: Houghton Mifflin.

Bettelheim, B. (1987). The importance of play. *Atlantic Monthly* (3), 35–46.

Frank, L. (1982). Play in personality development. In G. Landreth (Ed.), *Play therapy: Dynamics of the process of counseling with children* (pp. 19–32). Springfield, IL: Charles C. Thomas.

Ginott, H. (1994). *Group psychotherapy with children: The theory and practice of play therapy.* Northvale, NJ: Aronson.

Hendricks, S. (1971). A descriptive analysis of the process of client-centered play therapy (Doctoral dissertation, North Texas State University, Denton). *Dissertation Abstracts International, 32*, 3689A.

Howe, P., & Silvern, L. (1981). Behavioral observation during play therapy: Preliminary development of a research instrument. *Journal of Personality Assessment, 45*, 168–182.

Moustakas, C. (1955a). Emotional adjustment and the play therapy process. *Journal of Genetic Psychology, 86*, 79–99.

Moustakas, C. (1955b). The frequency and intensity of negative attitudes expressed in play therapy: A comparison of well adjusted and disturbed children. *Journal of Genetic Psychology, 86*, 309–324.

Oe, E. (1989). Comparison of initial session play therapy behaviors of maladjusted and adjusted children (Doctoral dissertation, University of North Texas, Denton).

Papalia, D., & Olds, S. (1986). *Human development.* New York: McGraw-Hill.

Perry, L. (1988). *Play therapy behavior of maladjusted and adjusted children* (Doctoral dissertation, North Texas State University, Denton).

Piaget, J. (1962). *Play, dreams, and imitation in childhood.* New York: Routledge.

Rogers, C. (1951). *Client-centered therapy.* Boston: Houghton Mifflin.

Smolen, E. (1959). Nonverbal aspects of therapy with children. *American Journal of Psychotherapy, 13*, 872–881.

Withee, K. (1975). A descriptive analysis of the process of play therapy (Doctoral dissertation, North Texas State University, Denton). *Dissertation Abstracts International, 36*, 6406B.

Woltmann, A. (1964). Concepts of play therapy techniques. In M. Haworth (Ed.), *Child psychotherapy: Practice and theory* (pp. 20–32). New York: Basic Books.

Chapter 3

History and Development of Play Therapy

Birds fly, fish swim, and children play.

Garry Landreth

Play has long been recognized as occupying a significant place in the lives of children. As early as the 18th century, Rousseau (1762/1930) wrote about the importance of observing play to learn about children and to understand them. In *Emile*, he expressed his ideas on the training and education of children and observed that they are not tiny adults. An interesting point to note is that 250 years later we are still struggling against this concept of children. Although Rousseau's comments on the play and games of children were more in accord with educative purposes than with the therapeutic uses of play, his writings reveal a sensitive understanding of the world of children. "Hold childhood in reverence, and do not be in any hurry to judge it for good or ill.... Give nature time to work before you take over her business, lest you interfere with her dealings.... Childhood is the sleep of reason" (Rousseau, 1762/1930, p. 71).

As early as 1903 Froebel emphasized the symbolic components of play. He proposed that play has a definite conscious and unconscious purpose regardless of the nature of the play, and therefore

27

can be looked to for meaning. "Play is the highest development in childhood, for it alone is the free expression of what is in the child's soul.... Children's play is not mere sport. It is full of meaning and import" (Froebel, 1903, p. 22).

The first published case describing the therapeutic use of play and a psychological approach to working with a child was Sigmund Freud's report in 1909 of the classic case of "Little Hans," a 5-year-old boy with a phobia. Freud (1909/1955) saw Hans only one time for a brief visit and conducted the treatment by advising Hans' father of ways to respond with suggestions based on the father's notes about Hans' play. "Little Hans" is the first case of record in which a child's difficulty was attributed to emotional causes. Today, emotional factors are so readily accepted that it is perhaps difficult to appreciate the magnitude of what was then a new concept of psychological disturbance in children. Reisman (1966) pointed out that at the dawning of the 20th century, professionals generally believed childhood disorders were the result of deficiencies in the child's education and training.

Kanner (1957) concluded from his research that when the 20th century began, no procedure or approach was being used with children that could in any sense be regarded as child psychiatry. Play therapy developed from efforts to apply psychoanalytic therapy to children. Considering how little was known about children in the early 1900s, one may be a bit surprised to realize that the formal and often highly structured approach utilized in adult analysis to obtain material for interpretation, primarily through the process of recall and recollections of the client, was so quickly recognized as being inadequate and inappropriate for child analysis.

Psychoanalytic Play Therapy

Following Freud's work with Hans, Hermine Hug-Hellmuth (1921) in the early 1900s seems to have been one of the first therapists to emphasize play as essential in child analysis and to provide children in therapy with play materials to express themselves. Although her work predates that of Anna Freud and Melanie Klein, she did not formulate a specific therapeutic approach. She did, however, call attention to the difficulty of applying methods of adult therapy to children. It seems that the same problem we face now existed then—that of attempting to apply established methods with adults to children and discovering that child therapy is distinct and different from adult therapy. In these early days, analysts found that children were unable to describe their anxieties verbally as adults did. Also, unlike adults, children seemed not the least bit interested in exploring their past or discussing their developmental stages, and many times refused to attempt to free associate. Consequently, most therapists who worked with children in the early 1900s resorted to indirect therapy contact by collecting observations of children.

In 1919, Melanie Klein (1955) began to employ the technique of play as a means of analyzing children under 6 years of age. She assumed that a child's play was as motivationally determined as the free association of adults. Analysis was carried out by substituting play for verbalized free association. Thus, play therapy provided direct access to the child's unconscious. She reported that additional material was exhibited in the child's play as a result of her interpretations. During this same period, Anna Freud (1946, 1965) began to use play as a way to encourage the child to form an alliance with her. Unlike Klein, Anna Freud emphasized the importance of developing the emotional relationship between the child and the therapist before interpreting the unconscious motivation behind the child's drawings and play. Both Klein and Freud stressed the importance of uncovering the past and strengthening the ego. Both also believed play to be the medium through which children express themselves most freely.

Melanie Klein (1955) used play as a way to encourage children to express fantasies, anxieties, and defenses, which she then interpreted. A major difference between Melanie Klein and Anna Freud was Klein's heavy reliance on interpretation of preconscious and unconscious meanings of children's play. She saw symbolic meaning, especially sexual, in almost every play activity. She believed exploration of the unconscious was the main task of therapy and that this could best be achieved through analysis of the child's transference relationship with the therapist. Klein stressed taking the desires and anxieties in the therapist–child relationship back to where they originated—to infancy—and in relation to the first love objects—the parents, especially the mother. She believed that reexperiencing early emotions and fantasies and understanding them, gaining insight through the therapist's interpretations, diminished the child's anxieties.

Klein (1955) explained the significance of interpretation by describing a play therapy episode with a child who surrounded a few toy figures with bricks:

> I would conclude and interpret that the child shows a room and that the figures symbolize people. Such an interpretation affects a first contact with the child's unconscious. For through the interpretation he comes to realize that the toys stand in his mind for people and therefore that the feelings he expresses toward the toys relate to people; also that preceding the interpretation he had not been aware of this. He is beginning to gain insight into the fact that one part of his mind is unknown to him, in other words, that the unconscious exists. Moreover, it becomes clearer to him what the analyst is doing with him. (p. 225)

The toys and materials Klein used were primarily simple, small, unstructured, and nonmechanical: little wooden men and women, animals, cars, houses, balls, marbles, paper, scissors, clay, paints, glue, and pencils. She kept each child's playthings locked in a drawer, which represented the private and intimate relationship between child and therapist. Klein did not allow physical attacks on herself, but she provided opportunities for children to act out aggressive fantasies in other ways, including verbal attacks on her. She stated that she was usually able to interpret children's deeper motives in time to keep the situation under control.

Anna Freud (1946, 1965) used children's play primarily as a means for facilitating children's positive emotional attachment to the therapist, as a way to gain access to the child's inner life. A major objective was to influence the child to like her. Direct interpretation of play was minimal, and she cautioned against viewing everything in the play situation as symbolic. She believed some play had little emotional value, because it was merely conscious repetitions of recent experiences. Freud believed that children do not form a transference neurosis. She delayed offering direct interpretations to children concerning the real meaning of their play until she had gained extensive knowledge from play observations and interviews with parents.

Because free association as developed by Sigmund Freud was cognitive in nature, Anna Freud modified the structure by involving the child in a feeling-level experience. She encouraged the child to verbalize daydreams or fantasies, and when the child had difficulty discussing feelings and attitudes, she encouraged the child to sit quietly and "see pictures." By using this technique, the child learned to verbalize his innermost thoughts and, using the interpretations of the analyst, to discover the meaning of these thoughts. Thus the child gained insight into his unconscious. As the relationship with the therapist developed, the emphasis of the sessions was shifted from play to more verbal interactions.

Klein (1955) visited the United States in 1929 and later reported that play, as a part of the therapeutic procedure with children, was little used here. The works of Hermine Hug-Hellmuth, Anna Freud, and Melanie Klein were revolutionary in changing attitudes about children and their problems.

Release Play Therapy

The second major development in formulating play therapy occurred in the 1930s with the work of David Levy (1938) in developing release therapy, a structured play therapy approach for children who had experienced a specific stressful/anxiety-provoking situation. Levy felt there was no need for interpretation and based his approach primarily on a belief in the abreactive effect of play. In this approach, the major role of the therapist is to be a shifter of scenes, to recreate through selected toys the experience that precipitated the child's anxiety reaction. The child is permitted to engage in free play to gain familiarity with the room and the therapist, and then the therapist uses play materials to introduce the stress-producing situation when he feels it is appropriate. The reenactment of the traumatic event allows the child to release the pain and tension it caused. At other times, the child may be allowed to select her own free play. In this process of "playing out" or reenacting the experience, the child is in control of the play and thus moves out of the passive role of having been "done to" and into an active role of being the "doer." As the child plays, the therapist reflects the verbal and nonverbal feelings expressed.

Three forms of activities of release therapy occur in the playroom:

1. Release of aggressive behavior in throwing objects or bursting balloons or release of infantile pleasures in sucking a nursing bottle
2. Release of feelings in standardized situations such as stimulating feelings of sibling rivalry by presenting a baby doll at a mother's breast
3. Release of feelings by recreating in play a particular stressful experience in a child's life

The following case described by Levy (1939) presents the essence of the release therapy approach:

A girl, aged two years, was referred because of night terrors, onset two days before referral. She awoke frightened and screamed that there was a fish in her bed.... The night terror was related to a visit to a fish market on that very day. The fish merchant...lifted her up to see the fish.

A second complaint was stammering, which had its onset five months before referral, although speech had developed normally up to that time.... There were ten play sessions. A fish made of clay was introduced in the second session. To the question, why was the doll afraid of the fish, the answer was that the fish would bite, and the fish would go "in here," pointing to her eye, her ears, and her vagina. A few days before the night terror the patient had inquired about sex differences after seeing the father naked. Other than the introduction of the fish in various parts of the play sessions, the method was chiefly to facilitate her own type of play.... For example, she saw finger paint and wanted to play with it. I showed her how, but she wouldn't touch it, nor let me put a dot of paint on her hand.... By playing with it myself and getting her to handle it gradually, she got to prefer it....

Following her first appointment there was no change in behavior.... Fear of the fish left after the third or fourth session and the stammering showed improvement after the sixth, disappearing two weeks before the last session. A follow-up was made seven months later. Improvement was maintained. (p. 220)

Gove Hambidge (1955) extended the work of Levy under the title "Structured Play Therapy" and was more direct in introducing events. Following the establishment of a therapeutic relationship, the format consisted of directly recreating the anxiety-producing situation, playing out the situation, and then allowing the child free play to recover from the intrusive procedure.

Relationship Play Therapy

The emergence of the work of Jesse Taft (1933) and Frederick Allen (1934), referred to as relationship therapy, constituted the third significant development in play therapy. The philosophical basis for relationship play therapy evolved from the work of Otto Rank (1936), who deemphasized the importance of past history and the unconscious and stressed the development of the therapist–client relationship as crucial, with a consistent focus on the present, the here and now.

In relationship play therapy, the primary emphasis is placed on the curative power of the emotional relationship between the therapist and the child. As Allen (1934) stated,

> I am interested in creating a natural relation in which the patient can acquire a more adequate acceptance of himself, a clear conception of what he can do and feel in relation to the world in which he continues to live…. I am not afraid to let the patient feel that I am interested in him as a person. (p. 198)

No effort is made to explain or interpret past experiences. Present feelings and reactions are the primary focus of attention, and this approach reportedly led to considerable reduction in the length of the therapy. Allen and Taft stressed regarding children as persons of inner strength with the capacity to alter their behaviors constructively. Therefore, children were given freedom to choose to play or not to play and to direct their own activity. The hypothesis was that children gradually come to realize that they are separate persons with their own strivings and that they can exist in a relationship with other persons with their own qualities. In this approach, the child has to assume responsibility in the growth process, and the therapist concentrates on those difficulties that concern the child, rather than on those concerning the therapist.

Nondirective/Child-Centered Play Therapy

The work of the relationship therapists was studied and expanded by Carl Rogers (1942), who extended these concepts and developed nondirective therapy, later referred to as client-centered therapy (Rogers, 1951) and today as person-centered therapy.

The fourth major development in play therapy was the work of Virginia Axline (1947), a student and later colleague of Carl Rogers. She effectively operationalized the philosophy and principles of Rogers' nondirective/person-centered theory (i.e., belief in the individual's natural strivings for growth and the individual's capacity for self-direction) for application in relationships with children in play therapy. Nondirective play therapy makes no effort to control or change the child and is based on the theory that the child's behavior is at all times caused by the drive for complete self-realization. The objectives of nondirective play therapy are self-awareness and self-direction by the child. The therapist has a well-stocked playroom, and the child has the freedom to play as she chooses or to remain silent. The therapist actively reflects the child's thoughts and feelings, believing that when a child's feelings are expressed, identified, and accepted, the child can accept them and then is free to deal with these feelings.

In summarizing her concept of play therapy, Axline (1950) stated, "A play experience is therapeutic because it provides a secure relationship between the child and the adult, so that the child has the freedom and room to state himself in his own terms, exactly as he is at that moment in his own way and in his own time" (p. 68). This approach was later referred to as client-centered play therapy and then as child-centered play therapy. Although there are several well-established theoretical approaches to play therapy, among those in current use, child-centered play therapy has the longest history of use, the strongest research support, and according to recent surveys of practicing play therapists, is most used by play therapy practitioners (Lambert et al., 2007).

Play Therapy in Elementary Schools

The establishment of guidance and counseling programs in elementary schools in the 1960s opened the door to the fifth major development in play therapy. Until the 1960s, play therapy was largely the domain of the private practitioner with a focus on treatment of maladjusted children, and the literature related to play therapy reflected this condition. However, with the addition of counselors to elementary schools, counselor educators such as Alexander (1964); Landreth (1972); Landreth, Allen, and Jacquot (1969); Muro (1968); Myrick and Holdin (1971); Nelson (1966); and Waterland (1970) were quick to describe their play therapy experiences in the literature. These authors encouraged the use of play therapy in school settings to meet a broad range of the developmental needs of all children, not just the maladjusted. This trend toward the preventive role of play therapy has continued.

Dimick and Huff (1970) suggested that until children reach a level of facility and sophistication with verbal communication that allows them to express themselves fully and effectively to others, the use of play media is mandatory if significant communication is to take place between child and counselor. They proposed that the main question is not whether the elementary school counselor, school psychologist, or social worker should use play therapy, but rather *how* play therapy should be used in elementary schools.

The ultimate objective of elementary schools is to assist the intellectual, emotional, physical, and social development of children by providing adequate learning opportunities. Therefore, a major objective of using play therapy with children in an elementary school setting is to help children get ready to profit from the learning experiences offered. Children cannot be made to learn. Even the most effective teachers cannot teach children who are not yet ready to learn. Play therapy, then, is an adjunct to the learning environment, an experience that helps children maximize their opportunities to learn.

In recent years, growth in the number of elementary school counselors who utilize play therapy has been impressive and accounts for a large percentage of the total number of mental health professionals who use play therapy. Some university counselor education programs now require play therapy training in their school counseling tracks.

Association for Play Therapy

The establishment of the Association for Play Therapy (APT) in 1982 constitutes the sixth major development in the progressive growth of the field of play therapy. The organization of APT was the brainchild of Charles Schaefer and Kevin O'Connor, who envisioned an international society dedicated to the advancement of play therapy. The APT is interdisciplinary and eclectic in orientation. The association publishes an excellent quarterly newsmagazine, the *International Journal of Play Therapy*, and sponsors a conference each year in October in a different region of the United States. Membership in APT increased from a total of 450 in 1988 to over 5,670 in 2011. This rapid increase graphically demonstrates how fast the field of play therapy is developing. APT encourages membership from mental health professionals interested in working with children. For a membership application, write to the Association for Play Therapy, 2050 North Winery Avenue, Suite 101, Fresno, California, 93703, or go online to www.info@a4pt.org. Contact can also be made by consulting the Membership and Networking link on the Web site home page www.a4pt.org/.

University Training

An increasing number of universities are offering courses and supervised experience in play therapy in response to the heightened interest in play therapy training by professionals in the field and preprofessionals in training. According to APT data, in 2011 at least 171 universities in the United States were offering play therapy training in the form of one or more full-semester courses. In 1989, only 33 universities offered a course in play therapy. The

APT provides an online directory of universities offering play therapy training at Find University Play Therapy Directory on their Web site.

Center for Play Therapy

The national Center for Play Therapy established on the University of North Texas campus has been a significant development in the field of play therapy. The center serves as a clearinghouse for information regarding play therapy literature, training, and research as well as a site for ongoing play therapy training and research. The center has eight fully equipped play therapy rooms and three activity therapy rooms, each with video equipment and one-way mirrors. The Center for Play Therapy in the Department of Counseling, Development, and Higher Education offers eight master's- and doctoral-level courses in play therapy, including supervised practicum and internship experiences each semester; provides a 2-week Summer Play Therapy Institute in July; sponsors an Annual Play Therapy Conference in October; publishes results of surveys and research, including a *Bibliography of Play Therapy Literature;* has produced a video series of clinical play therapy sessions featuring distinguished contributors to play therapy; and provides scholarships for master's degree and doctoral degree study. The Center for Play Therapy is recognized as the largest play therapy training program in the world, and scholars, researchers, and university professors from numerous countries have studied in the center or used the facilities for their university research sabbatical. For information, write to the Center for Play Therapy, University of North Texas, 1155 Union Circle No. 310829, Denton, Texas, 76203-5017 or check out the Web site at www.coe.unt.edu/cpt.

Filial Therapy

The nature of parent–child relationships is of primary importance to the present and future mental health of children. Therefore, clearly, if the mental health of future adult populations is to be significantly impacted in positive ways, greater effort must be made to substantially improve the mental health of all children. The skills of those in the mental health professions must be given away through training to parents, who are in the best position to profoundly impact the lives of future adults. Filial therapy, the training of parents to be therapeutic agents with their children using basic child-centered play therapy skills, has been one of the most important developments in the field of play therapy. This innovative approach was developed in the 1960s by Bernard and Louise Guerney, a husband and wife team, and has gained widespread acceptance as a model for enhancement of the parent–child relationship. The filial therapy model, as conceived by the Guerneys, trains parents in basic child-centered play therapy skills to become the therapeutic agent in their children's lives by conducting weekly special play times in their own homes.

Perhaps a more complete picture of filial therapy could be achieved by presenting a definition of filial therapy. In my work, *filial therapy is defined as a unique approach used by professionals trained in play therapy to train parents to be therapeutic agents with their own children through a format of didactic instruction, demonstration play sessions, required at-home laboratory play sessions, and supervision in a supportive atmosphere. Parents are taught basic child-centered play therapy principles and skills, including reflective listening, recognizing and responding to children's feelings, therapeutic limit setting, building children's self-esteem, and structuring required weekly play sessions with their children using a special kit of selected toys. Parents learn how to create a nonjudgmental, understanding, and accepting environment that enhances the parent–child relationship, thus facilitating personal growth and change for both child and parent.*

Building on the work of the Guerneys, I developed a more condensed, 10-session parent training format (Landreth, 1991, 2002) based on my experience that time and financial constraints often hindered parents' participation. Landreth and Bratton (2006) formalized the 10-session format in a text, *Child Parent Relationship Therapy (CPRT): A 10-Session Filial Therapy Model*. The CPRT protocol has been manualized (Bratton, Landreth, Kellam, and Blackard, 2006) allowing for replication of the model. This manualized treatment approach is a first in the field of play therapy. Filial therapy is an encouraging development in the mental health field. Therapeutic skills should be shared with parents. If what the therapist does with children in the playroom is helpful to children, those same behaviors exhibited by parents can be helpful to children's overall growth and development.

Trends in Play Therapy

Adult Play Therapy

A developing interest is occurring in the use of play therapy with adults in therapy settings. In these play sessions, the adult becomes absorbed in the activity of play itself and thus engages in a kind of awareness that is not possible through mere verbalization. Through play the adult has a conversation with self that is a very personal experience because direct involvement is called for. The dollhouse, sandbox, dart gun, paints, and Bobo and other typical play therapy toys can be facilitative materials for adults. Play therapy sessions with elderly residents in nursing homes are described in my book, *Innovations in Play Therapy: Issues, Process, and Special Populations* (2001), as being highly effective. Some therapists have reported exciting results allowing adults to choose toys freely in the playroom. Other therapists conduct group therapy sessions in the playroom and ask the adult members to choose objects that represent symbols for themselves. These objects then become the points of focus for sharing by the member and for feedback from other members.

Play Therapy Techniques in Family Therapy

Family therapists are beginning to recognize the value of bringing toys and art materials to their sessions to facilitate involvement and expressions of children and parents. Children below the age of 9 or 10 do not possess the verbal facility necessary to participate effectively in family interviews. Without the inclusion of play media, many family therapy sessions consist primarily of verbal interactions between the participating adults, with the children either fulfilling the role of spectator or wandering aimlessly around the room in actuality or in their thoughts. Handing a child the family doll figures and asking him to show what happens at home is far more effective than asking the child to verbally describe or confirm what an interaction is like at home. At other times, involving the whole family in a play activity can be very facilitative and quite therapeutic for all involved. When parents are asked to participate with their children in planning play activities, they learn problem-solving methods that will be helpful to them in future family interactions. Family play therapy allows the therapist to assume a variety of roles in interacting with the family, including play facilitator, role model, participant, and teacher or educator.

Group Play Therapy

Although group play therapy has been used throughout most of the developmental history of play therapy, utilization has been very limited. Haim Ginott's *Group Psychotherapy with Children: The Theory and Practice of Play Therapy* published in 1961 and republished in 1994 and Daniel Sweeney and Linda Homeyer's *Handbook of Group Play Therapy* published in 1999 are the only texts published on the topic of group play therapy. Workshop training in group play therapy is an increasing point of focus at play therapy conferences. It is for these reasons that group play therapy is listed here under trends rather than in the section on significant developments.

As in group counseling for adolescents and adults, group play therapy is basically a psychological and social process in which children, in the natural course of interacting with one another in the playroom, learn not only about other children but also about themselves. In the process of interacting, children help one another assume responsibility in interpersonal relationships. Children are then able to naturally and immediately extend these interactions with peers outside the setting of group play therapy. Unlike most other approaches to group counseling, in group play therapy there are no group goals, and group cohesion is not an essential part of the developing process. By watching other children, a child gains the courage to attempt the things she wants to do.

Play Therapy in Hospitals

Hospitalization can be a frightening and stressful experience for the young child, because the child is in a strange environment where all sorts of invasive procedures are carried out. Because of these activities and new surroundings, children often experience anxiety and a feeling of loss of control. Golden (1983) believed that the play therapist's toys are every bit as important as the surgeon's knife in assisting children to leave the hospital healthier than when they arrived. If children do not have an opportunity to appropriately express and deal with their fears and apprehensions, emotional problems may emerge, and healthy adjustment will be altered.

The application of play therapy principles and procedures can be found in hospitals internationally. In the United States, Child Life Programs have been instrumental in incorporating playrooms and play therapy procedures into what would otherwise be a sterile environment. Using hospital equipment, syringes, stethoscopes, masks, and so forth, in combination with dolls or puppets, the therapist can acquaint children with medical procedures through directed play and thereby significantly reduce children's hospital-related anxiety. Positive results also have been achieved by allowing children to choose materials and direct their own play. Children often will act out in their play procedures what they have just experienced. This could be viewed as the child's way of trying to understand what has been experienced or as the child's way of developing control.

References

Alexander, E. (1964). School centered play therapy program. *Personnel and Guidance Journal, 43,* 256–261.

Allen, F. (1934). Therapeutic work with children. *American Journal of Orthopsychiatry, 4,* 193–202.

Axline, V. (1950). Entering the child's world via play experiences. *Progressive Education, 27,* 68–75.

Axline, V. (1947). Nondirective play therapy for poor readers. *Journal of Consulting Psychology, 11,* 61–69.

Bratton, S., Landreth, G., Kellam, T., & Blackard, S. (2006). *Child parent relationship therapy (CPRT) treatment manual.* New York: Routledge.

Dimick, K., & Huff, V. (1970). *Child counseling.* Dubuque, IA: William C. Brown.

Freud, A. (1946). *The psychoanalytic treatment of children.* London: Imago.

Freud, A. (1965). *The psycho-analytical treatment of children.* New York: International Universities Press.

Freud, S. (1909/1955). *The case of "Little Hans" and the "Rat Man."* London: Hogarth Press.

Froebel, F. (1903). *The education of man.* New York: D. Appleton.

Ginott, H. (1961/1994). *Group psychotherapy with children: The theory and practice of play therapy.* Northvale, NJ: Aronson.

Golden, D. (1983). Play therapy for hospitalized children. In C. Schaefer & K. O'Conner (Eds.), *Handbook of play therapy* (pp. 213–233). New York: John Wiley.

Hambidge, G. (1955). Structured play therapy. *American Journal of Orthopsychiatry, 25,* 601–617.

Hug-Hellmuth, H. (1921). On the technique of child analysis. *International Journal of Psychoanalysis, 2,* 287.

Kanner, L. (1957). *Child psychiatry.* Springfield, IL: Thomas.

Klein, M. (1955). The psychoanalytic play technique. *American Journal of Orthopsychiatry, 25,* 223–237.

Lambert, S., LeBlanc, M., Mullen, J., Ray, D., Baggerly, J., White, J., & Kaplan, D. (2007). Learning more about those who play in session: The national play therapy in counseling practices project (Phase I). *International Journal of Play Therapy, 14,* 7–23.

Landreth, G. (1972). Why play therapy? *Texas Personnel and Guidance Association Guidelines, 21,* 1.

Landreth, G. (1991). *Play therapy: The art of the relationship.* New York: Accelerated Development.

Landreth, G. (2001). *Innovations in play therapy: Issues, process and special populations.* Philadelphia: Brunner-Routledge.

Landreth, G. (2002). *Play therapy: The art of the relationship* (2nd ed.). New York: Routledge.

Landreth, G., Allen, L., & Jacquot, W. (1969). A team approach to learning disabilities. *Journal of Learning Disabilities, 2,* 82–87.

Landreth, G., & Bratton, S. (2006). *Child parent relationship therapy (CPRT): A 10-session filial therapy model.* New York: Routledge.

Levy, D. (1938). Release therapy in young children. *Psychiatry, 1,* 387–389.

Levy, D. (1939). Release therapy. *American Journal of Orthopsychiatry, 9,* 713–736.

Muro, J. (1968). Play media in counseling: A brief report of experience and some opinions. *Elementary School Guidance and Counseling Journal, 2,* 104–110.

Myrick, R., & Holdin, W. (1971). A study of play process in counseling. *Elementary School Guidance and Counseling Journal, 5,* 256–265.

Nelson, R. (1966). Elementary school counseling with unstructured play media. *Personnel and Guidance Journal, 45,* 24–27.

Rank, O. (1936). *Will therapy.* New York: Knopf.

Reisman, J. (1966). *The development of clinical psychology.* New York: Appleton-Century-Crofts.

Rogers, C. (1942). *Counseling and psychotherapy.* Boston: Houghton Mifflin.

Rogers, C. (1951). *Client-centered therapy.* Boston: Houghton Mifflin.

Rousseau, J. (1762/1930). *Emile.* New York: J. M. Dent & Sons.

Sweeney, D., & Homeyer, L. (1999). *Handbook of group play therapy.* San Francisco: Jossey-Bass.

Taft, J. (1933). *The dynamics of therapy in a controlled relationship.* New York: Macmillan.

Waterland, J. (1970). Actions instead of words: Play therapy for the young child. *Elementary School Guidance and Counseling Journal, 4,* 180–197.

Chapter 4

A View of Children

To grow up to be healthy, very young children do not need to know how to read, but they do need to know how to play.

Fred Rogers

Although some people have said space is our last frontier to explore, childhood may in fact be our last frontier. We know so little about the complex intricacies of childhood and are limited in our efforts to discover and understand the meanings in childhood because we are forced to allow children to teach us.

RULE OF THUMB:

What is most important about children can be learned only from children.

Only the child the play therapist is with in the play therapy relationship can teach the therapist what he does not know about the child that is important. We can only learn about children *from* children. Children bring to the relationship with the therapist a rich tapestry of emotional possibilities from which they weave the intricacies of their personalities. The direction these emotional possibilities take is affected by the person of the therapist, the kinds of responses the therapist makes, and what children sense in the therapist.

Tenets for Relating to Children

The process of relating to children from a child-centered frame of reference is based on the following tenets about children that compose, for the therapist, the framework for an experiential self-projecting attitude about children. The tenets are as follows:

1. **Children are not miniature adults.** The therapist does not respond to them as if they were.
2. **Children are people.** They are capable of experiencing deep emotional pain and joy.
3. **Children are unique and worthy of respect.** The therapist prizes the uniqueness of each child and respects the person the child is.
4. **Children are resilient.** Children possess a tremendous capacity to overcome obstacles and circumstances in their lives.
5. **Children have an inherent tendency toward growth and maturity.** They possess an inner intuitive wisdom.
6. **Children are capable of positive self-direction.** They are capable of dealing with their world in creative ways.
7. **Children's natural language is play.** This is the medium of self-expression with which they are most comfortable.
8. **Children have a right to remain silent.** The therapist respects a child's decision not to talk.
9. **Children will take the therapeutic experience to where they need to be.** The therapist does not attempt to determine when or how a child should play.
10. **Children's growth cannot be speeded up.** The therapist recognizes this and is patient with the child's developmental process.

Children are persons in their own right. They do not become persons upon the attainment of some predetermined age or after having met certain criteria. Each child is a unique personality, and that uniqueness is not dependent on any significant person in the child's life; neither is personal significance limited to or a function of the child's behavior. Therefore, children are worthy of respect because they have worth and dignity as individuals. Their uniqueness is prized and appreciated by the therapist, who responds to the child as a person. Children are people. They do not have to earn that distinction.

The child is not an object for study but, rather, is a person to be known in the dynamics of the moment. The child standing before the therapist in the playroom is not a problem to be analyzed but a whole person to be related to and understood. Children, indeed all persons, have a longing to be heard, to be recognized as persons of value. For some children, it is as though they go through their lives day after day tapping out their message: "Hey, up there! Does anyone hear me? Does anyone see me? Does anyone care that no one seems to care about me? My heart aches. Do you see it? Do you care?" And day after day adults in their lives ignore these emotional messages. In the playroom, however, children are noticed, listened to, heard, responded to, and allowed to chart their own lives. This is a freeing process for children which allows them to draw on their inner resources for growth and self-direction. The acceptance, safety, and permissiveness experienced in the playroom allow children to express the fullness of their personalities.

Children Are Resilient

Children possess an inner strength and are resilient. They bounce back. Attempting to explain that they are products of their home environment seems to be far too simplistic and does not account for the differences and variability in children reared in the same environment. How do we account for some children who seem to be invulnerable to what would appear to be devastating experiences in their lives? Some children experience regular beatings by unloving and insensitive parents but are not beaten down psychologically in the process. Some children are reared in poverty but grow up rich in spirit and outlook on life. Some children have alcoholic parents but, unlike "codependent brothers and sisters," are themselves independent and well adjusted. Some children are reared by emotionally disturbed parents and are themselves quite successful and well-adjusted as teenagers and adults. A possible explanation seems to be the way these experiences have been internalized and the integration that has occurred within individuals

FIGURE 4.1 Children possess an innate capacity to strive toward growth and maturity. The play therapy relationship facilitates the development of that capacity.

as they have interacted with their environment. Such examples emphasize the capacity and striving of the human organism to grow toward fulfillment and maturity even in the midst of adverse circumstances (Figure 4.1).

Significant variables that researchers have suggested as contributing factors to making some children invulnerable are high self-regard, self-control, inner motivation, and a sense of personal identity. These children have confidence in themselves. They *feel* capable of exerting control over their environment and are goal directed. Researchers have found that parents of such children have allowed considerable self-direction (Segal & Yahraes, 1979). These findings echo the dynamics and process of the play therapy relationship as experienced by children.

When I think of resilient children, I am reminded of 18-month-old Jessica McClure, who fell down an abandoned well shaft in west Texas and captured the attention of people around the world.

What a horrible and terrifying experience for a small child, surely as frightening as anything an adult could possibly experience. She was stuck in that small shaft for almost 2 whole days, with no one to talk to her, no one to touch her, no one to comfort her. There was no way for her to know where she was or what had happened to her. Those 2 days must surely have been an eternity for Jessica. When rescue workers first made contact with her through a microphone after she had been wedged into that dark shaft and all alone for 46 hours, they heard this tiny toddler singing softly to herself. What a remarkable demonstration of the inner natural motivation of children to comfort and take care of themselves. We adults are not wise enough to know the capacity and potential of children. Our view of children is typically much too narrow and restrictive. Some adults want to limit children to their finite comprehension; the capacity of the human organism surpasses our level of understanding.

Normally, children have fun. They are exuberant. When provided with opportunities to do so, children approach life with excitement, openness, and wonder. All children should experience some joy in their life every day, and this should be the goal of all adults who interact with children on a regular basis. Children are deprived of joy when they are rushed to complete tasks and hurried to grow up. Places of calmness and patience should exist in all children's lives for, in the midst of calmness and patience, children can discover and test their inner resources. Children are basically trusting and are, therefore, vulnerable. Adults must be careful that they not take advantage of children's trust. Adults must be very sensitive to the inner experiencing of children.

Children do not hold onto yesterdays. The world of the child is now. We cannot say to children, "Wait," because their world is a world of experiencing now. The world of the child is a world of slow, amply punctuated with whirlwind activity. Children appreciate simple things. They do not try to make things more complex. Children are constantly growing and changing inwardly and outwardly, and this dynamic process must be matched with an equally dynamic therapeutic approach.

Some Children Are Like Popcorn, and Some Are Like Molasses

Anyone who has ever been in the presence of children for any extended period of time is well acquainted with the personality and behavioral variability they exhibit as they go about exploring their world in their own individual, unique ways. Some children are like popcorn: They do everything with great bursts of energy and activity. When something occurs to them, they pop forth with exuberance to activate this new and wonderful idea. They are like bumblebees, capable of seemingly motionless hovering when something captures their attention; then they zoom off with a great burst of motion and buzz of noise to find something else of interest.

Other children are like molasses and can barely be poured from one place to another. They do everything with great deliberateness and careful consideration, caught up in their own seeming inertia, impervious to activity being generated around them. They are like gyroscopes: Everything is functioning and spinning on the inside as it should, but little if any movement or change is observable on the outside.

Some children are like mushrooms; they pop forth overnight. Other children are like orchids; they take 7 to 12 years to bloom (Nutt, 1971). The effective play therapist is the kind of person who waits for orchids but is patient with mushrooms. Each child has his unique approach to the solution to problems and how life should be lived. Therefore, as the child already possesses those qualities necessary for growing and becoming a well-adjusted, mature individual, the therapist waits patiently for the child to discover that unique self. The therapist has a sincere belief in the child's ability to work out difficulties and so does not, out of his or her impatience, suggest that the child become involved in other activities or talk about more important topics—which, after all, other significant adults have said are important and should be explored because this child needs to change. Because the therapist respects the child, he or she does not interrupt or "talk down" to the child, nor does the therapist discount what the child says or the feelings he experiences.

References

Nutt, G. (1971). *Being me: Self you bug me.* Nashville, TN: Broadman.

Segal, J., & Yahraes, H. (1979). *A child's journey: Forces that shape the lives of our young.* New York: McGraw-Hill.

Chapter 5

Child-Centered Play Therapy

The best discovery the discoverer makes for himself.

Ralph W. Emerson

The child-centered play therapy approach is an encompassing philosophy for living one's life in relationships with children—not a cloak of techniques the play therapist puts on upon entering the playroom and takes off when leaving, but a philosophy resulting in attitudes and behaviors for living one's life in relationships with children. It is a way of being based on an intentional commitment to certain beliefs about children and their innate capacity to strive toward growth and maturity. *Child-centered play therapy is a complete therapeutic system, not just the application of a few rapport-building techniques, and is based on a deep and abiding belief in the capacity and resiliency of children to be constructively self-directing.* Children are quite capable of appropriately directing their own growth, and they are granted freedom in the play therapy relationship to be themselves in the process of playing out feelings and experiences. Children create their own histories in the playroom, and the therapist respects the direction determined by each child.

The child-centered play therapist believes deeply in and trusts explicitly the inner person of the child. Therefore, **the play therapist's objective is to relate to the child in ways that will release**

the child's inner-directional, constructive, forward-moving, creative, self-healing power. When this philosophical belief is lived out with children in the playroom, they are empowered and their developmental capabilities are released for self-exploration and self-discovery, resulting in constructive change. The child-centered therapist is concerned with developing the kind of relationship that facilitates inner emotional growth and children's belief in themselves. Child-centered play therapy is an attitude, a philosophy, and a way of being with children rather than a way of doing something to or for children.

Personality Theory

What a child knows—some intellectual knowledge or some "important" information the therapist can provide—is not what is important to personality development; *how a child feels about herself is what makes a significant difference in behavior.* Each child possesses a personal perceptual view of self and the world that is reality for the child, and this view of self provides a basis for individual functioning in whatever daily experiences occur in the child's life. This view of self and the limitless potentialities within each child are the basis for the theory of personality structure on which the child-centered approach to play therapy is based. These principles provide a framework for understanding the complex intricacies of the therapist's beliefs, motivation, and attitude that form a lifestyle approach to children.

At this point, my tendency is to go on writing about children and the wonderfully fresh and exciting ways they approach the creative living of life; but a discussion of theory is necessary. *An understanding of and adherence to a system of theoretical personality constructs provides consistency to the therapist's approach to children and enhances the therapist's sensitivity to the child's internal world of experiencing.*

I feel the need to point out that a counseling theory is based on a theory of personality and behavior that is not age restricted. In teaching my play therapy courses, I have at times been disturbingly puzzled by the reactions of some graduate students and mental health practitioners who are excited about utilizing a child-centered approach in their play therapy sessions with children, but do not believe that the same theoretical constructs of personality and behavior are applicable to adolescents and adults in counseling experiences. A counseling theory is an inclusive theory of development that explains personality development and behavior across all ages and does not change when applied to older or younger persons. How is it possible to believe that a 5-year-old child has an innate self-actualizing tendency and, therefore, the therapist needs to follow the lead of the child, and then in the next moment explain that a 30-year-old adult is predisposed to cognitive vulnerabilities that lead to psychological distress, and therefore, the therapist's role is to educate the adult about what is rational or irrational? I am unable to sort through the incongruities generated by the application of such opposing views to individuals dependent on their age.

Having said that, let's return to an exploration of theory. The theoretical constructs of child-centered play therapy are focused on the inner dynamics of the child's process of relating to and discovering the self that the child is capable of becoming. The child-centered theory of personality structure is based on three central constructs: (a) the person, (b) the phenomenal field, and (c) the self (Rogers, 1951).

Person

The *person* is all that a child is: the child's thoughts, behaviors, feelings, and physical being. A basic proposition is that every child "exists in a continually changing world of experience of which he is the center" (Rogers, 1951, p. 483). As the child reacts to this changing world of experience, the child does so as an organized whole, so that a change in any one part results in changes in other parts. Therefore, a continuous dynamic interpersonal interaction occurs in which the child, as a total system, is striving toward actualizing the self. This active process is toward becoming a more positively functioning person, toward improvement, independence, maturity, and enhancement of self as a person. The child's behavior in this process is goal directed in an effort to satisfy personal needs as experienced in the unique phenomenal field which for that child constitutes reality.

Phenomenal Field

The *phenomenal field* consists of everything the child experiences (whether or not at a conscious level), internal as well as external—including perceptions, thoughts, feelings, and behaviors. The phenomenal field forms the basis of internal reference for viewing life. Whatever the child perceives to be occurring is reality for that child. Therefore, a basic tenet in child-centered play therapy is that the child's perception of reality is what must be understood if the child and the behaviors of the child are to be understood. The child's phenomenal world is the point of focus and must be understood if a significant relationship is to be established with the child. The child's behavior is viewed as being goal-directed in an effort to satisfy personal needs as experienced in the unique phenomenal field which for the child constitutes reality.

Whatever the child perceives in the phenomenal field, therefore, assumes primary importance as opposed to the actual reality of events. Because reality is subjectively determined, **the child's behavior must always be understood by looking through the child's eyes.** Thus, the therapist intentionally avoids judging or evaluating even the simplest of the child's behaviors (i.e., a picture, stacked blocks, attempts at spelling, playdough creations) and works hard to try to understand the child's internal frame of reference. If the therapist is to make contact with the person of the child, the child's phenomenal world must be the point of focus and must be understood. The child is not expected to meet predetermined criteria or fit a set of preconceived categories.

The constantly changing interaction of the person of the child—thoughts, behaviors, feelings, and physical being—with the experiential environment is such that the child's perspective, attitude, and thoughts are constantly changing. This dynamic has great significance for the therapist, who may see the child only once a week. The child this week is in some ways different, and the therapist must "catch up." Events that were reacted to one way last week may be reacted to differently this week, as the child's inner world of reality changes. This constantly changing integration within the child seems to explain the tremendous resiliency within children and the generating effect on hope. Life is a constant process of personal dynamic experiences, and children are constantly experiencing an internal reorganization of thoughts, feelings, and attitudes. Therefore, past experiences are not experienced with the same degree of intensity or impact day after day. Thus, the therapist has no need to take the child back to past experiences, because the child has grown since former events, and past experiences no longer have the same impact they formerly had. Therefore, the therapist allows the child to lead, to take the current playroom experience to where the child needs to be.

Self

The *self* is the third central construct of the child-centered theory of personality structure. Rogers (1951) hypothesized that every child exists in a continually changing world of experience, of which the child is the center. The child reacts as an organized whole to this field as it is experienced and perceived, which for the child is reality. As the developing infant interacts with the environment, especially through interactions with significant others, a portion of the child's total private world (perceptual field) gradually becomes recognized as "me" (differentiated as the self), and concepts are formed about himself or herself, about the environment, and about himself or herself in relation to the environment. The self, then, is the totality of those perceptions of the child.

According to Patterson (1974), the child can become a person and develop a self only in interactions with other persons. The self grows and changes as a result of continuing interaction with the phenomenal field. Rogers (1951) described the structure of the self as

[A]n organized configuration of perceptions of the self which are admissible to awareness. It is composed of such elements as the perceptions of one's characteristics and abilities; the percepts and concepts of the self in relation to others and to the environment; the value qualities which are perceived as associated with experiences and objects; and the goals and ideals which are perceived as having positive or negative valence. (p. 501)

The child's behavior, therefore, is generally consistent with the child's concept of self.

As the child develops, the child experiences reactions and evaluations from parents and significant others, and perceives himself as good or bad dependent on these evaluations. A child whose parents react to him as stupid and incapable comes to view himself as stupid and incapable. How can a child feel capable if no one responds to her as capable? How can a child like herself if no one likes her? How can a child trust herself if no one trusts her? How can a child feel acceptable if no one accepts her? How can a child feel wanted and important if no one wants to be with him? How can a child believe in himself if no one believes in him? How can a child discover what self-responsibility feels like if no one provides opportunities for him to assume self-responsibility?

Rogers hypothesized that the self grows and changes as a result of continuing interaction with the phenomenal field. The child's behavior is viewed as being consistent with the concept of self. Therefore, the play therapy experience can facilitate positive change in self-concept. In the child-centered play therapy relationship, a child experiences an adult who genuinely cares for him, accepts as he is, wants to be with him, believes he is capable, trusts him to make responsible decisions, believes in him as a person, and returns responsibility to him in an atmosphere of permissiveness and acceptance. In this kind of safe relationship, the therapist becomes a significant person in the child's life. The child then internalizes the therapist's attitudes and responses to the person he is and comes to feel adequate, accept himself, believe in himself, see himself as capable, trust himself, like himself, and act responsibly.

A Child-Centered View of Personality and Behavior

Rogers (1951) articulated 19 propositions regarding personality and behavior that provide a conceptual framework for understanding human development, behavior, and motivation. His hypotheses reflect the philosophical core of child-centered play therapy and also explain the facilitative nature of the therapeutic relationship and how psychological change occurs in a child. These propositions, summarized below as they apply to children, describe a child-centered view of the person and behavior of the child and provide a basis for relating to children in play therapy.

Every child exists in a continually changing world of experience, of which the child is the center. The child reacts as an organized whole to this field as it is experienced and perceived. This perceptual field is, for the child, "reality." As the child develops and interacts with the environment, a portion of the child's total private world (perceptual field) gradually becomes recognized as "me" (differentiated as the self), and the child forms concepts about himself or herself, about the environment, and about himself or herself in relation to the environment.

The child has a basic tendency to strive to actualize, maintain, and enhance the experiencing self. The resulting behavior is basically the goal-directed, emotionally influenced attempt of the child to satisfy needs as experienced, in the field as perceived. **Therefore, the best vantage point for understanding the child's behavior is from the internal frame of reference of the child.**

Most of a child's behavior is consistent with the child's concept of self, and behaviors inconsistent with the self-concept are not owned. Psychological freedom or adjustment exists when the self-concept is congruent with all of the child's experiences. When this is not the case, the child experiences tension or maladjustment. Experiences that are inconsistent with the self-concept may be perceived as a threat, resulting in the child becoming behaviorally rigid in an effort to defend the existing self-concept.

When there is a complete absence of any threat to the perception of self, the child is free to revise his or her self-concept to assimilate and include experiences previously inconsistent with the self-concept. The resulting well-integrated or positive self-concept enables the child to be more understanding of others and thus to have better interpersonal relationships. The child moves from external motivation to internal motivation that incorporates realization of the value within himself or herself (Rogers, 1951, pp. 481–533).

Rogers' 19 propositions are further delineated as follows:

The child is viewed as:
1. Being the best determiner of a personal reality. The child's perceptual field is "reality."
2. Behaving as an organized whole.
3. Striving toward independence, maturity and enhancement of self.
4. Goal directed in an effort to satisfy needs.
5. Being behaviorally influenced by feelings that affect rationality.
6. Behaving in ways that are consistent with the self-concept.
7. Not owning behavior that is inconsistent with the self-concept.
8. Responding to threat by becoming behaviorally rigid.
9. Admitting into awareness experiences that are inconsistent with the self if the self is free from threat. (Rogers, 1951, pp. 481–533)

An understanding of and grounding in these theoretical constructs of personality and behavior provide the play therapist with the necessary dimensions for understanding the person and behavior of a child and help the play therapist to see more clearly what a child sees in her world of perceptual reality. Thus, the role of the play therapist in the play therapy relationship will be more consistent and effective.

Key Concepts of Child-Centered Play Therapy

Child-centered play therapy is both a basic philosophy of the innate human capacity of children to strive toward growth and maturity and an attitude of deep and abiding belief in children's ability to be constructively self-directing. It is based on an understanding of the observable natural forward movement of the human organism through developmental stages of growth that are normally progressive and always toward greater maturity. This tendency is innate and is not externally motivated or taught. Children are naturally curious, delight in mastery and accomplishment, and energetically live life in their continual pursuit of discovery of their world and themselves in relation to the world.

Speaking of the process of self-discovery and self-growth, Moustakas (1981) said:

> The challenge of therapy is to serve, to wait with interest and concern for the child to activate the will and to choose to act, to dare to pursue what is present in the way of interest and desire. This calls for unusual patience and an unshakable belief in the child's capacity to find the way, to come to terms with the restraints and tensions of living, a belief in the child's powers to listen inwardly and to make choices that are self enhancing. (p. 18)

An inherent tendency exists within children to move in subtle directness toward adjustment, mental health, developmental growth, independence, autonomy of personhood, and what can be generally described as self-actualization. The basic character or nature of children's lives is activity. Their approach to living is an active process, and this can perhaps best be seen in a close observation of their play, which is active and forward moving, not passive, toward enhancing self-sufficiency in the activity of living life. This **inherent push toward discovery, development, and growth** is readily observable in the developmental stages of infants and young children. When they experience difficulty or frustration in their attempts to accomplish or master a physical developmental task, infants naturally strive forward toward mastery using their own unique coping skills and the propensity to try again with renewed vigor, effort, and determination.

Infants are not content to continue crawling from one place to another. An inner urge to stand up, followed by a developmental forward-moving continuation of the inner striving, results in their learning to walk. This is not a conscious decision, a well-thought-out plan, or the result of some significant adult's efforts to teach walking. It occurs spontaneously as a result of growth and development inherent in a child's nature, if the necessary conditions are present. This inherent directional process does not automatically ensure a smooth succession of transitional steps. The infant pulls up to a standing position, turns loose, takes a faltering, wobbly step forward, falls, stands up, wobbles forward for a few steps, and falls again.

Although some pain may be experienced in this process, the infant continues this forward-striving directional process toward growth. It is not necessary for someone to explain to the infant what causes the pain, what is being done the wrong way, how his behavior affects significant adults, or what behaviors need to be changed in order to achieve the desired goal. This **directional striving** will occur spontaneously when the infant is ready to take the next step, even though a period of temporary regression to crawling may occur. The infant will try again and again until walking is mastered to his satisfaction. Because in these experiences the infant has been responsible for self, the accomplishment and accompanying satisfaction are internalized and strengthen the self. This continual striving for growth makes mature behavior more satisfying than immature behavior.

Although this example may seem to be an oversimplification of a very complex process, it clearly highlights the point that children are capable of self-determination. This propensity to move in the direction of increasing independence, self-regulation, and autonomy and away from control by external forces is not limited to developmental accomplishments in infants or toddlers but can be seen as a primary motivating force of the whole person at all developmental levels and phases of life as individuals strive for meaningful interpersonal relationships and enhancement of self. Children have a far greater capacity for self-direction than is readily recognized, and they are capable of making appropriate decisions.

A powerful force exists within every child that strives continuously for self-actualization. This inherent striving is toward independence, maturity, and self-direction. The child's mind and conscious thoughts are not what direct her behavior to areas of emotional need; rather, it is the child's natural striving toward inner balance that takes the child to where she needs to be:

> The behavior of the individual at all times seems to be caused by one drive, the drive for complete self-realization. When an individual reaches a barrier which makes it more difficult for him to achieve the complete realization of the self, there is set up an area of resistance and friction and tension. The drive toward self-realization continues, and the individual's behavior demonstrates that he is

satisfying this inner drive by outwardly fighting to establish his self-concept in the world of reality, or that he is satisfying it vicariously by confining it to his inner world where he can build it up with less struggle. (Axline, 1969, p. 13)

Adjustment and Maladjustment

The inner drive toward self-realization and affirmation of the worthwhileness of self are basic needs, and each child is striving continually to satisfy these needs:

An adjusted person seems to be an individual who does not encounter too many obstacles in his path—and who has been given the opportunity to become free and independent in his own right. The maladjusted person seems to be the one who, by some means or other, is denied the right to achieve this without a struggle. (Axline, 1969, p. 21)

Manifestation of these principles can readily be seen in the lives of some children, such as in the following case of Matt.

Seven-year-old Matt walked methodically beside me into the counseling center, hands stuffed into his pockets, shoulders hunched, and a hollow look on his face. He looked older, defeated by the jarring, awful reality of having been locked in a hot, smelly, dark jail cell on the upper floor of a county government office building for 4 days, without anyone with whom he was familiar to comfort him. His parents lived within walking distance of the jail, but they had not visited him, their reason locked somewhere deep inside and either unknown to them or deliberately withheld.

When I saw Matt standing in the cell earlier that morning, he tried hard to appear calm and almost nonchalant, but the fright in his eyes and the bright red half-circle outlining his bottom lip betrayed his inner anxiety and revealed a frightened little boy, the victim of a system not prepared to understand or provide for the needs of children and that had no juvenile detention facility.

Earlier in the school year Matt had been referred to the Center for Play Therapy by his second-grade teacher for "aggressive behavior, short attention span, frequently tardy, and being moody." Test results were inconclusive but did indicate satisfactory academic progress potential. He was recommended for play therapy and walked the one block from his school to the center, accompanied by a school staff member, once a week for six sessions. When Matt missed his seventh session, I called the school and was informed that he was in jail. Matt had been caught stealing empty soft drink bottles from a grocery store and, as this was the second such incident in a month, the county judge, having been given legal jurisdiction over Matt by his parents because, "We can't do anything with him," declared Matt incorrigible and ordered him sent to jail.

I persuaded the court to release Matt to my custody, and now here we were in the play therapy room together again. As he banged out his frustration on Bobo, he said, "Sometimes a guy gets to wondering if his parents really love him, and what you gotta do is go out and do something kinda bad. Then when your parents find out about it, if they beat up on you, you know they love you." Matt was striving to enhance his self and yet, at the same time, was pushing the very thing he wanted farther away because his behavior made him unacceptable to his parents.

Matt wanted to feel that he was a lovable person, to be accepted and included in the family as a worthy member. He found himself, however, in a home environment where the relationships were not lovingly supportive enough to provide the security and sense of belonging necessary for him to demonstrate directly in a constructive way that part of himself that longed to be appreciated and responded to as a lovable person. Because Matt was not able to express outwardly his inner drive to enhance his self, he resorted to indirect and ultimately self-defeating ways of affirming the worthwhileness of his self.

Axline (1969) explained the difference between well-adjusted behavior and maladjusted behavior this way:

> When the individual develops sufficient self-confidence…consciously and purposefully to direct his behavior by evaluation, selectivity, and application to achieve his ultimate goal in life—self-realization—then he seems to be well-adjusted.
>
> On the other hand, when the individual lacks sufficient self-confidence to chart his course of actions openly, seems content

to grow in self-realization vicariously rather than directly, and does little or nothing about channeling this drive in more constructive and productive directions, then he is said to be maladjusted.... The individual's behavior is not consistent with the inner concept of the self which the individual has created in his attempt to achieve complete self-realization. The further apart the behavior and the concept, the greater the degree of maladjustment. (pp. 13–14)

All maladjustments result from an incongruence between what is actually experienced and the concept of self. Whenever a child's perception of an experience is distorted or denied, a state of incongruence between the self-concept and experience exists, resulting in psychological maladjustment. Incongruence between the child's self-concept and experience basically results in incongruence in behavior. Therefore, **the child-centered play therapist is intentional about looking through the child's eyes to understand the child's perception of self and experiences** and builds an understanding and accepting relationship in which the child feels safe enough to express himself and explore experiences as he perceives them. As previously stated, children possess the capacity to experience the factors of their psychological maladjustments and the capacity and the tendency to move away from a state of maladjustment toward a state of psychological health in the context of a safe relationship.

Therapeutic Conditions for Growth

This forward-moving, actualizing tendency previously described is the central tenet of the child-centered approach to play therapy and was succinctly described by Rogers (1980) as "Individuals have within themselves vast resources for self-understanding and for altering their self-concepts, basic attitudes, and self-directed behavior; these resources can be tapped if a definable climate of facilitative psychological attitudes can be provided" (p. 115). The attitudes of the play therapist that form the basis for the therapeutic relationship and facilitate the release of the child's inner resources for growth are genuineness (being real), nonpossessive warmth (warm caring and acceptance), and empathy (sensitive understanding) (Rogers, 1986).

Being Real

The child-centered play therapy relationship is not an experience in which the therapist assumes a certain role or tries to do things in a prescribed manner. That would not be real or genuine. An attitude is a way of living life, not a technique to be applied when it seems to be needed. Genuineness is a basic and fundamental attitude that is for the therapist **a way of being rather than a way of doing.** Realness is not something to be "put on" but, rather, a "living out" of self at the moment in the relationship. The extent to which this is possible is a function of the therapist's awareness of his own feelings and attitudes. Genuineness or realness implies that the therapist possesses a high degree of self-understanding and self-acceptance and is congruent in what he feels and what he expresses in the relationship. This concept does not imply that the play therapist must be fully self-actualized; rather, it is a statement regarding the importance and necessity of the therapist having insight and being congruent in the relationship with the child.

The play therapist must have ample self-understanding and insight into personal feelings in areas such as rejection, which may be experienced in relation to a child's behavior in the playroom. This area of self-understanding is especially important for beginning play therapists, whose experiences and value systems may result in their experiencing feelings of rejection or even dislike of a child who exhibits messy behavior, tries to manipulate, or is verbally abusive to the therapist. A play therapist who lacks self-understanding of her own motivation in this area may inappropriately project rejection to the child. Play therapists should work through such issues in supervisory or consultation relationships outside the play therapy experience.

Realness is being aware of and accepting one's own feelings and reactions with insight into the accompanying motivation and being willing to be oneself and to express these feelings and reactions when appropriate. At such times the therapist is being real or genuine and is experienced by the child as a person, rather than as a professional. If the therapist feels uncomfortable about something the child has asked her to do, expressing those feelings of being uncomfortable is being very real. Children are sensitive to the play therapist's way of being and are keenly aware of any false front or professional role presented. The experience of being with an adult who is living a life of realness at the moment with the child can be very rewarding for a child. Such an experience was summed up by one child who said, "You don't seem like a counselor. You just seem like a real person."

Warm Caring and Acceptance

A discussion of warm caring and acceptance must first focus on the necessity of the play therapist's acceptance of self. The time with the child is not an objective relationship in which some kind of mechanical acceptance of the child exists but, rather, is an extension of self as being acceptable to self and relating on that basis. Children are nonassuming in their acceptance, and their acceptance is basically unconditional. I have learned from my experiences with children that they like and accept me for the person I am, for the way I am. They do not try to analyze or diagnose me. They accept me, my strengths, and my weaknesses. Experiencing their acceptance has freed me to be more accepting of the person I am. How can a play therapist extend to a child genuine warmth if the therapist does not feel that for himself? How can the therapist be accepting of the child if the therapist experiences self-rejection or nonacceptance of the person he is? How can I respect the child if I do not respect myself? Acceptance, like genuineness, is an attitude, a way of being, an extension of the person of the therapist and all that the therapist is at that moment.

This kind of acceptance and warm caring is characterized by positive respect for the child as a person of worth. The therapist experiences a genuine feeling of warmth and caring for the child which is unconditional. This caring is experientially felt; it is not some abstract attitude of respect and acceptance of the worth and dignity of other persons one can pick up from readings or

FIGURE 5.1   Warm caring and acceptance grant the child freedom and permission to be fully himself or herself in the emerging togetherness of the relationship in the playroom. The therapist really cares for the child, and there is an absence of evaluation or judgment.

graduate courses in counseling or psychology. The therapist really cares for the child and experiences a genuine prizing of the person of the child, so what occurs is an absence of evaluation or judgment. Experiential caring is based on interactions within a relationship, getting to know the person of the child, and therefore does not automatically exist at the deepest levels possible within the first few minutes of encountering the child. Neither is it likely, as Rogers (1977) has pointed out, that the therapist will experience unconditional caring at all times. Unconditional caring and acceptance is not an all-or-none characteristic but is best thought of as a matter of degree, experienced in relation to the child out of the play therapist's deep, abiding feeling for, faith in, and appreciation of children's lives. The child is respected and prized just as much when she is defiant, moody, angry, or resistive as when she is cooperative, happy, or pleasantly engaging the therapist (Figure 5.1).

Warm caring and acceptance grant the child freedom and permission to be fully himself in the emerging togetherness of the relationship in the playroom. The therapist does not wish that the child were different in some way. The attitudinal message consistently projected is, "I accept you as you are," not "I'll accept you if...." Acceptance does not imply approval of all of the child's behavior. As is discussed in Chapter 11, many behaviors are considered unacceptable in the playroom necessitating the setting of therapeutic limits. However, the central concept here is that **none of the child's behaviors is evaluated as making the child any more or any less worthy of being accepted or prized as a unique person.** Such nonevaluative acceptance is absolutely essential to establishing the kind of relationship in which the child feels safe enough to express and reveal her innermost feelings and thoughts.

Most children have a strong desire to please adults and are quite sensitive to even the most subtle cues of rejection by the therapist. Children are keenly aware of and sensitive to whatever the play therapist experiences. Therefore, the importance of therapist self-awareness and self-understanding needs to be emphasized again. Children are egocentric and are likely to internalize a therapist's feelings of boredom, impatience, veiled criticism, or other negative behaviors as rejection of themselves. Because children have been developmentally dependent on "reading" nonverbal communication cues of adults, they are sensitive to whatever the therapist is feeling.

If the therapist experiences some inner tenseness as the child takes a fist full of playdough and repeatedly squishes it in the cup of brown tempera paint, that will be sensed by the child and will inhibit further experiential communication and exploration. Impatience with a child who stands in silence in the middle of the playroom and is slow to begin playing may show in a slightly different tone of voice or verbal expression such as, "You don't want to play with any of the toys here?" or a suggestion, "Beth, maybe you would like to play with some of those dolls right there." Beth hears these as messages of rejection, that she is not pleasing the therapist. In response to a 10-year-old boy filling the nursing bottle with water and sucking on it at length, the therapist's reaction may be, "Now what! He's too big to do that! Maybe he's regressing, and I should do something to stop it." Such a critical reaction may show in raised eyebrows, squinted eyes, or clinched teeth and will be quickly perceived by the child as disapproval. The child's reaction, then, is likely to be feelings of guilt for engaging in "baby" play. If the therapist readily responds to some play activities by the child and not so readily to others, the child takes note of that as disapproval of the play that is not readily responded to.

These are subtle but significant forces in the play therapy relationship, and they have a major impact on the degree of acceptance experienced by the child. Warm caring and acceptance are basically an attitude of receptiveness toward the experiential world of the child and facilitate in the child an awareness that the therapist can be trusted.

Sensitive Understanding

The typical approach in most adult–child interactions is characterized by an attitude of evaluation of children based on what is known about them. Seldom do adults strive to understand the internal frame of reference of children, their subjective world. **Children are not free to explore, to test boundaries, to share frightening parts of their lives, or to change until they experience a relationship in which their subjective experiential world is understood and accepted.** Sensitive understanding of children occurs to the extent the therapist is able to put aside his own experiences and expectations and appreciate the personhood of children, their activities, their experiences, their feelings, and their thoughts. According to Rogers (1961), this kind of empathy is the ability to see the world of another by assuming the internal frame of reference of that person: "To sense the client's private world as if it were your own but without ever losing the 'as if' quality—this is empathy, and it seems essential to therapy" (p. 284).

Attempting to sensitively understand children from their viewpoint may be one of the most difficult and also potentially most critical factors of the therapeutic relationship, for as children feel understood by the play therapist, they are encouraged to share more of themselves. Such understanding seems to have a magnetic quality for children. As they feel understood, they feel safe enough to venture forth further in the relationship, and their perception of their world is changed.

This process of coming forth and familiar objects taking on new meaning is graphically described in the delightful story of *The Little Prince* (de Saint Exupery, 1943). The fox in the story tries to convince the little prince to tame him (to establish a relationship with him). He tells the little prince his life is monotonous and boring, that he hunts chickens and men hunt him. There is no change in expectation or the routine. He describes the chickens as all being just alike, and all the men as just alike. Then the fox says,

> But if you tame me, it will be as if the sun came to shine on my life. I shall know the sound of a step that will be different from all the others. Other steps send me hurrying back underneath the ground. Yours will call me, like music, out of my burrow. And then look: you see the grain-fields down yonder? I do not eat bread. Wheat is of no use to me. The wheat fields have nothing to say to me. And that is sad. But you have hair that is the color of gold. Think how wonderful that will be when you have tamed me! The grain, which is also golden, will bring me back the thought of you. And I shall love to listen to the wind in the wheat. (p. 83)

The similarity between this description and the impact an understanding and accepting relationship in play therapy can have in changing a child's perception is striking. What a wonderful description of the healing power of a relationship to alter a person's perception of the world and in the process that which had little meaning takes on new and significant meaning. **Perceptions are changed as a result of meaningful relationships.**

In a play therapy relationship, the therapist anticipates the child's inner rhythm and is sensitive to the emotional movement of the child in the flow of the play therapy process. Being empathic with a child often is regarded as a passive process of sitting in a chair in a playroom and allowing the child to do whatever comes to mind, with little or no reaction or response from the play therapist. Nothing could be further from the truth. This relationship of being fully with a child is a highly interactive mental and verbal process on the part of the therapist. Sensitive understanding that is accurate requires the therapist to maintain a high level of emotional interaction with the child. The therapist has a sense of personal identification (as if) with the child, rather than a mere reflection of feelings now and then as the child plays.

This process of being fully with the child and sensitively and accurately understanding the child requires a commitment of self to the relationship with the child. Being fully committed to the relationship with the child results in one of the most active experiences in which a therapist can be engaged, necessitating significant emotional and mental involvement and verbal responsiveness on the part of the therapist. This is not some objective observational activity to be entered into lightly. Mental and emotional effort is required to accurately sense and enter into the child's private world with understanding. Children know when they have been "touched" in this way (Figure 5.2).

FIGURE 5.2 The relationship with a child is a continual prizing of the uniqueness of the child and an empathic experiencing of the moment-by-moment living out of the child's world at a pace of unfolding determined by the inner direction of the emerging child.

Sensitive understanding means the play therapist is in full emotional contact with the child's perceptual, experiential world of reality. No questioning or evaluation is made of the child's verbal or acted out description of feelings or experiences in relation to this personal world of experiencing. The therapist tries hard to be fully in tune with all that the child is experiencing and expressing at the moment. The therapist does not try to think ahead of the child's experience or to analyze the content in some way to derive meaning. The attitude of the therapist is to sense as deeply as possible the experiencing of the child at that moment and to accept as fully as possible the emerging intuitive empathic response within herself as being sufficient for the moment. Thus, the relationship with the child is a continual prizing of the child's uniqueness and an empathic experiencing of the moment-by-moment living out of the child's world at a pace of unfolding determined by the inner direction of the emerging child.

The therapist does not try to send painful experiences of the child away by unnecessary reassurance, such as reassuring a frightened child that "Everything will be okay" or attempting to comfort a child with, "But your mother really does love you." To do so would be to reject what the child is feeling at the moment. Such responses give a clear message to the child that it is not permissible to experience pain. Whatever the child feels is considered by the therapist to be a legitimate feeling. If Bobby feels sad over the loss of a favorite crayon, the therapist experiences that sadness, perhaps not to the extent the child feels it, but nevertheless an experiencing occurs of the sadness "as if." Even though the therapist may never have been physically abused by an alcoholic father, the terror and anger felt by Kevin are experienced within the intuitive experiencing of the therapist "as if" and verbally communicated with feeling to Kevin. "You felt completely helpless and were so scared of your father. You feel really angry at him." The therapist must be careful not to allow his life experiences to encroach upon and color such feelings and experiences.

The Therapeutic Relationship

Attempting to describe the almost imperceptible but fully present subtle nuances characteristic of a shared relationship with the person of a child is a bit like trying to pick up a small bubble of mercury with your fingers. The very nature of the mercury is such that it defies being picked up. How does one adequately describe the shared experience, the exuberance of a child who struggles to express the unbelievable emotional release experienced in the safety of being fully accepted as a person of worth? Are there words that will adequately describe the emotion experienced in such moments? If so, they are unknown to me, for words always seem to be such an inadequate means for attempting to convey the essence of such a shared moment with a child.

Perhaps we should look to children who live out such experiences in the playroom for descriptions of the meaning of the relationship. Five-year-old Philip stood in the middle of the playroom flinging his arms up and down and excitedly repeated, "Who would have thought there was such a place like this in the whole world!" Indeed, this relationship is for most children like no other they have experienced. Here the adult allows the child to be—just that, to be! The child is accepted for the person she is and what she is at that time.

This kind of relating, of truly experiencing being with a child with the permission of the child to know her inner world, is not learned by training or by sharpening our intellect. It is a learning open only to the heart. The importance of responding out of one's heart in a relationship with a child is vividly described by the Tin Woodman in his conversation with the Scarecrow in *The Wizard of Oz*:

> "I don't know enough," replied the Scarecrow cheerfully. "My head is stuffed with straw, you know, and that is why I am going to Oz to ask him for some brains."
> "O, I see," said the Tin Woodman. "But, after all, brains are not the best things in the world."
> "Have you any?" inquired the Scarecrow.
> "No, my head is quite empty," answered the Woodman, "but once I had brains, and a heart also; so having tried them both, I should much rather have a heart." (Baum, 1956, pp. 55–56)

Respect for the person of the child and a prizing of the child's world are not activities of the mind. They are genuinely felt and experienced in the inner person of the therapist and are sensed and felt by the child, who deeply appreciates and values the therapist for such unconditional acceptance. This relationship with the child in the playroom, then, is a mutually shared relationship of acceptance and appreciation in which each person is regarded as an individual.

This is a unique relationship based on **expectancy not expectation.** Expectation focuses on behavior, expecting the child to be a certain way, to exhibit certain behaviors that have previously been identified, to play a certain way, what the child is supposed to do. A relationship of expectations is based on performance as the basis for identity and value. Expectations restrict and box a child in. Because I have no expectations of Bryan in the playroom, I will never be disappointed in Bryan.

Expectancy has a dynamic quality of anticipation of being together. What will Bryan be like today? Expectancy is an attitude of eagerness. Expectancy is alive, dynamic, an unknown potential. **A relationship of expectancy does not rely on the past or information about a child.**

I have sometimes experienced a fantasy that the developing relationship with a child in play therapy is like going into a completely dark room, in which someone has placed a beautiful and very valuable vase on a stand. I enter the pitch-black room with eager expectancy knowing the vase is in there somewhere and wanting to make contact with it so that I can discover what it is like and appreciate its beauty. Under such conditions I would not stride right into the darkness of the room and begin to grope for the location of the vase. Neither would I swing my arms rapidly to try to make contact, lest I unexpectedly and unintentionally strike the stand or the prized vase, causing it to topple to the floor. Such behavior would be unthinkable. Instead, I enter the darkness of the room with caution and first stand there to begin to adjust to these new surroundings, trying to sense the dimensions of the room. I focus all of my energy on being sensitively aware of the possible existence of nearby objects.

Having adjusted to the initial darkness of the room and being guided by great caution, I proceed to gently explore what is available to me in the room. My movements are slow. I begin to get acquainted with what I experience in the room, to see as clearly as I can in my mind that which I experience and sense with my total being. Everything about me is straining to sense the presence of the vase. After a few moments of not being successful in my efforts to locate the vase, I do not change my approach and move ahead quickly or try a new procedure and start crawling around on the floor. Quite the contrary, I know the vase is here somewhere; so I proceed with great patience to gently feel for the vase.

I do not try to rush the discovery. Instead, I persevere with persistent patience in my effort to make contact with the vase. Finally, one of my gentle hand movements touches something; I am very still, knowing it is here! I experience a flood of relief, joy, anticipation, and wonder at what the vase will be like. Then I begin ever so gently to touch the vase, allowing my hands to explore its shape and beauty and to picture that beauty in my mind. The play therapy experience with a child is like this experience with the vase, and in like manner I want to approach, experience, and "touch" the emotionally vulnerable child.

When I am in a relationship with a child, I experience an unspoken inner struggle to touch what is untouchable in the child. To accomplish this, I have learned to appreciate and enjoy the child's inner quietness. Waiting is a part of the therapeutic process. *Waiting for the child conveys a belief in the child, a willingness to trust the child.* I want to be patient with the child's inner process. If I am to be successful in my effort to make contact with the child,

> I must be still within myself and *see* the child.
> I must be still and *listen* to the child.
> I must be still and *make contact* with the imagination of the child.
> I must be still and *follow* the lead of the child.
> I must be still and *experience* the child.
> I must be still within myself and *touch* the hidden inner person of the child.
> I must be still within myself and *wait* for the child.

If I am to be helpful to a child, I must make contact with the person of the child at all levels of experiencing in our shared time together. Being still within myself does not mean I am unresponsive and silent. A great deal is always being communicated verbally and nonverbally by a child, and I want to communicate what I hear and understand to the child. I would like to gently touch the child's emotional world and also to hear as fully as I can the child's expressed thoughts, reactions, and descriptions. I would like the total response of my person, verbally and nonverbally, to convey to the child the depth of my yearning to know and understand, to the extent to which I am fully capable, the child's experiential inner world of feelings and thoughts as known, experienced, felt, expressed, and lived out at the moment.

Just as I want to hear, the child has a longing to share what he may perceive as a frightening part of his life, or a part of his life that the child fears may be rejected by me or others. So the child ventures forth in this relationship in ways that may seem to lack focus or direction as he experiences this inner conflict of wanting to be heard and fearing evaluation and criticism. At such times a tentative and perhaps almost imperceptible sharing occurs of this vulnerable part of the child's self in what may be an obscure or oblique manner that could easily go unnoticed, because the message is so inconspicuous or veiled.

The child is perhaps at that moment only vaguely aware at some deeper level of this underlying part of herself or her experience that she would like to share, perhaps not even at a conscious level, in the immediacy of our experiencing relationship. At other times, one can sense at an immediate conscious level a deep longing on the part of the child to have this vulnerable part of self heard and accepted. In the midst of the child's behavior that may sometimes be bizarre or sometimes monotonous or sometimes seemingly out of control or deliberately provocative, there is the person of a child who is tapping out a message, "Does anyone hear me? Does anyone notice I am hurting? Does anyone care?" At these moments in our developing relationship, I would like by my attitude, words, feelings, tone of voice, facial and bodily expression, by the total person I am to communicate my hearing, understanding, and acceptance of this deeper message in a way that will help the child to feel safe, accepted, and appreciated. I want by all that I am at that moment to confirm the child's existence.

Sometimes by my response in such moments, it seems to me I am very gently opening a door the child has come to stand in front of in our journey together; and by that gesture, I am saying to the child, "I'm really not sure either what is on the other side of the door. I understand what is there may be frightening to you or something you would rather not face. But I am willing to walk through that door with you. I am not willing to lead you through the door, nor will I push you or follow you through the door. I will be fully present beside you, and we will discover together what is there. I trust you in this process to be able to face and cope with whatever we find there." This kind of relationship was described by Rogers (1952, p. 70) as "the process by which the structure of the self is relaxed in the safety of the relationship with the therapist, and previously denied experiences are perceived and then integrated into an altered self."

The beginning of this movement toward a different self is facilitated when the warmth, interest, caring, understanding, genuineness, and empathy experienced by the therapist are perceived and felt by the child. In this climate of facilitative psychological attitudes (Rogers, 1980), the child comes to rely on her own vast resources for self-directed behavior and for altering her self-concept and basic attitude. Thus, **the power to change resides within the child and is not a result of direction, advice, or information the therapist might have to offer.** As expressed by Rogers (1961, p. 33), "If I can provide a certain type of relationship, the other person will discover within himself the capacity to use that relationship for growth and change, and personal development will occur." The relationship then can be described as therapeutic and a function of basic key attitudes of the child-centered play therapist who is willing to know the child and to be known in the process of the developing relationship.

Child-centered play therapy is an immediate and present experience for children in which the therapeutic process emerges from a shared living relationship developed on the basis of the therapist's consistently conveyed acceptance of children and confidence in their ability to be of help to themselves, thus freeing children to risk using their own strengths. Experiencing this acceptance of themselves, children begin to value themselves and come to perceive and accept themselves as unique and separate.

As children gradually experience being themselves, they are free to experience living in the present and to make creative, responsible use of their individuality. The therapist can do nothing to make this happen. The therapist tries to see and experience the child's point of reference and understand the meaning to the child without imposing her beliefs or solutions on the child. This basic intent of the therapist does not vary with the presenting problem or the cultural background of the child. According to Glover (2001), "It is exactly this accepting and respectful relationship that makes child-centered play therapy an ideal intervention for children who are of a different culture than the therapist" (p. 32).

Because the motivation for learning and change spring from an intrinsic self-actualizing tendency in the child, I have no need to motivate the child, to supply energy, or to direct the child's behavior toward some predetermined goal. **I trust the child to lead our experience together to where the child needs to be. I am not wise enough to know where a child should be in our relationship, or what a child should do.** I trust the child's intuitive inner direction to take the experience to where the child needs to be. I can never be sure I know what the child should be working on in our time together. For example, only the child and the perpetrator may know about sexual abuse. Parents and teachers may know only that there are behaviors, such as a child waking up frightened or biting other children, about which they are concerned.

In the child-centered approach, the child selects the theme, content, and process of the play. The child chooses which toys to play with and sets the pace. The therapist does not make decisions for the child, no matter how insignificant the decision may seem to be. Thus, the child is encouraged to accept responsibility for himself and in the process discovers his own strengths.

The nature of the interaction between the therapist and child in the child-centered approach was clarified by Axline (1969) in her *Eight Basic Principles,* which serve as a guide for therapeutic contact with children. These principles in revised and extended form are listed here:

1. The therapist is genuinely interested in the child and develops a warm, caring relationship.
2. The therapist experiences unqualified acceptance of the child and does not wish that the child were different in some way.
3. The therapist creates a feeling of safety and permissiveness in the relationship, so the child feels free to explore and express herself completely.
4. The therapist is always sensitive to the child's feelings and gently reflects those feelings in such a manner that the child develops self-understanding.
5. The therapist believes deeply in the child's capacity to act responsibly, unwaveringly respects the child's ability to solve personal problems, and allows the child to do so.
6. The therapist trusts the child's inner direction, allows the child to lead in all areas of the relationship, and resists any urge to direct the child's play or conversation.
7. The therapist appreciates the gradual nature of the therapeutic process and does not attempt to hurry the process.
8. The therapist establishes only those therapeutic limits necessary to anchor the session to reality and which help the child accept personal and appropriate relationship responsibility.

In this approach, *the child and not the problem is the point of focus.* If the focus of the play therapist's interactions with a child is on solving the child's identified problem, then the message communicated to the child is, "Your problem is more important than you are."

RULE OF THUMB:

When you focus on the problem, you lose sight of the child.

The child is always more important than any problem the child may be experiencing. I would be dismayed if a child ever thought that I was more interested in or concerned about a problem she might have than I was about her as a person. Every child is so much more than anything the child has done or experienced. I have learned from children that **experiences do not define the persons they are.** Children are not bound by their experiences. They are not limited to what they have done or accomplished.

It is very likely that someone reading this book has experienced a shattering experience in his or her life, the destruction of a dream, an overwhelming tragedy, a deeply disturbing experience, a traumatic event, or a heartbreaking loss. The person you are is not defined by that experience. Perhaps you are reading this book because you are in graduate school and now have direction in your life. You have overcome that devastating experience, a testimony to the resiliency of the human organism and the fact that the person you are is not defined by that experience.

RULE OF THUMB:

The facts about a child do not tell very much about the person of a child.

The play therapist must avoid becoming blinded by her limited understanding of a child and a prisoner of her own solutions to complex problems. The child's identified problem may be only an observable symptom of a deeper issue, the cause. I do not assume that what I have been told about a child by parents, teachers, and other significant individuals in the child's life is the most important thing about the child or all there is to know about the child. Therefore, **my objective in the play therapy relationship is to discover that which I don't know that I don't know I don't know.** I am not wise enough to know what I should be looking for in a child. And because I don't know what to look for, how can I go looking for it?

There is so much I don't know about children. Perhaps what is most important is what I don't know. I am not wise enough to know what a child should be working on; therefore, I trust the child to take me in this relationship to where the child needs to be. I make no preconceived decisions about a child. To do so would block the creative growth of the child. I wait patiently with wonder and eager anticipation as the vulnerable inner person of the child emerges.

The journey of the relationship is what is significant, not the determining of the child's past history, not the determining of causes, not the uncovering of past behaviors, not the discovery of environmental factors, not the development of an educational plan, not direction provided by the therapist, not the structuring of interventions, not the solving of the child's problem, but *being with* the child, fully experiencing the child's world, seeing, experiencing, and taking in a part of the child I have not experienced before. A play therapist in a supervision group concluded, "Therapy is not something I have to do, but rather is something to be a part of. Play therapy is a journey I get to take with a child."

Diagnosis is not necessary, because child-centered play therapy is not a prescriptive approach. The therapist does not vary the approach to meet demands based on a specific referral problem. The relationship that develops and the creative forces this relationship releases in the child *generate* the process of change and growth for the child. **The relationship is the therapy; it is not preparation for therapy or behavioral change.**

Whatever develops in the child as a result of the play therapy relationship was already there. The therapist does not create anything in the child. The therapist only helps to release what already exists in the child. The potential for whatever positive behavioral changes or growth that occurs or whatever the child becomes already existed in the child before the therapist saw the child. Therefore, the therapist cannot take credit for the change. In this process, the child is responsible for himself and is quite capable of exercising that responsibility through self-direction resulting in more positive behavior.

In child-centered play therapy, the relationship, not the utilization of toys, or the application of techniques, or the interpretation of behavior, is the key to growth. Therefore, the relationship is always focused on the present, living experience with the child:

Person of the child... rather than ... problem
Present............. rather than ... past
Feelings .... rather than ... thoughts or acts
Understanding ...... rather than ... explaining
Accepting .... rather than ... correcting

Child's direction. . . . . rather than . . . therapist's instruction
Child's wisdom. . . . . . rather than . . . therapist's knowledge

The relationship provides consistent acceptance of the child, which is necessary for the development of enough inner freedom and security in the child for her to express herself in self-enhancing ways. The key facilitative elements in the relationship which are growth-promoting for the child can be summed up in the following **therapeutic dimensions in the play therapy relationship:**

Belief in the child
Respect for the child
Acceptance of the child
Hearing the inner child
Acceptance of the child's will
Focus on the child's needs
Freedom for the child to set his own direction
Opportunity for the child to make choices
Respect for the child's boundaries
Patience with the process

Objectives in Child-Centered Play Therapy

When we speak of objectives in the child-centered play therapy approach, the emphasis is on broadly defined therapeutic objectives rather than on individualized prescriptive goals for the child. Setting specific goals is inconsistent with child-centered philosophy because goals are evaluative and imply specific achievements required of the child which have been externally established. When specific objectives or goals are set for the individual child, the therapist will almost assuredly drift into the trap of subtly or directly pushing the child to work on the objective related to the identified problem and will thus restrict the child's opportunity for self-direction. Does this mean the therapist is not interested in the "problem" parents or teachers have identified? Not at all, for such information about the child is a part of the child's total life and can (but not necessarily) help the therapist to better understand what the child is communicating in the playroom.

An important caution to note is that knowing such pretherapy information about the child may bias the play therapist's perceptual view of the child and result in the therapist not "seeing" other parts of the child. Although this is a realistic concern, exposure to information about the child prior to encountering the child for the first time is largely unavoidable in that the therapist will often need to interview parents or teachers prior to working with the child, because the setting precludes the availability of another staff member to conduct the interview. This potential problem can largely be overcome if the therapist has a high degree of self-understanding, is aware of the potential perceptual bias, and is committed to the process of allowing the child to be fully the person she is at the moment with the therapist.

The general objectives of child-centered play therapy are consistent with the child's inner self-directed striving toward self-actualization. An overriding premise is the necessity for building a relationship with the child that will provide the child with a positive growth experience in the presence of an understanding, accepting, and supportive adult so the child will be able to discover internal strengths.

RULE OF THUMB:

It is not possible to establish a relationship with a problem.

Because child-centered play therapy focuses on the person of the child rather than on the child's problem, the emphasis is on facilitating the child's efforts to become more adequate, as a person, in coping with current and future problems that may affect his life. To that end, the broad therapeutic objectives of child-centered play therapy are to help the child

1. Develop a more positive self-concept.
2. Assume greater self-responsibility.
3. Become more self-directing.
4. Become more self-accepting.

5. Become more self-reliant.
6. Engage in self-determined decision making.
7. Experience a feeling of control.
8. Become sensitive to the process of coping.
9. Develop an internal source of evaluation.
10. Become more trusting of himself.

These objectives of child-centered play therapy provide a general framework for understanding the characteristics and the process of the approach. Because specific objectives are not set for the child, the therapist is free to facilitate the development of these person-focused objectives. This does not preclude the child from working on specific problems she feels a need to express, but frees the child to do so. In this child-centered relationship, the therapist believes in and trusts the child's capacity to set her own goals. Children in play therapy, however, seldom establish specific goals for themselves, at least not verbally and perhaps not consciously. A 4-year-old does not voluntarily say, "I need to stop hitting my 1-year-old brother," or a 5-year-old does not state, "My goal is to like myself better." Likewise, a 6-year-old does not say, "I'm here to work on the anger and rage I feel toward my father, who sexually abused me." Although such problems may not be stated as goals by children, such problems will be acted out through their play, and in the process of the relationship children *will* work on the problems in their own way. In this approach, children need not be aware they have a problem for play therapy to be beneficial.

In child-centered play therapy, no attempt is made to control a child, to have the child be a certain way, or to reach a conclusion the therapist has decided is important. The therapist is not the authority who decides what is best for the child, what the child should think, or how he should feel. If this were the case, the child would be deprived of the opportunity to discover his own strengths.

What Children Learn in Play Therapy

Because the majority of children who are referred for play therapy are involved in some sort of school experience, a pertinent topic to examine is that of learning. Most teachers spend their day involved in the process of helping children learn, so teachers naturally may want to know just what children learn in play therapy, especially if a child has to miss part of the instructional time in order to attend play therapy sessions. Actually, for children play therapy is a unique learning experience under the most favorable growth-promoting conditions possible and, as such, is viewed from a developmental perspective with objectives consistent with those of the school: to assist children in learning about themselves and their world.

Play therapy assists the development of children by helping them to know and accept themselves. Play therapy also assists in accomplishing the broader school objective of learning about the world by helping children to get ready to profit from the learning experiences provided by teachers. Children who are anxious or worried, have poor self-concepts, are experiencing a divorce in the home environment, or have poor peer relationships cannot achieve maximum learning from even the most masterful teacher. **Play therapy, therefore, is an adjunct to the learning environment, an experience that helps children maximize opportunities to learn in the classroom.**

Risk taking, self-exploration, and self-discovery are not likely to occur in the presence of threat or the absence of safety. The potential learning experiences available in play therapy are directly related to the degree to which the therapist is successful in creating a climate of safety within which children feel fully accepted and safe enough to risk being and expressing the innermost totality of their emotional being. This is not a conscious decision on the part of children but, rather, the result of a permissive climate void of criticism, suggestions, praise, disapproval, or efforts to change them.

Children are accepted just as they are; therefore, there is no need to please the adult in this relationship. As one child expressed it, "In here you can just be your own little ol' self." Because there is no threat to self, self-exploration and self-discovery occur naturally. This is not meant to imply that self-expression occurs with reckless abandon, as might be the case in the early stage of the therapeutic process. In response to the feeling of permissiveness established in the playroom, the safety to be fully one's self, and the careful use of therapeutic limits (which will be discussed later), *children learn self-control and responsible freedom of expression.*

Most of what is learned by children in the play therapy relationship is not a cognitive learning but a developing experiential, intuitive learning about the self that occurs over the course of the therapeutic experience. This kind of learning about self in the child-centered play therapy relationship is a result of the kind of relationship facilitated by the therapist. The following Eight Basic Learning Experiences About Self facilitate change in children:

- **Children learn to respect themselves.** The play therapist maintains and communicates a constant regard and respect for children, regardless of their behavior—whether they are playing passively, acting out aggression, or being whiny and dependently insisting on help with even the simplest tasks. Children sense and experience the therapist's respect, feel respected, and, because an absence of evaluation and an ever-present acceptance exists, they internalize the respect and thus learn to respect themselves. Once children have respect for themselves, they learn to respect others.

- **Children learn that their feelings are acceptable.** Through the process of playing out their feelings in the presence of an adult who understands and accepts even the intensity of the feelings, children learn that all of their feelings are acceptable. As children experience their feelings are acceptable, they begin to be more open in expressing their feelings.

- **Children learn to express their feelings responsibly.** Once children's feelings have been openly expressed and accepted, they lose their intensity and can more easily be controlled appropriately. *As children learn to responsibly control their feelings, they are no longer controlled by those feelings.* This, then, is a freeing process for children to experience in that they are free to go beyond those feelings.

- **Children learn to assume responsibility for themselves.** In the natural process of development, children strive toward independence and self-reliance but often are thwarted in their efforts by adults who, although well-intentioned, take charge by doing things *for* children and thus deprive them of opportunities to experience how being responsible for themselves feels. In the play therapy relationship, the therapist believes in children's ability to be resourceful and so resists doing anything that would deprive them of the opportunity to discover their own strength. As the therapist allows children to struggle to do things for themselves, children learn to assume responsibility for themselves and discover what that responsibility feels like.

- **Children learn to be creative and resourceful in confronting problems.** When children are allowed to figure things out for themselves, to derive their own solutions to problems, to complete their own tasks, their own creative resources are released and developed. With increasing frequency, then, children will tackle their own problems, even those that were formerly overwhelming, and experience the satisfaction of doing things all by themselves. Although a child may initially resist the opportunity to solve his own problems, the creative tendency of the self will come forth in response to the therapist's persistent patience.

- **Children learn self-control and self-direction.** If no opportunities are available to experience being in control, learning self-control and self-direction is not possible. Although this principle seems simplistically obvious, the absence of opportunities like this in children's lives is overwhelmingly conspicuous when one takes the time to carefully observe children's interactions with significant adults. Unlike most other adults in children's lives, the play therapist does not make decisions for children or try to control them either directly or subtly. Limits on children's behavior in the playroom are verbalized in such a way that children are allowed to control their own behavior. Because control is not applied externally, children learn self-control and self-direction as they are allowed to make their own decisions.

- **Children gradually learn, at a feeling level, to accept themselves.** As children experience being accepted just as they are with no conditional expectations from the therapist, they gradually, and in sometimes imperceptible ways, begin to accept themselves as worthwhile. This is both a direct and an indirect process of communication and learning about self. The therapist does not overtly tell children they are accepted, because that would have little or no positive impact on the relationship or the way children feel about themselves. Acceptance is an attitudinal message communicated verbally and nonverbally by all that the therapist is and does. Acceptance is first felt by children and then becomes known to them as they experience being accepted nonjudgmentally for who they are, just as they are, with no desire that they be different. This increased self-acceptance is a major contributing factor to the development of a positive self-concept.
- **Children learn to make choices and to be responsible for their choices.** Life entails a never-ending series of choices. But how can children learn how to make a choice or what making a choice feels like if they are not allowed to experience the process of making choices: the indecision, the struggle, wanting to avoid, feeling incapable, the anxiety, and the apprehension that one's choice will be unacceptable to others? Therefore, the therapist avoids making even simple choices for children, such as which color to use in a drawing or which toy to play with.

These are all desirable indices of growth in maturity.

Multicultural Approach of Child-Centered Play Therapy

Child-centered play therapy is a culturally sensitive approach because the facts about a child's socioeconomic strata or ethnic background

> [D]o not change the therapist's beliefs, philosophy, theory or approach to the child. Empathy, acceptance, understanding, and genuineness on the part of the therapist are provided to children

equally, irrespective of their color, condition, circumstance, concern or complaint. The child is free to communicate through play in a manner that is comfortable and typical for the child, including cultural adaptations of play and expression. (Sweeney & Landreth, 2009, p. 135)

Being sensitively attuned to a child and responding to a child's emotions transcends culture and is a multicultural language (Figure 5.3). As pointed out earlier in this chapter, the child-centered play therapist tries to see and experience the child's point of reference and understand the meaning to the child without imposing beliefs or solutions on the child. This basic intent of the therapist does not vary with the presenting problem or the cultural background of the child. According to Glover (2001), "It is exactly this accepting and respectful relationship that makes child-centered play therapy an ideal intervention for children who are of a

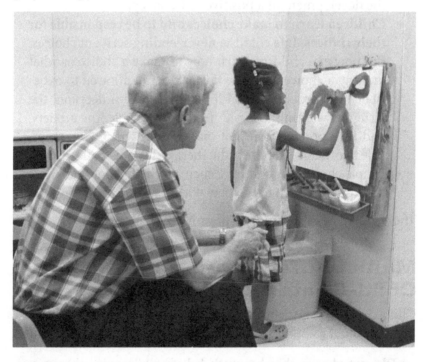

FIGURE 5.3 Child-centered play therapy is a culturally responsive intervention because children's self-directed play takes on aspects of their culture and transcends language barriers.

different culture than the therapist" (p. 32). When a child plays out his story and is responded to with empathy, genuine warmth, and acceptance by the therapist, the child begins to develop empathy and acceptance of self and others and acceptance of his culture because his cultural play is accepted.

Although some play therapists rely on a verbal approach and encourage children to express their feelings in words as a necessary part of resolving problems, the child-centered play therapist is respectful of differences, does not encourage or insist on direct verbal expression of affect, and allows children to choose the method of communication most comfortable to them. Because play is children's natural language of expression, children play out rather than talk out their experiences and feelings in direct but more often symbolic ways that allow them to distance themselves from the pain and stress involved in exploration of actual happenings and experiences. Thus, children in cultural groups where the direct expression of emotions is not encouraged are able to fully express and explore intense emotional reactions in the safety of their play in the child-centered play therapy relationship. Glover (2001) proposed that child-centered play therapy allows a child the freedom to be who the child is, thus providing the basis for a culturally sensitive relationship.

In some approaches to play therapy, the therapist expects children to volunteer information, especially information related to problems and their life experiences, so play therapy sessions can be structured to deal overtly with these issues in the course of therapy. Such an approach goes counter to the social values of many cultural groups that believe problems should not be disclosed to strangers and should be handled within the family. The child-centered play therapist does not question children about their problems because the child-centered approach is not a prescriptive approach and background information does not provide guidance for what the therapist does or how the therapist conducts herself in the relationship with a child in the playroom.

Lin (2011) found in his meta-analytic study of child-centered play therapy that non-Caucasian children demonstrated substantially greater improvement as a result of play therapy than Caucasian children. Lin hypothesized that a possible explanation lies in the child-centered play therapy approach that allows non-Caucasian children to utilize their self-directed play to transcend language barriers, thus allowing them a nonverbal means of expressing their inner feelings, thoughts, and experiences that they may be unable to express fully in an English-speaking world. Lin concluded his findings by strongly suggesting that practitioners can confidently consider child-centered play therapy as a culturally responsive intervention.

Garza (2010) studied the effects of child-centered play therapy with Hispanic children and concluded that the results of her study demonstrated

[S]trong support for CCPT as a viable treatment modality for Hispanic children. The results are noteworthy because this study compares CCPT to a research-supported intervention. There is a particularly strong indication that the behavioral outcomes of children who receive CCPT interfaces with a behaviorally focused value (obedience) of Hispanic parents. (p. 188)

Research studies have shown child-centered play therapy and child–parent relationship therapy (filial therapy based on child-centered play therapy philosophy, theory, and skills) to be effective with children across diverse cultures: African American children, Chinese children, German children, Hispanic children, Iranian children, Israeli children, Japanese children, Korean children, Native American children, and Puerto Rican children. (Research results are presented in Chapter 17 of this book.)

References

Axline, V. (1969). *Play therapy.* New York: Ballantine.

Baum, K. (1956). *The wizard of oz.* New York: Rand McNally.

de Saint Exupery, A. (1943). *The little prince.* New York: Harcourt, Brace.

Garza, Y. (2010). School-based child-centered play therapy with Hispanic children. In J. Baggerly, D. Ray , & S. Bratton (Eds.), *Child-centered play therapy research: The evidence base for effective practice* (pp. 177–191). Hoboken, NJ: Wiley.

Garza, Y., & Bratton, S. C. (2005). School-based child-centered play therapy with Hispanic children: Outcomes and cultural considerations. *International Journal of Play Therapy, 14(1)*, 51–79.

Glover, G. (2001). Cultural considerations in play therapy. In G. Landreth (Ed.), *Innovations in play therapy: Issues, process, and special populations* (pp. 31–41). Philadelphia: Brunner-Routledge.

Lin, Y. (2011). Contemporary Research of Child-Centered Play Therapy (CCPT) modalities: A Meta Analytic Review of Controlled Outcome Studies. (Unpublished doctoral dissertation, University of North Texas, Denton.)

Moustakas, C. (1981). *Rhythms, rituals and relationships*. Detroit, MI: Harlow Press.

Patterson, C. (1974). *Relationship counseling and psychotherapy*. New York: Harper & Row.

Rogers, C. (1951). *Client-centered therapy: Its current practice, implications, and theory*. Boston: Houghton Mifflin.

Rogers, C. (1952). Client-centered psychotherapy. *Scientific American, 187*, 70.

Rogers, C. (1961). *On becoming a person*. Boston: Houghton Mifflin.

Rogers, C. (1977). *Carl Rogers on personal power: Inner strength and its revolutionary impact*. New York: Delacorte.

Rogers, C. (1980). *A way of being*. Boston: Houghton Mifflin.

Rogers, C. (1986). Client-centered therapy. In J. L. Kutash & A. Wolf (Eds.), *Psychotherapist's casebook* (pp. 197–208). San Francisco: Jossey-Bass.

Sweeney, D., & Landreth, G. (2009). Child-centered play therapy. In K. O'Connor & L. Braverman (Ed.), *Play therapy theory and practice: Comparing theories and techniques* (2nd ed., pp. 123–162). Hoboken, NJ: Wiley.

6

The Play Therapist

Man is perfectly human only when he plays.

F. Schiller

The play therapist is a unique adult in children's lives, unique because the therapist responds out of his own humanness to the person of the child while controlling any desire to direct, probe, or teach, and instead provides responses that are freeing to the child's natural urge toward self-direction. That children are aware of this uniqueness may be seen in this excerpt from a play therapy session:

Chris: What color should I paint this frog?

Therapist: In here you can decide what color you want the frog to be.

Chris: I don't know. Would black be okay? Are some frogs black? My teacher said frogs are green.

Therapist: You would like to paint your frog black, but you're not sure that would be okay.

Chris: Yeah, you're supposed to tell me what color to use.

Therapist: You would like for me to make the decision for you.

Chris: Yeah, everybody else does.

Therapist: Everybody else would just decide for you so you think I should, too, but in here you can decide the color you want your frog to be.

Chris: It's going to be blue! The world's first blue frog! You're funny!

Therapist: I seem different to you because I don't tell you what to do.

Chris: Yeah!...Like a blue frog.

Creating Differences

Chris is right, of course. Therapists who use play therapy are "funny" people. They are not "funny" as in creating humor, but "funny" as in creating a new and different kind of adult–child relationship for the child to experience. The creation of this relationship is contributed to by the presence of play materials that provide unique opportunities for communication and relationship development that are not possible in verbally bound experiences with children. The playroom is not necessarily unique, for most children will have already played with many of the materials available. The playroom does, however, make it possible for the therapist to create those differences that make the therapist truly unique—"funny" in the child's thinking. This adult, the play therapist, exhibits characteristics children rarely experience with adults.

The characteristics of *acceptance of the child, respect for the child's uniqueness, and sensitivity to the child's feelings* identify the play therapist as a unique kind of adult. The therapist sees the child as an individual with thoughts, feelings, beliefs, ideas, desires, fantasies, and opinions worthy of respect. Many adults never see the child. They are too busy to notice the child. They have too many "important" things to do that must be done now, and after all, it is important that things be done in a hurry. Consequently, the child is not really seen. In such circumstances, the adult is only vaguely aware of the child's presence. For most children who come to the playroom, receiving the play therapist's complete and undivided attention for 45 minutes is a truly unique experience. The play therapist notices everything the child does and is genuinely interested in the child's feelings and play activities. Unlike most other adults, the therapist has a block of time devoted exclusively to the child.

The play therapist is *intentional* about creating an atmosphere. Therapists must be aware of what they do and why they do it. This makes therapists unique because they are not stumbling through a relationship with a child, but are being careful about their own words and actions. The therapist is working hard at creating an atmosphere conducive to the building of a relationship with the child. A difference is created because the time together is child centered, and the child is allowed to be separate from the therapist. The child is viewed as a capable and unique individual. A difference is created because the therapist has great respect for the child.

Being With

When a child first views the play therapist, no observable significant differences exist between the therapist and other adults. The therapist may be taller or shorter than most adults, or he or she may have a memorable face, but no physical differences exist that can signal to the child that this person will be special. The differences between an effective play therapist and other adults, therefore, must come from within as the self of the therapist is made fully present and available to the child.

Several qualities make the effective play therapist a different kind of adult to the child, and one of the most significant is the art of *being fully present*—that is, interacting with the child by observing, listening, and making statements of recognition. In many children's relationships with adults, being there rarely exists. Children are observed through the din of the television set or listened to from behind the evening paper and are recognized primarily when they do something wrong.

The play therapist is an adult who *intently observes, empathically listens, and encouragingly recognizes not only the child's play but also the child's wants, needs, and feelings.* The play therapist knows that being present with the child requires much more than a physical presence; **being with** is truly an art form that makes the play therapy experience unique for the child.

The play therapist is a person who hears the hurt in a child's heart; a person who cares enough to listen to the depth of a child's pain; a person who accepts without judgment the person of the child; a person who prizes the child's uniqueness in the midst of the child's despair; a person who appreciates the desperation of a child's loneliness; a person who understands and is willing to **be with** a child.

The uniqueness of the play therapist is heightened by listening actively not only to what the child verbalizes but also to the messages conveyed through the child's activity. The therapist understands that the toys and materials children select and how they play has meaning as a part of their total effort to communicate. The child receives the therapist's complete attention. Unlike many other adults, who are too busy and too involved with satisfying their own needs, the therapist is unhurried, and committed to understanding the child's needs, and really does want to hear the child. In fact, for the duration of the time they have together, to hear and understand are the therapist's primary objectives. The impact of this **being with** relationship can be seen in a child's reaction looking back on the play therapy experience several years later, "As I think back...you didn't seem to do a thing but be there. And yet, a harbor doesn't do anything either, except to stand there quietly with arms always outstretched waiting for the travelers to come home. I came home to myself through you" (Axline, 1950, p. 60).

Personality Characteristics

The following discussion may well sound like a description of an unattainable, perfect person. However, that is not the intent in attempting to describe personality characteristics that are conducive to helping children grow and develop in ways that are personally rewarding to them. The attainment of these characteristics is not nearly as important as the continual, self-motivating, never-ending process of striving to attain and incorporate these dimensions into one's life and relationships with children. The play therapist's *intentionality* in this striving is the dynamic therapeutic facilitative quality in the process, not the attainment of describable dimensions. Intentionality defies description but nevertheless exists in the inner recesses of the therapist's attitudes and motivations, and determines the extent to which the following characteristics are identifiable in the therapist's behavior.

Objective and Flexible. The effective play therapist is *objective* enough to allow the child to be a separate person and *flexible* in accepting and adapting to the unexpected with an attitude of willingness to be receptive to the new. These dimensions are based on an uncompromising resistance to imposing conforming behavior on children. The therapist has a genuine appreciation for the world of the child and attempts to understand that world on the basis of the child's own expressions. This appreciation is characterized by a sensitive understanding of, interest in, caring for, and liking of children.

RULE OF THUMB:

How the therapist feels about a child is more important than what the therapist knows about the child.

Does Not Judge or Evaluate. The therapist has no need to evaluate or judge children or what they produce or do not produce. An *unwillingness to judge or evaluate* stems from the therapist's experiential understanding of just how rewarding an experience can be when one is not being judged or evaluated. The therapist accepts the child's choice to play or not to play, to talk or not to talk. The child does not need to change or behave in any particular way to receive the therapist's acceptance. The therapist endeavors to meet the child where she is at the moment and moves with the child.

Open-Minded. The therapist is *open-minded* rather than close-minded. Openness and sensitivity to the child's world are basic prerequisites for play therapists. Children are considered and related to primarily on the basis of their own merit, who they are rather than who they have been described to be. There is an absence of any need to distort meanings, because the therapist is relatively free of threat and anxiety and is, therefore, open to receiving children as they are or will become. The therapist is able to turn loose of his world of reality and experience the child's world of reality. This open-minded dimension allows the therapist to receive fully and with accuracy the meanings communicated by children verbally, nonverbally, and in their play.

Patient. The play therapist is patient with the child in the moment, patient with the child's expression, patient with the child's process, and waits with eager expectancy for the child to come forth at the child's own pace. Patience allows the play therapist to take in, see, and experience what the child sees in her world. The process of this kind of patience is vividly described by White (1952):

> Raising plants is one of mankind's most successful activities. Perhaps success comes from the fact that the husbandman does not try to thrust impossible patterns on his plants. He respects their peculiarities, tries to provide suitable conditions, protects them from more serious kinds of injury—but he lets the plants do the growing. He does not poke at the seed in order to make it sprout more quickly, nor does he seize the shoot when it breaks ground and try to pull open the first leaves by hand. Neither does he trim the leaves of different kinds of plants in order to have them all look alike. The attitude of the husbandman is appropriate in dealing with children. It is the children who must do the growing, and they can do it only through the push of their own budding interests. (p. 363)

Such patience is anchored in the child-centered play therapist's unshakable belief in the child's inner-directional, constructive, forward-moving, creative, self-healing power.

High Tolerance for Ambiguity. Effective play therapists have a *high tolerance for ambiguity*, which enables them to enter into the child's world of experiencing as a follower, allowing the child to initiate activity, topic, direction, and content with encouragement from the therapist, who continually centers responsibility on the child. The child-centered play therapist does not need facts or answers about a child and is quite content with the process of not knowing what a child's behavior should mean. The therapist is comfortable living in the child's world of uncertainty.

Future-Minded. Because the child is always in a process of becoming, the play therapist is *future-minded* in relating to the child and responds to the child as a person who is capable of being more than he is at the moment. A friend of mine is a wood carver of western figures. He can see the potential in an old dead tree stump—a cowboy boot, a western hat, a rugged cowboy face. He does not respond to the present condition of the old dead tree stump, but rather to the potential that the stump holds. In his work, he intentionally and consistently responds to the potential he sees and focuses all of his energy on releasing what the stump is capable of becoming. In like manner, the child-centered play therapist relates to what the child is capable of becoming and does not restrict the child through attitude or verbal responses pertaining to the past, even the last session a few days ago.

The therapist is always trying to "catch up" to where the child is and so has no need to find out what happened yesterday, or last week, or last month, or a year ago—unless the child's leading goes in that direction. Then, the therapist is quite willing to follow. The therapist does not refer to the previous session, because the child is no longer at that point. Assuming once-a-week sessions, the child has had a whole week to grow, develop, and change since the therapist last saw him. Therefore, the therapist will need to catch up to where the child is this week and will avoid responding in ways that focus on the past. It is obvious the agenda of the play therapist in the following interaction in the sixth play therapy session is focused on the past.

Child:	(Painting a picture at the easel.)
Therapist:	Just like last time, you don't want any white spots on your picture.
Child:	(Later in session, plays a game.)
Therapist:	You're trying your new trick like you did last time.
Child:	(Shows therapist a plastic ring brought from home.)
Therapist:	You brought a ring from home just like last time.

The responses of this therapist are not therapeutic because they keep the child focused on the past and overlook the fact that there is a constantly changing interaction of the thoughts, behaviors, feelings, experiences, and physical being of a child. Thus, a child's perceptual world is constantly changing, and the child in the playroom this week is in some ways different. Therefore, past experiences are no longer perceived or experienced in the same way and the child does not feel understood because the child is focused on what he is doing now, not what he did last week. Future-mindedness does not project or lead the child into the future, but is an attitude of receptivity to the child being in a continuous process of becoming.

Personal Courage. The effective play therapist acts and responds out of *personal courage* by admitting mistakes, by being vulnerable at times, and by admitting inaccuracies in personal perceptions. Personal courage is needed to take risks and to act on intuitive feelings in response to the child's creative expressions of self at the moment. For the therapist to allow herself to be vulnerable enough to be impacted or touched emotionally by the child's experiences and feelings, personal courage is required along with an openness to risk by sharing herself in a personal way that is nondefensive. Personal courage based on inner confidence may be required when a child is testing the limits of the relationship, for example, threatening to throw a block of wood at the therapist or shooting the therapist with a dart gun. Therapists who have low tolerance for risk-taking behaviors may respond inappropriately in such situations by being punitive or threatening. Such situations also call for a high degree of *patience*.

Being Real, Warmth and Caring, Acceptance, and Sensitive Understanding. Because the dimensions of *being real, warmth and caring, acceptance, and sensitive understanding* were discussed in the previous chapter, they are mentioned here just to let the reader know that I recognize their worth as personality dimensions in the therapeutic process. These dimensions can be further described as being loving and compassionate.

Helen Keller (1954) described in her autobiography the significance a loving, compassionate person can have in facilitating a life-changing process:

> Once I knew the depth where no hope was and darkness lay on the face of all things. Then love came and set my soul free. Once I fretted and beat myself against the wall that shut me in. My life was without a past or future, and death a consummation devoutly to be wished. But a little word from the fingers of another fell into my hands that clutched at emptiness, and my heart leaped up with the rapture of living. I do not know the meaning of the darkness, but I have learned the overcoming of it. (p. 57)

Personally Secure. The effective play therapist is *personally secure* and thus recognizes and accepts personal limitations without any sense of threat to her feelings of adequacy. There is nothing a child can say about the therapist that will threaten the therapist (Figure 6.1). Some play therapists feel they must be helpful to all children. Out of their own fear of being perceived as inadequate, they continue to work with children far beyond their ability to be helpful, or they accept child clients whose emotional difficulties exceed the limits of their training. Knowing when to make a referral is an absolute must for the play therapist.

Sense of Humor. Children have fun. They enjoy playing and discovering. They laugh right out loud when something is funny to them. The play therapist should possess a *sense of humor* and be able to appreciate the humor in what the child experiences as being humorous. However, for the therapist to laugh at a child is never appropriate.

Therapist Self-Understanding

General agreement exists among authorities that, regardless of the age group worked with, all therapists need self-understanding and insight into their own motivations, needs, blind spots, biases, personal conflicts, and areas of emotional difficulty as well as personal strengths. Therapists should not assume they can keep their

FIGURE 6.1 The play therapist is personally secure and trusts the child to lead the relationship to where the child needs to be.

own values and needs compartmentalized and separate from their relationships with children. The therapist is a real person, not a robot. Therefore, personal needs and values are a part of the person and thus become a part of the relationship. The question, then, is not whether or not the therapist's personality will enter into the relationship but, rather, to what extent it will do so.

A responsibility of the therapist is to be involved in a process of self-exploration that will promote self-understanding, thus minimizing the potential impact of the therapist's motivations and needs. This process of knowing self can be facilitated through personal therapy, and either individual or group therapy is highly recommended to learn about self. Another source of self-exploration would be supervisory or consultative relationships, which allow the therapist, out of personal willingness, to explore his motivations and needs. Because self-understanding is a process and not an event, being involved in such a process throughout their professional career can be helpful to therapists. Exploring the following questions might enhance the process of self-understanding:

What needs of mine are being met in play therapy?
How strong is my need to be needed?
Do I like this child?
Do I want to be with this child?
What impact do my attitudes and feelings have on this child?
How does this child perceive me?

A therapist who is unaware of her own personal biases, values, emotional needs, fears, personal stresses, anxieties, and expectations of self and others probably will not be effectively sensitive to such dimensions in children. The therapist does not leave personality needs outside when entering the playroom with a child. Consequently, these needs become a part of the relationship and the developing therapeutic process. If the therapist is not fully aware of a need to be liked, a fear of rejection, guilt feelings related to limit setting, or a need to be admired or successful, these needs will emerge in subtle manipulative ways that control and restrict the exploration and expression of the child.

The play therapy relationship is much more than the result of observable criteria. Therapist attitudes, motivations, expectations, needs, and beliefs about the child constitute *intangibles* that can have a significant impact on the development and outcome of the therapeutic relationship. Some degree of subtle structuring is inherent in all therapeutic relationships and exists to a greater or lesser extent depending on the play therapist's awareness of his needs, motivation, intent, expectations, and beliefs about the child. These intangibles are sensed or felt by the child in the relationship and thus affect or structure the behavior of the child, whether the play therapist intends such structuring or not. Intangibles in the play therapy relationship of which the play therapist should be aware are listed below:

- *Is your intent to change the child?* Can there be genuine acceptance of the child if the play therapist's intent is to change the child?
- *Do you hope the child will play?* Is the child really free in the playroom to set his own direction if the play therapist hopes the child will play?

- *Are you more accepting of some behaviors than others?* Will the child feel liked and appreciated if the play therapist approves of only certain behaviors?
- *Do you have a low tolerance for messiness?* Is the child free to express her need to be messy if the play therapist has a low tolerance for messiness?
- *Do you have a need to rescue the child from pain or difficulty?* Will the child discover her inner strengths and resources if the play therapist has difficulty tolerating children's pain?
- *Do you have a need to be liked by the child?* Can therapeutic limits be set as needed if the play therapist is unaware of his need to be liked by the child?
- *Do you feel safe with the child?* Can the child feel safe in the play therapy relationship if the play therapist does not feel safe with the child?
- *Do you trust the child?* Is it possible for the child to trust herself if the play therapist is not able to trust her?
- *Do you expect the child to deal with certain issues?* Is the child really free to explore his inner issues and concerns if the play therapist expects the child to deal with certain issues?

These are nonquantifiable intangibles that subtly influence the dynamics of the process of play therapy. Play therapist self-understanding can lessen the impact of these variables on the play therapy relationship.

The most significant resources the therapist brings to the play therapy relationship are the dimensions of self. Skills are useful tools, but therapists' use of their own personalities is their greatest asset. As important as training and skills are in becoming a play therapist, they simply are not enough. The therapist must be the kind of person who appreciates the perceptual-experiential world of children, a person who delights in being with children and experiences their world as exciting. Although training and the use of therapeutic procedures are important, the therapist's ability to be human is of prime importance. **The person of the therapist is more important than anything the therapist knows how to do.** The therapist must be the kind of person with whom children feel safe, safe enough to explore, safe enough to risk being themselves; the kind of person children experience as being trustworthy and caring. With such a person, children will find satisfying encouragement for self-growth.

Therapist Self-Acceptance

The child-centered play therapy approach is a function of the therapist's attitude toward herself and the child. This attitude is characterized by an acceptance of herself and the child and a deep and abiding belief in the capacity of the child to be responsible for himself in the process of exercising self-direction resulting in more positive behaviors. The therapist must accept herself sufficiently enough to allow a child in the therapy experience to be different from her. Such self-acceptance is an inner strength that allows the therapist to be intentional about being with the child and accepting the child. This attitude of commitment respects children's right to make choices and recognizes the capacity of children to make choices that are both maturely satisfying to them and ultimately acceptable to society. A significant result of therapist self-acceptance is the building of a relationship in which a child will feel safe enough to change or not to change.

RULE OF THUMB:

A child will not change until the child is free not to change.

This therapeutic dimension is entirely dependent on the therapist's acceptance of self and acceptance of the child. The therapist does not wish the child were different in some way. The child is enough at this moment. The objective of the therapist is to create a climate in which the child feels free to be fully who she is at the moment in the shared experience of learning about self and each other. Out of a deep respect for the person of the child, the therapist gives full, complete, undivided attention and acceptance to the child.

Giving of herself in this way means the therapist is keenly sensitive to personal experiences and feelings that may be identified with the child and is careful to sort out or distinguish those feelings that are emotional reattachments to previous experiences. The therapist is careful to avoid projecting emotional reactions or needs onto the child. Thus, the play therapist must be engaged in a continual process of self-awareness and self-acceptance. Being in the process of self-discovery can be as rewarding to the therapist as to the child and is necessary for self-acceptance. Play therapists often begin this process of self-acceptance as a result of experiencing such acceptance in training programs. The impact can be seen in this self-evaluation by a graduate student:

> Play therapy is very rewarding to me because I am helping a child to accept himself. A great deal of the reward in play therapy comes from being able to keep my personal needs out of the child's way. I believe when a person is able to keep her needs in check that she is not only recognizing her own feelings, but accepting those feelings and, therefore, accepting herself. I began the process of accepting myself during this class. I was able to act responsibly and keep my needs out of the play sessions. Of course, the process of accepting one's self is continuous throughout life, but oh, what a beginning I have been able to make. Now, I want to begin generalizing my self-trust to the other areas of my life! Thank you for accepting me.

Another student wrote, "The feedback in my supervision sessions gave me permission to be more myself, to go with my intuitive responses. That's important. I needed that. As I relaxed more and really got into the experience, I thoroughly enjoyed it!"

The play therapist has faith in the nature of children, believes that a universal characteristic of children is the urge to unfold, and respects that unfolding as characterized in the uniqueness of each child. The inner dynamics of this urge may have been suppressed or thwarted but can be revitalized under the proper conditions. The therapist's belief in growth and change does not come from a static, intellectual decision position but is determined largely by an experiential process of being aware of her own continuous developmental unfolding of discovery about self in relationships and life experiences. This self-understanding and accompanying self-acceptance enables the therapist to wait expectantly for the emerging self within the child. No impatience is felt toward the current projected self of the child, because there is a willingness to accept personal imperfection and to forgive himself for not being perfect. The therapist accepts his own humanness. Therefore, no need exists to have the child be perfect.

RULE OF THUMB:

You cannot accept another person's weakness until you are able to accept your own.

The freeing aspect of self-understanding and self-acceptance is described by a beginning play therapist this way:

The more I understand myself and admit to being imperfect, the more I can let go of self-consciousness and the need to fulfill a role expectation of being a therapist. This preconceived image has deprived me of the freedom and spontaneity through which my best strengths may be developed. I no longer feel in the playroom that I am performing a stressful chore, but constructing a personally creative encounter with Michael. I am discovering that when I am uptight it is difficult to approach another, and that with increased relaxation I can see myself in action, to note the false moves or the extra steps I have unconsciously incorporated into my behavior.

The attitude of the play therapist sets the tone of the play therapy session and quickly permeates the entire experience. Play therapy is not a role; it is a way of being. The therapist who attempts to use a "method" or set of techniques will appear stilted and artificial and ultimately will be dissatisfied and unsuccessful. The inner person of the child is much more likely to emerge in growth-enhancing ways to the extent that the therapist is able to give up a role of authority and leadership in the play therapy experience. Such positions serve to create dependency expectations on the part of the child. The therapist's goal is to project a personal self as fully as possible. This in turn facilitates the movement of the child toward becoming the self he is in the developing relationship. Children are very sensitive to all the subtleties of the person of the therapist, and are therefore much more affected by the person of the therapist than by any technique the therapist may use. Effective therapists appreciate their own uniqueness and are therefore able to accept the uniqueness of others.

Role of the Play Therapist

The therapist has no need to direct or lead the child to a particular topic or activity. The therapist allows the child to lead the way and is content to follow. What is important is not the therapist's wisdom, but the wisdom of the child; not the therapist's direction, but the child's direction; not the therapist's solution, but the child's creativity. Therefore, the child is accepted for all that she is in order to free the child to be unique.

The child-centered play therapist is not a supervisor, teacher, peer, babysitter, investigator, playmate, or parent substitute. Dibs summed up his view of the therapist by saying, "You're not a mother. You're not a teacher, you're not a member of mother's bridge club. What are you? It does not really matter. You are the lady of the wonderful playroom" (Axline, 1964, p. 204). The therapist does not solve problems for the child, explain behavior, interpret motivation, rescue the child, or question intent. Taking on any of these roles would deprive the child of opportunities for self-exploration, self-creativity, self-evaluation, and self-discovery.

Does this mean, then, that the therapist is passive? Absolutely not! The therapist assumes an active role. Must the therapist do things for or to children before she can be described as being active? Does being active require the therapist to exhibit a high level of physical activity? Being active does not have to be an observable quality. The therapist is emotionally active, requiring sensitivity, an appreciation of what the child is doing and saying, and an attitude of receptive responsiveness. This emotional investment is characterized by an interactive quality that is both felt by the child and therapist and overtly experienced in the interactive verbal expressions of the therapist. The therapist maintains an active role in the process of play therapy, not in the sense of directing or managing the experience, but by being directly involved and genuinely interested in all of the child's feelings, actions, and decisions.

Can the therapist's efforts teach children about themselves? Can the wisdom of the therapist that comes from years of graduate study, reading, and experiencing children be imparted to child clients? Gibran's (1923) *The Prophet* addressed this issue, saying, "No man can reveal to you aught but that which already lies asleep in the dawning of your own knowledge....For the wisdom of one man lends not its wings to another man" (p. 32). The play therapist is not a person who tries to make things happen, for that is not an option within the possibilities that exist in reality. To *make* happen or create *for* others the inner wisdom necessary for living life simply is not possible. Whatever is important or necessary for children's growth already exists in children. The therapist's role or responsibility is not to reshape children's lives or make them change in some predetermined way but, rather, to respond in ways that facilitate release of the creative potential that already exists in them. The living of life is never a static occurrence; it is a process of relentless learning and renewal. Pasternak was reacting to this process when he said:

> When I hear people speak of reshaping life it makes me lose my self control and I fall into despair. Reshaping life! People who can say that have never understood a thing about life—they have never felt its breath, its heartbeat, however much they may have seen or done. They look on it as a lump of raw material that needs to be processed by them, to be ennobled by their touch. But life is never a material, a substance to be molded.... . Life is constantly renewing and remaking and changing and transfiguring itself. (Salisbury, 1958, p. 22)

The significance of the child-centered play therapy relationship for the child and the therapist, for the therapist is also affected by the person of the child and the relationship, is readily seen in the following description of my play therapy experiences with Ryan.

Ryan—A Dying Child in Play Therapy

Two brothers, ages 7 and 5, were wrestling, and the 7-year-old suffered a broken leg. A trip to the hospital resulted in a surprising and traumatic finding. Cancer had weakened the bone, necessitating immediate, radical surgery to amputate the leg at the hip in an effort to stop the spread of the cancer. The diagnosis: Ryan had only a few months to live.

Play Therapy

My first contact with Ryan came as a result of play therapy sessions with his 5-year-old brother, who had been referred to me by wise parents who recognized the potential emotional trauma for the 5-year-old and the possibility of deep personal guilt. Prior to the eighth session with the 5-year-old, his mother called to say the 5-year-old wanted to invite Ryan to come with him to the special playroom. I viewed this as a significant positive development in the 5-year-old's growth, that he was willing to share the playroom experience; that he perhaps recognized at some level that something in the play therapy relationship might be helpful to Ryan; and in our relationship, that he felt secure enough to bring Ryan.

When I met Mom and the two children in the waiting room, I was immediately emotionally impacted by Ryan's condition. Most of his hair was gone, there were purple marks on his face to direct the radiation treatment, and dark shadows circled his eyes. This was the first time I had seen Ryan, and I was overcome with a deep sadness and an ache that welled up in me. The 5-year-old showed Mom and Ryan the way to the playroom. Mom carried Ryan, sat him down in the middle of the playroom, and left.

Ryan's condition so captured my attention, and I was so caught up in my own emotion, that I forgot about Ryan's brother for a few moments. I was deeply immersed in the scene Ryan was portraying. He took the 10-inch-tall dinosaur, stuck a toy soldier in the wide-open, gaping mouth, and with his finger slowly pushed the soldier all the way into the mouth, until the soldier fell down the dinosaur's throat into the hollow body. He then stood the dinosaur on the floor and lined up three rows of toy soldiers facing the dinosaur. Ryan very carefully made sure all the weapons were pointed toward the dinosaur, then leaned back and studied the scene for several moments. Not one shot was fired—all that strategic placement of soldiers and they just stood there, unexpectedly impotent facing the huge monster. No, the feeling was clearer now. This was not a monster, this was the enemy within Ryan. The enemy that could not be stopped. The soldiers were powerless, their weapons useless. The monster was too powerful. He could not be stopped! Ryan did not say one word or make any kind of sound during this entire process, and he did not need to. I was in touch with him, and he was communicating.

This was one of those rare experiences in the living relationship of the playroom when, for a few brief moments, time and the reality of everything outside the fleeting experience of the moment did not exist in consciousness for either one of us. I was sensing Ryan's inner experiencing, captivated by the awesomeness of the scene before me. A moan of anguish moved slowly through my soul—"He knows. He knows the monster inside him can't be stopped." Then the moment was gone, and I was jarred back to the reality of his brother's presence by Ryan asking his brother for the can to put the soldiers in. His brother needed me as much as Ryan did. This began my brief but extraordinary journey of learning about living as Ryan shared living with me.

I saw Ryan in play therapy sessions during the last 2 months of his life. Ryan's condition deteriorated rapidly over the next few weeks, necessitating several trips to the hospital, and each time the pronounced diagnosis was, "He has only a few hours to live." A kind and sensitive mom asked a friend to call me on these occasions, and after I hung up the phone, I grieved for a dear, little friend I would not see again. Then I would receive word that Ryan had rallied, and a few days later he would be back in his home, asking to see me again.

During the last month of his life, Ryan was too weak to leave his bed, so I carried my traveling play therapy kit to his home. I was eager for the opportunity to be with Ryan, but each time I parked in front of his home, I sat there a few minutes fully experiencing a rush of sadness, a lump in my throat, and an urge not to go in, because so much about Ryan reminded me of his impending death—purple marks on his face from the radiation treatment, the protruding growth on the side of his head, his large stomach, the thinness of his whole body. I experienced each session as probably our last one. Uttering a deep sigh of resignation to the feeling and acceptance as my problem, not Ryan's, I would prepare myself to meet Ryan, to be open to his world of experiencing, to share in what he wanted to share.

Although weak and emaciated, Ryan delighted in our sessions together. While I held the newsprint tablet, he drew pictures of Mickey Mouse with huge hands and 40 fingers thrust outward, a porcupine, and a buzzard, which seemed to me to represent his struggle against cancer. Ryan was delightfully uninhibited. I had never imagined I would need to assist a child with a urine bottle in the middle of a play therapy session; thus, my initial reaction to his request to "use the bathroom" was an awkward and fumbling, "I'll go get the nurse." Ryan's reaction was, "We don't need her." And indeed we did not. Ryan trusted me and was patient with my awkwardness.

The next week Ryan was in the hospital again, made another dramatic recovery, and asked to see me again the next week. In this session, Ryan drew the Mickey Mouse figure again, but with a smaller body and hands. He colored Mickey dark purple, and the face looked hollow, with very dark eyes. It did indeed look like death. Ryan then chose an egg carton from the kit, colored each of the egg cells a bright color, closed the carton, and colored it black all over. Yes, beauty and color and brightness and hope are on the inside. Next, Ryan drew a picture of a straw house, a stick house, and a brick house; he talked about the straw house and stick house being blown down and the three pigs being safe in the brick house. An interesting feature of the houses was that the brick house had the largest door. I believe Ryan somehow intuitively felt death was near, and that he would be in a safe place. Ryan then announced that he was tired, so I left.

That was the last time I saw Ryan. He died 3 days later. During our times together Ryan had led the focus and exploration of the sessions into those areas important to him, had walked down the road he had chosen, and had played in the way he wanted to play. In our relationship, I discovered that even under the most personally stressful of circumstances, children can experience the pleasure of playing and can feel in control even when circumstances seem to be out of control.

What I Learned About Me

I know so little about what it is like for a child to face death.
> Therefore, I will be open to learning what Ryan taught me.

I experience sadness when I think of a child dying.
> Therefore, I will need to protect children from my feelings.

I know so little about life.
> Therefore, I will be open to the continuous wonderment of living as experienced by children.

I sometimes focus too much on problems—on what is not working out.
> Therefore, I will work hard to look beyond to the experiential world of the child.

I am not capable of knowing what should be significant or important for another person.
> Therefore, I will resolve in my relationships with children to discover their needs.

I like it, too, when another person "sees" my world.
> Therefore, I will struggle to be sensitive to the child's world.

I am more fully me when I feel safe.
> Therefore, with all that I am capable, I will try hard to help children to feel safe with me.

What I Learned About Ryan

I wanted to withdraw from the reminder of his pain,
> But Ryan wanted to be with me.

I could not solve his problem,
> But he did not expect me to.

I thought about him dying,
> But he focused on living.

I experienced deep sadness as I approached our times together,
> But he was eager and excited.

I saw an emaciated body,
> But he saw a friend.

I wanted to protect him,
> But he wanted to share with me a relationship.

Ryan Lives

Society will report that Ryan died, but I have recorded in my heart his struggle to live, the oxygen mask, the bright splotches of color he chose, the pain he endured, the fatigue laden with delight in his squeaky little voice, the enthusiasm and vigor with which he drew pictures. So, he lives. Not the part they see, but what I see. This dying little person taught me lessons for living.

I remember Ryan saying, "This is our special time, just for me and you. No one will ever know about it, Garry. It's just for us." I wonder what Ryan remembers.

The Relationship With Ryan

This special relationship with a special little person at a crucial time in his life gave me an unusual perspective on allowing children to lead the relationship into areas important to them rather than in a direction I might think important. I experienced a genuine prizing of this unique child, an appreciation for his expressive eagerness, which was only temporarily dimmed by overwhelming fatigue from the physical struggle. Our times together seemed to be an oasis in his life, a time when he was free to be in control of the direction of his experiences, even though reality dictated that he could not control what he was experiencing in his body.

During our times together, Ryan focused on living rather than dying, on joy rather than on sadness, on creative expression rather than on apathy, and on his appreciation of our relationship rather than on the loss of relationships. It was with wonder and awe that I experienced with this dying child the shared joy, release, and excitement of the moment as he played out our living relationship. Play was special to Ryan, and he prized our relationship. I learned that success, then, might not be what I perceive to be needed, or the correcting of a problem. It may indeed be the brief momentary experiencing of a caring, safe relationship in which the child is free to be all that he is capable of being at that time. Ryan, a child who was dying, taught me lessons for living (Landreth adaptation).

Supervised Practice Facilitates Self-Insight

Graduate class work, discussions, reading, workshops, role-playing, and observing experienced play therapists are necessary and significant prerequisites in learning to be a play therapist. However, the most important learnings are those derived from experiences, and the possibilities for learning about self, children, and play therapy from supervised play therapy experiences are limitless. Not until children are experienced can they be known. Not until the therapist experiences the struggle to relate to a child can the play therapy relationship be understood. Not until the therapist experiences being with a child can apprehensions be discarded. Not until the therapist attempts to apply training can developed skill be appreciated.

All play therapists should be engaged in a process of never-ending self-critique, and viewing one's own videotaped sessions is by far the best possible means of self-supervision and supervision by other professionals. Seeing oneself on video is essential for self-growth and is considered a must in supervision. It is simply not possible for a play therapist to really know what kind of play therapist she is without having seen videos of her play therapy sessions. With the availability of inexpensive video equipment, a play therapist's reluctance to video some of his play therapy sessions may reveal defensiveness or insecurity. Any play therapist, regardless of years of experience, should be open to continued learning about self.

The Play Therapy Skills Checklist (PTSC) (see Table 6.1) developed by the Center for Play Therapy at the University of North Texas is an excellent scale for use in supervision/consultation to help play therapists focus on child-centered play therapy verbal responses and nonverbal skills. The PTSC is filled out while observing a play therapy session and can be used in self-supervision of video-recorded sessions and also by a supervisor to provide feedback to play therapists whose play therapy sessions have been video recorded or are observed live through a one-way mirror. The scale is best utilized as a stimulus for discussion as well as supervisor feedback. Play therapist insight can be

TABLE 6.1 Play Therapy Skills Checklist (Center for Play Therapy, University of North Texas, Denton, Texas).

Play Therapy Skills Checklist Center for Play Therapy University of North Texas						
Therapist: _____ Child (age): _____ (____)						
Observer: _____ Date: ____/____/____						
Therapist Non Verbal Communication	**Too Much**	**Appropriate**	**Need More**	**None**	**Therapist Responses/ Examples**	**Other Possible Responses**
Lean Forward/Open						
Appeared Interested						
Relaxed Comfortable						
Tone/Expression Congruent with Child's Affect						
Tone/Expression Congruent with Therapist's Responses						
Therapist Responses	**Too Much**	**Appropriate**	**Need More**	**None**	**Therapist Responses/ Examples**	**Other Possible Responses**
Tracking						
Reflecting Feelings						
Reflecting Content						
Facilitating Decision Making/Responsibility						
Facilitating Creativity/Spontaneity						
Esteem Building/Encouraging						
Facilitating Understanding						

Limit Setting: Protect Child and Therapist, Maintain Therapist Acceptance/Relationship, Protect Room/Toys, Structuring, Reality Testing

Immediacy/Spontaneity:

Child Made Contact/Connection:

Therapist's Strengths:

Areas for Growth:

expanded by asking play therapists to rate themselves, compare their ratings to the supervisor's ratings, and discuss the discrepancies. Supervision/consultation is essential in helping play therapists develop a consistent theoretical model and approach.

As is true in child-centered play therapy where the primary focus is the child rather than the child's behaviors, in supervision, the primary focus is on the person of the therapist and skill development is secondary. The supervisor is sensitive to the underlying dimensions in the therapist–child relationship such as therapist intangibles discussed earlier in this chapter: Is the therapist aware of his own needs? How does he feel about the child? Does he trust himself? Does he feel safe with the child? Is he more accepting of some behaviors than others? Is he tolerant of the ambiguity of the child's uncertainty?

The following self-evaluations from play therapists in training give a glimpse into the impact and insight derived from supervised play therapy experiences.

Play Therapist: Margaret

Through experiencing children in play therapy, I have come to understand the living nature of the therapeutic relationship. I more fully understand and feel the dynamic experience of encountering a child, finding in Jeffrey what I can never discover in textbooks—myself *in action* with the child. I needed to move beyond intellectual descriptions and classification, beyond the abstract view of helping, and to encounter my own inner experience. It is not easy to be in intense relations with a child.

Play Therapist: Keith

One of the clearest discoveries I have had in my play therapy sessions has been a realization that I am too impatient. I have not learned to wait, and this compounds the experience of stress. Perhaps this is why it is difficult for me to see things from any perspective but my own. I have learned that I need to respond to the child instead of trying to make a good response. When Justin refused to leave the playroom, I was able to stand patiently by the door and experience how effective acceptance of feelings and permissiveness can be when he walked out the door under his own steam after only a couple of minutes.

Play Therapist: Douglas

This second session brought with it the realization of one of my worst apprehensions—the child who continually asks questions. It was obvious from the types of questions Eric asked that he had a poor self-concept. It seemed to be difficult for him to rely on his own judgment, or to decide for himself how to use his time in the playroom. For me, it was difficult to answer his questions simply and then give the lead back to Eric. He sought my approval on almost every new activity he took on. Some of my responses were facilitative, others were not. I learned that this inconsistency can facilitate more questions which, in turn, increases my anxiety and my inappropriate responses. I think it is extremely important to remember that the child learns something from what I say. It is important to communicate that I have faith in the child's own judgment so that he can learn to rely on his own judgments. The responsibility to change or not to change is in the child's hands. What a boost for the child's self-confidence, self-respect, and self-esteem.

Play Therapist: Ching

During my play therapy sessions, I found that initially the child felt strange with me because of my differences in nationality and speech pattern and also because I was too quiet and not responsive enough. The initial difference set an unfamiliar stage for the child, and then my reserved or quiet behavior added to the unfamiliarity. I learned that I must increase my rate of response to help put the child at ease.

Recommended Training Program

Commitment to children demands that the therapist make every effort possible to ensure that children receive quality help from competent play therapists. The field of play therapy is experiencing a growing and enthusiastic interest as a viable approach for meeting children's needs, and because children cannot speak for themselves on this matter, professionals in the field must try to ensure that individuals who practice play therapy possess specialized knowledge and skills that render them effective in play therapy to serve the best interests of children. With this commitment in mind, the following, tentative guidelines are suggested for training play therapists. A basic premise is that the professional standards required for using play therapy in counseling with children should be no less than those required for working with adults in a counseling relationship:

- A master's degree in an area of the helping professions, such as counseling, psychology, social work, or a related area
- Content areas of study in child development, theories of counseling and psychotherapy, clinical counseling skills, and group counseling
- Content area of study in play therapy equivalent to 90 clock hours of instruction
- Personal counseling, either as a member of a counseling group, individual counseling, or other pertinent experience that provides opportunities to examine the self over an extended period of time
- Observation and case analysis of children from the normal population as well as maladjusted children
- Observation of experienced play therapists with opportunity to discuss and critique the sessions
- Supervised experience in play therapy by a professional who has experience in play therapy

In my Introduction to Play Therapy course, which is a one-semester, 3-hour graduate credit course, students are involved in the following sequence of laboratory experiences in addition to lectures, discussions, reading, and writing papers related to various aspects of play therapy:

- Observe play therapy sessions of master's and doctoral practicum students in our Center for Play Therapy.
- Observe and critique videotapes of my play therapy sessions.

- Observe at least one of my current play therapy sessions or a special demonstration for the class.
- Role play, with me playing the part of the child, to improve responding skills and to become comfortable with the unexpected things children may do in the playroom.
- Role play in pairs in the playrooms, taking turns being the child to gain insight into children's feelings and their perception of the experience.
- Conduct play sessions with volunteer adjusted children in an undisturbed room in a nursery school, day-care center, church Sunday School classroom, or room in their home. Students bring a box of appropriate toys, audiotape the sessions, and write a critique of the experience focusing on what they learned about the child, play therapy, and themselves.
- Participate in live supervised play therapy sessions with volunteer adjusted children in the Center playrooms and receive immediate feedback. Sessions are supervised by doctoral students and play therapists in private practice. Students write a critique of the experience.

In addition to this introductory course, master's degree students are required to take a course in advanced play therapy, group play therapy, or filial therapy. Students receive live supervision with immediate feedback in a one-semester on-campus supervised play therapy practicum in the Center for Play Therapy. Following successful completion of the practicum, the graduate students are placed in an internship in an elementary school, agency, or clinic where they can continue their supervised play therapy experience.

These guidelines for training are made with full recognition that, until more university programs offer training in play therapy, some of these requirements will need to be fulfilled in non-traditional academic ways, such as intensive training workshops. These workshops could be offered in a format of 45-hour sequencing that builds on previous workshop training. The typical 1- and 2-day general overview introductory workshop will not suffice. The crucial factor is supervised experience, and although no substitute exists for that, a variety of ways are available so that the play therapist can receive supervision other than through a traditional, organized campus practicum. A qualified play therapist could be contracted for individual supervision, or with several staff members in an agency on a regular basis, or arrangements could be made for a university play therapy program to provide a condensed, short-term, 45-hour, supervised practicum in play therapy. One of the most dynamic experiences I engage in is the supervision of 12 practicing play therapists who are private-practice and agency professionals in a 3-day 8-hours-per-day, individual and group play therapy practicum each summer, assisted by four of my advanced doctoral students. This model of supervision is described in Bratton, Landreth, and Homeyer (1990). The suggestions in this chapter are intended as minimum procedures and should not be taken as recommended standard procedures.

References

Axline, V. (1950). Play therapy experiences as described by child participants. *Journal of Consulting Psychology, 14*(1), 53–63.

Axline, V. (1964). *Dibs: In search of self.* New York: Ballantine.

Bratton, S., Landreth, G., & Homeyer, L. (1990). An intensive three day play therapy supervision/training model. *International Journal of Play Therapy, 2*(2), 61–78.

Gibran, K. (1923). *The prophet.* New York: Alfred Knopf.

Keller, H. (1954). *The story of my life.* New York: Grossett & Dunlap.

Landreth, G. L. (Adaptation) This case is an adaptation of "*The Case of Ryan—A Dying Child*" from Landreth (1988). Reprinted with permission of the American Association for Counseling and Development.

Salisbury, F. (1958). *Human development and learning.* New York: McGraw-Hill.

White, R. (1952). *Lives in progress.* Orlando, FL: Dryden Press.

Chapter 7

Parents as Partners in Play Therapy

Counseling with children requires consideration of certain dimensions and aspects of the relationship not encountered in counseling with adults. Children usually are dependent on a significant adult, most often the parent, in their life to make arrangements for scheduling play therapy. Therefore, *any effort by the therapist to be helpful to children must begin with consideration for the parameters of the relationship to be established with the parent.* Will the parent be involved in therapy? What are the complexities involved in informing parents of children's behavior in the playroom?

Maintaining sensitivity to the complexity of the changing parental role in our society is a major challenge requiring awareness and sensitivity to high divorce rates, increasing numbers of single parents, changing parental roles, increasing levels of stress in families, and greater personal isolation. Such factors critically impact the parent's level of involvement and directional intensity. Although parents today generally are more sophisticated about counseling, the therapist cannot assume they know anything about play therapy. Parents also need assistance in informing their children about play therapy and how to help in the separation process for the first session.

Background Information

Interviews with parents and teachers can provide useful information to help the therapist better understand what is going on in the child's life outside the playroom experience and can provide cues to understanding the meaning of a child's play. Such information can result in the therapist being more sensitive and empathic with the child and so is helpful in facilitating the process of the developing relationship. However, outside information also can "color" or structure the therapist's perception and stimulate the therapist's latent tendency to be interpretative with the child in a way the therapist would never be without such information. Consider the following case of 4-year-old Paula, who learned, along with her therapist, of her mother's pregnancy 4 weeks prior to the occurrence of the following events in the playroom:

> For two consecutive sessions, Paula busily arranged all the chairs in a tight cluster, bound them together with string, and covered the entire construction with paper. She left a small opening and crawled in and out with some nervous giggling. Armed with his knowledge of the pregnancy, the therapist "understood" the play as a symbolic acting out of fantasies about pregnancy and birth. After making some observations to Paula about her manifest behavior, her pleasure, and her "worried" giggle, he considers the best way for interpreting to her his "certain" interpretation of its latent meaning. However, since the second of these sessions is about to end, he decides to wait to deliver his interpretation until next week. In the intervening week, he meets with Paula's parents in a regularly scheduled interview. They tell him that three weeks earlier, the family had gone camping. They were very pleased that Paula was able to manage this experience without significant fears and say, "That's something she couldn't have done a few months ago." They did note that she was a bit anxious about sleeping in a tent with them and her older brother, but she was easily reassured. (Cooper & Wanerman, 1977, p. 185)

Clearly Paula's play behavior is related to the more recent camping trip and the tent episode. Typically, a play therapist knowing about the mother's pregnancy and not knowing about the camping trip would "read into" the child's playroom behavior anxiety about the mother's pregnancy. The child-centered play therapist intentionally focuses on the child and the relationship in the playroom and out of respect for and belief in the child does not take the residue of information learned outside the play therapy relationship into the unique developing relationship with a child in the playroom. Play therapists must never assume they know everything about a child. Our information is always incomplete.

Information received by the therapist does not result in a change in approach by the child-centered play therapist. This is not a prescriptive approach that varies with the presenting problem. No attempt is made to match a certain technique with a specific problem. The therapist's belief in the child is unwavering, regardless of the specific problem. Thus the therapist is consistent across sessions and with different children. The therapist at all times interacts with the child rather than focusing on a problem. Therefore, background information is not essential to the child-centered therapist but may be secondarily helpful in formulating an overall picture as a basis for assessing growth or change or may be used as a basis for offering parenting suggestions.

An ideal procedure would be for another therapist to interview and counsel with the parent(s), thereby removing the play therapist from the potential bind of having to disregard background information in order to remain perceptually open to the child. This also would alleviate the problem of interference with the therapist–child relationship when the child knows the therapist is talking with the parent(s). Because most play therapists do not work in a setting where another therapist is available to work with the parent(s), if counseling with parents is necessary, sessions can be scheduled for a separate time when the child is not with them. However, many parents' work schedules prohibit their making two trips to the therapist's office. When this is the case, the therapy hour may have to be split between the child and the parent(s) for periodic parental sessions. This procedure is not recommended as a standard course of action but may be the only course of action if the therapist considers working with the parent(s) to be essential.

If the therapy hour is split between the parent(s) and the child, the parent(s) should be seen first. This helps to diminish the tendency of children to feel the therapist is "telling on them," as may happen when the child is seen first. Children should always be informed of meetings with parents, so they will not be surprised to find out such a meeting has taken place. Older children may be allowed to choose to have their play therapy session before or after the therapist meets with the parent(s).

Must Parents Also Be in Therapy?

Without a doubt parents play a vital and significant role in the lives of their children and, therefore, should be included in some kind of therapeutic procedure whenever possible. Whether parents need therapy or training in better parenting skills is a question for the play therapist to determine. Frequently, filial therapy is the recommended intervention for parents. Filial therapy is a parent-training intervention designed to build and enhance the parent–child relationship through teaching parents child-centered play therapy skills to use in special play times with their children. Thus, parents become the agents of therapeutic change in their children's lives. Child Parent Relationship Therapy (Landreth & Bratton, 2006), a 10-session filial therapy model, has demonstrated significant positive results in multiple research studies with a variety of parent populations and child problems.

Many parents simply do not know how to be helpful to their children's emotional adjustment and cannot be expected to know, because they have had no appropriate training anywhere in their lifetime. However, when parents feel better about themselves, are less anxious, and are better adjusted, they are more likely to respond in positive, self-enhancing ways to their children. The point being made here is that parent training is the preferred but not the exclusive approach.

A frequently asked question is, "Can play therapy be effective if the parents do not receive therapy?" Although involving parents in therapy or parent training is always recommended if possible and positive results may be achieved in less time if they are, children in play therapy can and do change in significantly positive ways without their parents being involved in therapy or parent training. Children are not completely at the mercy of their environment. If they were, how would we account for those children who have grown up in absolutely terrible home environments, yet go on to be quite well-adjusted and successful adults? Although this is possible, it is not typical—but it does point to the individual's capacity to grow and to overcome. Play therapy can be effective without parents receiving therapy or parent training.

Further evidence of this can be seen in elementary school counseling programs. Many parents work and are not available during the day for counseling sessions. To expect an elementary school counselor to work with the parents of every child seen in a counseling relationship is unrealistic. In most elementary schools, counselors report significant changes in children's behavior even though they have only limited contact with a minimum number of parents.

And what of residential institutions for children where parents are not available? Can therapy with children in these settings be effective? Is help to be withheld because parents are not there? Or is help to be withheld until a newly placed child forms a relationship with a significant adult staff member in the institution so the significant adult can be worked with?

The answer to such questions is obvious. Experiences in schools and residential institutions have demonstrated children's capability to cope, adjust, change, and grow even though parents did not receive counseling. To insist that children not be seen in therapy until their parents can be worked with is to deny the growth potential and coping ability of children and the ability of parents to alter their own behavior in relation to a child's change in behavior. When the behavior of a child changes as a result of the play therapy experience, parents unconsciously perceive the change, be it ever so slight, and in turn respond to the child in a slightly altered way, thus encouraging the change in the child. Said another way, the child goes home and is a little different; so the parents respond a little differently. Some obviously gross exceptions do exist to this premise, as in the case of severely emotionally disturbed parents or parents who habitually abuse drugs, but generally this premise is true.

How this process of change works can be seen in the following case. Three-year-old Sarah's father described her this way: "We don't dare leave her alone for one minute or something will be destroyed. She messes everything up, colors on the walls. She just can't be trusted." In play therapy, as Sarah experienced the therapist's consistent acceptance of her, her persistent demands, her "baby" behavior (sucking on the nursing bottle, etc.), and her need to be messy, she became less demanding and much more agreeable. Some of her messy behavior resulted in therapeutic limit setting, thus allowing her to learn to control her terrible mess in the bathroom at bath time, which was her father's task to clean up. As Sarah began to demonstrate greater self-control, her father became more accepting of her, relaxed with her, and began to play with her spontaneously. They began to have fun together, and Sarah felt accepted.

Sarah no longer tried to pinch or hurt her 5-month-old baby brother, began to play by herself more, and, in her mother's words, "She doesn't follow me around whining all the time." Mother also relaxed with Sarah, became more trusting of her, responded more readily to her need for nurturing, and was able to say, "I have my lovable little girl back." Neither parent was worked with in therapy, nor were they told anything about what Sarah did in the playroom. As is demonstrated in this case, children not only can change but do, without concomitant parent therapy.

Parents as Partners in the Play Therapy Process

Prior to the first play session, the play therapist meets with the parents without the child present. The child is not included as a precaution to protect the child from hearing parents describe a stream of negative descriptions and complaints about the child and the child's behavior that would be harmful for the child to hear. Many parents are considering play therapy for their child because they are frustrated with the child, at their "wits end," angry at the child, feel hopeless, are desperate, and may dump pent-up emotions focused on the child. Children should not experience the brunt of such venting from parents and, therefore, are seldom involved in consultations with parents.

The therapist's primary task during this session is to build a relationship with the parents, focusing on the parents' needs and concerns and conveying to them their importance in their child's therapy. Parents bring to this initial meeting the intensity of their concerns about their children and accompanying emotional reactions. Some parents feel overwhelmed, and the sensitive therapist will respond to these feelings with the same empathic caring that comes forth in the relationship with a child in the playroom. Emotional contact with parents helps them to trust the therapist, an absolutely essential element if parents are to be consistent in bringing their children to play therapy. Parents need to know they have been heard and understood. In this initial parent consultation, the sensitive therapist will respond equally to parents' concerns about their children's problems and the deeper level of parents' emotional reactions, moving back and forth between these dimensions in the interview process. This is not a time for education and instruction, which can quickly become overwhelming and feel judgmental to parents.

The initial parent consultation provides the play therapist with the opportunity to inform parents about play therapy: what play therapy is, why it is used with children (toys are like children's words, etc.), how play therapy works (how it is helpful to a child), what to expect during the process, and to show the parents the playroom so they will be familiar with where the child is spending time in their absence. The experience of standing in the middle of the playroom usually helps parents relax.

The therapist will also want to prepare parents for unexpected happenings in the waiting room such as how to respond if their child resists separating and clings to them, and how to respond when their child reenters the waiting room at the end of the session. (How to respond to happenings in the initial experience in the waiting room is explained in the next section.) I have found that it is best to anticipate happenings and coach parents on how to respond. In the Center for Play Therapy at the University of North Texas, we provide parents with a small brochure that gives examples of how we hope parents will respond to anticipated happenings in the waiting room as well as what to tell their child about coming to the playroom. Special considerations for the child that might impact the therapeutic process will also be inquired about in this initial parent consultation: medications, child's fears, allergic reactions to sandbox dust, toilet training for very young children, and so forth.

The importance and characteristics of confidentiality will need to be discussed. Although, in most states, children do not have the legal right to confidentiality, the play therapist emphasizes the need for children to experience confidentiality of specific actions and words in the playroom. In play therapy, parents are not allowed to observe their children's play therapy session so that the child can feel free to fully express thoughts, feelings, and actions. In the first consultation, the therapist reviews the importance of attendance, indicating that sporadic participation in play therapy interferes with progress. The play therapist highlights the need for a final session if the parents decide to prematurely terminate therapy.

Meeting with parents on a regular basis, at least once a month, is considered to be essential in that this helps keep parents involved in the process, provides an opportunity for parental feedback regarding developmental progress and emotional/behavioral change, and continues the process of building a relationship with parents. Frequency of meetings with parents is determined by the unique needs of the child and the parents. If a child has been traumatized or has experienced a crisis situation, meeting more frequently may be needed to provide the parent needed support. These continuing consultations provide opportunities for brief training of parents in skills to help them respond to their child in more positive ways. These skills are introduced in the context of parents' discussing their child's behavior. Typically parents are taught basic Child Parent Relationship Therapy (CPRT) skills of reflection of content and feelings, choice giving, building self-esteem, returning responsibility, and limit setting (Bratton, Landreth, Kellam, & Blackard, 2006; Landreth & Bratton, 2006).

Explaining Play Therapy to Parents

Helping parents understand what play therapy is may be one of the most important things the play therapist does because, in most cases, the cooperation of the parent is essential in bringing the child to the sessions. Parents immediately think of fun and games when they hear the term *play therapy* and wonder why they are being asked to bring their child to play when the child already plays at home. If parents do not understand how play therapy works, they cannot be expected to trust the process or to have faith in the therapist, and if they do not, their negative attitude may affect the child's feelings about the sessions. Comments like, "It's costing a lot of money for you to just go in there to play. And besides, you're still wetting the bed," are sure to make the child feel guilty and undermine the therapeutic relationship. The following explanation about play therapy could be given, modified to allow the therapist's own uniqueness and approach to be communicated:

I know you are concerned about Lisa. She seems to be having a difficult time coping (at home, at school, with the divorce, with other children, etc.). In the process of growing up, most children experience difficulty adjusting at some time. Some children may need more help than others in some areas and less help in certain areas. Children have a hard time sitting in a big chair, like the one you are sitting in, and talking about what bothers them. They don't know the words to describe what they are feeling inside or what they are thinking, so sometimes they act out or show how they feel.

In play therapy we provide toys, and I will show you the playroom in a few minutes, for children to use, to say with the toys what they have difficulty saying with words. In the play therapy experience, toys are like the child's words, and play is the child's language. When children can communicate or play out how they feel to someone who understands, they feel better because the feelings have been released. You have probably experienced the same thing when you were bothered or worried about something and told someone who really cared about you and understood, then you felt better and could handle the problem better. Well, play therapy is like that for children. They can use the dolls, puppets, paints, or other toys to say what they think or how they feel. Therefore, how children play or what they do in the playroom is very important, just like what you say here is very important. In play therapy, children learn how to express their thoughts and feelings in constructive ways, to control their behavior, to make decisions, and to accept responsibility.

After the play therapy sessions, if you were to ask Lisa what she did, she would probably say she just played. And if someone asked you what you did here today, you would probably say we just talked. But what we have talked about is very important. What children do in the playroom is also very important. They work through their problems with the help of the counselor. Children are sometimes unaware at the moment that something important has happened in the playroom; so they don't have anything important to say. Sometimes it is easier for children to explore feelings, especially their fears or anger, with someone who can be objective and accepting than it is with parents or teachers. Therefore, it is best that you refrain from quizzing Lisa about what she did, what happened, or if she had fun.

The time in the playroom is a special, private time for children. They should not feel they have to give a report to anyone, even parents. Play therapy sessions with children are confidential, just like counseling sessions with adults. I want to respect Lisa just as much as I respect you as an adult. Therefore, I will be happy to share with you my general impressions and to offer suggestions, but I am not free to tell you the specifics of what Lisa says or does in the playroom. I will share with you general information I think you should know. If you came to see me for counseling and shared something you were concerned about, I would not later tell your spouse or your employer. Our time together would be confidential. When Lisa and I come out of the playroom, it would be best if you didn't ask, "How did things go?" or, "Did you have fun?" Just say, "Hi. We can go home now."

Sometimes Lisa may take a painting or drawing home with her. If you praise the painting, she may feel she should make other paintings for you. It would be best just to make comments about what you see in the painting. "You used lots of colors. There's some blue, and green, and a lot of brown all the way across the bottom of the picture." Because paints can sometimes be messy and the playroom floor may have sand spilled on it, I suggest you let Lisa wear some old play clothes you won't mind getting soiled. Please do not reprimand Lisa or be surprised if she has paint smeared on her hands or arms. Most children get some paint on them when they paint in the playroom. The paint is washable. Some children really enjoy the freedom to be messy with paints, and that can be a part of the therapeutic process.

I am sure you are wondering what to tell Lisa about coming to see me. You may tell her she will be coming to be with Mr. Landreth in his special playroom every week, where there are lots of toys for her to play with. If Lisa wants to know why she is going to the playroom, you can tell her something general like, "Things don't seem to be going very well for you at home (or other general statement related to the identified problem), and sometimes it helps to have a special time just for yourself to share with a special person."

This explanation is given in bits and pieces interspersed with comments and questions for the parent that allow the parent to comment. Giving a parent the entire explanation without a break would be more than a parent could take in and assimilate. As a part of the initial interview, a tour of the playroom or opening cabinet doors in your office to reveal play materials will help the parent to better understand what you have been trying to explain about play therapy. Don't rush this part of the process. Be sure to encourage the parent to ask questions. This is a good time to explain further the purpose of play.

Preparing Parents for Separation

Parents often feel awkward and embarrassed if their child is reluctant to go to the playroom and may make some very inappropriate statements in an effort to get their child to leave the waiting room with the therapist. A parent who says, "If you don't go with the nice man to his playroom, he will think you are ugly" has doomed the beginning of the relationship to a difficult start. A reluctant child is just expressing herself in the only way he or she knows how at that moment—no more and no less. Being reluctant and saying, "I don't want to go to the playroom," does not mean the child is ugly or bad or anything negative. It just means the child does not want to leave her mother or father or does not want to go to the playroom or some other reason the adults do not understand at the moment. When parents know what to expect on their first visit with their children to the playroom and have been told how to respond, the process of separation usually is less difficult for parent and child and a relief to the therapist. With preparation, parents are better able to help their children assume more independence. The therapist may find the following explanation helpful to parents:

When children come here for the first time, they are sometimes reluctant to go with me to the playroom because this is a strange place to them and they have never seen me before. Most children, though, are quite eager to go see the playroom. When I come into the waiting room and introduce myself to Robert, I will say, "We can go to the playroom now." It would be helpful if you would say, "Fine. I'll wait here, and I'll be here when you're finished in the playroom, Robert." (Parents should not say "Bye bye," because that may result in the child feeling he is going to be gone for a long time or perhaps even forever! Always remember how things may seem to the child.) Please do not tell Robert to "Be nice" or any other instructions.

If Robert is reluctant to go to the playroom with me, I will be patient with his reluctance and will reflect his feeling. He may need a minute or two to decide he is willing to go to the playroom. During this time, I hope you will just sit quietly and allow me to do all the work. I am comfortable with a child's reluctance to go to the playroom and believe we will get to the playroom. It just may take a few minutes. If after several minutes, Robert is still reluctant to go to the playroom, I may ask you to walk down the hall to the playroom with us. When we get to the door of the playroom, I will let you know if I think you need to go into the playroom with us. If I should ask you to go into the playroom, just go right in, sit in the chair I point to, and watch. If Robert wants to show you toys or interact with you during the play time, I will respond for you.

Parents should be forewarned that they may hear their child yelling or throwing things, and that such noises are not unusual, because children play hard in the playroom. Or they may hear their child crying, because the child wants to leave the playroom. This behavior also is acceptable. Loud noises and crying do not mean anything is wrong.

Often parents want to tell the therapist something about their child just as soon as the therapist enters the waiting room. The therapist should remind parents that he wants to give their child full attention in the waiting room. Therefore, the best procedure would be for parents to hold their comment until a scheduled meeting time.

If doubts or concerns exist about the child's physical functioning, advise parents to consult their pediatrician. This is always an appropriate suggestion when problems such as bedwetting or enuresis are discussed.

The Parent Interview

Admitting that they or their child need help is a very sensitive and difficult area for most parents. The tendency is to put off asking for help as long as possible, hoping "things will get better." And so in many cases, when the parent finally contacts the therapist, the area of concern is long-standing or has escalated in intensity to the point of frightening or frustrating the parent. The therapist should be especially sensitive to the struggle the parent has undergone to reach the point of asking for help and should relate to that struggle with understanding, rather than rushing to focus on the presenting problem. The parent may feel guilty, frustrated, inadequate, or angry, and these feelings will need to be related to first by employing the same empathic approach utilized in the playroom. Consistent with the child-centered play therapy approach, the relationship established with the parent is considered to be crucial.

The parent's own emotional adjustment and level of frustration tolerance may be the determining factor in whether the parent seeks therapy for the child. A study by Shepherd, Oppenheim, and Mitchell (1966) of 50 children referred to a child guidance clinic and a group of 50 children matched for age and symptom who had not been referred for therapy found that the mothers who had been seen in the clinic were depressed, upset by stress, anxious, perplexed by their children's problems, and worried about what to do. Mothers in the matched group tended to be casual about their children's behaviors and viewed their children's problems as temporary, requiring patience and time to overcome. They seemed to have more self-confidence.

The findings of this study and others highlight the need for the therapist to be sensitive and responsive to the emotional dynamics underlying the parent's reactions. The skillful therapist will, with the help of the parent, weave an intricate tapestry of interaction going in and out of focusing on the presenting problem and the parent's feelings as the therapist follows the parent's movement back and forth between these issues in the initial interview. If the session were to be dissected, some parts would be just like a therapy session, other parts would clearly portray typical intake interview material, and other parts would reveal a parental guidance function with the offering of suggestions for the parent to consider. For example, in a case involving difficulty in getting a child to bed at night, upon learning that the parent did not read to the child, I suggested the parent read a short story to the child just before tucking her into bed. The therapist must be very cautious in making such suggestions before the parent, child, and the relationship are more fully understood. This process of smoothly responding to all levels of the parent's concerns is illustrated in the following initial interview I had just prior to seeing a child for a preliminary diagnostic session in the playroom to determine the need for play therapy.

Parent: I have five kids put into one.
Therapist: He must keep you very busy.

Parent: Yes, I work a full-time job and keep a house and him. As far as school, he does pretty good as long as he's on his medication. Now, if he's not on his medication, that kid, there's no controlling him.

Therapist: What kind of medication is he taking?

Parent: He's on Ritalin.

Therapist: Did you give him medication this morning?

Parent: Uh huh. He gets two before he goes to school in the afternoon and another one after school. He seems to get a streak of energy right at nighttime when the medication has worn off. That kid's got energy.

Therapist: Sounds like that's a busy time, a hard time for you, when he gets that streak of energy.

Parent: Yes. It's nighttime and that's when I'm tired and I want to relax. It's hard trying to work a full-time job and take care of him and the house and with all his energy. He's had that energy since day one.

Therapist: Working full-time and taking care of Anthony is just about all you can keep up with, and he has been overly active ever since he was a tiny baby.

Parent: Yes. Nobody would agree with me. I said he was hyper and had a lot of energy, but no one would agree with me. I was home almost 2 years with him. When we put him in day care and started having trouble, that was when people finally started listening to me and said, "This kid has something wrong." He's very artistic. He can be good when he wants to be, but the majority of the time he's not.

Therapist: But you know that he can control his behavior when he decides to, is that what you're saying?

Parent: Sometimes.

Therapist: You're not very sure he really can.

Parent: Not very often. And you really got to get after him, and I mean you got to get on him hard.

Therapist: What does that mean, you have to be hard on him?

Parent: You have to keep after him constantly, I mean stay on him. You know, you tell him to do something, and he won't do it.

Therapist: You have to follow him around and see that he does it.

Parent: More or less, and there's times that he's gotten pad-dlings for not doing what he's told, and he's got a very smart mouth.

Therapist: So he talks back to you.

Parent: Yes. He tries.

Therapist: How often would you say that you paddle Anthony?

Parent: It's hard to say because I try to avoid it. Like I was saying, when he breaks the camel's back.

Therapist: The last resort.

Parent: Yes, it's not something that happens every day, and I try to avoid it unless he just gets to the point where I can't take anymore of it.

Therapist: Uh huh.

Parent: Then—you see, now I don't even have to use it. Some-times all I have to do is threaten to use it.

Therapist: And then he stops the behavior.

Parent: He starts doing what he's told.

Therapist: So it sounds like he can control himself, but then at other times he's so active that he doesn't think about controlling himself.

Parent: Right. That's about it. He's got too much energy—if we could drain the energy out of him I think everything would be all right. (Laughs.) But there's no way to do that except with the medication, which slows him down.

Therapist: How long has he been on the medication?

Parent: About 2 years now.

Therapist: When was the last time the pediatrician adjusted his medication?

Parent: It was about maybe a month ago. We alter the dos-age depending on what he goes through. The doctor more or less goes by what I feel. If I see that he's doing good then we bring the dosage down. We brought it down for a while because he seemed to be doing better. Then once he started school again, he started getting up again, so we increased it.

Therapist: You said a minute ago that the medication seems to wear off by nighttime. What are bedtimes like for Anthony?

Parent: Horrible!

Therapist: What does that mean, horrible?

Parent: Well, it's not really that bad going to bed; he usually falls asleep on the couch with me. I'll be sitting on the couch relaxing, and he'll fall asleep. But it's usually 10 o'clock before he falls asleep. Now, he's waking me up between 4 and 5 o'clock every morning, and I'm not up at 4 o'clock in the morning! (Laughs.)

Therapist: That's really early for you. You're not functioning very well.

Parent: Very early! And he wants to lay in bed with me, and I won't have it. There's not enough room, and I want to sleep comfortably with the little bit of sleep I do get. I finally put him back in bed or on the couch, and he'll sleep for awhile. Sometimes he'll argue with me, sometimes he won't. But he doesn't need a lot of sleep. We also have a problem with bedwetting. I can't get him to quit. And, it's getting to be a pain. I mean he's 6 years old. It's got to quit. Now his doctor said she could give him medication, but I didn't want to push another medication on him. I think that one is enough.

Therapist: You're really frustrated with the bedwetting. Has there ever been a period when he did not wet his bed at night?

Parent: Yes. We've gone through periods off and on, going back a few years, where he would get up in the middle of the night, go to the bathroom, and go back to bed without ever disturbing me. He did that for awhile. But it's been going on for quite awhile now. I would guess 6 months, a year.

Therapist: That must seem like a long time.

Parent: Yes, it's been a long time.

Therapist: So he wets his bed every night or almost every night.

Parent: Almost every night.

Therapist: There are some nights when he doesn't.

Parent: Yes, but the majority of the time he's wetting his bed at night. I think it's laziness. He doesn't want to get up out of bed and go to the bathroom is what I think it is.

Therapist: So you've decided he could stop if he wanted to.

Parent: Yes, if he would. If he could get his mind when he's sleeping, to get him up, yes.

Therapist: Have you ever tried a routine of waking him up and taking him to the bathroom?

Parent: No. (Laughs.) I don't get enough sleep as it is to think about that. He wakes me up so early.

Therapist: This is a hard time for you, not enough rest. How about Dad, does he ever get up with him?

Parent: Daddy goes to bed, he puts his head down, and he doesn't know anything until the next morning. A bomb could go off under the bed, and he wouldn't know it.

Therapist: Nothing bothers him. It's all up to you, then.

Parent: Not in the least. The only time he gets his sleep disturbed is when one of us is very sick. I mean we've got to be deathly sick is the only time he would hear anything. Anthony comes jumping in the bed at 3, 4, 5 o'clock in the morning, and Daddy doesn't know anything. So as far as that goes, that wouldn't work.

Therapist: So you don't think you could depend on Dad for any help.

Parent: No. Not when he comes to bed late.

Therapist: Sounds like, from some of the things that you've said, that you're primarily responsible for taking care of Anthony and trying to help him change his behavior.

Parent: Pretty much, the majority. Until a month ago, Anthony spent 2 months home with Daddy because Dad was out of work, and I couldn't pay for a babysitter as long as he was out of work; so he did take care of Anthony at that time. And things seemed to be pretty good. I mean he still was overactive. They got along and were pretty good at it, hardly any problems in school or anything, but now we're back to babysitters. Now, I can't keep him in a day care. I've gone through four or five different day cares and none of them can handle him because of his activeness. Right now, he's at a home sitter, which seems to be working pretty good. And it's a one-on-one.

Therapist: So things are a lot better at home and school when Anthony has lots of close attention.

Parent: He needs one-on-one attention is what I've been told by the majority of the people. He needs one-on-one. I've threatened him to quit working and stay with him 24 hours a day because of trying to keep him someplace, and he doesn't like the idea. He doesn't want Mommy to quit working, because then there's no more toys, there's no more extras.

Therapist: Sounds like you're so exasperated you are willing to try almost anything to get him to control himself.

Parent: Yes, but to get him to control himself totally, he doesn't understand that. I don't know if it's that he doesn't want to or he can't.

Therapist: I really hear the confusion there for you. There's a part of you that thinks, "Well, maybe if he really worked hard at it he could control himself." But there's another part of you that kind of knows it's not something he really can control sometimes.

Parent: I don't know.

Therapist: Just not sure about that.

Parent: No. What I'd like and what happens are two different things. I mean I've been putting up with it for so long. My major problem, though, is I'm afraid about what will happen when he's finished kindergarten. We've got the medication to control him pretty much now, but what's going to happen when he goes to school all day? And he's very big for his age. And that's another problem I'm afraid of—I mean he is tall.

Therapist: So you're looking ahead to first grade and knowing that if this is still going on, he is going to have some real problems.

Parent: And I'm going to have the problems.

Therapist: And you're also going to have problems with him. I hear your frustration. There are times when you just get so frustrated, almost too much for you to take care of.

Parent: Yes, and other people don't see it, what I go through, and there have been a couple of times over the last 6 months that I thought I was going to have a nervous breakdown trying to control everything. At one point I thought I almost did. Something has just got to be done, and if it's not done soon, it's not going to be a question of Anthony surviving, it's going to be Mommy surviving.

Therapist: The pressure has really been hard on you. You've been working hard a long time to keep everything together, and now you're just almost at the breaking point sometimes.

Parent: Yes, I am, and it's got to change, that's all there is to it. But I'm the one who has been pushing this, and I'm the one who needs it, and I just feel that—at one time I had a hard time even getting my husband to go to this stuff. It's hard to get him—I mean my husband is a lot older. My husband is 58 years old, and he's set in his ways. And that's another thing that I'm fighting against, is that he's set.

Therapist: It's hard for you to get him involved, and you feel you need some help. It's almost overwhelming to you trying to take care of everything by yourself.

Parent: Yes. I mean he's been getting more involved lately than he had ever before because I've been doing a lot of screaming and yelling, because I'm at the point of no return and I can't handle it.

Therapist: So you're finally getting your message across to him that you really need some help, but even that you have had to work so hard at. You just feel so desperate.

Parent: Yes, that's pretty much the way it is, and I've just got to have some help.

The session ended with an explanation of play therapy and a visit to one of the playrooms. It is obvious this mother needs therapy for herself, so she will be better able to cope with her son.

Ethical and Legal Issues in Play Therapy

Because play therapists have received training in a specific area of the field of mental health such as counseling, psychology, or social work, it is assumed that they have received thorough training in and have a working knowledge of the general areas of ethical and legal issues related to their area of study as prescribed by their state licensing board and professional organizations to which they belong. It does seem important, though, to focus some attention on legal and ethical issues specifically related to working with young children because they are a dependent population. The intent of this section is to call attention to fundamental guidelines related to the unique setting of working with children in play therapy, a sort of reminder. The purpose of this section is not to provide an exhaustive review of legal and ethical issues.

Play therapists are advised to follow ethical guidelines and standards of practice of professional organizations which require that they take appropriate precautions such as obtaining informed consent, professional consultation, and supervision to ensure clients are protected, and that they are practicing within the boundaries of their profession. State laws differ regarding therapy with minors, and play therapists are advised to familiarize themselves with the laws of the state in which they practice.

Legal and ethical considerations dictate that parents should be involved when mental health professionals are working with children. Sweeney (2001) noted:

> When working with children, it is imperative to remember that while the child may be the focus of treatment, the legal guardian is essentially the client from a legal and ethical perspective. This is simply because the presumption of the state is that minors are legally incompetent. This means that children are not considered to have the legal capacity to consent (or refuse) services, or the right to obtain and retain privilege in regard to confidential information. It is the legal guardian, which is most often the parent, who is the holder of these rights. This can make the legal and ethical aspect of counseling children occasionally ambiguous for all involved persons. (p. 65)

Thompson and Rudolph (2000) noted that "The rights of minors and the rights of parents to serve in a 'guiding role' can cause confusion. While adults agree on the worth and dignity of children, it must be recognized that legally, minors have fewer rights than adults because of their supposed limited experiences and cognitive abilities to make decisions" (p. 502). Parents must be informed about the purpose and process of play therapy and appropriate informed consent secured. Obtaining informed consent is a complex issue for play therapists. According to Sweeney (2001),

> To satisfy the principle of informed consent, which is essentially a legal and ethical doctrine, the consent of clients must be given in a voluntary, knowledgeable, and competent state. Because of their minor status, children are not considered voluntary, knowledgeable, and competent clients. Play therapists choose to use play as a means of communicating with children because they lack the developmental skills to engage in therapy in the same manner as adult clients. The very concept of informed consent is sophisticated and abstract, and as such is counter to this basic rationale for using play therapy. Since children are generally considered legally incapable of consenting to the process of play therapy, a substitute must make the decision. In most cases, this will be the parent or legal guardian. (p. 68)

Permission must be obtained from the child's legal guardian prior to scheduling for play therapy. The therapist would be well advised not to assume that the parent who arranges for the child to be in play therapy has custody of the child. The adult in your office discussing the child may indeed be the child's mother, but she may be divorced and the father has full custody. In cases involving divorced parents, it is recommended that the therapist obtain copies of the most current designated court orders pertaining to the child's issues. Obtaining a divorce decree may not result in the most current information. As a precaution, the play therapist's notes should reflect their request for the most recent court order in addition to obtaining a copy for their file. The therapist must obtain informed consent from the legally appropriate guardian giving permission for the named child to be in play therapy and verifying that the parent is the legal guardian. A separate form is needed for granting permission for release of information and to make audio and video recordings of the sessions.

Always obtain parental permission before discussing a child's case with school personnel, an agency, and so on. This point cannot be overemphasized. Never release information or discuss a child with teachers or other significant individuals in the child's life, other than the child's legal guardians, without obtaining permission from the legal guardian. This rule would not apply in many elementary schools, where the counselor is viewed as a part of the educational team and discussions with teachers are recommended.

Psychiatric Referral

In cases such as potential suicide, a psychiatric evaluation may be needed. If residential care is deemed necessary, the therapist may need to be reminded that many psychiatric facilities are not equipped to adequately care for young children. The therapist will want to visit facilities and ask important questions of the staff. What kind of training and experience do they have in working with children? What degrees and licensure or certification do the staff members hold? What procedures are used with children below the developmental age of 10? Do they use the same approach with all ages—that is, only group work based on verbal interaction with groups of eight children ages 5 to 12? Do the staff members seem to really care about and understand children? Are they warm persons? Is there a play therapy room? If so, ask to see it. You cannot assume a highly qualified staff exists in all areas just because the program is a part of a psychiatric facility. This is information the therapist will need in order to assist in referrals.

References

Bratton, S., Landreth, G., Kellam, T., & Blackard, S. (2006). *Child parent relationship therapy (CPRT) treatment manual: A 10-session filial therapy model for training parents* (includes CD-ROM). New York: Routledge.

Cooper, S., & Wanerman, L. (1977). *Children in treatment: A primer for beginning psychotherapists.* New York: Brunner/Mazel.

Landreth, G., & Bratton, S. (2006). *Child parent relationship therapy (CPRT): A 10-session filial therapy model.* New York: Routledge.

Shepherd, M., Oppenheim, A., & Mitchell, S. (1966). Childhood behavior disorders and the child-guidance clinic. *Journal of Child Psychology and Psychiatry, 7,* 39–52.

Sweeney, D. (2001). Legal and ethical issues in play therapy. In G. Landreth (Ed.), *Innovations in play therapy: Issues, process, and special populations* (pp. 65–81). Philadelphia: Brunner-Routledge.

Thompson, C., & Rudolph, L. (2000). *Counseling children* (5th ed.). Pacific Grove, CA: Brooks/Cole.

8

The Playroom and Materials

The atmosphere in the playroom is of critical importance, because that is what impacts the child first. The playroom should have an atmosphere of its own that conveys warmth and a clear message: "This is a place for children." Creating an environment friendly to children requires planning, effort, and a sensitive understanding of how it feels to be a child. Children are more likely to feel comfortable in places where a sense of openness exists that says to the child, "You are free to use what is here. Be yourself. Explore." The feeling in the playroom should be like putting on a well-worn, warm sweater. The look of the toys and materials should say, "Use me." It is difficult to accomplish this kind of feeling in a new room with all new toys. The feeling in such rooms often is cold. Great effort and creativity are required to transform a new playroom into a comfortable place that invites the child's interaction. A well-worn feeling is preferred.

Playroom Location

Because children are sometimes noisy, the playroom should be located in an area of the agency, school, or suite of offices least likely to distract or disturb other clients and staff members. If parents or other children hear what is going on in the playroom, the child may feel that his privacy has been violated and the relationship may suffer. Likewise, parents may unnecessarily question the child about what they heard, thus threatening the child. Although some writers have recommended the playroom be soundproof, that seems to be unrealistic and largely unattainable. When a child yells, throws the blocks, or pounds with the mallet, the noise will be heard outside the playroom. Acoustical tile on the ceiling will reduce the noise level considerably. Do not put acoustical tile on the walls, because the texture invites children to pick, poke, and pull pieces off. Also, there is absolutely no way paint can be washed off or removed from the porous material.

Complete isolation of the playroom is probably an unrealistic goal, although I once worked for several years in a private counseling agency that had a small house located on the back of the property that we converted into a children's place with two play therapy rooms. It was a wonderful experience, and the children quickly identified with the "little house."

Playroom Size

A room approximately 12 feet by 15 feet seems to meet the purposes of play therapy best. Although I have worked in playrooms with smaller dimensions, an area of 150 to 200 square feet feels almost ideal, because the child is never too far away. A long narrow room or a larger room would defeat this purpose. In larger rooms, the therapist may "chase" the child around the room in an effort to be close and in the process deprive the child of the opportunity to take the lead in approaching the therapist on the child's terms.

A room of the size recommended here provides ample space for group play therapy with two or three children but no more, because the typical high activity level causes too many conflicts resulting from physical encroachments on other children's activities, or on the child who wants to play alone for a few minutes, or on the child who wants to sit contemplatively. Enough space must be available for children to have their own activity space if they desire without continually bumping into each other or disrupting each other's play. Yes, children do need to learn to play together. However, the play therapy setting can be a very intense, emotional experience, and some children need the opportunity to pull aside, to be alone, to regroup psychologically; they are not able to ask for such space, nor are other children likely to recognize the need in the midst of their own self-motivated period of high activity. A combination of not enough space and too many children is potentially chaotic and damaging to children. For larger play therapy groups of five children, a playroom of approximately 300 square feet is desirable.

Playroom Characteristics

The room should provide privacy from view, with no windows on inside walls or in the door. A window on an outside wall will probably not present a problem, but curtains that can be drawn or miniblinds of some kind will be needed. No windows to contend with is the best plan.

Durability and ease of cleaning makes vinyl tile squares the preferred floor covering, and damaged squares can be easily and inexpensively replaced. For that reason, solid sheet vinyl is not cost-effective. Carpet of any kind is avoided. Carpet is difficult to keep clean, almost impossible to sweep sand out of, and spilled paint makes a real mess. In playrooms and play areas where carpet cannot be replaced, a large piece of sheet vinyl can be placed under the easel. However, this procedure may convey to children that they should be careful and clean. Carpet can present the same message.

The walls of the playroom will need to be painted with washable enamel because ease of cleaning is a major consideration. Vibrant, dark, and somber colors are avoided. An off-white color is preferable, because it contributes to a bright, cheerful atmosphere.

If funds permit, a special addition is the inclusion of a one-way mirror and wiring for sound for supervision and training purposes. Play therapy sessions can be filmed through the one-way mirror, thus avoiding distracting the child with the presence of the video camera in the playroom. Having a video camera in the playroom usually results in children "hamming it up," and the therapist's anxiety level will be heightened if an expensive camera has to be protected.

Although parents are typically not allowed to watch play therapy sessions, a highly desirable procedure is for parents to watch demonstration sessions with their children when parent training, as in filial therapy, is employed. For parent training, the one-way mirror can be the most valuable tool available. The opportunity for parents to see the therapist demonstrate what has been discussed in the training, and then having the opportunity to have their own session with their child supervised, is invaluable.

A sink with cold running water is recommended. Hot water is potentially dangerous and is not needed. Disconnect or turn off the hot water valve underneath the sink and screw the cold water valve about half closed, so the child can turn the water on all the way without it splashing all over the place. The sink also is less likely to overflow with less water coming out of the faucet. This kind of planning ahead allows the therapist to be more permissive and eliminates the need for so many limits.

A chalkboard with a tray across the bottom can be mounted to the wall approximately 21 inches from the floor, to best accommodate the wide variability in children's height. An eraser and white and colored chalk are made available. Break the new chalk into pieces, so children will not feel they have to be careful.

Mount a polished metal mirror, no glass, on the wall. Children use the mirror to check out their facial expressions, to study themselves, and to enact play scenes involving their home.

The typical playroom will probably need shelves on two walls to provide enough space for the toys and materials to be displayed without being crowded or piled on top of each other. Self-contained, boxed shelves sturdy enough to be climbed on and permanently fastened to the wall are ideal. The top shelf should be no higher than 38 inches, so that small children will be able to reach the toys without assistance and without having to climb on top of something (Figure 8.1). If you have the opportunity to design a playroom for a new building or remodeled space, a very small bathroom with just enough space for a commode and designed for the door to open into the playroom will eliminate the problems associated with children having to leave the playroom to go to the bathroom. The therapist's dilemma of how many times to allow a trip to the bathroom and whether or not the request is based on genuine need will be eliminated. Children also will use the bathroom as an extension of the playroom to act out bathroom

FIGURE 8.1 Sturdy shelves make a great place to hide when feeling small and vulnerable.

scenes, as a place to hide or retreat from the therapist, and to find out what it is like to completely shut out and ignore an adult.

Sturdy, wood, or hard-surface child-sized furniture is needed in the playroom. A table and three chairs, one adult size, will be needed. A storage cabinet with a countertop for painting, play-dough, finger painting, and so on is highly recommended. This could be a part of the sink area.

Other Settings for Play Therapy

Although desirable, a fully equipped playroom is not essential for children to express themselves. I never accept the excuse that there is no space for play therapy. What is important is that children be provided with an opportunity to choose the mode of communication that is most natural for them. For some children, this may be a combination of the two modes available—play and verbalization. An immediate therapeutic dividend resulting from being allowed to choose is that children can set their own directions and assume responsibility for doing so.

One creative elementary school counselor in west Texas, who serves five elementary schools, converted the back half of a school bus into a play therapy room. A partition separates the play area from the front half, which serves as a group guidance area. She drives this traveling play therapy room to each school 1 day a week and conducts play therapy sessions while parked in the parking lot.

Many therapists in private practice and agencies are quite effective in conducting play therapy sessions in one end of their office. In elementary schools, where the counselor often serves more than one school and has a tiny "cubby hole" for an office or shares an office with other staff members, play therapy sessions can be held in the corner of a regular classroom when vacated, a workroom, the nurse's office, or the corner of the cafeteria after the cooks have left for the day. One innovative elementary school counselor uses space in the bookroom after textbooks have been removed and distributed at the start of the school term. She displays the toys and materials on several of the empty bookshelves, and the children play in the floor space and on the shelves. She reports significant results in this setting. Another counselor obtained permission from a church adjoining the school grounds to use one of its Sunday School classrooms. Other counselors have reported satisfactory results using the stage of the auditorium or cafeteria. These areas often are unused, and a portion of the stage or off-stage area can be made more private by closing the stage curtains.

In settings such as the cafeteria or classroom, a physical approximation of the boundaries for the session can be indicated by using chairs or tables to indicate the designated play area. The child should not be allowed to roam over the entire cafeteria. The development of a therapeutic relationship would be almost impossible under such conditions. In these settings the therapist must be ready to set more stringent limits. Wherever play therapy sessions are held, every effort must be made to protect the confidentiality of the sessions. When complete privacy and confidentiality are not possible, children should be informed that they may be heard or seen by others.

In these modified settings, the therapist can keep a selection of toys and materials stored in a box or totebag under the desk, in a corner, or in a closet, and the play materials can be arranged on the corner of the desk, on a chair seat, and on the floor just before each play therapy session. A bookcase with a curtain across the front or a cabinet with doors makes an excellent place to house play materials. Open display of play materials prior to each session helps children feel more comfortable, invites participation, and conveys permissiveness in a setting that seems to say, "This is just for you."

Rationale for Selecting Toys and Materials

The intent in this chapter is to present some guidelines for the therapist to use in selecting toys and materials that will serve as a medium for children to express feelings, explore relationships, and understand themselves.

Some general guidelines for selecting toys are that the toys are durable and communicate a message of, "Be yourself in playing," rather than a message of, "Be careful." Toys and materials are needed that provide children with variety in choice of medium of expression. The toys do not need to be elaborate. Remember, the first toys used by humans in play were sticks and stones. Age-appropriate, noncomplex, nonmechanical toys that can be easily manipulated by children avoid frustration. No toy should require the child to seek the therapist's help to manipulate. Many children in need of play therapy are already prone to be dependent, and the therapist will want to avoid reinforcing such behavior. Therefore, toys are selected that children can manipulate by themselves. Many games do not fit these criteria and, by their very nature, necessitate the direct involvement of the therapist, often in a competitive role. The therapist is then forced into a position of either defeating the child or being dishonest and allowing the child to win. Children usually are sensitive to the latter position and thus do not feel the satisfaction that is so important to the development of positive self-esteem. Noncompetitive board games can be quite facilitative with older children.

Selecting toys and play media materials is a deliberate process based on a sound rationale and always takes into account the basic rationale for using play therapy with children in the first place: a recognition of children's developmental level, which is expressed naturally through their play and activity. As I pointed out earlier, toys are children's words and play is their language. Therefore, toys and materials (words) are selected that facilitate children's expression by providing a wide range of play activity (language). Because children can express their feelings and reactions more fully through their play, the toys and materials selected for play therapy are a significant therapeutic variable. Toys and materials are selected that

1. Facilitate a wide range of creative expression.
2. Facilitate a wide range of emotional expression.
3. Engage children's interests.
4. Facilitate expressive and exploratory play.
5. Allow exploration and expression without verbalization.
6. Allow success without prescribed structure.
7. Allow for noncommittal play.
8. Have sturdy construction for active use.

Because toys and materials are part of the communicative process for children, careful attention must be given to the selection of appropriate items. The rule is *selection* rather than *accumulation*. Play areas and playrooms containing an assortment of randomly acquired toys and materials often resemble junk rooms and doom the play therapy process to failure.

RULE OF THUMB:

Toys and materials should be selected, not collected.

Toys and materials should be carefully selected for (a) the contribution they make to the accomplishment of the objectives of play therapy and (b) the extent to which they are consistent with the rationale for play therapy. All play materials do not automatically encourage the expression of children's needs, feelings, and experiences. Mechanical and electronic toys or electronic games are not appropriate for play therapy. Electronic games do not facilitate the development of a relationship or a child's creativity. They also do not allow symbolic play because the game is preprogrammed. *The item should do only what the child prescribes.*

Toys and materials are used by the child in the act of play to communicate the child's personal world. Therefore, toys and materials should be selected that facilitate the **Seven Essentials in Play Therapy**: establishment of a positive relationship with the child, expression of a wide range of feelings, exploration of real-life experiences, reality testing of limits, development of a positive self-image, development of self-understanding, and opportunity to develop self-control.

Establishment of a Positive Relationship With the Child

The relationship between therapist and child is based on the ability of the therapist to understand the child's communications and to create an environment that allows the child to communicate freely. Selecting toys that promote clear understanding for the therapist and allow the child to play out themes of real life, aggression, and creative expression helps to establish clear communication. Therefore, providing a family of dolls that represent all members of the child's family will give the child opportunity to create scenes that the therapist can understand more readily than if the same scene were played out with less identifiable objects.

The importance to the therapeutic relationship of understanding the meaning of children's communication and how appropriately selected toys can make it easier for the therapist to understand the meaning of children's play is underscored in some excellent examples by Ginott (1994):

> Children usually play out family themes by using dolls that represent mother, father, and siblings. In the absence of such dolls, a child may symbolically play out family themes by using big and little wooden blocks. But the exact meaning of the message may

escape the therapist. Banging two blocks together may represent spanking or intercourse, or it may merely be a test of the therapist's tolerance for noise. Inserting a pencil into a pencil-sharpener may represent intercourse, but it may also mean that the pencil needs sharpening. However, when a father doll is put on top of a mother doll, the therapist has less room for misinterpretation. For the child, pencil and doll may be equally useful as a means of expression, but to the therapist they are not. The presence of a doll family enables the child to assist the therapist in understanding him. (p. 54)

Expression of a Wide Range of Feelings

The expression of a wide range of feelings can be promoted when toys such as puppets are available, which lend themselves to the expression of those feelings. Choosing toys that are easily used in the expression of feelings will facilitate the expression of those feelings when the need arises within the child. If the need arises and the means to express a particular feeling are not available, the child is stymied in that area. Puppets provide a safe way to express feelings without being threatened, because the characters of the puppets are the ones expressing the feelings. Very few, if any, board games meet the criteria of facilitating a wide range of feelings, exploration of real-life experiences, or testing of limits. What board game can be used by a child to act out her sexual abuse or the accompanying terror?

Exploration of Real-Life Experiences

The expression of real-life experiences is an essential ingredient in any therapy, whether for the child or adult, because real-life experiences are what lead to the need for therapy. Selecting toys, such as a medical kit, that the child can use to develop a feeling of control in life situations promotes inner balance in the child. When the child is able to express real-life experiences in play and have those experiences understood and accepted by the therapist, then those real-life experiences are trimmed to a manageable size.

Reality Testing of Limits

Children will act out aggression, so toys such as a dart gun give the child an opportunity to test the limits of what is permissible and what is not. In the process of play therapy, the child can learn where to draw the line between the two. Testing of limits enables the child to find out where the boundaries are in the relationship with the therapist. The testing of limits also is a reality experience in what could otherwise be fantasy. Pent-up feelings can be expressed with great vigor as limits are tested.

Development of a Positive Self-Image

Many children in need of play therapy have poor self-images, so providing toys and materials such as playdough, crayons, and blocks, which can be mastered and manipulated easily, are necessary for building up a feeling of, "In here I can do things for myself. I can be successful." These feelings are then generalized to the rest of the child's life. Complicated and mechanical toys make mastery difficult and may reinforce an already existing poor self-concept.

Development of Self-Understanding

Self-understanding grows out of the interaction with the play therapist in which the child feels safe enough to be, to express feelings. Many of these feelings are negative. As the child expresses these feelings and experiences the therapist's acceptance and reflection of those feelings, the child comes first to introject the therapist's acceptance and then seems to understand himself or herself better. A variety of toys and materials, such as the bop bag and dolls, facilitate the expression of a wide range of feelings and thus contribute to self-understanding.

Opportunity to Develop Self-Control

The development of self-control grows out of the interaction between the child's responsibility to make decisions, to choose without adult interference or guidance, and the child's redirection of unacceptable behaviors into controlled, acceptable avenues. Sand is an excellent medium for expressing feelings and provides ample opportunity for limit setting and the development of self-control.

Categories of Toys

Although in this chapter a great deal of emphasis is placed on the selection of appropriate toys and materials, the intent is not to imply that toys and materials are considered to be of primary importance in establishing a therapeutic relationship with the child. Nothing can take the place of the emotional climate that develops as a result of the therapist's attitude, use of his or her own personality, and the spontaneous interaction between the therapist and child. Toys and materials can, however, determine or structure the kind and degree of expression by the child and the interaction with the therapist and, therefore, must receive careful attention as to their selection. Some toys and materials, by the very nature of their construction and design, are prone to elicit certain kinds of behaviors more than others and to some extent structure the behavior of the child. Crayons and paint suggest drawing and painting. Sand encourages digging and burying. This initial structuring based on the qualities of the toy or material is more likely to occur in the early stages of therapy, when the child does not feel safe enough to be creative.

Suggestions offered in this chapter are intended to provide the play therapist with some broad guidelines for selecting a variety of structured and unstructured toys and materials that seem to facilitate children's exploration and expression. Appropriate toys and materials for play therapy can be grouped into three broad categories.

1. Real-Life Toys

A doll family, dollhouse, puppets, and nondescript figures (e.g., Gumby) can represent family members in the child's life and thus provide for the direct expression of feelings. Anger, fear, sibling rivalry, crises, and family conflicts can be directly

FIGURE 8.2   Real-life toys provide children opportunities to play out happenings and events they have experienced but do not have words to describe.

expressed as the child acts out scenes with the doll family figures. A car, truck, boat, and cash register are especially important for the resistive, anxious, cautious ("shy"), or withdrawn child because they can be played with in noncommittal ways without revealing any feelings. When children are ready, they will choose play media that will help them express their feelings more fully and openly. When the therapist is ready, or when the therapist wants certain feelings expressed, is not important. A child should never be pressured to discuss topics or express feelings. When the child feels safe, experiences being accepted, and knows the therapist can be trusted, the child will express his feelings spontaneously (Figure 8.2).

The cash register provides for a quick feeling of being in control as a child manipulates the keys and calls out numbers. The car or truck gives an excuse for moving about and exploring the room. This also is a safe way to approach the therapist, "to find out what the therapist feels like" when the child gets physically close. There are subtle reasons children do many of the things they do in the playroom, and the therapist should be sensitive to these possible motivations. The presence of a chalkboard conveys permissiveness to many children, who come to the playroom from classrooms where the rule is, "Don't mess with the chalkboard!" An atmosphere of permissiveness is crucial if the therapist is to make contact with the inner person of the child.

2. Acting-Out Aggressive-Release Toys

Children in play therapy often have intense pent-up emotions for which they do not have verbal labels to describe or express. Toys and materials such as the Bobo (bop bag), toy soldiers, alligator puppet, guns (absolutely no realistic looking guns), and rubber knives can be used by children to express anger, hostility, and frustration.

Inclusion of aggressive toys, especially the Bobo in the playroom, is an area of concern and controversy for some play therapists who believe the presence of a Bobo encourages aggressive behavior in children. Such a view reveals a lack of understanding of the process of child-centered play therapy that focuses on children's feelings and needs rather than on behaviors in a relationship that allows the acting out of aggression on inanimate objects within appropriate boundaries. A key element in the presence of aggressive behavior is the use of therapeutic limit setting that focuses first on understanding the child's feeling. In this accepting, understanding, and caring relationship, children express/play out deeply felt emotions of anger that have been buried inside. In the process of playing out anger, children get their feelings out into the open and in the context of therapeutic limit setting, they learn to cope with, control, and express these feelings in a self-enhancing and acceptable way that is more maturely satisfying. It is the therapist's acceptance of the accompanying feelings of anger or aggression as well as acceptance of the child's desire to break limits that constitutes the therapeutic dimension that facilitates a decrease in the need for acting out the behavior and thus a decrease in the acting out of aggressive behavior. This change can appropriately be referred to as the development of self-control.

As to the position that the presence of a Bobo invites aggression, experience and a study of children's play therapy sessions at the University of North Texas Center for Play Therapy refute this position. A study of the case notes of 205 play therapy sessions for 20 children found that 65% of the 205 sessions contained no play with the Bobo. Aggressive play with the Bobo was reported in 22% of the sessions, nurturing play was found in 11% of the sessions, and noncommittal types of play with the Bobo were reported in 0.05% of the play therapy sessions (Trotter, Eshelman, & Landreth, 2004). These findings support the observation of Smith (2002) that the Bobo was played with very little by the 12 children in his play therapy research study. *The way children use items in the playroom is generally more a function of their personal needs, than the design of the item.*

Returning to the topic of toys recommended for play therapy, every play therapy experience should contain something a child can destroy. Egg cartons serve this purpose well. They can be stomped, cut, ripped apart, painted, and so on. Popsicle sticks can be snapped in two or jabbed into the playdough aggressively. Aggressive children seem to experience the permission to release aggressive feelings in the accepting environment of the playroom as satisfying and are able to move on to more self-enhancing positive feelings. Shooting, burying, hitting, and stabbing the toys are acceptable behaviors in the playroom, because they are expressed symbolically.

The intensity with which angry and aggressive feelings are expressed in the playroom can sometimes be unsettling to the beginning play therapist. In such situations the therapist must be aware of a personal need to protect himself from his own awkward, unsettled feelings and will need to refrain from moving quickly to intervene in the child's expression. However, at times setting a limit on some of the child's behavior may be necessary—if, for example, the child begins to throw sand all over the room. Hammering on a pounding bench toy releases feelings and at the same time facilitates the focusing of attention and energy in a manner that increases concentration.

Animal toys that represent wild animals are necessary, because some children in the early stages of play therapy find it difficult to express aggressive feelings even against human figure dolls. These children, for example, will not hit a father doll but will hit a lion. Some children will express their aggression through the alligator puppet by biting, chewing, and crunching. Playdough is an example of a material that fits into two categories—creative and aggressive. It can be pounded, smashed, rolled out with great vigor, and pinched into pieces as a way to express anger or frustration. Playdough also can be used by the child to create figures for play.

3. Toys for Creative Expression and Emotional Release

Sand and water (Figure 8.3) are probably the most used unstructured play media by children, but they are the least likely materials

FIGURE 8.3 Sand lacks structure and can be whatever the child wants it to be: the surface of the moon, quicksand, the beach, something to clean with—the possibilities are limitless.

to be found in play therapy settings, even though water is one of the most effective therapeutic mediums of all playroom materials. The absence of sand and water in play therapy settings is most likely the result of therapists' low tolerance for messiness and a need to keep things neat and clean. Reluctance also may stem from a legitimate concern about having to clean up. However, this does not seem to be a valid reason, as appropriate limit setting likely will keep most of the sand and water confined to receptacles. In nonplayroom, limited-space settings, a dishpan with an inch of sand and a bucket with a couple of inches of water would serve the purpose quite well. Sand and water lack structure and can be whatever the child wants them to be: the surface of the moon, quicksand, the beach, something to clean with—the possibilities are limitless. There is no right or wrong way to play with sand and water. Therefore, the child is assured of success. This is especially helpful for cautious ("shy") or withdrawn children.

Blocks can be houses, they can be thrown, they can be stacked and kicked down, allowing the child to explore what being constructive and destructive feels like. As with water and sand, the child can experience a feeling of satisfaction, because there is no correct way to play with blocks. Easel paints afford the child an opportunity to be creative, to be messy, to pretend bathroom scenes and smear, or to express feelings (Figure 8.4).

Tote Bag Playroom

Until children reach a developmental level of expressive competence with verbal communication that allows them to express and explore fully the persons they are and their inner world of emotions, toys and materials should be carefully selected to facilitate this process. My experience has been that children can communicate a wide range of messages and feelings with a limited number of toys and materials. Secondary considerations, then, in selecting toys and materials for use in a modified play therapy setting are their size and portability. The following toys and materials are considered to be the minimal requirements for conducting a play therapy session and are recommended because they facilitate a

FIGURE 8.4   Easel paints afford the child an opportunity to be creative, to be messy, to pretend bathroom scenes, to smear, and to express feelings.

wide range of expressions and can easily be transported in a tote bag or stored out of the way in a corner or in a closet:

Aggressive hand puppet (alligator, wolf, or dragon)
Band-aids
Bendable doll family
Bendable Gumby (nondescript figure)
Blunt scissors
Costume jewelry
Cotton rope
Crayons (eight-count box)
Dart gun
Doll
Dollhouse (use box that holds reams of paper, box lid serves
    as dollhouse, draw lines on inside of lid to mark rooms;
    box doubles as storage container for toys)
Dollhouse furniture (at least bedroom, kitchen, and bathroom)

Handcuffs
Lone Ranger–type mask
Medical mask (white dust mask will suffice)
Nerf ball (a rubber ball bounces too much)
Newsprint
Nursing bottle (plastic)
Pipe cleaners
Playdough
Popsicle sticks
Rubber knife
Small airplane
Small car
Spoons (avoid forks because of sharp points)
Telephone (two)
Toy soldiers (20-count size is sufficient)
Transparent tape
Two play dishes and cups (plastic or tin)

If storage space is available, an inflatable vinyl bop bag (Bobo) would be a special asset. A dishpan-size plastic container with an inch of sand in the bottom also would be useful in a more permanent setting. Rice could be used in place of the sand if clean-up is a problem. A bucket with an inch or so of water would be helpful.

Recommended Toys and Materials for the Playroom

The following toys and materials for a fully equipped playroom have been found to be useful in facilitating children's expressions in the Center for Play Therapy playrooms at the University of North Texas. This list is the result of years of experimentation resulting in discarding items and adding others and keeping those items that a wide range of children consistently used in a variety of ways to express themselves:

Balls (large and small)
Band-aids
Barbie doll

Bendable doll family
Blunt scissors
Bobo (bop bag)
Broom, dustpan
Building blocks (different shapes and sizes)
Cereal boxes
Chalkboard, chalk
Colored chalk, eraser
Construction paper (several colors)
Crayons, pencils, paper
Cymbals
Dart gun
Dinosaurs, shark
Dishes (plastic or tin)
Dishpan
Doll bed, clothes, blanket
Doll furniture (sturdy wood)
Dollhouse (open-on-floor type that child can lean into)
Dolls, baby clothes
Dress-up clothes
Drum
Egg cartons
Empty fruit and vegetable cans
Erasable nontoxic markers
Flashlight
Gumby (bendable nondescript figure)
Hand puppets (doctor, nurse, police officer, mother, father,
    sister, brother, baby, alligator, wolf)
Handcuffs
Hats: fireman, policeman, tiara, crown
Lone Ranger–type mask and other masks
Medical kit
Medical mask (white dust mask will suffice)
Nursing bottle (plastic)
Pacifier
Paints, easel, newsprint, brushes
Pitcher
Play camera

Play money and cash register
Pots, pans, silverware
Pounding bench and hammer
Puppet theater
Purse and jewelry
Rags or old towels
Refrigerator (wood)
Rope
Rubber knife
Rubber snake, alligator
Sandbox, large spoon, funnel, sieve, pail
School bus (Fisher Price type)
Soap, brush, comb
Spider and other insects
Sponge, towel
Stove (wood)
Stuffed animals (two or three)
Telephone (two)
Tinker toys
Tissues
Tongue depressors, popsicle sticks
Toy noise-making gun
Toy soldiers and army equipment
Toy watch
Transparent tape, nontoxic glue
Truck, car, airplane, tractor, boat, ambulance
Watercolor paints
Xylophone
Zoo animal and farm animal families

The play therapist is always sensitive to issues of culture and diversity in the toy selection process. Many of these toys and materials can be obtained inexpensively from garage sales or donations from parents whose children have outgrown them. Community agency therapists could present their play therapy program to civic groups, outlining their needs for materials and asking for financial support. Elementary school counselors could do the same with their parent–teacher association (PTA) and request sponsorship of the play therapy program with an annual donation for specific materials. A list of the above items could be posted in the agency or teacher's lounge, asking for donations of the items children have outgrown. This should only be done after the counselor has explained the play therapy program in a teacher's meeting. Avoid a random request for toys, because many items will be "collected" that are not appropriate for play therapy.

Displaying the toys in an organized manner on shelves so they are readily visible presents a visual picture of order and stability and facilitates children's exploration and creativity. Grouping toys together in laundry-type baskets scattered around the room or using plastic containers on shelves to hold bunches of toys presents an image of confusion and inhibits the therapeutic process of expression. Children who are cautious or have poor self-concepts do not feel safe enough to rummage through a basket full of toys to find what is at the bottom of the basket. My experience in visiting such play therapy rooms is that the use of baskets and containers to hold toys typically means there are far too many toys in the room. Ten small cars and a dozen stuffed toys are not needed. Two to three items that are similar is the general rule.

Special Considerations

Although the successful completion of puzzles can facilitate the development of frustration tolerance and a sense of adequacy, they are not recommended because at least one puzzle piece will invariably get lost, thus frustrating a child who already may be frustrated. Experiences in the playroom should not perpetuate negative experiences in children's lives. Children who suffer from feelings of inadequacy and have difficulty completing tasks should be able to experience success with the toys and the resulting feeling of satisfaction.

Children's storybooks are highly recommended in other settings, but not in the playroom because books in the playroom do not fulfill the roll of facilitating children's expression and the acting out of experiences. Books can be a major distraction, and their presence invites children to sit for long periods of time looking at pictures or reading. Children will often ask the therapist to read a story, and this takes the therapist out of her customary role in the playroom and puts the therapist in the lead as she reads a story, thus shifting the focus from the child to the therapist.

Lego-type construction toys for building are avoided because they have too many pieces. Even small boxes of such toys may contain as many 100 to 200 pieces. Finding all the pieces and putting them back in the container can be a real problem for the therapist. The patience and acceptance of an already stressed or tired play therapist can be severely tested when a child picks up a box containing 200 small pieces and with great glee flings all 200 pieces into the four corners of the playroom. The therapist is very likely to groan inwardly when faced with the task of finding and picking up 200 small Lego-type pieces.

Children are not allowed to bring food into the playroom because food items are distracting and become the point of focus. Parents are advised to give their children a snack to eat before they are brought to the playroom. When the therapist enters the waiting room and discovers the child is sipping on a bottle of juice, the therapist can respond, "Looks like you are drinking juice. Juice is for staying in this room. You can put it right there (pointing) while we go to the playroom. It will be there when we come back."

Remove broken toys. Whatever is in the playroom should be intact, complete, and should work. Many children referred for play therapy come from confusing and frustrating environments. What is in the playroom should not add to that confusion or frustration by being incomplete or broken.

Washable tempera paints should be kept fresh. Nothing inhibits or frustrates a child more than the discovery of cups of dried, caked paints. Paints also sour and develop a terrible odor and need to be replaced periodically. When mixing tempera paints, squirt some liquid detergent into each cup of paint to help retard the growth of the odor-producing bacteria. The detergent also makes removal of the paint from clothes easier, even though the paints are labeled washable. The use of small disposable coffee cups inserted into the paint containers also makes the job of cleaning and changing paints an easier task. Place only an inch or so of paint in each cup as a precaution against paints being spilled and to make the job of clean-up easier. Children do not need full cups of paint. That's asking for trouble.

A sturdy, small plastic storage container can make an excellent sandbox. The sand should be heavily sprinkled with water periodically to keep the dust down.

Children need a place to escape or hide from the therapist. The puppet theater makes hiding possible, and the playroom can be arranged so that some item such as the stove sits out into the room. Children can then play on the other side of the stove, out of the view of the therapist, when they feel the need to do so. Such separation or rejection of the therapist is significant in the development of freedom in the relationship.

The playroom should not be used as a place for babysitting. Other staff members who do not work with children often have a tendency to view the playroom as just that, a place for their parent clients' children to play while the parent is in a counseling session. This rule also applies to children who are in play therapy. The play therapy relationship is a special emotional relationship that takes place in the special playroom. *The play therapy room is an emotional place.* Allowing a child to play unattended in the playroom while the parent is being seen by the play therapist interferes with the development of this important emotional relationship.

The playroom is cleaned up and toys put back in their proper place by the play therapist after each session. (The rationale for this position and the issue of asking children to clean up is dealt with in Chapter 13.) Because toys are the child's words, the child should not have to go searching for the toys needed for expression. Children in play therapy often come from chaotic, confused family settings. If toys are strewn carelessly around the playroom and in different places from session to session, the play therapist is reinforcing the child's experience that life is always chaotic and confused. It is important that the playroom present an image of order and consistency. These are therapeutic dimensions.

A part of consistency is that toys are in the same place in the playroom every time the child enters the room. The baby bottle is not sometimes on one side of the playroom and at other times on the opposite side of the room. Items are always somewhere on their designated shelf. This does not mean the playroom must be neat and clean, only orderly. Children feel more secure when they always know where things are. That helps to make the room and the relationship predictable. An organized playroom promotes consistency of the environment, symbolizes the world can be orderly, and ensures the child's play is not influenced by the play of previous children.

When several staff members use the same playroom, an advisable procedure is to schedule a once-a-month cleaning time when everyone who uses the room meets in the room to give it a general cleaning and put the room in order. If this is not done, the room can get to be a real mess in a hurry, and a playroom that looks and feels like a junk room is not therapeutic.

Suggested Titles for the Play Therapy Program in Schools

In view of the emotional reaction to the term *therapy* by some teachers, principals, and parents, the elementary school counselor may want to consider a title for the program other than play therapy program. Play therapy programs in schools could be referred to as "counseling with toys," "emotional growth through play," "developmental growth through play," or a similar title. The elementary school counselor will be the best judge of the potential reaction to the term *play therapy* in the local setting. Such an important program for children should not be prevented from functioning simply because someone objects to the term. The elementary school counselor is encouraged to take a creative approach to developing a title that best describes the spontaneous and expressive use children make of toys and materials provided for their use in communicating their world to the counselor. When using play therapy, elementary school counselors are encouraged to emphasize that they are employing an approach that helps them in their efforts to effectively assist children in their developmental growth. The ultimate objective of play therapy in a school is to help children get ready to profit fully from what teachers have to offer.

References

Ginott, H. (1994). *Group psychotherapy with children: The theory and practice of play therapy.* Northvale, NJ: Aronson.

Smith, M. (2002). Filial therapy with teachers of deaf and hard of hearing preschool children. (Unpublished doctoral dissertation, University of North Texas, Denton).

Trotter, K., Eshelman, D., & Landreth, G. (2004). Yes, Bobo should be in the playroom! *Association for Play Therapy Newsletter, 23*(2), 25–26.

Chapter **9**

Beginning the Relationship: The Child's Time

Who would have thought there was a place like this in the whole world?

Child in play therapy

Just what is that, really, the child's hour? It is one of those rare times, one of those rare relationships in which the child directs herself, a time when the child determines how time will be used. No effort is made to direct the child's play. This is a special time belonging to the child to do with in accordance with his wishes, to make of as he chooses. The child can be just as slow as he wants, inch along, and no one says, "Hurry up." The child can be grumpy, act grumpy, look grumpy, and no one says, "Be happy." The child can do nothing, accomplish nothing, and no one says, "Get busy. Do something." The child can be loud, noisy, bang things together, and no one says, "Be quiet." The child can be silly, giggle, laugh right out loud, and no one says, "Act your age." The child can be small, tiny, suck on a bottle, and no one says, "You're too big for that." The child can use the glue, scissors, paste, make a spaceship, and no one says, "You're too little to do that." This is an extraordinary, singularly uncommon time, place, and relationship when the child can be, experience, and express all she is at the moment and be accepted fully. That makes this the child's time.

The therapist recognizes that growth is a slow process, not to be pushed, prodded, and hurried along. This is a time when the child can relax, a place where growth takes place naturally without being forced, a special relationship. Standing in the middle of the playroom, 5-year-old Rafael summed up his feeling about the uniqueness of the hour by saying, "I wish I could come live here." His statement catches the essence of this special time, place, and relationship for the child.

Objectives of the Relationship

The child-centered play therapist does not attempt to establish objectives for the child to accomplish but is concerned about objectives as they relate to facilitating the development of a therapeutic relationship with the child. The focus is the child. The objective is to become so absorbed in the relationship with the child that everything the therapist does becomes a response to the relationship. The following objectives express that purpose.

1. **To Establish an Atmosphere of Safety for the Child.** The play therapist cannot make a child feel safe. The child discovers that in the developing relationship. The child cannot feel safe in a relationship that has no limits. A feeling of safety is also promoted by the consistency of the therapist.

2. **To Understand and Accept the Child's World.** Acceptance of the child's world is conveyed by being eagerly and genuinely interested in whatever the child chooses to do in the playroom. Acceptance also means being patient with the pace of the child's exploration. Understanding is accomplished by relinquishing adult reality and seeing things from the child's perspective.

3. **To Encourage the Expression of the Child's Emotional World.** Although the play materials are important, they are secondary to the expression of feelings by the child, which they facilitate. In play therapy, there is an absence of

evaluation of feelings. Whatever the child feels is accepted without judgment.

4. **To Establish a Feeling of Permissiveness.** This is not a totally permissive relationship. An important aspect, however, of play therapy is that the child feel or sense the freedom available in this setting. Allowing the child to make choices creates a feeling of permissiveness.

5. **To Facilitate Decision Making by the Child.** This is accomplished largely by refraining from being an answer source for the child. The opportunity to choose what toy to play with, how to play with it, what color to use, or how something will turn out creates decision-making opportunities, which, in turn, promote self-responsibility.

6. **To Provide the Child With an Opportunity to Assume Responsibility and to Develop a Feeling of Control.** Actually being in control of one's environment may not always be possible. The significant variable is that children *feel* in control. Children are responsible for what they do for themselves in the playroom. When the play therapist does for children what they can do for themselves, children are deprived of the opportunity to experience what self-responsibility feels like. *Feeling in control* is a powerful variable and helps children develop positive self-esteem. A survey of 2,800 children from inner-city schools showed that the best predictor of academic achievement was the child's sense of control over the environment (Segal & Yahraes, 1979).

Making Contact With the Child

Because the child probably has not made a self-referral to play therapy, the implied assumption is that significant adults in the child's life think the child needs to be changed. Therefore, the child comes to the first play therapy session with the expectation that the therapist also wants him to change. Consequently, when viewed from the child's frame of reference, one can understand that the child initially may be resistive, angry, or withdrawn, feeling the need to protect or defend himself. Whatever the feeling, that is the existence of the child at that moment, and the child has brought to the relationship what is being experienced. The therapist does not view these initial reactions and feelings as extraneous and something to get past to the "real reason the child is here." That is the child, and *whatever the child is feeling is accepted as a declaration of the person of the child at that moment under those conditions.*

The process of making emotional contact with a child begins when I first come into the child's presence. I experience a challenge of, "What will we, the child and I, be able to create here? What is the person of this child like? What does this child want? How does this child feel right now? How does this child perceive me? What does this child need from me?" Uppermost in my mind at such times is the thought, "I don't want to be like most other adults in my interactions with this child." Actually, it is more than a thought, for I experience a genuine desire to be different. I do not want to crowd the child physically, to come into the child's presence too quickly, or to get too close.

This child has never seen me before. "I wonder what I look like to this child? What does this child see in my face? What does this child hear in my tone of voice? Does the liking, the warmth I feel for children show in my face? Does my tone of voice reveal kindness? I would like somehow to be smaller at this moment in order to enter more fully into this child's world. Does the child know that I think he is important, the most important person in this room, more important to me than even his mother? Do my eyes show that? Is my caring about how the child feels inside being communicated? Do my words convey that caring?" In most experiences and relationships, especially those that are new, children are always wondering:

Am I safe? I don't know you. Will I be safe with you? Is this a safe place? What is going to happen to me here? What are you going to do to me?

Can I cope? What if I can't do what you ask me to do? What if I don't know the answers to your questions? What do I do if you don't tell me what you want? What if I make the wrong choice?

Will I be accepted? Will you like me? Will you like what
I do? What can I do to make sure you like me?

The building of a relationship begins with what the child sees
and perceives in the therapist and is dependent on the therapist's
sensitivity to the child's experiencing at the moment. Making contact with the child means responding with gentleness, kindness,
and softness to the child's communication of self. Through the
process of accepting the child's attitudes, feelings, and thoughts,
the therapist enters the child's world. Once contact with the child
has been made in this way, a trusting relationship can begin to
develop. According to Moustakas (1981), making contact with a
child "can happen only when therapy is approached with a pas-
sion, with a courage to pursue in depth, with a determination to
stay on the path with the child, no matter what" (p. 11).

RULE OF THUMB:

Be sensitive to how the child sees his or her world.

Being sensitive also means being aware that in most other
places where children are taken for a required purpose someone
does something to them: doctor, dentist, testing for school placement, and so on. That children expect the play therapist also to
do something to them is understandable. How does the setting
look to children? Is it an inviting looking place, or austere like
a hospital? Are the hallways sterile looking? Is there any color
anywhere? Are the pictures on the walls of the hall or waiting
room ones children appreciate? Are they hung at children's eye
level? Does the image of the waiting room say this is a place for
children? Therapists will find it helpful to look at themselves and
the surroundings through children's eyes.

The Initial Encounter in
the Waiting Room

Building the relationship begins with the initial interactions
between the therapist and child in the waiting room. The therapist

enters the waiting room with eager anticipation of the exciting possibilities this new relationship may bring and is usually met by a concerned parent who is prepared to inform the therapist about concerns related to the child's behavior. The parent has what she considers to be important information about the child that the therapist should know, and she may have rehearsed the points so the therapist will know exactly the nature of the problem. The therapist greets the parent, and immediately the parent begins to bring the therapist up-to-date. This is not an appropriate time for the therapist to practice active listening or to be patient and hear the parent out. While the therapist stands there talking to the parent, the obvious message is that the therapist considers the parent more important than a child. That is not a recommended way to begin a significant relationship with the child. The child probably already feels insignificant and like a nonperson because he has experienced this scene many times—the parent talking about the child in the third person as though he was not present.

Perhaps the therapist will find it helpful to ponder what it would feel like to be an appendage, just stuck on, no real useful purpose, jerked here and there at the whim of giants. Surely that is how some children feel, unimportant and unnoticed—unless, of course, they cause one of those giants a problem. Then they get plenty of attention. Well...even negative attention is better than no attention. Certainly the therapist does not want to perpetuate such a perception of self for the child. Therefore, the therapist will politely inform the parent that now is not a good time to discuss those issues, because they are important and time is needed to explore them, and a time will be arranged later for that purpose. The therapist will then immediately crouch down and greet the child.

The therapist will find it helpful to enter the waiting room, give the parent a short warm greeting, immediately crouch down, make eye contact, give a warm smile, and make an introduction to the child without giving the parent a chance to initiate conversation. The child is the most important person in the whole building at that moment. The therapist is there to build a relationship with this important little person and to communicate the child's importance. Therefore, the therapist does not stand in the child's presence and discuss the child.

Following the short introduction to the child, the therapist can say, "We can go to the playroom now. Your mother will wait here so she will be here when we come back from the playroom." The therapist then stands up, giving a visual cue to support the verbal statement. This is not a time for questions such as, "Would you like to go to the playroom?" or "We can go to the playroom now, ok?" because such questions just ask for trouble from a skeptical or resistive child who then responds, "No." Also, a choice is implied when one is not intended. If the child does indeed wish she did not have to go into the playroom, that is best dealt with inside the playroom, where the child is free to express feelings and desires with materials selected for that purpose.

The development of a relationship with a child begins in the waiting room, and asking questions is not a recommended way to begin a relationship with a child. On the way down the hall to the playroom, if the therapist tries to engage the child by asking "How old are you?" or "Where do you go to school?" the child will expect the same approach once in the playroom and will wait dutifully for the therapist to ask more questions. Questions keep the therapist in the lead. The child-centered play therapist allows the child to lead the experience and the relationship to where the child needs to be and therefore avoids questions.

Outside the playroom, the presence of parents or other observers may interfere with or stimulate reactions in the child that otherwise might not originate. Stating that the parent will wait in the waiting room and will be there when the child comes back from the playroom reassures the child. The therapist must always remember that the child is going off with a perfect stranger, to an unknown place, and for what could be a "forever" time in the child's perception.

The play therapist might respond to a child who is reluctant to go to the playroom with, "You need more time to decide about going to the playroom. I'm going back to my office. You can choose to have 1 more minute or 3 more minutes before you go to the playroom. Which do you choose?" Choices elicit cooperation, because control is returned to the child.

After the chosen time has passed, if the child is still reluctant, the therapist can say, "Mom, you may go down the hall with us to the playroom, so Robert will know you know where the playroom is." Robert can participate in this decision by the giving of a choice to decide if he wants to walk beside Mom or hold her hand. This almost always results in the child moving toward the playroom, because he is not about to stay in the waiting room by himself while his mother walks away down the hall with the therapist. Usually the child will go right into the playroom without the parent. If the child does not, the therapist can ask the parent to accompany the child into the playroom by saying, "Mom, it looks like Chad would like to have you in the playroom for a while. You can come in with us." As mom enters the playroom, the therapist says, "You can sit there, points to chair, and I will talk for you if Chad needs a response from you." As the session progresses and the child relaxes, the therapist can indicate to the parent an appropriate time to leave the playroom. The parent should leave the room with no comment.

Whether or not to allow the parent into the playroom is at the discretion of the therapist. The therapist does need to anticipate that once in the playroom it may be even more difficult for the child to separate, because the child has already experienced reluctant behavior getting the parent to stay. Generally, the longer the parent stays in the playroom, the more difficult the separation is for both parent and child. The therapist should recognize that the issue of separation may be more difficult for the parent than it is for the child and consequently the child, sensing that, reacts to the parent's feelings. If that is the case, the issue of separation may as well be dealt with at the door of the playroom. Another factor to be considered is the therapist's feelings. The therapist may be much more comfortable allowing the parent into the playroom than having to deal with a reluctant child. However, as long as the parent is in the playroom, the definite possibility exists that the child will not feel safe enough to explore some areas of importance.

Whether or not to go for therapy is much too weighty an issue for a 4-year-old to decide. Parents would not allow a child whose tonsils were so swollen she could not swallow to decide whether or not to take medication; a 4-year-old is not mature enough to handle that kind of responsibility. A parent would not allow an 8-year-old with a broken leg to choose whether or not to be taken to the hospital. Likewise, the decision of whether or not to go for therapy is too much responsibility to grant a child. A suicidal 10-year-old would not be allowed to make a choice about receiving therapy. However, once inside the playroom, the child is free to decide whether or not to participate in the experience, to take advantage of the opportunity to change. Children can be provided with opportunities for change, but they cannot be made to change. That is for the child to decide.

The child could be allowed to choose which day to go, or whether to go to the playroom or an office, but eventually there must come a time when a decision has to be made. A child's emotional well-being is no less important than his or her physical or educational well-being. This is a time for the courage of conviction tempered by great patience. The decision to be made is that of the parent and the child. Some writers recommend the therapist may have to carry the reluctant child to the playroom. I do not feel comfortable in that position. As an absolute last resort, the parent may decide to carry the child to the playroom, but physical struggles are to be avoided if possible. Although I have never had to use this approach, I have been involved in some experiences that required 20 to 30 minutes of patient work to help the child get ready to go to the playroom.

Developing the Relationship in the Playroom

Structuring in child-centered play therapy is minimal and is in keeping with the general philosophy and objectives of the approach: the facilitation of freedom, safety, and self-control.

Introduction to the Playroom

Minimal structuring of the relationship begins with introducing the child to the playroom experience as the therapist and child enter the playroom. The therapist projects a warm and friendly image with tone of voice and facial expression. This is not a time to be overly serious or stern. Smile. The therapist's facial expression is animated and conveys what words cannot.

Verbal communication is kept to a minimum at this point. This is not the time to try to convince the child that a wonderful time will be had. The value of the therapeutic experience cannot be explained verbally to a child who has lived with fears of criticism, condemnation, or rejection throughout life. The value of the relationship can only be known and felt as it is being experienced. Attempting to explain too much about the relationship may unintentionally set limits on the relationship that will inhibit the child's exploration and expression. The mystery of the playroom cannot be removed with words. That can only happen as the child risks exploring.

Words are chosen carefully to communicate to the child freedom, self-direction, and the parameters of the relationship. The therapist might say something like, *"Melissa, this is our playroom, and this is a place where you can play with the toys in a lot of the ways you would like to."* Actually, this statement might seem a bit directing and structuring, because the seemingly implied expectation is that the child will play when, in fact, the child is just as free not to play. However, expressing to a child that she is free not to play is difficult without getting caught up in a lengthy explanation. The statement is freeing and allows the child to be self-directing in that it conveys to the child responsibility for direction.

Boundaries on freedom are conveyed by the words "in a lot of the ways" which, in effect, communicate limits on behavior. This is a key phrase. The words "any way you want" are avoided because this is not a place of complete freedom. Inexperienced therapists often introduce a child to the playroom with, "This is our playroom, and this is a place where you can play with the toys any way you wish," only to have to withdraw their absolute approval as they are about to be shot with the dart gun or as the child throws the airplane at the observation mirror. The therapist is encouraged to give considerable thought to the initial structuring phrase used.

Allow the Child to Lead

After the introduction to the playroom, the therapist now sits down, further communicating to the child willingness to allow the child to lead. The therapist's chair is the only neutral place in the playroom, and the therapist sits there until invited by the child to enter the child's physical space or play. Beginning each session by sitting in the same place communicates a message of predictability to the child and helps the child feel safe. Predictability contributes to a feeling of safety and both are therapeutic dimensions. Sitting down also communicates returning of responsibility to the child. Remaining standing may result in the therapist towering over the child and conveys that the therapist is in charge or is about to do something else, so the child waits expectantly. Also, the tendency while standing is to follow the child around the room, which will cause the child to feel overly self-conscious with the therapist watching over her shoulder.

When the play therapist allows a child to lead in the play therapy relationship, the therapist is living out both a basic philosophy of the innate human capacity of the child to strive toward growth and maturity and an attitude of deep and abiding belief in the child's ability to be constructively self-directing. This philosophy and the resulting attitudes and beliefs result in the therapist trusting the child to take the play therapy experience to where the child needs to be. The therapist allows a child to lead in all areas of the relationship. The essence of this inner dimension of trusting the child is summed up in a self-critique statement made by a play therapist in one of my supervision groups. "For the first time, I fully experienced trusting myself and the child enough to allow the child to go where the child needed to go and do what the child needed to do, and I was struck by the resourcefulness and vast creative language of the child."

Within the structure of time limits and a minimal number of limits in the playroom, the child experiences the freedom of choosing to play or not to play, to talk and what to talk about or not to talk, to sit or stand silently in the middle of the room, to include or exclude the therapist in her play, to hide or not to hide from the

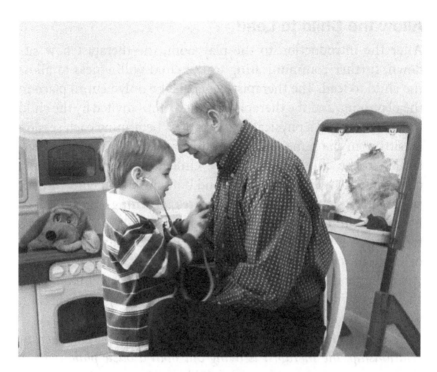

FIGURE 9.1 Children often use toys as a way to make contact with the therapist in the building of the relationship.

therapist, to sit on the floor or run around the room, to play fast or slow, to accept or reject the therapist, to listen or not to listen to the therapist, to be loud or quiet (Figure 9.1). Making choices is a critical part of the therapeutic process in child-centered play therapy. The opportunity to choose whether or not to play or which toy to play with first may seem inconsequential, but for the child each choice made represents some control over her life.

In an attempt to communicate friendliness and a relaxed atmosphere, some play therapists may sit on the floor. A result is that the child is very likely to interpret the therapist sitting on the floor to mean the therapist expects to be invited to play, and the child will dutifully do so even though he had not intended to invite the therapist to play. If the therapist had not sat on the floor, the child might never have asked the therapist to play. The floor is the child's territory, and the therapist respects that until the child invites the therapist to enter. Following the child's lead does not eliminate participation in the child's play, but this participation is done at the direction or invitation of the child.

When participating in the child's play, the therapist is careful to keep the child in the lead. Participation involves taking cues from the child. The child is the director and choreographer of the drama and nothing happens in the play unless it is the child's decision. Interference in the child's play may involve asking questions, offering solutions or suggestions, or allowing the child to manipulate the therapist into becoming a teacher or doing things for the child. Children do not learn self-direction and responsibility when the therapist provides solutions or direction.

Of course, there are reasonable limitations to following a child's direction. The therapist would not undress if directed to do so by a child, but would respond, "You want me to take my clothes off. My clothes are not for taking off. You can pretend the doll (points to doll) is me and take the doll's clothes off." The therapist is not the child's playmate, and maintains his therapeutic role while participating in the child's play.

An abused child creates a play scenario in which an abusive father verbally attacks her. She then directs the therapist, "You be my dad and yell and scream really loud at me and call me names. Tell me I'm stupid, and you hate my guts!" Under no circumstances would I be able to carry out such a role that so violently violates my value system and caring for a child. I could never scream abuses or yell at a child even in play. Such abusive language would be too emotionally penetrating even in play. I would be deeply troubled if a child ever thought that I might even consider doing her harm. How could she ever feel safe with me after such an experience? The therapist should be absolutely consistent and predictable in the play therapy relationship. My response to the child would be, "I wouldn't feel comfortable yelling at you or calling you names even in play. I wouldn't want you to think I might hurt you even in play. You can pretend the Bobo (punching bag) is me and have the Bobo yell at you." This transition allows the child to continue to express and explore what is needed. (My response has 44 words, far more than the recommended 10 or less, probably a result of the fact that this is a strong emotional issue for me.)

Five-year-old Toby sets up a row of toy soldiers in front of the therapist and a row in front of himself, hands the therapist a loaded dart gun, retrieves a dart gun for himself, and puts the dart in the gun. He shoots one of the therapist's toy soldiers and says, "Now it's your turn. You shoot one of mine." Before taking action, the therapist will find it helpful to examine what is known about child development and how young children perceive their world. We know from child development literature that young children view their possessions as extensions of themselves. This information should cause the therapist pause. If he shoots Toby's toy soldiers, there is the possibility that Toby might internalize the behavior as an act against his person. Knowing that the therapist responds, "You can play my part and shoot your soldiers," as he hands his dart gun to Toby. I am deeply sensitive to the possibility that I might do something that would cause a child to view me as unpredictable, or that a child might think I would do him harm. I want to be so *consistent* in my behavior that a child can *predict* how I will respond or how I will be. The child will then feel *safe* with me. *Consistency produces predictability, and predictability facilitates a feeling of safety.*

Allowing the child to lead in the relationship communicates the therapist's respect for the child. I trust the child to take me in this developing relationship to where he needs to be, to what the child needs to be working on in his life. Therefore, I am eager to follow the child's lead, to be a part of the child's journey into self. What a precious privilege to be allowed to experience a child's creative discoveries about himself.

Hearing Nonverbal Expressions

Most mental health professionals are more dependent on client verbal expressions than they realize. The effective play therapist listens carefully to what is not verbalized by the child, what the child has experienced, feels, desires, wants, thinks, wonders about, and is not able to express verbally. A child is at all times communicating something about the person he is but not necessarily in words.

RULE OF THUMB:

Listen to the child with your eyes as well as your ears.

Most of what the play therapist needs to hear from a child cannot be heard with ears. It is not possible to hear fright in a child's face with your ears. Fright can only be heard with your eyes. You cannot hear a tear trickle down a child's cheek with your ears. That can only be heard with your eyes. The most important messages in the play therapy relationship can only be heard with your eyes. A child may play silently with toys and yet speak volumes through his play. Isn't that why play therapy is the developmentally responsive therapeutic modality of choice with children? Play is the child's natural medium of expression, and verbal communication is not necessary.

Respecting the Child's Space

The child is allowed to separate from the therapist and maintain the physical distance that feels comfortable for her. There is a reason why Karla sits playing with farm animals across the room, with her back to the therapist, and that reason is respected. The child will approach the therapist when she feels comfortable in doing so or when she needs to do so. The therapist is being very child centered when this dimension of the relationship is respected. Such behaviors on the part of the therapist communicate subtle but powerful messages about the relationship.

Physically Tracking the Child

The child can be followed around the room without doing so physically, although that also might be appropriate at times in later sessions when the therapist is asked to do so by the child. The therapist can be quite active without leaving the chair by shifting body posture forward on the edge of the chair as the child moves away or by leaning forward, arms folded across legs, to be closer to the child's activity in the dollhouse, for example, which may be 4 or 5 feet from the therapist's chair. This brings the therapist's head down to a lower level and seems to project the therapist into the child's play, conveying interest and involvement. Sustained involvement also is conveyed when the therapist moves her whole body to swing around from one side of the chair to the other as the child moves around the room.

RULE OF THUMB:

The therapist's toes should follow his or her nose.

The child should be like a magnet attracting the whole person of the therapist, including the physical part. Wherever the child is in the playroom, the therapist's nose and toes are pointed in the child's direction. In supervising play therapists, I have often observed therapists turning their head 90 degrees to track children with their eyes while the rest of their body remained motionless and projected away from the child, communicating only minimal involvement with the child. When the therapist's whole body swings around and the toes are pointed toward the child, the child feels the therapist's presence.

The therapist also can follow the child around the room by thinking about the child and by being totally absorbed in the child and the child's activity, trying to feel the child's intensity, sensing his involvement, wondering at his creativity, puzzling over the possible meaning in his play, feeling the atmosphere of the moment, and communicating this feeling of **being with** in facial expression, tone of voice, and general attitude. The therapist can be involved in and a part of the child's activity without physically following the child around the room. No amount of routinely physically following a child around the room will ever communicate the kind of involvement that is projected through an attitude of genuine caring, unwavering interest, and heartfelt desire to know the child's internal frame of reference.

After the child and therapist have begun to know and trust each other, the therapist may feel comfortable moving his chair to a different vantage point in the room to interact with the child. Because this is meeting the therapist's need and not the child's, a helpful procedure is to inform the child of what is about to take place so the child will not be startled or his activity disrupted. This could be accomplished by saying, "Carlos, I'm going to move my chair (as the therapist now begins to move the chair) right over here by the sandbox, so I will be closer to your play." To say "so I can see what you are doing" sounds like a parent checking on a child and does not convey the therapist's intent. Again, these are subtle differences, but the impact on the relationship is significant.

Reflecting Nonverbal Play Behavior: Tracking

The therapist responds to the child's actions and nonverbal play expressions by making tracking responses that describe with words what she hears with her eyes. Tracking responses put into words what the therapist sees and observes the child doing. Evan has just been introduced to the playroom for his first play therapy session and is walking around the room looking at some of the toys, puts his hands on his hips, and looks wonderingly across the room. The therapist tracks Evan's behavior, "Hmmm, you're trying to decide what to play with first." Evan walks across the room, picks up a car, sits on the floor, and begins to move the car back and forth. The therapist tracks Evan's behavior, "You decided to play with that. You're moving it forward and backward." Tracking responses communicate the therapist's interest in the child and what the child is doing. This therapeutic skill is explained more fully in the next chapter.

Reflecting Content

Reflecting verbal content in play therapy is similar to reflecting content in talk therapy with adolescents and adults. The play therapist summarizes or paraphrases and reflects back the verbal interaction of the child during the play session. A child then knows she has been heard. Reflecting the content of the child's verbal expression helps the therapist immerse himself in the child's world. Jennifer picks up a dinosaur and proceeds to share detailed information about dinosaurs. The therapist responds, "You know a lot about dinosaurs." Jeff (pretends a bomb is dropped near a car with people in it): "The people aren't hurt. They're hiding in the car, and the guy who dropped the bomb doesn't know." Therapist: "They're safe, and the guy doesn't know." These reflections of content show understanding, acceptance, and allow the child to lead. Reflecting content is explained more fully in the next chapter.

Reflecting Feelings

Some therapists try to rush rapport building by unnecessarily reassuring the child that everything is okay, and in the process they run roughshod over the child's feelings. Seven-year-old Clarice sits in a chair whining, "You don't have any good stuff. I don't wanna stay here." The therapist says, "Clarice, honey, other children really have a lot of fun here. See the dolls over there. Maybe you would like to play with them for a little while." The therapist now feels better because a suggestion has been offered, but the child feels worse because her feelings have been ignored.

If Clarice does follow the therapist's suggestion, dependency has been fostered. An accepting therapist does not push the child to play or talk. That is for the child to decide. A response is needed that focuses on the child feelings, "You don't like what's in this playroom, and you want to leave." Clarice now feels understood. Permissiveness implies the child can choose to play or not to play. Pushing the child to play or talk ignores the child's feelings and deprives her of decision making. In like manner, the accepting therapist does not ask probing questions to "get the child started." The child is allowed to lead the conversation as well as the play (Figure 9.2).

Angelina sets play dishes on the table and smiles as she states, "I know just where everything goes." Therapist response, "You're proud of yourself." Reflecting feelings is explained more fully in the next chapter.

Responding to the Reluctant, Anxious Child

The child is free to direct the interaction in the way she chooses. However, what if the child is anxious, stands in the middle of the

FIGURE 9.2 A being-with relationship is experienced as the therapist emotionally experiences sharing the moment with a child and reflects the child's feelings.

playroom, and says nothing? Then what? Assuming nothing is happening to which one can respond just because the child is nonverbal and not playing would be a therapeutic mistake. Children are at all times communicating something about themselves. Therefore, something is always present to be responded to by the therapist. Four-year-old Angela entered the playroom for her first session and said nothing. She obviously was very anxious and unsure of what to do or of what was expected in the playroom. The therapist already had made an introductory statement about the playroom.

Angela: (Stands right in front of therapist, twisting her hands, looking at therapist, and then looks at toys on the shelf.)
Therapist: You're looking at the toys over there. (Pause.)
Angela: (Looks at observation mirror, sees herself and grins.)
Therapist: And you saw yourself in the mirror there. (Pause.) I guess sometimes, maybe...it's just hard to decide

	what to do first (Pause, Angela glances at the toys again.), but this is a place where you can play with any of the toys you want to play with.
Angela:	(Begins to pick at a frayed piece of fingernail on one of her fingers.)
Therapist:	Hmmmm…you've got something right…there (Pause, points to Angela's fingernail.), right there on your finger. (Pause.) Hmmmm, looks like you are trying to pick something off your fingernail.
Angela:	This thread. I picked the other one off…
Therapist:	Oh, you have already picked one off.
Angela:	At school.
Therapist:	At school you did it. Uhmmm, so now you're doing this one.

The therapist's responsiveness to Angela's nonverbal cues helped her to relax, and the therapist's verbalized attentiveness resulted in Angela verbally joining in the interaction. Even without a verbalized response everything would have been fine, because Angela was already communicating with her eyes, face, and hands. When a child is nonverbal because she feels anxious or awkward in the playroom, that is not the time for the therapist to be nonverbal. That only increases the child's feeling of being on the spot and not knowing what to do. This point was experienced by a beginning play therapist: "I learned that I can inhibit a child by my silence, my facial expression, and my size, and that I can free a child in purposive ways having to do with acceptance, permissiveness, and feelings. I must be careful how I use myself. Children can be more easily injured by me than I by them."

The Child's View of the Play Therapy Relationship

The following monologue draws on accumulated experiences with children in play therapy and is the hypothesized interaction of a play therapist and child, the child's view of the experience, and his reaction to his first play therapy experience.

My mom says I'm going to have fun. Yeah, I've heard that line before! She's telling me that I'll be in a room with lots of toys and things 6-year-olds like to do. She says I'll be spending time with some lady they call a counselor. But who is this lady who wants to spend time playing with me? What is she like? Will I like her? Will she like me? What's she going to do to me? Maybe I'll never go back home again. I don't even know what she looks like. Oh, no, I hear footsteps…could it be…Gulp….

This lady must be the person they call the counselor. She is warm and friendly and she says "Hello" to my mom and introduces herself to me. She smiles a lot. That makes me feel more comfortable now so I say, "Hi." She bends down close to me, says "Hi," and notices my Spiderman shirt and my new tennis shoes with red stripes. She says they look like racing shoes. They sure are! Oh, I like her better now! Maybe she'll be okay after all.

Well, here we go down the hall. She's also noticing that I'm a little afraid. She says this must seem strange because I haven't seen her or her special playroom before and sometimes that's a little scary to children. Guess she's kinda saying that it's okay to be afraid. It's funny to hear that coming from an adult! She must be an understanding person, and she seems to care about me. Maybe she was afraid once in her life, too.

She takes me to what she calls her special playroom. Boy, it is different! There are toys in here! She tells me we'll be together in the playroom for 45 minutes. Hmmm, that's strange. No one has ever told me how long we would be together or how long I would have to play. She says this is a place where I can play with the toys in a lot of ways I would like to. Wow, can she really mean that? Yeah, she seems to care about me and she seems to like me, even though she hardly knows me. That's strange! I wonder if she treats every kid like that. Maybe I had better wait and see what she wants me to do. Other adults always tell me what to do. I'm going to be kinda quiet for a few minutes. She notices me looking at the paints and says sometimes it's hard to decide just what to do first, but that this is a place where I really can decide for myself. This whole thing sure is different. I pick up the paintbrush and splash red all over the paper…feels good.

I think I'll paint a purple apple tree. Wonder if that will be okay? Maybe I should just make it red and green, but I hate green—reminds me of asparagus. Yuk! I'll ask her what color

I should use. She says that's something I can decide. Boy, everybody else would have told me just what colors to use. Seems like I make most of the decisions in here. Well, here goes the purple paint. She says it looks like I've decided to use lots of purple. Yep, I sure have! It's kinda hard to get this thing to look just right. Hmmm, that's a funny looking apple tree, but I like it because it's big. Wonder if she thinks it looks okay. I'll just ask if she likes it. She says it looks like I worked hard to get it just the way I want it. Yep, that's right. It's just like I wanted it to be—all purple. This lady lets me please myself.

This is a funny place. I bet it would be fun to paint her nose purple! A lady with a purple nose. Now, that will be something! Boy, I'll just paint this whole blob of purple on her. I bet that will get her out of the chair. She'll probably run clear around the room! Hmmm, she doesn't look scared. She doesn't even yell at me to stop. She just says she knows I would like to put paint on her, but she's not for painting. She says I can paint on the paper or I can pretend the Bobo is her and paint on the Bobo. She's so calm about everything. It's no fun to put paint on her if she's not scared. Anyway, that sounds like a super idea to paint the Bobo. I hadn't thought of that.

I'm starting to play with some other toys now. Funny, this person they call the counselor seems to really be noticing what I'm doing. I like what I'm doing. Wonder if she thinks it's important? She's paying attention to me. Most adults don't do that. She's smart and catches on to what I'm doing. She even comments on what things I enjoy playing with the most. Yeah, she knows that the clay is my favorite. She's really interested in me and in what I'm doing.

Gosh, I like it here already. I think I'll try a few more things, like playing in the sandbox. I'd like for her to play in the sandbox with me, but she says she'll just watch me play in the sandbox. I like the way she's so straightforward about it. Most adults would just say, "I'll play with you in a few minutes," and then they'd forget all about it. Anyway, I think I'm only going to stay in here for a few minutes. I start to leave. She says we have 15 more minutes together in the playroom and then I can leave. She seems to believe I'll just do what needs to be done. That feels good.

Let's see—what'll I do next? It's fun getting to decide what I want to do next. At home, I hardly ever get to do what I want to do. The sitter always says what we're going to do at such-and-such time, or my brothers are always pushing me to do something I don't want to do, or my parents make me try something that I'm not ready to try. Not this lady—she's not pushy at all; she waits for me to make the move that I want to make. And she doesn't criticize me for being slow like all the kids at school do. She likes me because I'm me. Or at least, I think she does!

I think I'll play ball with this person they call the counselor. It's fun because we can talk and catch the ball at the same time. Gosh, she's so interested in whatever I do. And she's got a lot of what grown-ups call self-discipline. When I throw the ball away from her so she will miss it, she just lets the ball go, and she stays where she is. She says that if I want the ball, I can go and get it. It would be a lot easier for her to get the ball because she's closer. But she knows that I'm trying to trick her. I like the way she doesn't let me get away with that. My Mom would have finally picked up the ball—IF I had asked her enough times. But then, my Mom would end up screaming. This lady just never gets upset about anything.

I'm really enjoying spending time with this person they call the counselor. She believes I can do things without her help. When I asked her to take the top off the glue jar because I was afraid I couldn't get it off, she said that was something I could do. I did try, and you know what? It came off! I wish I knew I could do things outside this room. Then I could hit home runs at the ball game instead of always striking out and embarrassing my dad. Hmmm, maybe I can do some things like she believes I can. This lady is lots of fun. This is a fun place to be. It feels good to do things all by myself...just the way I decide.

I think I'll try to paint a picture of a police car. Boy, it's looking neat...all bright blue! Drat! The red paint for the light on top is running right down the side of my car! That really makes me mad. She says I look angry about that. Well, I am! But how did she know? Nobody else ever recognized my feelings. Does that mean it's okay to get mad about some things? Must be okay. She doesn't seem to mind my being mad.

Wonder what she will think if I pretend this big throwing dart is a rocket ship. Guess I could ask her what it's for. She says in here it can be anything I want it to be. Imagine that! An adult who lets it be what I want it to be. Wow, now I can zoom around the room and pretend I'm going to the moon where no one can boss me…kinda like in here where I'm the boss of me.

I wish it wasn't time to leave now. There are so many things I wanted to tell her but didn't get a chance to say. It's funny how sometimes it's so hard to tell my parents just little things. But I feel like I could say anything to her. She tells me to come back next week—that she looks forward to spending some time with me again. She sounds like she really means it. I feel so good right now, because she's the first person who has ever treated me like a real person, not just a kid. She respects me—that's what it is. And she knows that I can do great things. Or at least, that's the way I feel now!!!

Questioning Techniques of Children

A common practice of children is to ask the therapist a multitude of questions, which may be their way of making contact with the therapist and beginning to build the relationship. However, the therapist will find it helpful to consider that children already know the answers to many of the questions they ask. Examined from this perspective, responding to children's questions becomes a matter of trying to understand the motivation behind the questions rather than attempting to provide an answer. Providing answers to questions can inhibit children's use of items by binding children to the therapist's world of reality. When 5-year-old Hershel holds up the handcuffs and asks, "What are these?" and the therapist answers, "Handcuffs," they can no longer be the special new kind of spaceship he was thinking about. The therapist could facilitate the coming forth of Hershel's creativity and imagination by responding, "*That can be whatever you want it to be.*" Hershel is then free to proceed with what he already had in mind but had not verbalized. When Judy asks, "Who broke this doll?" she very well may be wondering what happens to children who break toys in the playroom. A sensitive therapist would respond, "*Sometimes accidents happen in here.*" Judy then knows this is not a place of punishment or a place where you must be careful. This is an adult who understands that accidents do happen. She then feels free to express herself more spontaneously and completely.

RULE OF THUMB:

Don't answer questions that have not been asked.

Answers to obvious questions can result in lengthy question-and-answer routines that increase children's dependency. When children ask questions in play therapy, the therapist considers what the underlying meanings are before responding to what seems to be the objective of their questions. Rather than answering the child's question, the therapist asks himself, "What is this child trying to tell me?" When Scott picks up the baby bottle and asks, "Is this a rocketship?" Scott is telling the therapist the baby bottle looks like a rocketship to him. Therefore, the therapist responds, "Must look like a rocketship to you." When a child points to the sandbox and asks, "Is that a sandbox?" the therapist responds, "Must look like a sandbox to you," thus accepting the child's perception that it is a sandbox. Trying to anticipate what children are saying in their questions rather than attempting to answer the questions is much more facilitative of expression and exploration. What the therapist senses at the moment would determine the kind of response to be made. The following questions and possible meanings underneath the obvious questions are provided for consideration in stimulating awareness of what children may be communicating.

1. Do other children come here?
   David might be
   a. Wanting reassurance he is special;
   b. Establishing a sense of belonging in the playroom—"my place," a sense of possessiveness;
   c. Curious about the playroom because of its uniqueness;
   d. Wanting to feel secure in knowing the room is his for this time;
   e. Wanting to know if other children play with the toys;

    f. Wanting to know if there are going to be other children with him in the room;

    g. Wanting to know if he can bring a friend; or

    h. Noticing something is different about the room this week.

2. Do you know what I'm going to do next?

   Laura might be

    a. Indicating that she has something definite in mind that she plans to do;

    b. Wanting to include the play therapist in her plans; or

    c. Finishing a project or changing the theme of play—a way of closure on one aspect of play.

3. Can I come back tomorrow? Or, when can I come again?

   Dwight might be

    a. Involved in a project that is important to him and wanting to finish it;

    b. Enjoying what he has been doing and wanting the opportunity to do it again;

    c. Saying, "This is an important place to me";

    d. Seeking reassurance of his time—that he does have a time in the playroom that belongs to him;

    e. Unsure about trusting his world to be consistent and not disappointing him in this situation as it has in others; or

    f. Saying, "I really like to come here," "It is important to me that I can come again."

4. Does anybody play with this?

   Rachel might be

    a. Saying, "Is it okay for me to play with this?";

    b. Unsure of the permissiveness of the playroom, seeking permission or reassurance of that permissiveness;

    c. Unsure of what the toy is or what she wants to do with the toy;

    d. Trying to decide what she wants to do; or

    e. Wanting to make contact with the therapist.

5. Do you know what this is?

   Mike might be

    a. Proud of something he has made;

    b. Wanting to make contact with the therapist;

  c. Ready to use the toy for a specific purpose—has plans for the use of the toy; or

  d. Asking for information.

6. What is this?

  Valerie might be

  a. Unfamiliar with the toy or play material and unsure of how it could be used;

  b. Trying to decide what she would like to do with the toy

  c. Unsure of the permissiveness of the playroom and saying, "Is it okay for me to play with this?" or testing the permissiveness of the playroom;

  d. Wanting to make contact with the therapist;

  e. Seeking direction or approval from the therapist;

  f. Wanting to use the item for something other than the apparent use;

  g. Trying to establish a superficial relationship with the play therapist while she checks out the room and the play therapist; or

  h. Trying to put things back on a "safe" level—often the play therapist will have touched on a sensitive issue or feeling.

7. Do you like children? Or, do you have any kids?

  Kevin might be

  a. Establishing rapport with the play therapist;

  b. Trying to find out more about the play therapist;

  c. Affirming that he does indeed feel liked and accepted by the play therapist (this question usually seems to be followed by the statement, "I like coming here.");

  d. Showing possessiveness toward the play therapist;

  e. Trying to take the focus off himself;

  f. Trying to make "polite" conversation; or

  g. Leading up to "whose side are you on?" type questions.

8. What time is it? Or, how much time is left?

  Theresa might be

  a. Enjoying herself and not wanting to leave;

  b. Wanting the feeling of certainty that there is time left;

  c. Wanting to feel in control that she knows how much time remains;

  d. Anxious to go; or

   e. Planning a project and wanting to be sure it can be finished.
9. Why do you talk like that?
   Robert might be
   a. Unaccustomed to talking with adults;
   b. Having a surprise reaction to the verbal attention;
   c. Annoyed by too much reflection of words; or
   d. Saying he notices the difference in the play therapist's reflective-type responses.
10. Will you fix this or do this for me?
    Cheryl might be
    a. dependent and lacking confidence in her ability to do things;
    b. trying to make contact with the play therapist; or
    c. testing the freedom of the experience together.
11. What would happen if I did this?
    Kent might be
    a. Testing the limits of his environment;
    b. Expressing curiosity; or
    c. Wanting attention.
12. Do I have to clean this up?
    Wendy might be
    a. Becoming acquainted with the playroom and learning to feel secure there;
    b. Wanting to be messy;
    c. Wondering where the boundaries are; or
    d. Trying to find out if this place is different.
13. Do children ever play together in here?
    Kirk might be
    a. Feeling lonely;
    b. Feeling insecure;
    c. Trying to avoid building a relationship with the play therapist; or
    d. Wanting to bring a friend.
14. Will you tell my mother?
    Serena might be
    a. Afraid of being punished for doing something;
    b. Getting ready to break a limit; or

    c. Wanting to confirm the confidentiality of the relationship.
15. Did you get any new toys?

    Jeff might be

    a. Having difficulty making decisions about what to do;

    b. Bored and saying he would like new materials; or

    c. Indicating he is getting ready to terminate.

16. How does this work?

    Sarah might be

    a. Actually wanting to know;

    b. Trying to manipulate the play therapist;

    c. Expressing dependence, getting the play therapist to show her so she doesn't have to figure it out by herself; or

    d. Wanting to establish some contact with the play therapist.

17. When will I come back?

    Jason might be

    a. Wanting reassurance that he will get to come back;

    b. Wanting to know when he will come again;

    c. Having anxiety about coming and wanting to know if he has to come back; or

    d. Feeling his behavior has been so bad the therapist won't let him come back.

18. What should I do?

    Nicole might be

    a. Wanting to shift responsibility to the play therapist;

    b. Wanting to know what she is allowed to do;

    c. Seeking permission to play; or

    d. Wanting to please the play therapist.

19. Who broke this?

    Greg might be

    a. Curious about who broke the item;

    b. Wondering what happens when someone breaks something;

    c. Upset about the toy being broken.

20. Where did you get this?

    Monica might be

    a. Curious about where it came from;

    b. Wanting to make contact with the therapist; or

    c. Wanting time to check out the room and the therapist.

21. Can I take this home?

     Chuck might be
     a. Wanting permission to take the item;
     b. Wanting to know what will happen to him if he takes it;
     c. Wanting to extend the experience or relationship;
     d. Feeling possessive of the playroom;
     e. Trying to take the focus off himself;
     f. Trying to make "polite" conversation; or
     g. Leading up to "whose side are you on?" type questions.

22. How do you play with this?

     Anita might be
     a. Wanting the play therapist to interact with her;
     b. Afraid she will do something wrong; or
     c. Feeling insecure or dependent.

Explaining the Observation Mirror and Recording

Trying to explain videotaping through a one-way mirror to young children can be a confusing task and in many cases does not seem to be necessary. Young children have difficulty comprehending being able to see through a mirror when all their experiences have been with mirrors at home that cannot be seen through. Some young children think there is a room and people inside the mirror, and that can be a very strange experience. Although taking young children into the observation room for a look through the mirror into the playroom does not seem to help them comprehend, they can be shown the observation room if they express an interest in seeing "the other room and those people." The process can be explained, however, to older children, and reassurance given that parents, teachers, and others will not be watching.

If an audio recording is made, children probably will notice the recorder in the playroom and may want to listen to the tape. The last few minutes of the session seem to be the best time for this. If videotaping is used and children express curiosity about what is on the video or want to see themselves, their request should be honored. Typically children do not request to listen to or view recordings.

However, those who do may react with awkwardness and embarrassment to some of their negative behavior. They also may be genuinely amused at themselves and some of their antics in the playroom. Viewing their own behavior can result in new insights as well as facilitation of the expression of additional feelings. Seeing himself drip paint on the floor while painting at the easel, Jeremy remarked, "I thought you were going to get on to me for splattering that paint." (Viewing of self on video is an area in need of research.)

Taking Notes During the Session

In my initial experiences with play therapy I took notes, but I found that to be distracting to me and the child. I would look down at my note writing and look back up to discover the child was in a different place, and I had missed some of the child's play behavior. Therefore, I had missed some of the child's communication, as the child's play is his language. I also noticed that I only took notes on certain happenings, not everything the child did, only those things I felt were important. The child also noticed that, and I became aware of the child doing more of some of the things that I made an effort to record. I was influencing and structuring the child's play, although that was not my intention. Knowing that something is being written down may be threatening to some children and consequently may restrict their play.

In one of my initial play therapy experiences, as I was writing notes during a session with 6-year-old Matthew, he came over and wanted to see my notes, so I handed them to him. (There should be no secrets in the playroom.) Matthew took my tablet over to the easel, promptly painted the whole page with black paint, and handed the tablet back to me. I experienced that as a very powerful message about his reaction to my writing down what he did. That was the last time I ever took notes during a play therapy session with any child. Sometimes I learn quickly! I am able to give the child my attention more fully when I am not concerned about recording what the child is doing. Notes on the session can be recorded immediately following the session and are important for the therapist's understanding of the development of themes in the child's play and to determine progress. One innovative play therapist I know in private practice clips a voice-activated cassette recorder to his belt while he straightens the playroom after each session and talks his notes into the tape recorder.

Preparing to End Each Session

Children often become intensely emotionally and physically involved in their experiences in the playroom and are not aware of the passing of time. A sensitive play therapist will help a child anticipate the ending of each play therapy session by providing the child with a 5-minute caution so the child is not suddenly surprised by an announcement that time is up. "Kim, we have 5 more minutes in the playroom, and then it will be time to go to the waiting room where your mom is." Time is always stated in a specific amount. The therapist would not say, "We have *about* 5 more minutes." "About" is an ambiguous term, and no one knows how long "about" is. For some individuals, "about" means probably another 10 or 15 minutes, for others it means as long as they want it to be. Time is a part of the structure of the play therapy experience, and the therapist is precise about the structure of the experience. This 5-minute caution provides the child an opportunity to bring herself under control and prepare to leave what is often a deeply satisfying or fun experience. Sometimes when a child is intently involved, an additional 1-minute caution may be needed. Avoid surprising children with an abrupt ending. Providing a 5-minute caution shows great respect for the child.

The play therapy experience is a permissive relationship, within established boundaries, and children often express themselves in creative and expressive ways. A common occurrence is that children use the paints at the easel to paint more surfaces than just the paper on the easel. As they experiment with the permissiveness of the playroom, children may paint their hands or arms and this is acceptable. A limit is set on painting clothes, walls, chairs, and so forth in the playroom.

Sometimes the paint finds its way to a child's face, deliberately so. Seven-year-old Jason had missed our two previous play therapy sessions, and in the process of telling me he had chicken pox, he showed me what his face looked like by putting spots of red tempera paint all over his face. I thought this was very creative. He then moved on to other play, and when I gave the 5-minute caution, the paint was still on his face. There is now an additional issue of concern for the therapist: How will mom react to the permissiveness of the playroom that allows her son to paint himself? Even though the play therapist as a matter of routine informs parents in the initial interview that children may paint their hands or arms, a parent may react with extreme rejection when actually confronted with such a spectacle. My concern is that a parent can with one quick emotional burst of anger undo what I have been working toward.

I waited 2 minutes to give Jason time to realize there was paint on his face and wash it off. When he didn't, I said, "Jason, the paint on your face is for washing off before we go to the waiting room where your mom is." If there is not water in the playroom, on the way to the waiting room, the therapist can stop by the bathroom and wait outside while the child washes. If Jason does not wash the paint off, I will walk into the waiting room before Jason and say to mom, "Jason has some paint on him (to prepare her). You can take him to the bathroom and help him wash it off." Allowing a child to proceed to the car with paint on his hands or arms can be catastrophic when the child gets paint on the inside of the car. The cautions presented here are essential in maintaining parental support for the play therapy process.

Play Therapists' Reactions to Their First Play Therapy Sessions

Kathy

It had all begun before I had a chance to realize that it had. There I was sitting in that chair reserved for that person they call a counselor who has a playroom, the one I'd heard about, read about, and was supposed to be about this very moment. Diverse thoughts flooded my mind, and although I wasn't counting, I could have sworn several butterflies had found their way to my stomach. I don't recall being nervous as much as I remember being eager for the experience and for whatever it might bring. It was a strange, but special feeling. I had experienced some apprehension, but for that brief 30 minutes that passed like seconds, all that was, strangely enough, the furthest thing from my thoughts.

Bill

I thought I was ready. I thought everything would come naturally, but I honestly had to struggle with the process. I wanted to direct the child's actions, to tell him what to play with, to literally "move him on." I wanted to explain what things were and "lead" the way, to do things for him, e.g., fix, put together, open, close, etc. I had to experience my frustration and leave him to struggle with his own frustration so we could both grow. I think this session was actually more therapeutic for me than it was for Brian. I learned so much about me and my needs, especially my need to help, to lead, to direct, to make things easier for children. Most importantly, I learned to hold me down in order to give children a chance to grow.

Marilyn

Before my first play therapy session I felt myself becoming nervous and uptight. My mind seemed to go blank as I tried to remember the "right" things to say. It was one of the best things that could have happened. As I walked hand-in-hand to the playroom with Karen, I felt myself relaxing and enjoying the child at my side. As we entered the playroom, I no longer felt that my mind was blank and in place of that feeling, I felt open, receptive, and ready to experience with her the marvelous relationship that was beginning.

Stephen

My first experience in the playroom was an exhilarating experience. I was able to drop the role of authority and healer and to accept the child and let her take the lead. I did not feel that I had to persuade or teach her. I could watch her and try to understand her world. I was able to concentrate on her, not my technique. I know now that I was feeling as much freedom as the child.

Basic Dimensions of the Relationship

The development of the relationship with a child, which we refer to as play therapy, is facilitated by the therapist's subtle use of self in responding to the child's communication of self in the process of play and is dependent on the therapist's sensitivity to and understanding of the dynamics of the child's world, as well as the child's emotional expression communicated in the relationship. Only when the child begins to feel safe with the therapist will the child begin to express and explore the emotionally meaningful and sometimes frightening experiences that have been experienced. The therapist must wait for this development. It cannot be rushed or made to happen. This is the child's time, and the child's readiness or lack of readiness to play, talk, or explore must be respected.

When the child experiences the freedom and permissiveness of directing his own play in the context of an empathic and caring relationship, the child develops self-discipline and perseverance that comes from the sustained effort required to carry through or complete a self-selected activity or project. The process of independently choosing an activity, directing the action, and relying on self for the outcome enhances self and develops self-reliance.

The therapist's responsibility in the relationship can be summed up in the following **four healing messages** that the child-centered therapist works hard to communicate to the child at all times, not just in words but with his total person:

I am here. Nothing will distract me. I will be fully present physically, mentally, and emotionally. I want to be so fully present that there will be no distance between myself and the child. I want to enter fully into the child's world, to move about freely in the child's world, to sense what the child senses, to feel what the child feels. Once I have achieved this kind of knowing contact, it is easy to know when I am not in touch with the child. Can I enter so fully into the child's world that I have no need to evaluate the child?

I hear you. I will listen fully with my ears and eyes to everything about the child, what is expressed and what is not expressed. I want to hear the child completely. Can I experience, hear, this child as she is? To accomplish this kind of hearing, I must be secure enough within myself to allow this child to be separate from me.

I understand. I want the child to know I understand what he is communicating, feeling, experiencing, and playing and so will work hard to communicate that understanding to the child. I want to understand the inner depth and meaning of this child's experience and feelings, the loneliness of feeling no one cares, the hollowness of failure, the desperation that can accompany sadness. The crucial dimension in therapy is the communication of this kind of understanding and acceptance to the child.

I care. I really do care about this little person and want her to know that. If I am successful in communicating fully the first three messages, I will not be perceived as a threat, and the child will allow me into her world. Then, and only then, will the child know I care. What I have experienced is that this kind of caring releases the dynamic potential that already exists in the child. I don't create anything. Whatever change or growth the child makes already existed in the child.

References

Moustakas, C. (1981). *Rhythms, rituals and relationships*. Detroit, MI: Harlow Press.

Segal, J., & Yahraes, H. (1979). *A child's journey: Forces that shape the lives of our young*. New York: McGraw-Hill.

Chapter 10

Characteristics of Facilitative Responses

The natural response of many adults to children is to question, command, or provide answers and is the consequence of an attitude that children only need to be told what to do to "straighten them out." *Responding to children in a way that communicates sensitivity, understanding, and acceptance and conveys freedom and responsibility is for many beginning play therapists like learning a foreign language.* A drastic shift in attitude and a restructuring of words used in responses are required. A beginning play therapist expressed the change this way, "I know *how* to respond. I just don't know *how* to put it into words."

From this new perspective, children are viewed as being capable, creative, resilient, and responsible. An objective of the adult–child relationship, then, is to respond to children in ways that release or facilitate the development of these existing capacities. The therapist genuinely believes children are capable of figuring things out for themselves, trusts their decisions as being appropriate for them within the boundaries of their developmental capabilities, and communicates this attitude through responses to children.

Sensitive Understanding: Being With

Rachel was a small first-grader who always walked the few blocks home from school with other children. Her mother constantly reminded her that she was to come directly home immediately after school was over for the day. This was drummed into Rachel repeatedly, and her mother's concern was understandable when Rachel was a few minutes late getting home one day. Rachel's mother walked to the sidewalk and looked down the street, no sign of Rachel. She paced the driveway for 10 minutes, and still no sign of Rachel. After 15 minutes, Mother became almost frantic. Twenty minutes had passed when Rachel finally came into view.

Mother was relieved, but then became quite angry. She yelled at Rachel in a loud voice, grabbed her by the arm, and ushered her into the house. After several minutes of angry reaction, Mother finally asked Rachel for an explanation. Rachel told her mother that on the way home she had passed by Sally's house and found Sally outside in the yard crying because she had lost her doll. "Oh," Rachel's mother replied, "and you stopped to find Sally's doll for her?" "No, Mommy," Rachel said, "I stopped to help Sally cry."

This story is a child's description of the child-centered play therapy philosophy and portrays so vividly a child's intuitive inclination to be child centered. The mother's focus was to help solve the problem of the lost doll. Rachel's first response was to **be with** Sally, to take in Sally's emotional world, to empathically respond to Sally's pain and distress. It did not occur to Rachel to solve Sally's problem, to go looking for Sally's doll. Rachel intuitively knew "When you focus on the problem, you lose sight of the child." Play therapists and perhaps all adults should learn from Rachel the importance of **being with** a child.

Rachel's empathic **being with** describes the relationship the play therapist strives for, not to the point of tears, but to that kind of understanding that comes from being with. The typical approach in adult–child interactions is characterized by problem solving and an attitude of evaluation of the child based on what is known about the child and previous circumstances. Seldom do adults strive to understand the child's immediate internal frame of reference, the child's subjective world, to genuinely be with the child. Sensitive understanding of the child occurs to the extent the therapist is able to put aside his personal experiences and expectations and appreciate the personhood of the child, as well as the child's activities, experiences, feelings, and thoughts. Children are not free to explore, to test boundaries, to share frightening parts of their lives, or to change until they experience a relationship in which their subjective experiential world is understood and accepted.

As with other therapeutic dimensions, the attitude of the therapist is critical in making contact with children in such a way that they feel understood and accepted for who they are. This depth dimension understanding means remaining free of a stylized role and participating deeply and meaningfully in the work of understanding the child. This means putting aside the tendency to evaluate and judge and to see instead from the viewpoint of the child. When understanding and acceptance are lacking, little if any effective therapeutic work is going on in the relationship.

Caring Acceptance

Acceptance grows out of a genuine and sincere interest in children, a sensitivity to their rights, and a belief that they can assume responsibility for themselves. Children who experience such an atmosphere of acceptance in the playroom learn that they can depend on others for support while developing their own sense of adequacy and independence. Acceptance is communicated through the therapist's patience and willingness to trust the process. The therapist is always patient with children. Patience allows the therapist to see things from the child's perspective. The therapist's acceptance is reflected in refraining from offering advice, suggestions, or explanations, and in not questioning or interrupting children. The therapist's empathic responses communicate understanding and acceptance to children, thus freeing them to be more creative and expressive (Figure 10.1).

Whether or not a child's actions, behaviors, or feelings are good or bad simply does not occur to the therapist. They are accepted as they occur, without being screened through any hint of judgmental attitude. By empathically reflecting happenings and feelings, the

FIGURE 10.1 When a child feels understood and accepted, the child feels safe enough to express himself or herself at his or her own pace.

therapist expresses respect for the child and affirms the child's right to have feelings and to express herself through actions. Acceptance, then, occurs in conjunction with permissiveness but does not necessarily imply approval of what the child is doing. An important dimension in the therapeutic process is the child's need to be accepted as a person of worth, regardless of inadequacies, deficiencies, or behaviors. The creation of this kind of relationship allows the child to express himself at his own pace without any hurry or pressure from the therapist. That is the epitome of respect: to be accepted just as one is without even the possibility of criticism, evaluation, judgment, rejection, disapproval, censure, condemnation, punishment, penalty, rebuke, reprimand, praise, compliment, reward, or accolade.

The therapist's accepting responsiveness encourages a child to explore her thoughts and feelings further. *When a child's feelings are expressed and accepted by the therapist, they are experienced with less intensity by the child, and the child's acceptance of those feelings is facilitated. The child then is more fully able to integrate and deal with feelings by expressing positive and negative emotions in a more focused and specific way.* This is a central postulate of child-centered play therapy and is the basis for the therapist's empathic responsiveness. Focusing on the child's feelings validates the person of the child rather than the importance of the problem.

Distinctive Qualities of Therapeutic Responses

The following qualities of therapeutic responses are therapist skills considered to be essential to the child-centered play therapy process. The extent to which these facilitative skills are used is a function of the therapist's intuitive sensitivity to the child in the immediacy of the moment.

Brief and Interactive

Most therapists have a tendency to use too many words when responding to children. Lengthy responses are confusing to children and often communicate a lack of understanding on the part of the therapist. A therapist will often respond to a child or tell a child something, immediately assume the child did not understand, and then in an effort to help the child understand, will add to or restate what was said in a slightly different way. Lengthy responses from the therapist result in the child being caught up in using energy to try to understand what the therapist is saying, thus disrupting the child's focus and interfering with the process of the child's play. Typically, this kind of interruption tends to change the direction of the child's play expression, and interferes with completion of the child's exploration and expression. Children do not remember lengthy responses and cannot internalize the intended meaning of the response.

Lengthy responses interrupt the child's focus on her play because she must divert energy to try to understand all the words coming into her awareness. Therapeutic responses are short,

---

RULE OF THUMB:

Responses should be short, 10 words or less.

---

succinct, focused on the child, have an interactive quality with the child that feels like the rhythmic flow of a conversation, not just static statements or simple word reflections, and match the flow and emotional intensity of the child. Lengthy responses are typically the result of the therapist's attempts to point out something to the child, educate the child, or explain the child's behavior to the child. Short responses tend to be a communication of the therapist's empathy and understanding and are guided by the therapist's desire to be with the child as fully as possible.

Help the Child to Go On

I like my responses to a child best when they fit smoothly into the child's expression without interrupting the natural flow of the child's play or verbal communication. The response has been offered at just the right moment, interjected into the plane of the child's communication with no disturbance of the surface, and the blending has been so harmonious that the child hardly takes any conscious notice. I would like my responses to be like a world-class diver who, with seemingly little effort, gracefully springs off the diving board at just the right moment and gently intersects the surface of the water with hardly a ripple to show that the diver has been there. My responses to a child are most facilitative when they are like that with no disruption of the flow of the child's expression. At such moments, I feel a oneness with the child, a genuine understanding, and a "living with" that transcends the circumstances of both our lives. We are here together, and a mutual acceptance exists.

The therapist is sensitively aware of a child's reaction to his responses. When a child reacts frequently to the therapist's responses by stopping her play, changing the direction of the play, or changing the process of the play in some way, the child may be giving a clear message that the therapist's responses are interfering with the child's expression. Consultation should be sought to help the therapist respond differently.

Reflect Nonverbal Play Behavior: Tracking

The therapist is an involved, verbally responsive participant with the child. The relationship will deteriorate when a child feels watched. A child's question of, "Why are you looking at me?" typically means the therapist has not been verbally active enough. The therapist responds to the child's actions and nonverbal play expressions by making tracking responses that describe with words what she hears with her eyes. Tracking responses put into words what the therapist sees and observes the child doing and thus validate the child. "You're painting lots of colors on that." "Now, you're putting that one in there." "That one just crashed right into the other one." (Note the items are not labeled for the child.) "You're pushing that (car) right through there (tunnel)." The focus of these responses is on the child, thus helping the child to feel in control and empowered. It is generally helpful to begin a tracking response with "You're" or "You are" Maegan takes the stethoscope out of the medical kit and listens to her heart. "You're listening to your heart."

In some instances it is appropriate to describe the happening. "Hmmm, that just fell over," or the child is painting at the easel, paint drips on the floor, and the child looks down at the paint, "That dripped right on the floor." Tracking responses acknowledge the child's play expression, *help the child to feel the therapist is interested in him and his play, demonstrate the therapist is striving to understand the child's world, communicate the therapist's involvement, and help the child to feel the therapist is participating with him.*

If the therapist is silent during a child's play, the child will begin to feel watched or that the therapist is not interested. Sitting and watching without responding to a child can also increase the child's anxiety. Feelings of security and warmth are promoted as the child hears the therapist's voice and the description of his activities. Tracking responses convey interest in the child and what the child is doing.

A word of caution: Tracking can be overdone to the point of making a child feel self-conscious as in the following example that occurred in 10 seconds. "You're walking over there. You're bending down." "You're picking that up. You're looking inside that. You're putting that back on the floor. Now you are looking for something else." Such rapid fire tracking responses do not sound genuine or conversational, and a child would probably experience the comments as intrusive. Tracking responses should not follow the child's activity or play expression too closely, and they need to be stated in a genuine, warm, caring, and conversational manner. The play therapy relationship is similar to being in a counseling session with an adult. Adults know that the therapist cares and hears them when the therapist listens and verbally responds. In like manner, the play therapist listens with ears and eyes and verbalizes what she hears and sees.

Reflect Content

Just as is true with adults, children need to know they have been heard and understood. Hearing a child confirms the child's existence and worth. Reflecting the content of what a child verbalizes in play therapy is the same skill process that occurs in counseling sessions with adults. The play therapist summarizes or paraphrases and reflects back the verbal interaction of the child during the play session. A child then knows he has been heard and understood. Reflecting content validates children's perception of their experience and helps to clarify children's understanding of themselves. Reflecting the content of a child's verbalized communication is one of the four basic healing messages the play therapist is intentional about communicating to a child. The following interaction in a play therapy session demonstrates reflection of content:

Scott: (picks up can of playdough) What do you do with this?
Therapist: In here you can decide.
Scott: Hey, it's a bomb! (drops the can of playdough on top of a small car in the sandbox) Blam! Did you see that car!
Therapist: Just blew that car up!

Scott: Yeah. (grabs sand scoop, quickly digs hole, and buries car) Blew such a big hole it covered the car up.

Therapist: Yep, that's a big hole. The car can't be seen anymore.

Scott: The people aren't hurt. They're hiding in the car, and the guy who dropped the bomb doesn't know.

Therapist: The people are safe, and the guy doesn't know.

The therapist's reflective responses in this interaction are short, succinct, interactive with the child's actions and verbal descriptions, reflect content, communicate the therapist's acceptance, understanding, and allow the child to continue to lead as his story unfolds. It is obvious the child feels understood and free to continue his exploration.

Reflect Feelings

By playing out their feelings in the presence of the play therapist who understands and accepts even the intensity of the feelings, children learn that all of their feelings are acceptable. As children begin to experience that their feelings are acceptable, they begin to be more open in expressing them. The play therapist communicates understanding and acceptance of a child's feelings by verbally labeling the feeling. (You're frustrated with that.) When feelings are accepted by the therapist and reflected to children, they learn to trust their feelings. Reflecting a child's feelings validates the child and her feelings and facilitates the child's trusting of herself. The essential quality in reflecting a child's feeling is the communication of empathy, a feeling of being with in the experience.

Chad: (picks up handcuffs) How do you lock this?

Therapist: You're wondering how you lock that. (This is an accurate reflection but does not communicate a feeling of being with.)

A more empathic response would be:

Therapist: Hmmm, wonder how that locks? (If a child is wondering about something, then the therapist who is being empathic is also wondering. This response communicates a being with quality.)

The accepting therapist recognizes each feeling as being valid and so accepts each feeling. No attempt is made to convince the child that there is no good reason for feeling the way she does. Some therapists, unaware of their own needs, reject a child's feelings in the process of trying to unnecessarily reassure the child or make the child feel "better." Andy acted out an elaborate scene in the dollhouse involving a child playing alone in a room and the mother doll coming into the room and stabbing the child doll repeatedly. Considerable fear was acted out as the child doll tried to escape. In a following scene, the mother doll came into the child doll's bedroom, carried the sleeping doll outside the dollhouse, and threw the child doll into the lake (sandbox).

During this enactment, Andy verbalized his fear that, "Mother will get me. She's going to do something real mean to me." Having interacted with the mother in initial interviews and follow-up sessions, the therapist responded, "Andy, you know your mother loves you, and she would never ever do anything to hurt you." Although the therapist may have substantial evidence on which to base her conclusion, the therapist can never be completely sure of another person's behavior. We cannot speak for other people. We simply do not know what may take place in another person's home.

In her need to reassure Andy, the therapist ignored his feelings and so Andy did not feel understood. The therapist felt better, but at what expense? A more appropriate response that would reflect Andy's feeling would be, "You're really scared that your mother will do something mean to you, that she might hurt you. That's frightening."

Cristina, age 6, was referred to the therapist for being manipulative in her relationships with her parents and teacher. Her parents described Cristina as "bossy" and having difficulty getting along with other children. The following excerpt from Christina's play therapy session is an example of several of her attempts to manipulate the therapist, and the therapist's acceptance and reflection of her feelings.

Cristina: (Seated at the table painting) Get those paints and bring them over here. I want to use them. (Cristina is actually much closer to the paints.)

Therapist: You want me to get the paints for you, but in here you can get the paints if you want them.

Cristina: But I'm busy. Can't you see that?

Therapist: You're just so busy that you want me to get them for you.

Cristina: Yes! Now would you just get the paints!

Therapist: You're angry at me because I won't get the paints for you, but that's something you can do if you want the paints. (Cristina gets up, retrieves the paints, and proceeds to paint.)

Cristina: (Moves her paintbrush from the paper to a paint container for more paint, and the therapist's head turns slightly to follow the movement of the brush) Without moving your head, you can watch me paint at the same time.

Therapist: Some of the things I do bother you sometimes.

Cristina: Yes.

The presence of the toys and materials allowed Cristina, in the immediacy of the relationship with the therapist, to exhibit a significant behavior for which she had been referred. The therapist was able to demonstrate acceptance of Cristina's anger and to relate in a matter of fact way to the deeper issue of her doing things for herself. Reflection and acceptance of feeling are also demonstrated in the following excerpt:

Ricardo: (Picks up gun, looks angry, and pretends to shoot therapist.)

Therapist: You're mad at me. (Therapist reflects child's feelings and shows understanding.)

Ricardo: I'm not mad at you. (Ricardo may feel anger is not acceptable and so corrects the therapist.)

Therapist: Oh, you're not mad at me.

Ricardo: But I'm really sick of it.

Therapist: So, you're not mad at me, you're just sick of it.

A therapeutic relationship emerges as the therapist communicates acceptance and understanding. In this kind of relationship, children begin to recognize their inner value when the play therapist responds sensitively to the inner emotional part of their person by accepting and reflecting feelings, whether verbally or nonverbally expressed.

An empathic response that reflects a child's feelings matches the child's affect with facial expression, words, and tone of voice. Possible response beginnings that reflect feelings are

You like …
You don't like …
You're curious about …
You're wondering about …
You feel frustrated when …
You're really angry about …
That's really funny to you.

Build Self-Esteem

The behavior of children is largely a function of how they feel about themselves; so the play therapist is intentional about responding to children in ways that build up their self-esteem. A self-esteem building response gives the child credit for knowing or doing. Four-year-old Christina counts all the family figures. Therapist: "You know how to count." Recognizing and responding to a child's effort and energy enhances the child's sense of self. Esteem-building statements help children experience themselves as capable when the therapist responds to the effort rather than the product. "You made that just the way you wanted it to be." "You're working hard on that." A child struggles in the play therapy session to fit two objects together and accomplishes the task, "There, you figured that out."

Other possible self-esteem building responses might be

You know how to make that work.
You have something in mind.
Looks like you know how to ….
You remembered where that was.
You decided ….
You know just how you want it to look.
There, you got it open.
There, you made it stay together.

Self-esteem building responses help children to feel capable, facilitate development of a child's intrinsic sense of self, and thus build up intrinsic motivation.

Match Child's Level of Affect

When responding to a child, the therapist's facial expression and tone of voice can communicate more meaning than the words used. Being empathic means being with a child so fully that the child's experiences and feelings are felt. In communicating this being with to the child, the therapist's tone of voice and degree of affect match the level of affect/intensity expressed by the child. Rate of therapist response also conveys understanding and being with the child by matching the degree of interaction of the child. If the child is speaking thoughtfully or trying to figure something out, the pace of the therapist's response matches the child's pace.

The therapist avoids getting overly excited beyond the child's level of affect about little happenings. Erica runs her hand through the sand in the sandbox, comes up with a small green rock, and matter-of-factly states, "I found a rock." The therapist responds, "Oh, my! Isn't that wonderful! You found a colored rock in the sandbox!" This kind of excitement may cause the child to feel something is wrong or to distrust her own reaction because she does not feel equally excited. Expressing affect beyond the level expressed by the child is structuring and will lead the child into expressing affect and behaviors beyond what she is genuinely feeling. This can be seen when David hits the Bobo with minimum effort and the therapist responds with, "Wow! You really socked him that time!" Following the therapist's lead, David then hits Bobo with all the force he can muster.

Some therapists have a tendency to raise the tone of their voice when around small children, as though talking to a baby or talking down to the child. Such behavior projects a basic attitude about children being incapable and has no place in the therapeutic relationship. The therapist also avoids slipping into a monotone; that can be deadly. Use voice inflection to convey meaning and feeling.

Avoid Asking Questions

Questioning a child about the reasons for behavior generally is not facilitative of exploration because the child is expected to verbally communicate cognitive insight, and this is a contradiction of the rationale for placing children in play therapy. If the child were able to fully express himself through verbal means, he would not be in play therapy in the first place. Questions place the therapist in a leading, controlling position and are seldom facilitative. Even questions asking for clarification usually are not helpful or needed.

RULE OF THUMB:

If you have enough information on which to base a question, you have enough information on which to make a statement.

Questions imply nonunderstanding. It is not possible to communicate understanding through a question. "Did that make you angry?" communicates the therapist's lack of understanding, yet the therapist senses that the child feels angry or she would not ask the question. She either saw something in the child's facial expression or physical activity or heard something in the child's tone of voice that indicated anger. The therapist should trust what has emerged in her own intuitive system and make a statement, "You feel angry." Empathic statements go into the child's heart and soul. Questions go into the mind to be processed and evaluated. In like manner, questions about a child's play also interfere with the process of the play.

Questions designed to satisfy the therapist's curiosity such as, "How many times have you been sent to the principal's office?" or guesses such as, "Does your mother get angry when you do that at home?" are inappropriate. Will the therapist do anything differently once such information is obtained? Likewise, questions that attempt to produce insight, such as, "Have you noticed you use a lot of dark colors?" usually are beyond the level of the child's awareness and thus are ineffective.

At one point, a therapist asked 5-year-old Aaron to make up a story, and at the end of his story asked, "What is the moral of your

story?" to which Aaron asked, "What does that mean?" A therapist sensitive to the developmental level of children should know a
5-year-old probably will not know what the word "moral" means.
In addition, such a question calls for abstract reasoning beyond
the child's developmental level. Later, Aaron was acting out a loud
fight between a dinosaur and a snake, and the therapist asked,
"Wonder what would happen if all dinosaurs and snakes were
friends instead of fighting each other?" Aaron did not respond,
and no wonder! Even the ability of most adults to give an adequate response to such an abstract question is questionable.

The therapist was completely out of touch with Aaron, and he
expressed frustration with the therapist by throwing the dinosaur
at her. The therapist's response was equally ineffective: "Aaron,
seems like you're pretty mad at me. I'm guessing maybe that you
don't like coming here. And maybe you're a little mad at Mom for
making you come here. 'Cause, by making you come here, that
means she's in charge, and you don't like it when she's in charge."
The therapist completely avoided the personal issue between herself and the child and placed the blame on the parent with an
interpretative response that was much too lengthy for a 5-year-old.
She also drew a series of abstract associations that were bewilder-
ing to the child. The therapist probably felt quite satisfied, but we
must wonder how Aaron felt. The therapist gave very little indication that she understood Aaron.

Questions tend to move children (or clients of any age) from
the world of emotion into the world of cognition, which essen-
tially defeats the developmental rationale for using play therapy.
Questions also structure the relationship according to the therapist's agenda, thus placing the focus of the relationship on the
therapist rather than the child.

Facilitate Decision Making and Return Responsibility

Allowing a child the freedom to engage in the process of decision
making provides opportunities for the child to project his own
personal meaning onto the item or material. This inner experience of making decisions strengthens the child's self-concept and

provides the child with experiences that can become incorporated into a changed perceptual view of himself. This is a growth process that will enable the child to respond emotionally to future problems and situations in a more effective way. Therefore, the therapist refuses to accept responsibility for making decisions for the child, no matter how insignificant the decision may seem. To the child's question, "What color is the moon?" the therapist replies, "The moon can be any color you want the moon to be." Thus, the child is encouraged to accept responsibility for herself, and, in the process, discovers personal strengths. The process of choosing helps the child to feel in control of her life.

Children cannot discover and develop their inner resources and, in the process, experience the power of their potential unless opportunities to do so exist. Responsibility for self cannot be taught; responsibility can only be learned through experiencing. When therapists make decisions for children that deprive them of the opportunity for potential use of their own creativity, they interfere with the development of responsibility. Most child therapists would readily state the development of children's self-responsibility as one of their major objectives in therapy but, in reality, many limit children's opportunities to assume responsibility by making decisions for children that foster dependence. This does not happen in some major, catastrophic way but, rather, in little, almost imperceptible parts of their interactions with children by giving answers, making choices for children, helping when help is not needed, and leading children when children should be allowed to lead.

RULE OF THUMB:

When you do for a child what she can do for herself,
you teach the child that she is weak.

The following interactions return responsibility to the child, facilitate decision making, and allow the child's creativity to come forth:

David: I want to play in the sand. Will you take my shoes off?
Therapist: You have decided to play in the sand and want your shoes
            off first. You can take your shoes off if you want them off.

• • •

Sally: (Without trying to open the bottle of glue) Will you open this for me?

Therapist: In here that's something you can do. (Of course, the therapist would only return responsibility if it is determined that the child is capable of the action.)

• • •

Janet: I'm going to paint a picture of a fish. What color are fish?

Therapist: You can decide what color you want the fish to be.

• • •

Timothy: I like to draw pictures. What pictures do other kids draw?

Therapist: Oh, so you like drawing pictures. Well, in here, the important thing is the kind of picture *you* like to draw.

• • •

Mary: I don't know what to do. What do you want me to play with first?

Therapist: Sometimes it's hard to decide. What you play with first is for you to decide.

The ease with which the therapist can create dependence is recognized by a therapist who wrote,

> There were other times that my responses slipped into my old ways of making children dependent. April asked if she could play with a baby doll, and before my brain had turned on, I realized I had answered "Sure." I must eliminate that word from my vocabulary. This session again reinforced the need for constant connectedness with the child. A split second can mean the difference between a therapeutic response and one that encourages dependence.

Therapeutically facilitative responses return responsibility to children, thus helping children to feel in control and to become intrinsically motivated. The child-centered therapist believes in the child, is willing to allow the child to make decisions, and is committed to providing opportunities for self-direction by avoiding interfering with the process. What is being described here is the therapist's understanding of self and a deep, abiding attitude that becomes a way of being with children. A play therapist described this process as

> I am beginning to grasp in a very small way that giving responsibility isn't something one does verbally, although responsibility may be facilitated in that manner. I think giving responsibility must also have to do with freeing myself from responsibility. The session certainly would have been different if I had not been so concerned with putting Nina at ease and with things being done right. I mean, who am I? What makes me so special that I can "fix it" for her? And to what end? Whose needs would that satisfy? Who does that make feel adequate?

At the beginning of the first play therapy session, a child will often ask the therapist to identify what the therapist wants the child to do first, what things are used for, and for help with simple tasks such as how to take lids off items. The child may hold up a toy that she obviously knows the name for and ask, "What's this?" This is a moment when the therapist does not know for sure the motivation behind the question. To name the item may inhibit the child's creativity, structure the child's expression, or keep responsibility in the hands of the therapist. Responsibility could be returned to the child by responding, "*That can be whatever you want it to be.*" Similar responses, depending on the child's request, might be, "*You can decide,*" or "*That's something you can do.*" These responses allow a child to assume responsibility and to make a decision. Typically, the result of therapist's responses returning responsibility is that by the end of the first session the child is stating what things are without asking for the therapist's decision.

If a 3-year-old child picks up the can of playdough, looks at the lid, and asks, "Will you take this lid off for me?" the therapist can respond, "*Show me what you want me to do.*" There is a huge gulf between this response and responding to the request with, "*Tell me what you want me to do.*" This latter response places the focus on the therapist and implies that if the child will tell the therapist what he wants done, the therapist will then do it. The response "*Show me what you want me to do,*" keeps the focus on the child, allows the child to assume responsibility, and keeps the child in the lead. In the process of showing the therapist how to do what he wants done, the child often will complete the task. The therapist can then make a self-esteem-building response, "*There, you figured it out,*" or "*There, you did it.*" If the child tries to take the lid off, following the "show me" response and has difficulty and asks for help again, the play therapist can assist by responding, "*Looks like you know your finger goes here,*" placing the end of his or her finger under the lid next to the child's and lifting up slightly, allowing the child to complete the task, and then making a self-esteem-building response. **Returning responsibility keeps children in the lead and empowers children** as can be seen in the following interaction in a third play therapy session:

Hector: (picked up the dart gun and dart) Put the dart in the gun for me.

Therapist: In here that's something you can do.

Hector: (smiled) I knew you were going to say that. (successfully put the dart in the gun on the third try) WOW!!! I am good at it!

A therapist's self-critique of her play therapy session described the process of returning responsibility this way:

Throughout the session, Angelina wanted me to give everything a name in the playroom. For example, she held up a Barbie doll hairpiece and asked, "What's this? Then she repeated this question with a Barbie doll dress, a compact, and an empty container. She wanted me to give each item a name. I responded by stating, "That can be whatever you would like it to be," and "You can decide what that is for." Each time she readily made her own decision. The hairpiece was a crown, the compact was something you put paints into, the Barbie dress was a dancing dress, and the small container was a holder for Barbie's hair rollers. If I had answered *for* her, I would have fostered dependence, and she could not have discovered the answers for herself. This approach to returning responsibility seems to be a real self-esteem booster. By the end of the first session, Angelina asked very few questions and made very decisive statements and actions. Her independence was showing, and she seemed self-assured. I think this was a direct result of redirecting the responsibility to her instead of the focus being on me being the answer source.

RULE OF THUMB:

Grant responsibility commensurate with the child's
ability to respond responsibly.

When responsibility is returned to children, they will think of
creative solutions that might never occur to the therapist. When
5-year-old Bret asked the therapist, "What do you want me to fix
you for lunch?" the therapist responded, "In here you can decide
what you would like to fix." Bret chose "smushed spider pie." Later
Bret held up a plastic round bracelet and asked, "Hey, what is
this?" The therapist responded, "That can be whatever you want it
to be." Bret decided it was a handcuff.

Children often will answer many of their own questions if
the therapist simply will not be so quick to reply. A thoughtful
"Hmmm" by the therapist may be all that is needed. Four-year-old
Zack picked up the airplane and asked, "Why does it have two
doors?" The therapist responded, "Hmmm ..." and Zack promptly
stated, "Because if children bought it, more people could get out.
That's maybe it." Maria sat down by the paints and made a comment
about painting. The lids were on the paint canisters (Lids should
have been removed prior to the session.), and the therapist started
to take the lids off, but then checked herself and waited. Maria
easily removed the lids. The therapist can so easily take responsibility away from the child. Responsibility also can be granted to
nonverbal requests, as in the following play therapist's account:

> Since Samantha talked so little, I couldn't be sure when she was
> looking for direction or help. When she was sitting next to the
> dollhouse, walking the teddy bear around the house, she took a
> piece of furniture from the box and put the bear and the piece of
> furniture into the house. Then she took both items out and gave me
> a quick look. I said, "You can decide what goes in the dollhouse."
> Samantha then proceeded to pile all the furniture into the house.

Responses Are Personalized

Responses should always be personalized and address the presence of the child. Responding to David who is busy banging on

Bobo by saying, "David really likes hitting that Bobo" denies the presence of the child, and causes him to feel talked about as a nonperson. "You really like hitting that Bobo" addresses the child personally. Michael paints a picture, and the therapist responds, "Michael painted a picture" as though someone else is in the playroom. "You" gives the child credit and recognizes ownership.

Some therapists are prone to inappropriately include themselves in the interaction. Beth talks about playing soccer and how much she wanted to win, but her team lost. The therapist responds with, "Sometimes it feels bad when we lose and want to win." The therapist was not a part of the happening, and the use of "we" shifts the focus away from the child. Nancy says, "Last year these people came to our house....Uh, I forgot their name," and the therapist inappropriately responds, "Sometimes we do forget people's names if they are hard names for us." Again, the therapist should use "you" to recognize the person of the child.

Avoid Labeling Toys

Toys in the playroom are not identified or labeled until the child has verbalized an identifying label for the toy. What may be obvious to the therapist (a truck), may not be at all what the child had in mind (an ambulance). A child will not feel understood by the therapist if a toy is incorrectly labeled. Labeling a toy anchors the child to the therapist's reality and interferes with the child's creativity and fantasy. Once the therapist has identified the item as a truck, it can no longer be a school bus, the family car, a tank, or an ambulance. Referring to a toy in nondescriptive ways as "it," "that," "them," or "those" allows the child to decide what he wants the toy to be.

A car is not a car until the child labels it as a car. When the child picks up the car and puts it into the sand, the therapist responds, "You just put that right in there." The child is now free to continue with her unverbalized intent that the car is a giant bug. This response also communicates to the child that the therapist is with her. Avoiding labeling toys helps create a more permissive relationship in which children feel safe enough to explore using the toys in nonconventional ways.

Are Nonevaluative and Do Not Praise

Most relationships are for children places of evaluation: home, school, games, playgrounds, sports activities. The play therapy relationship must be a place of acceptance where children feel safe, safe enough to explore, safe enough to risk, safe enough to be themselves, safe enough to be creative, safe enough to try new behaviors. Therefore, **there is no place for any form of evaluation in the play therapy relationship** because children do not feel safe when they are being evaluated. Evaluation is based on judgment about what is right or wrong, correct or incorrect, pretty or ugly, adequate or inadequate. It is not possible to be evaluative and communicate acceptance. The play therapist strictly avoids even the simplest kinds of evaluation. Evaluative statements deprive the child of inner motivation.

Seven-year-old Haley paints a picture, turns to the play therapist with a big smile on her face and asks, "Do you think my picture is pretty?" The play therapist responds, "Oh, it's beautiful." Praise statements are based on an external evaluation, result in children seeking external reinforcement, and encourage development of external motivation rather than internal motivation in children. Evaluation is a double-edged sword that cuts both ways. If the therapist has the power to evaluate a picture as being beautiful, then she also has the power to evaluate the picture as being ugly. Haley's fear may be that next time the therapist will think her picture is ugly; so now she does not feel free or creative. She feels inhibited. Judgment about Haley's painting should be left to Haley.

The response, "Oh, it's beautiful," ignores the child and praises the painting. Praise increases children's dependency, fosters development of external motivation, inhibits creativity, and results in lower self-esteem. The response, "Oh, it's beautiful," ignores what Haley is communicating with her facial expression. The therapist can keep the focus on the child by responding to what she hears with her eyes, "You're proud of your picture," or "You like your picture." This response reflects Haley's feeling, helps Haley to trust her own internal reactions, and facilitates development of her intrinsic motivation.

If the child's face reveals no affect, the therapist can respond by prizing with her tone of voice what she sees as she describes, "You put lots of colors on your painting, and that color goes all the way up there," as the therapist points and traces the painting in the air with her finger. Focusing on the child's affect, prizing what has been produced, and describing what is seen affirms the child and bolsters the child's self-esteem.

Facilitative Responses

The importance of making facilitative responses cannot be over-emphasized. Just because a therapist is trying to be helpful to a child does not ensure that he or she will be, as can be seen in the following responses made by inexperienced play therapists when asked to respond to the same play therapy episodes.

DIRECTIONS

Robert, a 7-year-old boy, won the second-grade spelling bee in his school but exhibits socially maladaptive behavior. In his first play therapy session, Robert writes "skool" on the chalkboard and asks, "Is this the right spelling?" Write the response you would make to Robert.

RESPONSES

1. You tell me if that is the right spelling. (Response is not freeing to the child and places emphasis on right and wrong.)
2. You wonder if this is the right spelling. (A delaying tactic. Yes, that is exactly what the words say, but it probably is not what the child is wondering.)
3. You're not sure if it's spelled right, so you want me to tell you if it is. (Response attempts to convey understanding but misunderstands the child's reason for asking. Also does not grant the child freedom.)
4. You would like me to tell you how to spell, but I know you can spell "school." (Reflects the child's obvious

request, places emphasis on the therapist, and puts pressure on the child.)

5. I think you can decide how you want to spell "school." (Focus is on the therapist and what the therapist thinks.)

6. Sounds like you would like me to tell you if that is right or wrong. In here you can spell that word any way you would like to. (First sentence indicates the therapist is not sure of the request, restates the obvious, and makes the response too long.)

7. You want me to tell you if that's right, but in here that's something you can decide. (A much more facilitative response by using the word "decide" conveys to the child that this is a place where he can make decisions. First part of response is really not needed.)

8. You can spell any way you like in this room. (Very specific, to the point, and grants the child freedom.)

The first few responses seem to disregard the fact that Robert won the spelling bee in his school and thus probably knows how to spell *school*. Another consideration is that the way he has spelled *skool* is correct if he is thinking about the way he has seen the word spelled on some toys by the Play Skool Company. An objective in play therapy is to grant children the opportunity to set their own direction. Children do not need the therapist to be their spelling teacher or their math teacher. Must things always be the way the therapist thinks they should be?

DIRECTIONS

Jim, an 8-year-old boy in his second play therapy session, picks up two large throwing darts with rubber suction cups and asks, "What do you do with these?" Write the response you would make to Jim.

RESPONSES

1. You would like for me to tell you how to use those darts. (Another delaying reflection that is inappropriate. The therapist should say at this point what she would say after this. The response also labels the items as darts

and thus interferes with the child's creativity. He may have been wondering if they could be used for something else.)

2. Those are for throwing at the dartboard or the wall but not at me or the mirror. (Response potentially structures and limits the child's activity and inhibits creativity. The therapist's anxiety results in premature limit setting. There is no indication the child was even thinking about throwing darts at the therapist or mirror.)

3. You would like me to tell you what to do with those. In here, you can decide. (The first sentence is not facilitative. The second sentence is freeing and allows the child to be creative.)

4. You may do anything you want with those in here. (The therapist is trying to make a freeing response, but this is not a true statement. There are limitations. The child cannot smash the therapist in the face with the darts.)

5. In here, that's something you can decide. (A response that allows the child to be creative and to experience making a decision.)

The therapist's response should not bind the child to the therapist's world of reality. The child might want to pretend the darts are rocketships, people, or bombs. They can be whatever he wants them to be to express himself at that moment.

DIRECTIONS

Connie, 7 years old and in her second play therapy session, walks into the playroom, looks around the room, and asks, "Is this room really for me?" Write the response you would make to Connie.

RESPONSES

1. You can use this room during the 45 minutes each Tuesday we meet. (Does not respond to the child's emphasis on herself.)

2. Some other children come here to play just like you. But right now this room is for you. You can play with the toys in a lot of the ways you like. (Attempts to provide

too much information and does not respond to the child's potential feelings.)

3. This room is for you to use during our time together. (Response focus is on activity and ignores the child's potential feelings.)

4. It's just kind of hard for you to believe this is all just for you. (Response shows understanding of the child's feelings.)

Facilitative responses touch on feelings whenever possible. In this way, the therapist shows an understanding of the inner child and avoids answering questions that have not been asked. The focus is on what the child is trying to say rather than on what the child is asking.

DIRECTIONS

Kathy, 8 years old and in her second play therapy session, says, "Today is my birthday...but...my mother said...she said I been too mean to my little brother...so...she's not going to bake me a birthday cake." Kathy looks very sad, tears begin to form in her eyes, her head drops, and she stares at the floor. Write the response you would make to Kathy.

RESPONSES

1. Oh, so you've been too mean for a birthday cake. I bet that makes you feel sad. (This response is really off-base! The first sentence states the child has been mean when, in fact, the child said, "My mother said I been too mean." That's the mother's perception, not a fact. This is a grossly insensitive response. The attempt to touch the child's feelings places emphasis on the therapist with, "I bet," and also conveys that the therapist is unsure—yet, the child is standing there crying!)

2. You feel sad and wish you could have a birthday cake from your mother. You're so worried that your mother doesn't love you anymore because you've been so mean to your little brother. (First sentence is appropriate. Second sentence is too interpretative. Response

confirms the child has been mean when that fact is not known and, besides, that is not the issue. How the child feels at this moment is what is important.)

3. Sometimes it hurts when people don't do what we want them to do. (Does identify the hurt, but the generalization to "people" weakens the impact. The therapist is not a part of this happening, so the use of "we" is inappropriate; it does not focus on the child.)

4. You seem disappointed that your mother is not going to bake you a cake. (A gross understatement of the child's feelings; it ignores the child's obvious tears and sadness.)

5. Sounds like you're pretty sad that your mom won't bake you a cake. Sounds like you're angry with her. (Inappropriate use of the common counseling phrase "sounds like." No, the child doesn't sound like she is sad and hurting. *She is experiencing and demonstrating sadness and hurt at that moment.* There is no indication the child is angry. That is a projection by the therapist.)

6. You're sad that your mother isn't going to bake you a cake for your birthday, because she thinks you have been too mean to your little brother. (This is better, but still does not capture the feeling of the child. No need to stick in the part about being mean, because that detracts from the main focus of the child's feelings.)

7. You're really sad about a birthday and no birthday cake. You just feel like crying. (Short, shows understanding by touching the child's feelings.)

Children do not need explanations or lengthy discourses about their experiences. The most important part of the relationship is what the child feels and experiences in the relationship. An interesting point to note is that only the last response gave recognition to the child's tears, which were the most obvious part of the child's feelings. The absence of therapist verbal recognition of obvious feelings may be interpreted by the child to mean such feelings or expressions are not acceptable.

Typical Nonfacilitative Responses

The following excerpts from play therapy sessions are examples of typical responses that are not facilitative. How the therapist responds, the words used, can make a significant difference in whether or not a child feels understood, accepted, or restricted. The suggested responses are just that, suggestions, and are not intended to imply that these are the only responses that can be helpful. The objective here is to help you become aware of your own response patterns to children.

Missed Feelings

Child: Do people come here lots? (Excited voice, eagerness in face.)

Therapist: Sometimes. (Child is not asking for an answer.)

Suggested: You really like coming here. (Recognizes feelings indicated.)

• • •

Child: My puppy got killed, and I cried.

Therapist: I'm sorry your puppy got killed. (The therapist's focus is on his own reaction, ignores child's feelings, does not allow the child to explore her feelings further.)

Suggested: You were so sad about your puppy dying. You just felt like crying. (Touches feelings and shows understanding.)

• • •

Child: (Therapist had just explained that the cassette tape recording was for her and the child to hear, and no one else.) I know what you're gonna' do! You're gonna' give it to my mother!

Therapist: The tape will not go to your mother. It's just for me to hear, and I'll let you hear it if you want to. After that I will erase it. (The therapist is a bit defensive. The child needs to know he has been understood.)

Suggested: I know you're really concerned. You don't want your mother to hear the tape. It is just for you and me to hear and no one else. (Recognizes feeling and reassures confidentiality.)

• • •

Child:	(What he is working on keeps coming apart.) No, it's not working right! (He sounds angry.)
Therapist:	Does that make you feel mad? (The therapist asks a question for which the answer is already known, and thus sounds like she does not understand the child's feeling.)
Child:	Yeah! What do you think it does! (The child does not feel understood and is justifiably angry at the therapist.)
Suggested:	Just makes you angry when you can't make that stay fixed. (Recognizes feeling.)

• • •

Child:	My dog died, and we buried him right in our backyard. It was amazing! He died right by his old doghouse. (No observable affect about dog's death.)
Therapist:	He died right by his old doghouse, and you buried him in the backyard? (Simple reflection of words and voice tone at end turns the statement into a question of what child has just said.)
Suggested:	That was really surprising that he died right by his doghouse. (Shows understanding of feeling.)

Labeling Objects Ahead of the Child

Child:	Vrrooom. Vrrooom. (Pushing block along on floor.)
Therapist:	You are having fun with the car. (The child has not identified the block as a car. The therapist projects an assumption.)
Child:	That's not a car. That's a boat.
Suggested:	That's sure making lots of noise. (Avoids labeling block and says, "I'm with you.")

• • •

Child:	(Places alligator puppet on her hand.)
Therapist:	Now you have the alligator. (Child has not identified puppet. By naming the puppet, the therapist limits the child's creativity and structures possible play activity.)
Suggested:	Now you put that one on. (Allows the child to continue to lead and identify the puppet.)

• • •

Child: (Had been examining the spaceship, but did not iden-
               tify it. Then he picked up two male figures from the
               doll family on the table.)

Therapist: Looks like you picked out two things to go in your
               spaceship. (The therapist takes the lead and labels
               the spaceship. The child had not indicated what he
               intended to do with the two male figures. This directs
               the child's play.)

Suggested: Looks like you have something in mind for those.
               (Communicates involvement in what the child is doing
               and allows the child freedom to continue to direct his
               own play.)

. . .

Child: (Uses crayons and draws a picture of a cat.) This is my
               kitty. (Draws legs and puts several points on the end of
               each leg.)

Therapist: I see you are putting toenails on the kitten. (The
               child had not identified them as such, so the therapist
               is leading.)

Child: No. (Proceeds to color over the cat. The child had been
               drawing toes on the cat, not toenails. The child felt she
               had done something wrong.)

Suggested: Now you're putting some of those on your kitty right
               there. (Response conveys that the therapist is noticing
               what the child is doing, conveys interest, and allows
               the child to identify what she is drawing.)

Evaluation and Praise

Child: (The child finds a comb, and combs the hair of
               two dolls.)

Therapist: You're making them so pretty. (Since children want
               to please, the child may continue the activity to get
               more praise.)

Suggested: You know just how to comb their hair. (This reflects
               the child's ability rather than making a judgment as to
               how the results turn out.)

. . .

Child: Maybe I'll paint after I finish this.

Therapist: That sounds like a good idea. (The child may now think painting is what the therapist wants him to do. The child is no longer free to change his mind.)

Suggested: You're thinking you might like to paint next. (Shows understanding; the child is free to decide.)

• • •

Child: I made an airplane. (She then flies the airplane around the room.)

Therapist: Oh, you made an airplane! That's a nice-looking airplane. (The therapist's excitement exceeds the child's level of feeling; this is a value judgment.)

Suggested: And you can make it fly around. (Avoids simple word reflection and gives the child credit.)

• • •

Child: (Pretends to cook eggs, gives them to therapist on a plate.) How do they taste?

Therapist: These eggs sure do taste good! (Evaluates and encourages external motivation.)

Suggested: You worked hard cooking these eggs just for me. (Recognizes effort, encourages internal motivation.)

Inappropriate Questions

Child: Me and Courtney played house and (goes into long discourse about activities, keeps mentioning Courtney).

Therapist: Is Courtney one of your friends? (Question meets the therapist's need. Whether or not Courtney is a friend is irrelevant.)

Suggested: Sounds like you and Courtney did lots of things together. (This shows understanding of content, and keeps the focus on the child.)

• • •

Child: (Routinely hits on Bobo but with some vigor; no affect observable.)

Therapist: How does it make you feel to hit Bobo? (Inappropriate because no affect is observable. This implies to the child she should be feeling something.)

Suggested: (A response is not needed to everything a child does in the playroom.)

• • •

Child: (Tells about his baseball team and excitedly says) I know we're going to win this afternoon!

Therapist: Do you like to win? (Asks a question for which the answer is obvious. Conveys a lack of understanding.)

Suggested: You really have fun winning. (Shows understanding.)

• • •

Child: (Finds a small container.) Where's the stuff that goes in here? (Then places Barbie's shoes into the container.)

Therapist: Do you think those go in there? (Questions the child's decision, causes her to doubt herself; this does not communicate understanding.)

Suggested: You decided those go in there. (Gives the child credit for making a decision.)

Statements Turned Into Questions

Child: The lightning's scary.

Therapist: The lightning is a little scary? (Use of the word "little" underplays the child's feeling, and the question at the end conveys that the therapist does not understand the child's feeling and has to check.)

Suggested: It scares you when there's lightning. (Communicates understanding of feeling.)

• • •

Child: I'm going to cook supper now.

Therapist: You've decided it's suppertime? (Questions imply a lack of understanding.)

Suggested: You've decided it's suppertime. (Avoiding voice inflection at the end communicates understanding and gives the child credit for making a decision.)

• • •

Child: I like puppet shows. Do you like puppet shows?

Therapist: You like playing with all the puppets? (Voice tone at the end of the statement turns the statement into a question and calls for a yes-or-no answer.)

Suggested: You have fun with puppet shows.

• • •

Child: (Playing with several toys.)

Therapist: Wesley, we have 5 more minutes in the playroom, okay? (The last word implies the child has a choice when no choice is intended.)

Suggested: (Same response, just take out the last word.)

Leading the Child

Child: (Uses a plastic knife to scrape paint off a jar lid. Works hard to scrape the paint off.)

Therapist: Even though things are hard, you don't give up. (The child will now have great difficulty in stopping, even if some of the paint is hard to get off, because she may fear the therapist will think she is giving up and will be disappointed in her.)

Suggested: You're working hard to get that off. (Acknowledges the child's effort.)

• • •

Child: This house is for you. What color do you want it to be?

Therapist: I like houses made out of red brick. (The child's focus will now be on trying to please the therapist. The child may think he is supposed to draw a whole house covered with individual bricks and so spend an excessive amount of time drawing hundreds of individual bricks. What will happen if the child has difficulty drawing bricks?)

Suggested: A special house for me. You can choose what color you want it to be. (This allows the child to make the decision and to lead and keeps the focus on the child. Total design of the house can be the responsibility of the child.)

• • •

Child: (Plays in the kitchen area with the baby and the pots and pans. She picks up the coffee pot.)

Therapist: Are you going to have some coffee? (The therapist inserts his own reality and interferes with the child's

creativity and direction. What if the child was planning something else? Could she be about to pour
orange juice or a glass of milk for the baby?)

Suggested: Now you're going to use that. (Shows attentiveness of
the therapist, avoids labeling, and allows the child to
continue to lead.)

• • •

Child: What can I make for us to eat?

Therapist: Oh, there are lots of different things you could make.
(Implies the therapist knows what the child could make
and will result in the child waiting for the therapist
to tell.)

Suggested: You can decide. (Grants the child freedom and allows
him to assume responsibility for deciding.)

This new language of empathic responding requires effort and
commitment on the part of the therapist and a sincere desire to
understand and to be fully with a child in nonobtrusive ways that
sufficiently allow the child the freedom to be completely the person
he is at that moment. The facilitative dimensions of the child-centered
play therapist's interactive focus on the child can be seen in the
following transcription of one of my play therapy sessions.

Paul—A Fearful, Acting-Out Child in Play Therapy

Paul had a very close relationship with his grandfather. They went
just about everywhere together in an old pickup truck. When Paul
was 4 years old, his grandfather died and, although Grandfather's
death did not seem to be a traumatic experience for Paul, he did
miss his grandfather. Two months after Grandfather's death, Paul
insisted that Mother take him to the cemetery to visit PawPaw.
At the cemetery, Paul ran over to the gravesite, got down on his
hands and knees, and began to talk to PawPaw through a hole in
the flat headstone. Evidently the hole was intended for a flower
vase. After talking to PawPaw for several minutes, Paul was ready
to go home. Two weeks later, Paul insisted Mother take him to the
cemetery again to talk to PawPaw. This, then, became the pattern

for the next 2 years; every other week they took an hour-long drive to the cemetery to talk to PawPaw. During the following 2 years, Paul developed an obsessive fear of death. As a 6-year-old in first grade, Paul was not learning to read, was very aggressive with other children on the playground, and was fearful. Paul was referred to the Center for Play Therapy by his mother. The following protocol is from my second play therapy session with Paul.

Paul: (Paul opened the door to the playroom, walked into the room, and immediately began hitting the bop bag—a punching-return toy.) What was that? Bam! (Hits the bop bag.)

Therapist: You really whammed him one.

Paul: I'm the policeman. I'm the policeman now.

Therapist: You're the policeman for awhile.

Paul: Ah huh. (Hits bop bag.) God! Did you see that?

Therapist: You made him spin all the way around.

Paul: I, you know who I really am? The police. No. I'm gonna play with the home (dollhouse) for awhile. I kind of like it.

Therapist: You kind of liked that last time.

Paul: Yeah. (Playing with the dollhouse, arranging furniture.) What happened to Batman (bop bag)? He's marked on.

Therapist: Looks like somebody marked on him.

Paul: Guess somebody did. (Returns attention to the dollhouse.) Oh, they have a television. What's this? (Discovers a toy soldier someone left in the doll box.) Somebody was in here before.

Therapist: You discovered someone was here before you came today.

Paul: Who?

Therapist: Other boys and girls come here sometimes.

Paul: Oh. (Satisfied, returns to the dollhouse.) This one. This must be the children's room for a little while, ain't it? Where's the car? I need the car. Oh. (Walking around the room, looking for the car; finds it and brings it to the dollhouse.) Here it is.

Therapist: That's the one you were looking for.

Paul: Yeah. (Pinches himself with the car.) Ouch! Ouch! Oh darn! Daddy has to buy a new television. He bought one. This one's for his bed. They just moved in. (Referring to the doll family.)

Therapist: So they're just now moving into this house.

Paul: Again, didn't they? The television…. They used to live in here, didn't they?

Therapist: And now they're going to live here again.

Paul: Yeah. Oh, know what they're gonna do? They're gonna take a trip. They've got to get on. (Gets a large Fisher Price airplane and begins to put the family dolls in the airplane.)

Therapist: They're going to fly somewhere.

Paul: Do you know where they are going really? They're going to…. (Pretends to turn off a cartoon.) And now it's time to go to New York.

Therapist: A long way away.

Paul: I'll bet it's fast. Wonder what the kids think of flying. They are going to be happy, aren't they? Aren't they?

Therapist: So they will really like that.

Paul: I know cuz they are going on a plane trip. I'm going to make them sit down, right?

Therapist: You're going to put them in there just right.

Paul: If they don't sit down and put on their seatbelts, you know what's going to happen? They're gonna have to stay home. They won't get to go on a plane trip, right?

Therapist: So they have to do just what they are supposed to, or they won't get to go.

Paul: Right. The baby won't cry cuz she is going to be happy too, I bet. The mother's gonna…. (Laughing.) The mother and family is too big for the plane, ain't they? (Said even though all the doll family members were inside the plane.) They're back. (Plane never left original spot.) They parked right by their home, didn't they?

Therapist: So they're just real close to their house.

Paul: (Removes dolls from plane. Returns to dollhouse.) God! That was pretty fast. Guess what? You know what the Daddy's gonna do? Buy a new truck.

Therapist: So he's going to buy a new truck.

Paul: Yeah. They got two of them. They might move in this truck. They're getting ready to move. (Playing with dolls in the dollhouse.)

Therapist: And they could move in their truck.

Paul: They might. They might move. The kids are watching cartoons. The baby's, the baby's playing. Know what? After cartoons they get to go outside.

Therapist: So they are going to watch TV and then go outside.

Paul: The Daddy's gonna get a new truck. So she's (mom) staying here cooking supper. Daddy couldn't find a new truck. (Gets another truck, returns to the dollhouse.) Here's one. He's gonna buy this one. (Moves the truck around.) Golly, that's a big truck, ain't it? He might not buy that truck. Oh. Ahhh. Look now. Look at this now. Daddy's at work. He can't buy a truck. He didn't find one.

Therapist: He didn't find one he liked.

Paul: (Going to sandbox.) He's going to find something he likes someday, ain't he? Do you have another truck? Now stay tuned for Batman. (Runs over to bop bag, punches bop bag fiercely nine times in the face, wrestles him, and pushes him down.) He's down for a little while. I'm gonna put him on this chair. (Puts Batman bop bag on a chair.) He's gonna.... I'm gonna shoot him. I got these many guns. I'm gonna shoot at him. (Picks up guns and a small plastic TV.) Ooooo! This can be a different TV.

Therapist: Uh huh.

Paul: (Paul puts the TV in the dollhouse.) I guess that's Daddy's TV.

Therapist: So he's going to have a special one.

Paul: Yeah. (Picks up a rifle that shoots ping-pong balls.) Hey, where's those round balls? (Picks up a ping-pong ball.) I'm gonna shoot him (Batman) for good, ain't I? Ain't I?

Therapist: So you know just what you're going to do. You've got it planned.

Paul:	Look! Ready for Batman? Batman's gonna be in big trouble, ain't he? (Shoots.) I got him, didn't I?
Therapist:	You got him the first shot.
Paul:	I'm gonna kill him more. (Aims, shoots, and misses.) Hmmm, better try another gun. (Tries a dart pistol.) There's another. I got it. (Shoots to the side of the bop bag.) I missed him, didn't I?
Therapist:	It went right past him.
Paul:	(Shoots again to the side of the bop bag.) It's a hard shot, ain't it?
Therapist:	It's hard to hit it from way over there.
Paul:	(Shoots again and misses.) I missed him a bunch, didn't I? (Picks up the darts.) When I get him, guess what I'm gonna do? I'm gonna tie him up and kill him. I'm gonna cut him up.
Therapist:	You're really going to kill him.
Paul:	(Shoots and misses again. Shoots the bop bag again.) Got him! (Runs over and puts the bop bag on the floor, its head under a chair so that the bop bag is horizontal.) Supposed to be dead for a little while. You know what I'm gonna do to Batman? Ahhh. (Gets a rubber knife and cuts the middle of Bobo. Goes to the kitchen and looks through the dishes.) You know what I'm gonna do?
Therapist:	You've got something planned now.
Paul:	I'm not gonna poison him. (He cooked poison last session and fed it to Batman.) You know what I am going to do this time? Nah. I'm not going to. I'm gonna kill him again. I'm gonna poison him. That's what I was gonna do. Let's see. (Picks up a handgun, walks over to Batman, aims the gun right next to Batman's face, and shoots.) Haha. (Goes to the sandbox, stands in the middle, and fills a bucket with sand.) Guess what I'm gonna do?
Therapist:	You can tell me what you're going to do.
Paul:	Well, I'm gonna put Batman in this. (Drops the bucket, starts sweeping in the sandbox and outside the sandbox.) Sweep the blood off. Haha. Sweep the blood. Batman's gonna be really dead this time cuz I'll really kill him.
Therapist:	This time you'll make sure you kill him.

Paul:	You're right. This time I'm going to make sure you're gonna get killed.
Therapist:	Oh, I'm going to get it too.
Paul:	I know. You're Robin.
Therapist:	You're going to kill both of us.
Paul:	Bet you're right. Hope I don't miss ya. (Said with a lilt to his voice and a big grin.)
Therapist:	I'm not for shooting. (Paul aims way over the therapist's head and shoots the wall.) I know you would like to shoot me. You can pretend the Batman is me (points to Batman) and shoot Batman. (Paul again shoots over the therapist's head. It is obvious he does not intend to shoot the therapist.)
Paul:	Ohhh. I missed you. (Shoots again.) Ahhhhh, gosh. (Begins to play with the phone.) You know who I'm gonna call? Mmm ammm. (Gets another phone and dials.) Yeah, Batman's dead. Hum hum, okay. (Leaves the phone and goes across the room.) Hey, I'm gonna make a little song to wake Batman up, ain't I? (Plays a xylophone and looks expectantly at Batman.) He's almost woke up. (Walks over to Batman.) Chop his neck off, ain't I? (Hits Batman.) Now he's dead. Now I'm going to play with Dad again, Mr. old Dad. (Plays in the dollhouse and with the scooter truck.) Here's his new truck. That's gonna work better. He bought a new television, didn't he?
Therapist:	So now they have two televisions.
Paul:	Right. Hey, does this work? You put it in there? (Examines the TV and figures out where a piece goes.)
Therapist:	There, you figured it out.
Paul:	Does it move? (Tries to make the picture screen move.)
Therapist:	I guess you're wondering, does this thing really work like a real one?
Paul:	It didn't move. Daddy bought a new television didn't he? Mr. Dad, for them.
Therapist:	Dad brought it home for them.

Paul: To watch… to watch. The kids saw the new truck Daddy bought. Daddy. The kids didn't know it yet. They start running.

Therapist: Oh, he sort of surprised them.

Paul: The kids didn't see nothing like it, didn't they?

Therapist: So it was a special surprise.

Paul: Dad's gonna, he's gonna have to take it back someday.

Therapist: So Dad can't keep it.

Paul: (Puts the dolls in the truck.) They're gonna have a ride. Where's the baby? Oh. Get in there. (Puts the doll family in the scooter truck.) They're gonna have fun, aren't they?

Therapist: So they're all going together in that new truck and have fun.

Paul: (Paul pushes the truck slowly around the dollhouse, makes motor noise, stays very close to the dollhouse.) They're almost home, aren't they?

Therapist: They're coming back.

Paul: Time for them to get out. (Takes the dolls out and puts them in the house.) Oh, the kids say, Oowh! Oowh!"

Therapist: They didn't want to.

Paul: They didn't want to go home. They liked their ride, didn't they?

Therapist: They were having lots of fun.

Paul: Guess what? He might buy a tractor. He gets to go to work.

Therapist: So, he bought a TV, and then a truck, and he might even buy a tractor.

Paul: They might move.

Therapist: Hmmm. They might move.

Paul: Yeah, they're gonna miss cartoons in a little while, aren't they? Daddy has to go. Mamma has to put baby in bed, don't she? (Picks up the baby.) I bet this baby's gonna be baldheaded, don't you?

Therapist: No hair on his head.

Paul: I know. That means he's gonna be baldheaded someday.

Therapist: Hmmm.

Paul: This baby sure is, ain't it? We don't want no baby to be baldheaded. It's like a little boy being baldheaded. They're gonna do something. Daddy has to go to work. He might move something. He might get a new tractor. I bet he is. He needs one. Then he might move. Ahh oh! Here they come! Here comes the new tractor. (Plays with a tractor.) I think the kids are gonna be happy with the tractor. Oh, God! It's too big with the steering wheel. (Tries to put the tractor inside the scooter car.)

Therapist: It won't quite fit in there.

Paul: I guess he has to buy another tractor. I got it. Turn it over. Nah. (Can't make it go inside the truck.) Do it backwards? Nah. I guess he can't buy one today. Here's a tractor for him. (Finds another that fits.) Watch the tractor. Here's the tractor now. Let's get going. The cartoons are over. They got to watch it, didn't they? (Said with glee.)

Therapist: That made them happy to get to watch cartoons.

Paul: (Begins loading furniture into the scooter car.) Yeah, but poor Mom can't cook anymore (as he loads kitchen stove). She was hungry. The dad was hungry. You know something, they can move that bathroom.

Therapist: Uh huh. They can move just about everything in that house.

Paul: In the truck. Oh God! And they moved, didn't they?

Therapist: Moved everything out of the house.

Paul: Yeah. They decided to live here again. (Puts the furniture back in the dollhouse.)

Therapist: So they moved out and then decided to move back in.

Paul: Know why? They were missing some more cartoons.

Therapist: So they wanted to get back and watch some.

Paul: Know what Dad has to do? (Moves to the sandbox with the father doll.)

Therapist: You can tell me what he's gonna do.

Paul: Okay. He's gonna…he died.

Therapist: Oh, Daddy died.

Paul: Yeah. So they're gonna bury him in the sand. (Scoops out a hole in the sand and begins to bury the father doll.)

Therapist: He died and now he's getting buried right there.
Paul: I know. I guess they have to have a new Daddy, right? (Continues covering the doll with sand.)
Therapist: So if that daddy died, they'll need to get another one.
Paul: Ooooh. He's all buried.
Therapist: Now he can't be seen.
Paul: There's where he's at. (Places a funnel upside down on top of the grave with the spout pointing up.) The kids came to see him. The baby's still asleep. (Goes to the dollhouse and gets the boy and girl dolls.)
Therapist: Hmm, so they're going to go and see where he is buried.
Paul: (Placed the boy doll's head at the funnel end.) They heard something. Uhhhhhh. (Sound coming from the grave.)
Therapist: They heard something where Daddy is buried.
Paul: Yeah. And guess what. They are going to unbury him. (Pulls the doll out of the sand.) Oh, God! He's alive!
Therapist: So he really wasn't dead. Now he's alive.
Paul: They were surprised at him. (Sounds really excited and glad.)
Therapist: They were surprised but happy.
Paul: Oh my God, look! They're having a tornado in this area by their home. They better hurry home, right?
Therapist: Tornados are dangerous.
Paul: I know. It can blow houses down. One of them's, one of them's in the graveyard. That's the girl. (Buries a doll in the sand. The therapist can't see the doll being buried.)
Therapist: So the girl got left in the graveyard.
Paul: Uh uh, she's buried.
Therapist: Oh, she's buried in the graveyard.
Paul: She does not want…. She does not want the tornado to get her.
Therapist: So the tornado can't get her there.
Paul: The tornado's past. Oooh. Look what happened! (Knocks over toys near the dollhouse.) God!
Therapist: The tornado wrecked some things.

Paul: Yeah, some, but it didn't wreck this. (Points to the scooter truck.) All the kids have to get in the house fast, lay down and rest.

Therapist: So they're hoping they'll be safe in the house.

Paul: And she told her to get in and rest, too, while Daddy got the pickup truck over. (Pulls the truck over.) Ah, oh. The tornado's out. Guess what. Daddy's gonna be surprising. Guess what. Stay tuned for Batman!

Therapist: Now its time for Batman again.

Paul: (Goes over to Batman and attempts to put handcuffs on himself.) Uh, oh, they caught me, didn't they?

Therapist: You got caught by somebody.

Paul: The police. (Continues trying to handcuff his hands behind his back.)

Therapist: Oh, the police caught you. Hmm.

Paul: For killing Batman.

Therapist: So you killed Batman, and then the policeman caught you.

Paul: Yeah. Batman is alive now. Ouch. No wonder I can't put these on when I have my hands behind my back. Here. (Brings handcuffs to the therapist for aid; the therapist fastens them behind his back.) Okay, I'm in jail.

Therapist: So the policeman handcuffed you and took you to jail.

Paul: I know. First he has to do something. He can't kill nobody. The police surrounded him, and he has to put this (knife) back.

Therapist: So they fixed him up so he can't kill anyone.

Paul: Yeah. They have to put the knife back. The Batman's alive. Better get him up. (Stands Batman up.)

Therapist: So he's okay now.

Paul: But first wait. (Moves Batman around.) There. Uh oh, I'm out of jail now. Help me. (Tries to take the handcuffs off.) Ouch, ouch. (The handcuffs pinch his wrists.)

Therapist: Sometimes those things pinch.

Paul: Yeah. (Takes the handcuffs off.)

Therapist: But you got them off.

Paul: Guess what. I'm the police now. I'm going to get to be a police, didn't I?

Therapist: So now you're going to be the one with the handcuffs.

Paul: I'm the police now. I'm Batman and I'll bring you in jail, okay?

Therapist: You can pretend that someone is doing that, and I'll watch.

Paul: Okay. That. Mr. Policeman is having trouble, ain't he? (Trying to hook the handcuffs together.)

Therapist: Looks like he's having a hard time getting those on there just right.

Paul: Oh, no. He got it. Now he don't have trouble.

Therapist: You figured it out.

Paul: Uh huh, I found the way. (Hooks the handcuffs on his pocket.)

Therapist: Hmmm. You found a way to do it. Paul, we have 5 more minutes in the playroom today.

Paul: Oooh. (Doesn't want to end. Makes a shooting noise, runs over, and dives on the floor. Pretends to wrestle someone.) Got him, didn't I?

Therapist: You caught him right there.

Paul: (Wrestles the imaginary person for several minutes.)

Therapist: You're really working hard.

Paul: Yeah, I know. He's a tough one.

Therapist: He's really tough but you're wrestling him.

Paul: I got him down.

Therapist: You won. Paul, our time is up for today. It's time to go to the waiting room where your mom is (stands up).

Paul: AAAAh! Okay. (Walks to the door and opens it.)

As is often true in play therapy, several themes were evident in this second session. Television seemed to be very important to Paul, as noted in his numerous references to TV. A theme of moving and leaving the security of home was evident in the scenes involving the airplane trip in which the people didn't fly away, the auto trip in which Paul stayed very close to the dollhouse, and his announcing the family was going to move, followed by loading all the furniture and fixtures into the truck and promptly stating,

"They decided to live here again." Another theme was his play and statements indicating that death is not permanent, "Supposed to be dead for a little while." The culmination of this theme was the burial of the father figure in the sandbox and the boy doll figure talking to the buried father doll through the spout of the funnel. This scene was dramatically similar to Paul's trips to the cemetery, to "talk" to his grandfather through the hole for a flower vase in the headstone. After Paul began play therapy, he only asked one time to go to the cemetery, indicating a significant change in him. In the fifth session, Paul announced, "My PawPaw died you know." This was the first clear indication of his acceptance of the death of his grandfather.

Chapter 11

Therapeutic Limit Setting

Limit setting is one of the most important aspects of play therapy and seems to be the most problematic area for play therapists. The inexperienced therapist often feels insecure and is slow to apply limits. Sometimes the therapist is reluctant because of a desire to be liked by the child. Limits provide structure for the development of the therapeutic relationship and help to make the experience a real-life relationship. Without limits a relationship would have little value. The fact that the therapist struggles with setting limits speaks loudly of the therapist's valuing of self, the child, and the relationship. Emotional and social growth is not likely to occur in disorganized, chaotic relationships, and according to Moustakas (1959), therapy cannot occur without limits.

Basic Guidelines in Limit Setting

Permissiveness in the child-centered play therapy approach does not mean the acceptance of all behaviors. Therapy is a learning experience, and limits provide children with an opportunity to learn self-control, that they have choices, what making choices feels like, and how responsibility feels. Therefore, when limits should be set and are not, children are deprived of an opportunity to learn something important about themselves. In therapeutic limit setting, children are given the opportunity to choose.

Therefore, they experience a life lesson in being responsible for themselves and their own well-being.

The therapist's belief that children will choose positive coopera- tive behavior is a significant and impactful variable in the thera- peutic process. Children are more likely to comply with limits when they experience respect for themselves and acceptance for their feelings and behaviors…both positive and negative. Therefore, the therapist focuses on the child's unexpressed need for defiance, for example, while continuing to express fundamental understanding, support, valuing of the child, and a genuine belief in the child.

Limits in the playroom should be minimal and enforceable. Children cannot learn about themselves and cannot adequately express themselves in the face of a multitude of limits. Unenforceable limits do great harm to the therapeutic relationship by interfering with the development of trust.

The establishment of total limits rather than conditional lim- its is more effective. Total limits are less confusing to children and help the therapist to feel more secure. "You may pinch me, but you may not hurt me" leaves the issue wide open as to how much pinching is hurtful. "You may put a little water in the sand" would likewise not be acceptable. How does a child know what is expected if the therapist says, "You probably shouldn't smear so much glue on the Bobo." Conditional limits become the basis for arguments. A total limit would be, "I'm not for pinching." The child now knows exactly what is not permissible. Conditional limits, "You can't kick the door hard," can become the basis for arguments. What the therapist thinks is hard may not be per- ceived by the child as hard, so the child may attempt to convince the therapist. The therapist should never engage in an argument with a child. The best procedure is to simply restate the original limit or issue and then reflect the child's feelings or desire. "You would like to convince me that you didn't shoot the mirror, but the mirror is not for shooting."

Limits should be stated in a calm, patient, matter-of-fact, and firm way. Limits that are rushed or stated quickly reveal the therapist's anxiety and lack of trust in the child. If the thera- pist's attitude really is one of trust and a belief that the child will respond responsibly, then the therapist will respond accordingly with calmness. The fact of the matter is that if a child is standing 10 feet away from the therapist threatening to shoot the therapist with the dart gun, the therapist cannot move fast enough to get across the room and stop the child before the trigger is pulled. Therefore, the therapist may as well sit there with calmness and trust that if she responds appropriately, the child will respond responsibly. If the therapist were to jump out of her chair and attempt to grab the gun, her behavior would communicate a message of, "I don't trust you." The child is then left to carry out the original intent because, "She really expects me to."

Such moments of intense interaction can be anxiety provoking for the therapist and quickly reveal deeper attitudes, beliefs, and motivation. Inexperienced play therapists may experience some anxiety or perhaps even a bit of rejection of a child who persists in pushing the limit, threatening to do what necessitated the limit, or actually breaking the limit. There is only one way the therapist can learn that children really can be trusted in such situations and that is to "weather the storm" and in the process discover children really can and will control their behavior if responded to appropriately. For this reason, supervised experience is a must in helping therapists process their own deeper levels of feelings and attitudes.

In therapeutic limit setting, *the focus and emphasis are always on the child, in order to clearly convey where the responsibility lies.* A response such as, "In here we don't take our pants off" is inappropriate because the therapist has not the least inclination to undress. Yet the use of "we" and "our" implies the therapist is a part of the process. *Children should be allowed to be separate.* The response, "In here we don't throw paint on the floor," does not focus on the child and so dilutes the impact of the limit. The therapist's inclusion of himself or herself in such responses is probably a function of cultural response habits but also may reveal a need and attitude of which the therapist is unaware.

When to Present Limits

A common question among play therapists is when to set limits. Should limits be set as a part of the general introduction to the playroom at the beginning of the first session, or should the therapist wait until the occasion calls for the setting of limits? Providing a long list of limits at the beginning of the first session is not necessary. This tends to set a negative tone and interferes with the therapeutic objective of establishing a climate of freedom and permissiveness. In play therapy, the therapist is always concerned with the attitude that is being projected about the child and the relationship.

For some children, a listing of limits would only serve to give them ideas. For cautious ("shy") and fearful children, the early introduction of limits only serves to inhibit them more. Some children never need limits set on their behavior. Because play therapy is a learning experience for children, the best time to learn is when the limit issue arises. Emotional learning is then possible at the point of need for a limit.

RULE OF THUMB:

Limits are not needed until they are needed.

Self-control cannot be learned until an opportunity to exercise self-control occurs. Therefore, a limitation on the child leaving the playroom is unnecessary until the child starts to leave the playroom. At that moment, responding with, "I know you want to leave the playroom, but (therapist glances at watch) we have 20 more minutes in the playroom, and then it will be time to leave," allows the child to struggle with the responsibility of following or not following the limit. In this case, the therapist uses "we" to emphasize the relationship, and the reality is that the therapist also will be leaving the playroom.

Rationale for Therapeutic Limits

Play therapists often experience difficulty applying limits because they do not have a rationale for setting limits, and consequently they are inconsistent, sometimes allowing a behavior and at other times setting a limit on the same behavior. Knowing the purpose of setting limits and when limits should be set can provide consistency in applying limits. At the moment a limit is needed in the playroom is not the time to begin thinking about whether or not a limit is needed on a specific behavior.

Therapeutic limit setting is based on sound principles and a well-thought-out formulation of general areas in which intervention through limit setting will probably be needed. Limit setting should not occur at the sporadic, insecure whims of the therapist. *Limits are based on clear and definable criteria supported by a clearly thought-out rationale with the furtherance of the therapeutic relationship in mind.* Limits are not set simply for the sake of limiting behavior. Limits are applied because they are recognized as facilitating the attainment of accepted psychological principles of growth.

Although it may seem strange to say so and even more difficult to appreciate in the midst of confrontation with an aggressive, angry child, **the child's desire to break the limit has greater therapeutic significance than the exhibited behavior.** For here we are dealing with intrinsic variables related to motivation, perception of self, independence, need for acceptance, and the working out of a relationship with a significant person. Although the behavior being expressed is really secondary, the child's behavior too often captivates the unskilled therapist's attention and energy in an attempt to stop it. **All feelings, desires, and wishes of the child are accepted, but not all behaviors are accepted.** Destructive behaviors cannot be accepted, but the child can be granted permission to express himself or herself symbolically without fear of reprimand or rejection. The rationale for therapeutic limits is contained in the following seven principles and accompanying discussions.

1. Limits Provide Physical and Emotional Security and Safety for Children

Although the atmosphere in the playroom is conducive to a greater feeling of permissiveness than usually exists in a child's relationships outside the playroom, basic commonsense health and safety limits prevail in the playroom. *Setting limits on the child's behavior demonstrates the therapist's respect and caring for the child and intent to provide physical and psychological safety for the child.* The result is a relationship and an atmosphere in which the child feels safe. A child may not shoot a pencil in the dart gun because of the sharp point, drink water from a rusty can, or cut himself or herself with the scissors. A session in which the therapist is on edge because the child is engaging in potentially harmful activities would seem to have very little therapeutic value. A child should never be allowed to stick objects in electrical wall outlets. As a precaution, outlets should be covered.

At times the child may need to be protected from potential guilt, as in the case of a child who wants to hit the therapist or smash the therapist over the head with a toy. The child may later worry about what was done to the therapist and become quite anxious, fearing the therapist was hurt or that the therapist would not like the child anymore. Similar feelings and reactions can result if the child is allowed to paint the therapist's face, pour paint on the therapist's clothes, or shoot the therapist with the dart gun. A child should not be allowed to hit, kick, scratch, or bite the therapist. Although a child may express a desire to hit the therapist, paint on the walls, or break equipment, such behaviors are limited in order to prevent accompanying feelings of guilt or anxiety. In responding to situations described here, the therapist always maintains an accepting attitude of the child's feelings and desires.

The growth potential in children cannot be maximized in settings where children feel insecure. When no boundaries and no limitations on behavior exist, children feel insecure and usually experience anxiety. **Limits provide structure to the environment and the relationship, so children can feel secure.** Some children have difficulty controlling their own impulsiveness and need the security of experiencing limits being set in a way that provides them with an opportunity to gain control of their own behavior. Limits, therefore, help to assure the emotional security of children. When children discover where the boundaries are in the play therapy relationship and experience those boundaries being adhered to consistently, they feel secure because there is predictability in the relationship and setting. Limits define the boundaries of the therapeutic relationship.

2. Limits Protect the Physical Well-Being of the Therapist and Facilitate Acceptance of the Child

The therapist's physical safety as well as emotional and physical comfort are important dimensions in the therapeutic process. A therapist who is being bombarded with blocks of wood thrown by a child from across the room will experience great difficulty trying to focus on understanding the underlying reason for the attack, or what the child is feeling at the moment. The therapist who can sit through sand being poured over her head or watch patiently as the child cuts tassels off her new shoes and still concentrate on the needs of the child is rare indeed. Physical comfort and safety are basic needs for everyone and will be attended to by the individual either consciously or unconsciously. Therapist self-awareness is essential to the appropriate handling and resolution of this issue.

The inherent growth potential in children is facilitated by the therapist's acceptance and warm caring, and it is limit setting which allows the therapist to remain empathic and accepting of the child throughout the therapy process. **Limits are set on children's behaviors that hinder the therapist's acceptance.** For the therapist to maintain a warm, caring, accepting attitude toward a child who is hitting him on the knee with a hammer is virtually impossible. In this situation, the therapist likely will experience feelings of resentment and rejection, which in turn will be communicated to the child at some level. A child should not be allowed to pull the therapist's hair, throw sand on the therapist, paint the therapist's shoes, or hit the therapist in any way. *Any form of direct aggressive physical acting out or attack on the therapist should be prohibited.* Such behaviors are not to be tolerated under any circumstances, because they will interfere with the therapist's empathic acceptance, respect for the child, and objectivity in relating to the child. Limits may be needed to help the therapist maintain a high level of acceptance of the child.

Play therapists are not "superpersons." They are subject to experiencing normal, sometimes uncontrollable emotional reactions, and once reactions of anger or rejection have been experienced, they will be sensed by the child. Therefore, appropriate timing in setting limits is crucial to maintaining an attitude of acceptance and positive regard for the child. Activities that are likely to arouse feelings of anger or anxiety in the therapist generally should be limited. However, some therapists experience anxiety and anger over what would be described as minor messiness by the child, and in such cases, it is strongly recommended that therapists carefully examine their own motivations. Are the limits being set to facilitate the therapeutic relationship, or to accommodate a therapist's rigid code of neatness?

3. Limits Facilitate the Development of Decision Making, Self-Control, and Self-Responsibility of Children

One of the things children learn in play therapy is that their feelings, whether positive or negative, are accepted. Therefore, rejection or denial of one's feelings is not necessary. In the playroom, acceptable ways are available for the expression of all feelings. *Before children can resist following through and expressing feelings in ways dictated by first impulses, they must have an awareness of their behavior; a feeling of responsibility, and exercise self-control.* In the midst of experiencing the welling up of intense emotion, children often are unaware of their behavior and so are equally devoid of feelings of responsibility. Limit setting addresses the immediate reality of the situation and indirectly calls attention to the child's behavior through statements such as, "The wall is not for painting on."

How can children develop a feeling of responsibility if they are unaware of what they are doing? And how can they experience a feeling of self-control if they are too defensive to change their behavior? Therapeutic limit setting does not stir up feelings of defensiveness that often accompany attempts to stop a behavior, because the child's behavior is not the focus. What is focused on are the child's feelings or desires and the recipient or object of the behavior. This can be seen clearly in the statement, "You would like to paint on the wall, but the wall is not for painting," as opposed to, "Don't paint on that wall."

The child's *need* to paint on the wall, to be messy, to break the limit is accepted and communicated to the child in very specific and concrete ways by providing acceptable alternatives, "You would like to paint on the wall. The wall is not for painting. The paper on the easel is for painting." No attempt is made to stop the expression of the *feeling* or the *need*. Such a statement clearly indicates to the child a permissible way to express herself. Now the child is confronted with a choice, to act on the original impulse or to express himself or herself through the alternative behavior. The choice is the child's, and the therapist allows the child to choose. *The decision is the child's, and responsibility accompanies decision making.* If the child chooses to paint on the easel paper, it will be because the child decided to and exercised self-control, not because the therapist made her.

4. Limits Anchor the Session to Reality and Emphasize the Here and Now

Some children become caught up in fantasy play in the playroom and could spend the entire time absorbed in the enactment of fantasy scenes, thus effectively avoiding any personal responsibility for actions or behaviors that may be socially unacceptable or destructive. When the therapist verbalizes a limit, the experience is quickly changed from fantasy to the reality of a relationship with an adult in which certain behaviors are unacceptable, as is true in the world outside the playroom, except that in the playroom substantially fewer limitations are established on behavior. When the therapist interjects, "You would really like to dump that paint on the floor, but the paint is not for pouring on the floor. The sink is for pouring paint into," the child is confronted with the reality of having crossed an unacceptable boundary, has been presented the opportunity to choose what will be done next, and experiences the accompanying responsibility. The child can no longer live in the enactment of fantasy, because the therapist refuses to be ignored once the limit is set. The child must now focus on the reality of making a decision in relation to the playroom and the therapist.

Limits, then, assure the play therapy experience will have a real-life quality. The therapeutic experience should not be so unlike life outside the playroom that no transfer of experiences and learning will occur. *Limits exist in every relationship that has any significance. A relationship without any limits surely would have little value to the participants.* When the therapist states a limit to protect herself from harm, the therapist's personhood and respect for herself are declared. At that moment, the experience with the child truly becomes a living relationship anchored in the dynamics of the process of the reality of the moment.

5. Limits Promote Consistency in the Playroom Environment

Children often come from homes and classroom settings characterized by inconsistency in behavior on the part of adults who have difficulty maintaining rules. In these settings, what was prohibited today may or may not be prohibited tomorrow. What was allowed today may or may not be allowed tomorrow. An accepting attitude on the part of the adult this morning may or may not be evident this afternoon. Consequently, children in such environments are never quite sure just what to expect and often attempt to cope accordingly by being very cautious or by overtly acting out in an attempt to find out just where the boundaries are. Children need to experience consistency in their lives if they are ever to achieve some degree of emotional balance. **Consistency of attitude and behavior on the part of the therapist helps children to feel secure, and this inner security enables them to move toward being the persons they are capable of being.**

One of the ways the play therapist establishes a consistent environment is through the introduction and use of consistent limits. Limits are presented in a consistently nonthreatening manner, and the therapist is consistent in seeing that the limits are adhered to—not in a rigid manner, but in a consistent manner. Rigid could perhaps imply punishment and the absence of an understanding and accepting attitude. On the other hand, understanding and acceptance do not imply license, unwillingness to follow through, or a "wishy-washy," anything-goes attitude. The therapist can be patiently understanding and accepting of the child's wish or desire and still not accept the behavior. *Limits, therefore, help to provide the structure for a consistent environment.* The therapist does not allow a child to break a toy in one session, no matter how many similar toys are in the storage closet, and then set a limit on breaking the same kind of toy in the next session. What was prohibited in the last session is prohibited in this session, and what was allowed in the last session is allowed in this session. Thus, the sessions have consistency and predictability. These are therapeutic dimensions.

Without consistency there can be no predictability, and without predictability there can be no security. Consistent limits unwaveringly enforced help to make the play therapy relationship predictable and thus increase the child's feeling of security. Consistency in limit setting is a function of the therapist's attitude and is a tangible demonstration of the therapist's commitment to the welfare and acceptance of the child. Consistent limit setting is a concrete manifestation of the therapist's willingness to put energy into the relationship with the child. By being consistent in such a tangible way, the therapist assures the child of the realness of the therapist's feelings and attitudes in other, less tangible areas, such as acceptance.

6. Limits Preserve the Professional, Ethical, and Socially Acceptable Relationship

The very nature of the play therapy setting and age of the clientele are potentially more likely to result in uninhibited or acting-out behaviors than other therapeutic settings. Although it is inconceivable for an adult or adolescent client to want to take their clothes off in the therapist's office, fondle the therapist, or urinate on the floor, such behaviors may not be uncommon in the playroom. The nature of the freedom, permissiveness, and structure of the playroom is more conducive to these behaviors than is the typical office. Sometimes a logical sequence to these behaviors occurs. First the child takes shoes and socks off to get into the sandbox, and later the child takes the rest of his clothes off to play in the sandbox or to pretend to be a baby.

Allowing a child to remove shoes and socks to play in the sandbox is appropriate. After all, this is a common practice on the school ground, in the park, and at the beach. Taking trousers and underwear off is neither common nor socially acceptable at these same places, and it is unacceptable in the play therapy experience. Urinating on the floor also is socially unacceptable and should be responded to with firm, consistent limit setting.

Some sexually abused children may attempt to act out on the therapist sexual or erotic behaviors they have been taught by perpetrating adults, because the children feel safe in the playroom or in an attempt to perhaps unconsciously communicate to the therapist what they have experienced. *The child should not be allowed to fondle the therapist or engage in other seductive behaviors.* Limits should be set on such behaviors. Any form of sexual contact between the therapist and the child is inappropriate, unprofessional, unethical, and a violation of laws. As with many other acting-out behaviors, therapeutic limit setting enables the child to express the behavior and accompanying feelings symbolically and allows the therapist to be an objective but involved participant, thus preserving the professional and ethical therapeutic relationship. These same limitations would apply to the group play therapy experience. Children should not be allowed to engage in these behaviors with one another.

7. Limits Protect the Play Therapy Materials and Room

Most play therapy programs are not blessed with unlimited budgets for keeping the playroom supplied with toys and materials. Allowing random destruction of toys could become an expensive process, and at the same time would not be helpful to the emotional growth of the child. Most play therapists cannot afford to frequently replace the triple thick, heavy gauge vinyl, canvas-enclosed Bobo punching toy, which costs over $150. Therefore, "Bobo is for hitting, not stabbing with the scissors."

Although it might be great fun for the child to jump on the wood dollhouse and smash it to pieces, it probably would not be repairable and should be protected with, "The dollhouse is not for jumping on." Less expensive items also are not for breaking or smashing. Likewise, the room is not for destroying. The child is not allowed to knock holes in the walls or floor with the wood blocks. These are opportunities for limit setting and thus opportunities for the child to learn something valuable: how to bring himself under control. **The playroom is not a place of limitless freedom, where the child can do just anything.** There are limits, and they are part of the therapeutic process.

An important consideration, however, is that children have an opportunity to appropriately express their feelings through acceptable items. Simply limiting the behavior is not sufficient. Therefore, every playroom should have some items that are for smashing, breaking, or throwing. Egg cartons seem to fit this purpose quite well. They can be stacked and kicked over, jumped on and smashed, broken apart, thrown, and painted. Playdough can be suggested as an acceptable substitute for smashing or throwing on the floor.

Actually, the number of limits set in play therapy is minimal and involves behaviors in the following areas: (a) harmful or dangerous behavior to the child and therapist, (b) behavior that disrupts the therapeutic routine or process (continually leaving the playroom, wanting to play after time is up), (c) destruction of the room or materials, (d) taking toys from the playroom, (e) socially unacceptable behavior, and (f) inappropriate displays of affection.

Procedures in Therapeutic Limit Setting

Setting limits is a carefully thought-out procedure designed to convey understanding, acceptance, and responsibility to the child. **The objective of the therapist is not to stop the behavior but, rather, to facilitate the expression of the motivating feeling, want, or need in a more acceptable manner.** *The play therapist is a facilitator of expression rather than a prohibitor of action.*

Therefore, the objective is to facilitate the child's expression through actions and behaviors that are more socially acceptable. In this process of facilitating expression of feelings in appropriate ways, the child learns to control initial behaviors, to say "no" to self.

As will quickly be recognized, some actions in the playroom must be limited. The attitude and objective of the therapist at these times will largely determine the impact of the therapist's approach to limit setting. If the therapist is determined to stop the objectionable behavior, the approach to limit setting likely will be a demanding statement such as, "Don't do that." The child then will feel rejected or that the therapist does not understand. If the therapist lacks confidence and is unsure of the limit-setting procedure, that too will be conveyed in statements such as, "I don't think you should do that." The child may then either feel insecure or continue the behavior because there is no good reason not to.

Many practicing play therapists will readily recognize that some children who persist in a behavior the therapist is seeking to limit do so because they pick up on the therapist's uncertainty or insecurity. When confronted with a demanding or authoritarian attitude and approach, "I've told you before you can't do that," children seem to feel they must protect themselves by persisting in their original behavior. In such instances, to change would almost be a loss of self. The result then is likely to be a power struggle.

Rather than attempting to stop behaviors, the therapist's objective is to respond to the child in such a way that the child is left with the responsibility for changing his behavior. If the therapist tells the child what to do, then the therapist is responsible. When the therapist trusts the child's capacity to respond responsibly and communicates, "The mirror is not for throwing at. The sandbox is for throwing at," the child is free to decide what to do next and is thus responsible.

The play therapist is encouraged to carefully examine his attitude and intent when faced with the need to set limits and to give thoughtful consideration as to how best to communicate the actual limit. A different message is obviously communicated in each of the following statements to a child who is about to paint the wall:

"It's probably not a good idea to paint the wall."

"We can't paint walls in here."

"You shouldn't paint the wall."

"You can't paint the wall."

"I can't let you paint the wall."

"Maybe you could paint something else, other than the wall."

"The rule is you can't paint the wall."

"The wall is not for painting on."

Steps in the Therapeutic Limit-Setting Process

Several specific steps may be used in the therapeutic limit-setting process. They are implemented to facilitate the process of communicating understanding and acceptance of the child's motives, to make the limit clear, and to provide acceptable alternative actions and behaviors.

Step 1: Acknowledge the Child's Feelings, Wishes, and Wants

Verbalizing understanding of the child's feeling or want conveys acceptance of the child's motivation. This is an important step, because it recognizes that the child does have feelings that are being expressed in the play activity, and that these feelings are acceptable. Simply setting the limit without acknowledging the feeling might indicate to the child that his emotions are not important.

Verbalizing an empathic understanding of the feeling often helps to defuse its intensity. This is especially true in the case of anger and is often all that is needed for the child to begin modifying his personal behavior. Acceptance of the motivation seems to be satisfying to the child, and a need for the act no longer exits. *Feelings should he reflected just as soon as they are recognized.* "You're angry at me." Once the block of wood is in flight across the room, acceptance of the feeling can no longer be a deterrent.

Step 2: Communicate the Limit

Limits should be specific, rather than general, and should clearly delineate exactly what is being limited. Limits that are general are confusing, problematic, and interfere with the development of security for children. When limits are set, there should be no doubt in the child's mind as to what is appropriate and what is inappropriate, or what is acceptable and what is unacceptable. Limits that are fuzzy or unclear interfere with the child's ability to accept responsibility and to act responsibly. Therefore, a therapist's statement, "You can't put very much paint on the wall," would be inappropriate. Such a statement is not explicit and is certainly unclear, especially to children who perceive themselves as always doing only a "little bit" of anything.

The therapist may not always be able to follow these steps in sequence. The urgency of the situation—the child is about to throw the truck at the window—may necessitate stating the limit first, "The window is not for hitting," and then reflect, "You want to throw the truck at the window." In this example, no feelings are evident, so the child's desire is reflected.

Step 3: Target Acceptable Alternatives

The child may not be aware of any other way to express what she is feeling. At that moment, the child can only think of one way to express herself. At this step in the process of limit setting, the therapist provides alternatives to the child for the expression of the action. This can involve pointing out a variety of different alternatives to the child. A more durable or appropriate object may need to be selected for the expression: "The dollhouse is not for standing on. The chair or the table is for standing on."

A different surface may be needed to paint on: "The wall is not for painting on. The easel paper or the block of wood is for painting on." A substitute may need to be selected to replace the therapist as the recipient of aggressive behavior: "Ellen, I'm not for hitting. The Bobo is for hitting." A nonverbal cue, pointing toward the alternative(s), in conjunction with the verbalized alternatives is especially helpful in diverting a child's attention from the original source of focus and facilitating the process of choice making. Using the child's name helps to get the child's attention.

When limit setting is needed, the therapist can remember to **ACT** in instituting the steps in the process sequence.

A—Acknowledge the child's feelings, wishes, and wants.
C—Communicate the limit.
T—Target acceptable alternatives.

In keeping with the focus of child-centered play therapy, it is more therapeutic and facilitative to the developing relationship for the therapist to *act* rather than *react* in response to behaviors requiring a limit. The following interaction shows how the steps are applied when 6-year-old Robert is just as angry as he can be at the play therapist, picks up the dart gun, and glares at the therapist as he begins to load the dart gun:

Therapist: You're really angry at me.
Robert: Yes! And I'm going to shoot you good!
Therapist: You are just so angry at me you would like to shoot me. (Robert now has the gun loaded and begins to take aim at the therapist.) But I'm not for shooting. (Robert interrupts before the therapist can go on with the limit.)
Robert: You can't stop me. Nobody can! (He points the gun at the therapist.)
Therapist: You're so powerful no one can stop you. But I'm not for shooting. You can pretend the Bobo is me (therapist points toward the Bobo) and shoot the Bobo.
Robert: (Swings the gun around, takes aim at the Bobo, and yells.) Take that! (He shoots the Bobo.)

The important consideration here is that the feeling is expressed and the child has assumed responsibility for both feelings and controlling behavior (Figure 11.1). This is a significant step in the therapeutic process of learning self-control and self-direction, and that feelings are acceptable. Limits allow the child to express negative feelings without causing harm, and the subsequent fear of retaliation.

FIGURE 11.1 The ACT model of limit setting facilitates development of self-control and self-responsibility.

At this point some of you who are reading this book are thinking, "Yes, Garry, but what if the child does shoot you?" I believe the child will not shoot me. I believe the child will bring himself under control. The important therapeutic dimension here is an attitude and belief in the child. Have I ever been shot by a dart gun? Yes, many times, but I still believe the child will not shoot me again. The child's behavior does not cause me to change my belief in the child. I still believe the child is capable of bringing himself under control and deciding not to shoot me. How can a child believe in himself if no one believes in him. This attitudinal belief in the child is unwavering and is central to the child-centered play therapy theory and approach.

When Limits Are Broken

A broken limit can mean anything from mild testing behavior to a battle of wills. Breaking limits often is a cry for help from a child with low self-esteem who really does want the security of knowing definite boundaries do exist. Therefore, at this time perhaps more than at any other time, the child needs understanding and acceptance. The therapist should stay right with the child with reflection of feelings and desires while stating with firmness the established limit. Debates and lengthy explanations should be avoided. Threatening the child with what may happen if a limit is broken is never acceptable. Limits are never used as a way to punish a child. This is a time for exercising patience, calmness, and firmness. Even though the limit has been broken, the therapist is still accepting of the child.

When a child is reluctant to abide by the limit and pushes the boundary, the therapist does not threaten the child or extend a consequence to the next session, as seen in the case of Eric, who continued to play in the sandbox after the therapist stated for the fourth time that time was up in the session. The therapist's statement, "If you choose to continue to play, you choose to have less time in the playroom next week," was inappropriate. Choices and consequences apply only to the current session. Next week Eric will be at a different place in his life. **Each session should be an opportunity for a new beginning for a child.**

When a child persists in expressing or pursuing the original behavior and continues to break an established limit, verbalizing an additional step to the limit-setting sequence may be necessary. Before explaining this step, a caution is in order. Too often therapists become overly involved in trying to force the acceptance of the limit and move much too quickly to implement this final step. **Patience is the rule of the day.** In most instances, the first three steps should be gone through in sequence at least three times before verbalizing the final step. This final step should rarely be used.

Step 4: State Final Choice

After going through **ACT** a minimum of three times, often more, an ultimate limit or final choice is presented to the child. The therapist either indicates the child can choose by his behavior to have the item placed off-limits for the rest of the session or in very rare instances presents leaving the room as the ultimate choice. (Let me hasten to point out that leaving the playroom should only be used as an absolutely last resort. This option is so rarely appropriate that perhaps I shouldn't even have mentioned it.) Leaving the playroom is not needed as an option in response to playing with a toy inappropriately unless the child is painting on a wall, banging on the two-way mirror, or similar destructive behavior. The therapist's selection of which final condition to present will depend on the situation, the child, and the therapist's tolerance. Leaving the playroom should not be presented as a choice to a child who is manipulative and already wants to leave.

This fourth step must be carefully stated so the child clearly understands he has a choice and that whatever happens will be the result of his choice. *"If you* **choose** *to shoot me again, you* **choose** *not to play with the gun anymore today. If you* **choose** *not to shoot me, you* **choose** *to get to play with the gun for the rest of our time in the playroom today."* Notice the word "choose" was used four times. This statement makes it very clear the choice/responsibility and positive or negative consequences reside with the child. Limits presented in this manner are neither punishment nor rejection of the child. If the child shoots the therapist one more time, the child has clearly indicated by action the choice to stop playing with the gun. The child has chosen not to play with the dart gun. The choice does not belong to the therapist. Therefore, the child is not rejected.

If the child chooses to shoot the therapist, the therapist calmly responds, "I see you have chosen not to play with the gun for the rest of our time together in the playroom. You can choose to put the gun on the table beside me or on the shelf over there (pointing)." At this point some children will begin a bargaining process. "I promise I won't shoot you anymore. Please let me play with the gun some more." This approach to limit setting is a learning experience and children learn what the process of choice making and accompanying results feel like. Therefore, **once a child has made a choice, the therapist does not under any circumstances undo a child's choice.** The therapist follows through to see that the child's choice is carried out if the child continues to play with the gun. This does not mean the therapist leaps out of his chair and wrestles the child for the gun. This is a time for persistent patience with the process and understanding of the child's desire while continuing to verbalize, "You would really like to continue to play with the gun, but when you chose to shoot me again, you chose not to play with the gun for the rest of our time in the playroom." This response may need to be repeated several times, always with caring and understanding, and the therapist may begin to think "I sound like a broken recorder" but the message eventually gets through to the child.

Other considerations are that every possible effort should be made to protect the child and therapist from harm or to keep valuable property from being broken. The therapist would not stay seated and go through the limit-setting steps two or three times while the child banged on the observation mirror with a truck. The shattered glass could severely injure the child. In this case, after presenting *ACT* once, the ultimate limit is presented when the child hits the mirror a second time. "If you choose to hit the mirror with the truck again, you choose to leave the playroom for today. If you choose not to hit the mirror again with the truck, you choose to get to stay in the playroom for the rest of our time today.

The therapist could tolerate being shot with the vinyl dart while going through the limit-setting sequence three times in order to give the child an opportunity to assume responsibility for herself and to limit her own behavior. Assumption of responsibility for self is a major objective, and the opportunity to exercise that responsibility may be more important than the therapist being shot one more time with a dart—but it is not more important than the possibility of personal injury.

Tentativeness in Limit Setting

When setting limits, the therapist should be matter-of-fact and speak with sureness and conviction that come from having already determined what limits are needed. The following examples are from supervision experiences with play therapists who were being tentative:

Child: (Starting to leave the room with 30 minutes left in the session.)

Therapist: Let's stay in here for the rest of the time rather than going in and out, okay? (The therapist sounds unsure and asks for the child's agreement.)

Suggested: Jason, our time in the playroom is not up for today. We have 30 more minutes, and then you can leave. (Sets a definite limit and indicates when the child will get to leave.)

• • •

Child: I want to go out there. (Points to the offices.)

Therapist: Let's wait a little longer before we leave. (Attempts to coax the child into staying, hoping the child will forget she wants to leave.)

Suggested: You want to go out where the other people are, but our time in the playroom is not finished for 10 more minutes; then you can go out there. (Shows understanding of what the child wants, sets a firm limit, and communicates what can be done later.)

• • •

Child: Can I put water in here? (Holds up the gun.)

Therapist: You would like to put water in there, but we won't do that now. (Does not set a definite limit, indicates there is the possibility of putting water in the gun later. Inclusion of "we" implies the therapist will assist in putting water in the gun.)

Suggested: You would like to put water in that, but that's not for putting water into. The pan is for putting water in. (Acknowledges the child's want, sets a firm limit, and communicates an acceptable alternative.)

• • •

Child: I think I'll throw this truck right through that window.

Therapist: Could you maybe do something else with it? (Implies that the original plan is acceptable if the child can't think of anything else.)

Suggested: You would like to throw that truck at the window, but the window is not for throwing at. The truck is for playing with on the floor. (Recognizes the child's want, sets a firm limit, and states an acceptable use of the truck.)

Situational Limits

Taking Toys or Materials From the Playroom

This experience can really tug at the therapist's emotions when a child begs ever so pitifully, "Can I please just take this little car home to play with? I don't have any cars to play with, and this is my most special one." The therapist's first reaction may be, "Sure, why not? There are lots of other toys here and even another one just like that one." There are *four basic reasons for not allowing toys to be taken home. First,* play therapy is based on an emotional relationship, and **what the child takes away internally is more significant than what is carried away externally.** In far too many homes, children have been taught by parental behavior that material sharing is more important than emotional sharing. Gifts are given as substitutes for the sharing of self, and children have learned, inappropriately, that tangible items express a relationship.

Second, equally important is the fact of budgetary considerations. Most playrooms operate on very limited budgets. A *third factor* involves consideration for other children, and the basic rationale for selecting the toys and materials in the first place: Toys are the child's words, and play is the child's language. Toys are the child's means for self-expression. Allowing toys to be removed from the playroom can interfere with other children's freedom of expression. Therefore, toys also should not be taken to the waiting room by other staff members for babysitting purposes. The fact that other children use the playroom should not be mentioned as in the case of a therapist who stated, "Toys are for staying in the playroom because other children use the toys." At that moment the child probably does not care about the other children. Also, the focus now is on other children. The child's internalized message may be, "Other children are more important than I am." A *fourth factor* is the issue of what to do if the child is allowed to take a toy home and does not bring it back. The therapist would then be placed in a different role of trying to get the toy back.

To a child's request to take a toy home, the therapist could respond, "Having that car to play with at home would be fun, but the toys are for staying in the playroom so they will be here when you come back next time." This response generalizes to all the toys, thus preventing the necessity for restating the limit on the next 10 items the child wants to take home, and shows great respect for the child with, "so they will be here when you come back next time."

If a child wants to show a parent a special item in the playroom, the child can invite the parent to the playroom to see the item after the session is concluded. Children are allowed to take their paintings home, but the therapist does not suggest they do so. If the therapist wants a record of the child's paintings, he could ask the child's permission to keep the painting until the next session and during the intervening time take a picture of the painting.

Therapists have reported that some children seem to paint pictures just to take home as gifts to parents and siblings. In these cases, the therapists felt little, if any, exploration or self-expression was evident in the activity, so they requested the child leave all paintings until the last session and then take them all home. Fewer paintings were produced after the limit was set, which seemed to confirm the therapists' hypothesis. Limits may or may not need to be set on taking home items created with the playdough, depending on the budget. Most play therapists will probably need to set a limit with the playdough, and that can be perfectly acceptable.

Leaving the Playroom

Allowing a child to go in and out of the playroom at random during the session is not advisable, because that severely restricts the development of the relationship and prevents follow through and completion of some interactions, especially when a limit has been set or the child has just expressed some angry or frightening feelings. *Children need to learn that they cannot run away from the responsibility of seeing things through, that commitment to a relationship means staying and working things out.* Allowing children to leave the room and return at will can turn the experience into little more than a game. The therapist may want to inform some children that, if they choose to leave, they choose not to come back to the playroom for that day.

In most cases, the preferable procedure is not to allow children to leave the playroom until the scheduled time is up, except to get a drink or to go to the bathroom. Usually a rule of one trip out for a drink and one trip out to the bathroom is sufficient. However, this cannot be adhered to rigidly because some children may genuinely need to go to the bathroom more than once, as many inexperienced therapists have discovered when a puddle suddenly appeared on the floor—and then the child felt awkward and embarrassed. To help avoid this problem, *parents can be given the responsibility of taking the child to the bathroom prior to each session.* Two of the playrooms in our Center for Play Therapy have a small bathroom that opens into the playrooms, thus eliminating these problems.

The following interaction in the playroom illustrates the process of setting limits about leaving the playroom:

Kathleen: I don't like any of your stuff in here. I'm leaving. (Moves quickly toward door.)

Therapist: Kathleen, our time is not up in the playroom. You just don't like anything here and want to leave, but our time is not up. (Therapist glances at his watch.) We have 15 more minutes, and then it will be time to leave.

As pointed out earlier, the therapist uses "our" and "we" because the therapist and the child are both a part of the relationship, and both will be leaving the room. Adding the last part of the statement, "and then it will be time to leave," conveys to the child that she will eventually get to leave. Otherwise the child, especially a very young child, may be afraid she will never get to leave, and "Mommy and Daddy will never see me again."

Time Limits

A 45-minute session is sufficient, and the 15 minutes between sessions often is needed to get the room ready on time for the next child. In some settings, such as elementary schools or women's shelters, where the counselor is burdened with huge case loads, 30-minute sessions may be quite sufficient. Whatever time span has been communicated to the child should be adhered to. The therapist should remind the child when 5 minutes are left in the session. Young children, who do not have a clear concept of time, and children who are completely immersed in their play may need an additional 1-minute time "caution."

These reminders help children to get ready to end the experience and give them an opportunity to complete the task at hand or to move quickly to something else they had planned to do. This latter behavior is typical of many children and speaks of their planning ahead in their play, or even before they come to the session, as shown in Paul's comment, "I was gonna play with that truck before I came, right?" Another possible explanation for children moving quickly to some other play activity is that they know they will soon leave the playroom and so feel safe to engage in play activities that touch more directly on their basic difficulties. This process is not unlike what is experienced with adults who sometimes wait until the last few minutes of a therapy session to discuss significant problems.

The objective is not to get the child out of the room but, rather, to provide the child with an opportunity to assume responsibility for leaving the room. Therefore, the therapist's patience and understanding are continued with the ending of the session. The therapist experiences no feeling of being rushed to get the child out of the room. When the therapist announces, "Our time is up for today. It's time to go to the waiting room where your mother is," the therapist stands up to give a visual cue and respects the child's need to finish a task by waiting the necessary few seconds or minute. The attitude of returning responsibility to the child is continued by allowing the child to precede the therapist out the door.

Limiting Noise

Generally all noise in a playroom is acceptable. Children may yell, scream, bang the blocks of wood together as loud as they wish and as long as they want. Noise level may have to be limited in some clinics and schools, however, where people and activities in adjoining rooms and offices will be interrupted. This is certainly situational and, although not desirable to have to do so, is necessitated by practicality. Noise level in play therapy can be a major problem in elementary schools, because the counselor's office is usually located near the administrative offices. In that case, limiting the noise level would be far better than to have an administrator prohibit the use of play therapy.

Personal Items Are Not for Playing

Prohibiting a child's play with the therapist's watch, glasses, appointment book in a shirt pocket, and other personal possessions will significantly increase the therapist's comfort level and acceptance of the child. Allowing a child to try on and wear the therapist's glasses can lead to disaster and feelings of anger and rejection toward the child. A simple "My glasses are for me to wear" is sufficient. If the child persists, the therapist can add, "My glasses are not for playing with."

In situations where a camcorder is taken into the playroom to record the session, the camcorder should be placed near the therapist's chair in an inconspicuous place and turned on prior to bringing the child into the room. This will avoid calling attention to the recorder. If the child begins to play with the recorder, the therapist can say, "The recorder is not one of the toys for playing with."

Limiting Water in the Sandbox

Children delight in pouring water into the sandbox and can get caught up in pouring bucket after bucket of water until the sand is soupy. Even though the therapist may be comfortable with soupy sand, several points may need to be considered. The next child in the playroom may have been planning to play in the sandbox but does not because the sand is too wet, thus limiting the second child's expression. Soupy sand may take days to dry out and, if the sandbox is made of wood, will quickly rot the bottom. It seems best to limit the amount of water to a specific number of containers rather than trying to limit a certain volume of water. "James, the rule is three containers of water in the sandbox," should be stated as the child heads back to the sink for the fourth pan full of water. This rule is adhered to regardless of the size of container chosen by the child, thus avoiding arguments about the amount of water.

Urinating in the Playroom

Allowing a child to urinate in the sandbox or on the playroom floor is highly questionable and shows little regard for other children who will play in the sandbox, unless the therapist plans to empty the sandbox each time and put in fresh sand. Children need to learn to control such acting-out behaviors. Likewise, children should not be allowed to urinate in the nursing bottle and then drink the urine.

Beginning Play Therapists' Reactions to Setting Limits

Joanna

I was very apprehensive about being able to handle unexpected situations in the playroom. In the first play therapy session, the child put his hand on the door knob as if to open the door and leave. I surprised myself by responding, "I know you would like to go now, but our time is not up." I did not become overanxious as I expected. In the second session, the child obviously did not want to leave the playroom at the end of the time. I was able to remain patient and calm and to follow through in getting the child to leave. In both instances the children followed my expectations without direct instruction.

Carmen

When Laura ran for the tape recorder, I overreacted. Instead of stating a limit and allowing her to decide, I pulled her hand away. However, in another session, when Sarah saw the microphone, I did not touch her. I simply said it was a microphone and not a toy. She accepted this easily. I guess I learned more from Laura and Sarah than I could have learned from a book or journal article.

Reference

Moustakas, C. (1959). *Psychotherapy with children: The living relationship.* New York: Harper & Row.

Chapter **12**

Typical Problems in Play Therapy and What to Do If...

The relationship with a child in the playroom is always new, creative, exciting, and different with each child. Therefore, predicting what an individual child will do in a given session is not possible. Trying to anticipate some of the things children might do and formulating a response ahead of time can be helpful, however, to the inexperienced therapist. Knowing how to respond when confronted with an unexpected occurrence can help the therapist to remain calm and accepting of the child. Planning what needs to be done and how to respond ahead of time should not diminish the therapist's creative and spontaneous use of self. No matter how often certain responses, verbal and otherwise, are used, they should never become perfunctory or routine. The therapist should always be responding with compassion, understanding, and the utmost concern for the child's feelings. With that in mind, the following common problems in the playroom and possible responses are presented for the therapist to consider.

What to Do If the Child Is Silent

The silent child presents an interesting paradox for the therapist and a perplexing problem. The therapist uses play therapy because of the belief that children communicate through play, and yet when confronted with a child who is verbally silent, may experience thoughts and feelings that the child should talk. Therapists who feel awkward with children's silence or secretly wish children would talk should examine their own value systems, expectations of children, and their willingness to allow children to be children.

Is there ever a time when a child is not communicating? Must a child verbalize for communication to occur? Whose needs are being met by trying to get a child to talk? An honest answer to this last question requires courage on the part of the therapist to look deep within herself. Does the child need to talk to complete what the child wants to accomplish? How accepting is the therapist who wants the child to talk? A reasonable assumption is that a therapist who feels uncomfortable with a child's silence is not very accepting of the child. Children are remarkably sensitive to these inner feelings and attitudes of the therapist, and often resist being verbal because they sense being nonverbal is unacceptable to the therapist, and so they feel rejected. Acceptance means accepting the child as she is—being silent. Acceptance that is contingent on the child's talking is not acceptance. *Acceptance is not conditional—there is no "if."*

In play therapy, the child is continually sending messages, whether they are verbalized or not (Figure 12.1). Therefore, the therapist must maintain an attitude of responsiveness that communicates verbally and nonverbally acceptance of the child's silence. The therapist must listen carefully to the child, whether the child speaks or not. The key to establishing contact with the silent child is to respond verbally to what the child is doing at the moment or to what is sensed within the child at the moment. *A responsive attitude is not dependent on the child talking.* The facilitative quality of this kind of responsiveness can be seen in the following interaction with a child who was verbally silent:

FIGURE 12.1 In the playroom, children can recreate scenes they have experienced, and words are not necessary for communication to occur.

Michael:	(Sat in sandbox methodically spooning sand on his shoes.)
Therapist:	You're putting lots of sand right on top of your shoes.
Michael:	(No response, does not even look up; continues to spoon sand and concentrates on completely covering one shoe.)
Therapist:	There, you got that one completely covered up. That one can't be seen.
Michael:	(Shifts activity to carefully spooning sand on top of his left hand, which is resting on the side of the sandbox. Spills a little sand on the floor and glances at the therapist.)
Therapist:	Looks like you are wondering what I might think about your spilling sand on the floor. Sometimes accidents happen in here.

Michael: (Returns to covering his other shoe with sand; completes the task.)

Therapist: Now they are both covered up and can't be seen.

Michael: (Whispers.) Nobody likes them, so they are hiding.

Michael had been referred for play therapy because he was an isolate on the playground and seemed to have no friends in his second grade. Other children did not seek him out in the classroom.

As this episode demonstrates, the therapist proceeds at the child's pace, allowing the child to continue to provide direction for the interaction. Patience is the rule of the day. The therapist must be careful to avoid trying to respond to every single thing the child does. That can be very irritating to the child and can also result in the child feeling self-conscious. The therapist needs to avoid any behavior that might result in any pressure for the child to talk. After enduring a long silence, the uncomfortable therapist might ask, "Do you know why you are here?" in a not-so-subtle attempt to get the child to say something. Also, the question implies the child has problems and needs to get on with the business of working on those problems. Such efforts only serve to alienate the child.

What to Do If the Child Wants to Bring Toys or Food Into the Playroom

Sometimes children bring a favorite toy or doll with them to the first session, and this may indicate the presence of some anxiety. Therefore, the child's desire to take a special doll to the playroom would be recognized and accepted. If the child cradles a special truck under one arm and accompanies the therapist down the hall toward the playroom, this would be permissible and could be used as a point of contact with the child as they walk down the hall. "Robert, I see you brought something with you to take to the playroom. That must be a special toy. It's all green with big black wheels." This response accepts the child's desire to take the truck to the playroom, implies permission, recognizes the importance of the truck, and shows appreciation or prizing of the truck.

Does this mean that all items that are special to children are allowed in the playroom? Absolutely not. **The general rule is to allow only those items that approximate what would normally be selected for the playroom.** Remote-control toys, mechanical toys, wind-up and watch games, cassette players with headsets, glass items, and the like do not facilitate interaction with children or children's expressions, and therefore would not be allowed. Favorite books also are not allowed in the playroom because defensive, cautions ("shy"), or withdrawn children can retreat into the book and spend the entire time avoiding interacting with the new environment or the therapist. Books seldom facilitate building a relationship with a child in the playroom.

Children may come to the waiting room munching on all sorts of snacks. Excluding food from the playroom is generally best, because of the distraction precipitated by eating. Munching on chips is not conducive to involved or intensive play and also presents problems when children offer the therapist some of the food. If the therapist does not take a drink of the child's soda, will the child feel rejected? Allowing food in the playroom usually results in the child later insisting that the therapist go get drinks or snacks. If the child shows up with a half-eaten ice cream bar, the therapist can show compassion and understanding by allowing the child to finish eating before going to the playroom. The same suggestion does not apply to waiting for a child to drink all 12 ounces of a can of soda. Have you ever watched a 4-year-old drink a can of soda? That can take hours!

In responding to a forbidden item, the therapist should be sensitive to the child's feelings. "I know you would like to take that game with you to the playroom, but it is for staying here in the waiting room. It will be here when you come back from the playroom." The therapist is then responsible for helping the child to remember 45 minutes later that the item is in the waiting room. Likewise, children are prone to forget they brought a special item into the playroom; so the therapist will need to remember at the end of the session.

What to Do If the Child Is Overly Dependent

Many children who are referred for play therapy have learned to depend on adults for getting their needs met. Parents and caregivers are notorious for doing things for children, thus fostering dependency and affecting children's feelings of competence and responsibility. *The objective of the therapist is to return responsibility to children and to facilitate their self-reliance.* Some children deluge the therapist with requests for help or insistence that the therapist make a decision for them. Children are quite capable of making decisions for themselves in the playroom and can only discover that strength by being allowed to struggle with making decisions. Children must be allowed to struggle with making decisions. Children also must be allowed to struggle with doing things for themselves.

The therapist is not the child's servant to run and fetch items for the child, or dress the child, or open containers the child can easily open, or choose colors, or decide what picture the child should paint, or decide what the child should play with first. Such behaviors only perpetuate the child's dependency and confirm an already existing perception of self as being inadequate and incapable. The therapist's responses should convey confidence in the child and return responsibility to the child.

The following examples are comments made by children and the therapist's response returning responsibility:

Robert: Go get those scissors for me.
Therapist: You would like to have the scissors. If you want the scissors, you can get them.

• • •

Melanie: When I play, do you want me to put the toys back where they are or just leave them out?
Therapist: That's something you can decide.

• • •

Will: Is this a cat or a tiger?
Therapist: It can be whatever you want it to be.

• • •

Judy: What do you want me to play?
Therapist: In here, you can decide what you want to play.

• • •

Riverto: (without attempting) Will you stack these blocks up for me?
Therapist: That's something you can do.

These responses clearly convey the parameters of the relationship and return responsibility for action and direction to the children, who now must struggle with the process of self-discovery. If children are not allowed to struggle with doing things for themselves, how can they discover their worth? If no one believes in them enough to allow them to set their own direction, how can they ever believe in themselves?

What to Do If the Child Persists in Seeking Praise

As in all interactions with children, when confronted with a child who persists in wanting the therapist's evaluation or judgment, the therapist should be sensitive to the child's feelings and perception of self. Is the child's persistent demand to know if the therapist likes the child's picture an indication of insecurity and poor self-esteem, or a need to control the interaction? Dealing with a child who angrily demands a specific answer can severely test the therapist's feelings of adequacy and acceptance of the child.

When confronted with, "Just tell me. I want to know. Do you think my picture is pretty or not?" the therapist may have a tremendous temptation to stall by giving the question back to the child in order to buy time to think of a good response. A faltering, "You're wondering if I think your picture is pretty," has little or no facilitative value in such situations and usually only frustrates or confuses the child, who is left to wonder if he is being understood and so insists all the more for an answer. Children also will sense the therapist's hesitating, tentative quality and try even harder to force a direct answer. Although it might seem to be a simple matter of just giving the child an answer, such as "I think your picture is very pretty," praise directs children's behavior, restricts their freedom, creates dependency, and fosters external motivation.

In child-centered play therapy the objective is to free children to evaluate their own behavior, to appreciate their own creative beauty, and to develop an internal system of reward and satisfaction. Praise does not contribute to the development of a therapeutic relationship and usually indicates the therapist is not in touch with the inner dynamics of the child, due to the therapist's need to have the child feel good. In this situation, the therapist's response should either clarify the relationship in the playroom or facilitate the child's prizing of the picture, as in the following excerpt:

Martin: (Shows the therapist a picture he has painted.) Do you think my picture of a house is pretty?

Therapist: (Pointing to the picture.) You painted a red house right there, and hmmm (thoughtfully studying the picture), you put three windows right there (pointing to the windows) and, oh, you made this whole top blue all the way across here. And I see you painted a whole bunch of orange in this corner. (Said with genuine interest and a real prizing shown in tone of voice.)

When the child's productions are responded to in this nonevaluative, careful attention to detail, esteeming manner, the child tends to forget the original question asked and begins to study her work, getting caught up in noticing what the therapist notices, and feeling good about what has been produced. Often the child will take over the therapist's role of prizing and will begin to make comments like, "And up here I painted a big yellow sun, and these birds right here were kinda hard to make," to which the therapist could respond, "Yes, I see that big yellow sun, and those do look like birds alright. They were hard to make, but you made them." The child is now free to evaluate and appreciate her own work. When the therapist judges or evaluates something the child has done or created and pronounces it pretty or makes some other praise response, the therapist also communicates that he has the power to judge something to be ugly or negative. Therefore, evaluative responses are avoided.

Some children will persist in their demand for the therapist to say whether or not the picture is pretty. When this occurs, the therapist can clarify the relationship in the playroom by saying, "In here the important thing is not whether or not I think your picture is pretty, but what you think about your picture." This response is too long for some children, and the therapist may want to say, "What is important is what you think about your picture." The child is now free to say whether or not she thinks the picture is pretty. Evaluation belongs to the child. Therefore, the therapist returns the power of judgment back to the child.

Although the above example deals with cognitive evaluation, the same approach is used when feelings about a picture or some other object are the focus:

Jimmy: See what I am doing?

Therapist: You are playing with the clay.

Jimmy: What should I make?

Therapist: You may choose to make whatever you wish.

Jimmy: All right. I'll make a hippopotamus.

Therapist: You have decided to make a hippopotamus.

Jimmy: (Shapes the clay with much care and holds up a form that somewhat resembles an animal.) What is it? Do you like it?

Therapist: You worked hard on that. It can be whatever you want it to be. (Said because once into the actual construction or shaping of an object, children sometimes change their mind about what they have created.)

Jimmy: But do you like it? ... Do you think it is good?

Therapist: What is important is how you feel about it.

What to Do If the Child Says You Talk Weird

That the therapist does not ask questions, offer suggestions, or tell what to do may seem strange to a child. In some ways, the therapist may sound to the child as though the therapist is speaking a foreign language, because the child is not accustomed to hearing her expressed thoughts and feelings verbalized by anyone. At other times, when a child says, "You talk funny," she may be referring to the fact that the therapist's responses or manner of responding do not sound natural. Often a stilted or rote quality is evident, and the interaction doesn't sound at all like a conversation.

When the therapist merely parrots the child's words or verbally tracks the child's play activity in a perfunctory, reporting way, the child has good reason to take notice and to be irritated. He may feel the therapist is just telling, reporting what is being done, which is an insult because the child already knows what is being done. The objective is to be with the child and to convey understanding, not to report what is seen or heard. "Now the car is on top of the table" and "You put that car—just—as—close—to the edge as you could get it" convey entirely different messages. The first response is objective, takes note of the facts; the other communicates a feeling of *being with.*

A statement of "You talk strange" should be accepted and could be responded to with, "Oh, so I sound different than other people to you." Or the therapist could respond with an explanation: "I'm just trying to let you know I'm interested in you and what you are doing. I guess maybe what I say does sound different." Sometimes the statement, "You talk weird," is the child's negative "put down" of the therapist or an expression of resistance; then it could be responded to with, "You don't like the way I talk," or "Sounds like you might want me to stop talking." How to respond would depend on the child's meaning, as sensed by the therapist.

What to Do If the Child Wants the Therapist to Play a Guessing Game

"Guess what I'm going to do," or "What do you think this is?" are frequently asked questions by children in play therapy. The tendency of many therapists when faced with these requests or questions is to become involved in a game of guessing, and in the process the therapist restricts children's freedom and assumes responsibility for direction. "Guess what I'm going to do" may not be a request but, rather, an excited child's way of including the therapist in the activity, with no expectation for an answer. "What do you think this is?" may indeed be a request for the therapist to identify an object or a painting by the child. Even so, what are the potential consequences of engaging in a game of guessing with a child who has a poor self-concept, is dependent, or has a strong need to please? The child may well take the therapist's guess to mean that is what the picture should be or that is what is expected next, and as a result change the original intent.

If the therapist guesses the picture is a tree and the child intended it to be a nuclear explosion, the child may think the therapist's message is that drawings of people being blown up are not acceptable. After the therapist has made an identification, the child may have difficulty changing the content of the picture or continuing the play activity because he may feel that doing so would be going against the therapist, and that the therapist would not like him.

Play therapy is not a time to get caught up in guessing games. This is a time when the therapist must be consistent in intent, attitude, acceptance, objective, and approach. The child is responsible and capable, and that message must be clearly communicated in all interactions. Therefore, when the child says, "Guess what I'm going to do next," an understanding and freeing response would be, "You have something in mind," or "You have something planned." We can assume that if a child says, "Guess what I'm going to do next," the child must have something in mind to do. If the child asks, "What do you think this is?" the therapist could respond simply, "You can tell me." Responsibility for leading is then returned to the child.

What to Do If the Child Asks for Expressions of Affection

Some children in play therapy may have experienced very little direct expression of affection and often are emotionally needy. They may be unsure of just where they stand in the relationship and may need reassurance that the therapist does indeed care for them. When a child asks, "Do you like me?" is no time to reflect with, "You're wondering if I like you." Yes, that is exactly what the child is wondering and is exactly what was asked. Therefore, telling the child what was just asked is not necessary. This is a time for sharing on the part of the therapist in the developing of a personal relationship. In the following interaction, the therapist avoided the child's emotional need and the child quickly changed the focus of the interaction. This was 8-year-old Frank's sixth session:

Frank: (Sitting in the sandbox.) I want to tell you something but ... (Sits silently for a moment, sifting sand through his fingers.)

Therapist: You have something to tell me, but you're not sure if you want to say it.

Frank: Yeah. It might hurt your feelings, and you might cry. (Buries his fingers in the sand and looks down.)

Therapist: You don't want to hurt my feelings.

Frank: Yeah, and ... (Avoids eye contact and digs his hands deeper into the sand; sits silently for a time then glances at the therapist.) It's about your children.

Therapist: So it's something about my children.

Frank: Yeah, and ... Well ... (then quickly, breathlessly) It's ... do you love me?

Therapist: You're wondering how I feel about you.

Frank: Yeah ... well, do you?

Therapist: It's important to you to know how I feel about you, if I love you or not.

Frank: (Continues to sit in the sand, eyes averted, hands deep in the sand, his fingers touch something.) Hey, what's this? (Pulls a toy soldier out of the sand.)

This emotional moment with Frank is lost for now. The opportunity to respond to his emotional needs will probably come up again, because such issues are so important to children. But this particular moment is gone forever.

The therapist always hopes that her genuine caring for and prizing of the child will be received and felt by the child. Some children, though, may need more concrete verification and may ask, "Do you like me?" At such moments, the therapist needs to be very warm, caring, and personally responsive, because the child's feelings of self-esteem are vulnerable. If the therapist really does care for and values the child, expressing that would be appropriate. In our society, the words "like" and "love" are tossed around like confetti, often with little meaning or significance. Therefore, in responding to the child, the therapist may want to convey her feelings with, "You are special to me, and this is a special time together." The same response would be appropriate if the child asked, "Do you love me?"

What to Do If the Child Wants to Hug or Sit in the Therapist's Lap

Requests for hugs, to sit in the therapist's lap, and so on should be responded to with caution about the underlying motive. Of course if the child hugged the therapist, it would be inappropriate for the therapist to sit there rigid as a board. The therapist would want to return the hug, but there is a need to be cautious. Is this a sexually abused child? Has the child been taught that if you like or love someone you will show the person sexually? Does liking to the child mean seductive behavior expressed by touching, fondling, and rubbing? What if a girl suddenly hops into the male therapist's lap and begins to wriggle playfully? Surely the therapist would be aware of the possibilities of such behavior and would respond accordingly with, "I know that's fun for you, but I know you like me without your sitting on my lap," as he gently lifts the child off his lap.

For some children, the most natural thing is to lean against the therapist's leg as they take in scenes in the playroom. They are comfortable, and this is an unconscious behavior. They are just being spontaneous and free. If the therapist reached out and hugged the child, then one could ask whose needs are being met. The therapist would then be taking over the direction of the relationship and the session.

Another child might get the nursing bottle, begin sucking on it, crawl into the therapist's lap, and want to be held like a baby. The therapist's own comfort level here may best determine the appropriate response. If the therapist senses that this is an innocent request, no subtle underlying motive, simply a child acting out a sequence or reexperiencing feelings of being a baby, a natural response might be to hold the child for a few minutes. The therapist must be prepared, however, for additional requests to sing, rock, and change the baby's diaper. At some point, a limit may need to be set on the role the therapist is asked to play.

This situation can be an awkward time in the therapeutic process. If the therapist does not allow the child to crawl onto her lap, the child may feel rejected. Will cradling a child on her lap stimulate parental feelings of rocking her own children and thus interfere with the therapist's acceptance of the child's separateness?

Physical and sexual abuse have reached such epidemic proportions and have become such emotionally charged issues in our society that no longer can a clear suggestion be given as to the appropriate response, except to be very cautious. If in doubt about the child's needs or intent, perhaps a response could be, "I know you want to pretend to be a baby and suck on the bottle. You can do that in the baby bed there." This response is included here with much reservation, because it may be misunderstood. However, such a response also may be necessary in order for the therapist to maintain the conditions necessary for growth by the child. Just because cuddling a child feels natural for the therapist may not justify the behavior if the therapist has not carefully examined her own needs in this area. In most cases, cradling and rocking a child at the child's request would be very natural and appropriate. As a protection for the play therapist in such experiences, videotaping of sessions is highly recommended.

What to Do If the Child Tries to Steal a Toy

Justin is 5 years old, and this is his second time to be in the wonderful playroom. The playroom contains more toys than he has ever seen in any place, except where you buy them. He can't remember the last time his parents bought him a toy, but now here is all this neat stuff with no price tags. He pretends to play with the truck while he crams a small car into his pocket with the other hand, making sure the therapist cannot see what he is doing. But she does see the car being shoved into his pocket. Justin continues to play with the truck until the therapist announces time is up.

Now, what is the therapist to do? Wait for Justin to be honest and confess? Allow him to take the car, and hope he will bring it back? Use this as an opportunity to teach him about honesty? Not worry about the car because it cost less than a dollar anyway? None of the above! We must be concerned about the potential guilt Justin might feel after taking the car home. The value of the car is immaterial. The child's behavior and feelings are what we are concerned about, not the cost. The playroom is a place where values are learned by the child, not taught by the therapist.

Some inexperienced therapists might ask, "Justin, have you forgotten anything?" They might respond with, "Justin, can you think of one more thing you need to do before you leave today?" Some might ask, "Did you take the car?" Questioning of this nature presents a mixed message to Justin, because he senses by the insistence that the therapist knows, but the question implies that the therapist does not know. Could it be that in such cases the therapist is really being dishonest? This does seem to be the case. Questions about what is already known are seldom helpful.

RULE OF THUMB:

Don't ask questions when you already know the answer. Make statements.

This is a time to be straightforward, understanding, and firm.

Therapist: I know you would like to take the car with you, but the car in your pocket (points to pocket) stays here so it will be here for you to play with next time.

Justin: What car? I don't have any car. (Pats an empty pocket.)

Therapist: You would like to pretend you don't know where the car is, but the car in that pocket (points to pocket) stays in the playroom.

Justin: (Puts his hand into his pocket and retrieves the car.)

Questioning Justin about why he wanted to take the car, moralizing with, "You know you shouldn't take things that don't belong to you," or trying to get him to discuss related happenings by asking, "Wonder what happens when you take things at school?"

increases the intensity of the episode and the possibility of guilt feelings. These responses also take responsibility for leadership and direction away from the child and put the therapist in charge of deciding what is important. In addition, asking a child to verbally engage in insightful comparisons ignores the developmental reasons for placing children in play therapy. The child's play in play therapy is not merely preparation for the presumed more significant activity of verbal exploration.

What to Do If the Child Refuses to Leave the Playroom

Some children may express their resistance or need to test limits by refusing to leave the playroom at the end of the session. The child's reluctance to leave may be manipulation, to see how far the time limits and the patience of the therapist can be stretched. An indication of possible manipulation is that usually when the child is being manipulative, the child tends to observe the therapist's reactions. The child's facial expression lacks intensity and her body language indicates an incomplete and superficial involvement. Other children may want to stay longer because they are having so much fun. In this instance, the importance of the project to the child is conveyed in intensity and sincerity of facial expression as the child concentrates on the project. Regardless of the reason, sessions should not be prolonged. *A part of the therapeutic process for the child is developing enough self-control to stop, to say no to her own wishes or desires.* Therefore, the following procedure is recommended for ending a session with a child who is reluctant to leave.

Therapist: Our time in the playroom is up for today. (Therapist stands up.) It's time to go to the waiting room where your mother is.

Jessica: But I haven't played in the sandbox yet. (She runs over and begins to play in the sand.)

Therapist: You would like to stay longer to play in the sand, but Jessica, time is up for today. (Takes two steps toward door, while continuing to look at Jessica.)

Jessica:	(Big smile.) This is neat stuff. Can't I just stay a little longer? (Begins to pour sand through the funnel.)
Therapist:	(Takes two more steps toward the door.) That's really a lot of fun for you, but it's time to leave.
Jessica:	You don't like me. If you really liked me, you would let me stay. (Continues pouring sand.)
Therapist:	Oh, so you think if I liked you I would let you stay. I know you really want to stay longer, but it's time to leave the playroom. (Takes two more steps, reaches out and turns the doorknob, and pushes the door open a couple of inches.)
Jessica:	(Looks up and sees the therapist holding the door open.) I'm almost through. Just one more minute.
Therapist:	(Opens the door wider.) Jessica, I know you want to stay for as long as you decide, but time is up. (Takes a step through the door while looking expectantly at Jessica.)
Jessica:	(Slowly stands up, drops the funnel, and shuffles toward the open door.)

This episode took approximately 4 minutes, which can seem like 40 if the therapist gets caught up in the pressure of trying to make the child leave. Even if Jessica had taken 5 or 6 minutes to leave the room, the most important consideration is that she took herself out of the playroom even though she wanted to stay, and in the process her dignity as a person and her self-respect as an individual were not only preserved but enhanced.

What to Do If the Therapist Unexpectedly Cannot Keep an Appointment

Children deserve just as much consideration and courtesy as adults with respect to making, keeping, and informing about the canceling of appointments. Preferably the therapist would inform the child at the beginning of the session prior to the anticipated absence, followed by a reminder at the end of the session, with a clear statement that the child will get to come back to the playroom in 2 weeks or whenever the next regular appointment time would be. The anticipated coming absence should be mentioned at the beginning of the session so the child will not think the absence is some kind of punishment for something he just did in the playroom. A general statement about the reason for the absence, "I'm going to be in another town at a meeting," also helps the child to understand that the reason for the absence is not something he has done.

If an unexpected occurrence between sessions prevents the keeping of the next appointment, a postcard or telephone call informing the child about the absence would be a warm expression of the importance of the relationship. In those rare instances when an emergency prevents the keeping of an appointment, and notifying the child prior to the appointment time is not possible, the therapist could leave a personal phone message for the child or a printed note for the child to read or to be read to the child. **Concern for the child's feelings is always the rule of the day.**

Chapter **13**

Issues in Play Therapy

The therapeutic relationship in play therapy probably raises more questions about procedures and process than any other relationship in the helping professions. Although the therapist could not possibly anticipate all of the issues that may arise in the playroom, thinking through issues prior to beginning relationships with children can help the therapist to react with assurance so as not to confuse children by indecisiveness. The issues discussed here can provide a starting point for that kind of self-exploration. The therapist will need to ask the what and why of his positions on these issues.

Confidentiality

Very young children typically are not concerned about the issue of confidentiality, and yet they need to be informed that this is a safe, confidential time. Older children are more perceptive and socially aware, and thus are more likely to wonder who the therapist might tell and what the therapist might tell, as they have heard parents tell specifics of their behavior to friends and relatives. Caution must be exercised in how the child is informed, lest the child feel this is a secretive time and feel guilty about keeping it from her parents. This is an especially sensitive area when dealing with sexually abused children who have been emotionally seduced or frightened into secrecy. It should be sufficient to say to most children, "In this special time, what you say or do is private. I will not tell your parents or teacher or anyone unless it is necessary to keep you safe. If you want them to know what you do here, you can tell them. That will be fine. You can decide."

Children's artwork should not be displayed on the playroom wall or in the hallway, because this would be a violation of their privacy. A transcript of a counseling session with an adult would not be hung on the wall or displayed in the hallway. Children's artwork is their way of communicating and should not be shown to teachers or parents unless a child decides to do so. Displaying artwork can influence and structure the activities of other children who enter the playroom, see the artwork on the wall, and assume that is what they are supposed to do. Also, children invariably feel in competition with displayed artwork.

A general guideline when working with children in play therapy is never to reveal the specifics of what a child has said or done in the playroom unless permitted to do so by a professional code of ethics. A child's exact comments and specific play behavior are for the therapist's eyes and ears only and for professional colleagues who are in a consultative role. What, then, can be shared with parents? The therapist must use discretion in trying to assess just how parents will react to or use such information. Generally, when the issue of confidentiality is involved, the best procedure is to err on the side of caution. The therapist's impressions of the child and the behavior must be conveyed to the parent without violating the strict rules of confidentiality.

Showing understanding in the face of a parent's desire to know some confidential information can help to avoid the parent feeling "put off" and resentful or angry. Conveying only general information to parents without them feeling put off requires great skill by the therapist. **A general rule is to discuss general observations and avoid revealing specific behaviors,** as in the following interaction with a parent: "Chris seems to be angry. How is his anger expressed at home?" It would be inappropriate to say, "Chris is really angry. He spent 15 minutes beating on the Bobo so hard I thought he would break it."

Confidentiality is a difficult issue when working with children. The parents are, after all, legally responsible for the child, and they may genuinely want to know how they can be helpful. They also pay the bills for therapy and may feel they have a right to know what they are paying for and what is going on in the sessions. Where does the parent's right to know end and the child's right to privacy begin? This is a difficult question to answer, and the decision is always dependent on the parent's ability to use the information appropriately, the content of the information, the emotional vulnerability of the child, and the physical safety of all parties involved.

Children must always be protected from potential physical harm from themselves and others, as in the case of threatened suicide or a threat to run away. Parents must be informed, and the therapist will need to be well versed in taking parents through precautionary steps to help ensure children's safety when suicide is a possibility. As a part of the procedure, parents need to be cautioned to hide medications, weapons, kitchen agents for clogged drains, caustic cleaners, and so on.

Participation in Child's Play

Whether or not to participate in children's play is an important decision the therapist must make prior to the onset of therapy, and although it is largely a function of the therapist's personality, it should be based on a rationale consistent with the therapist's objectives. The child-centered play therapist is committed to a belief in the child's capacity for self-direction and avoids intrusion of her personality into the child's play. This is the child's special time to direct his own life, to make decisions, to play without unnecessary interference, to bring forth in play whatever is yearning to be expressed. The session belongs to the child, and the therapist's needs and directions are to be kept out. This is not a social time, and the child does not need a playmate. The therapist is there to help the child hear herself, see herself, understand herself, and be herself in the safety of an accepting relationship.

Although the child invites the therapist to play, the child may not particularly want a playmate. Some children feel obligated to

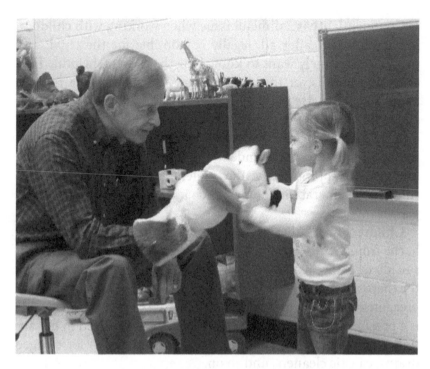

FIGURE 13.1 The therapist relies on the child for direction when participating in child's play, thus keeping the child in the lead.

invite the therapist to participate. The child may be asking for the therapist's participation because of a belief that doing so is what is expected or because the child wants to be liked by the therapist. An invitation to play could mean the child is looking for approval or for the security of having someone else determine the direction of the play (Figure 13.1). Such a request could be the child's way of testing the therapist's level of permissiveness.

The therapist must struggle with the question of what is the objective of participation and what will be accomplished. Is the real motivation to make contact with the child or to meet the therapist's need to be included? When faced with a nonverbal child who stands in the middle of the playroom, a therapist might pick up a doll, begin to straighten the doll's clothes, and put a shoe on the doll's foot hoping the child will follow his lead and begin to play. Is the therapist's motivation to free the child or to have the child do something so the therapist will feel comfortable?

Participation in child's play does not guarantee the child will feel more included, nor does it assure emotional involvement with the child. **The attitude of the therapist is the crucial variable, not the actual play participation.** When the therapist is being with, is fully involved and experiencing with the child, and is successfully communicating that involvement to the child, the child seldom asks the therapist to overtly participate. When the therapist is asked to participate, sometimes an underlying message is present. The child's message could be, "I don't feel I have your attention. You don't seem to be involved with me or interested in what I am doing." Perhaps the central issue is whether or not the child feels the therapist is participating.

The therapist can be actively involved with the child without playing. The attitude of the therapist is more important than the participation. Choosing not to be directly involved in the child's play does not necessarily predispose the therapist to be a passive observer, as some writers have claimed. A nonplaying emotionally involved relationship with the child in which the therapist indirectly participates in the child's play mentally and emotionally is quite possible. Just as words are sometimes not necessary for two people to be involved with each other, so too participation in play is not necessary for involvement. The therapist's genuine involvement and feeling with the child will be sensed by the child, just as a lack of involvement and interest will be sensed and felt by the child.

Although the therapist must guard against intruding in the child's play or inhibiting the child, participation in the child's play does not automatically impede the therapeutic process. Some experienced play therapists do an artful job of participating in an unobtrusive way. If the therapist chooses to participate in the child's play, the therapist must (a) keep the child in the lead, (b) keep the child in view, (c) maintain an adult–therapeutic role (the therapist is not the child's playmate), and (d) maintain appropriate boundaries through limit setting. If the therapist chooses to participate in the child's play, that would be done as a following participant, taking cues from the child. Asking the child to define the role or activity of the therapist allows the child to lead the way.

Following the child's lead does not imply doing just anything the child directs the therapist to do. The therapist would not drink the red tempera paint, spank the child, yell obscenities at the child, allow the child to pour sand or water inside the therapist's blouse, and so on just because the child directed that. I once consulted on a court case involving an episode in which the "play therapist" (I use the term loosely here) at the direction of a 5-year-old child who was pretending to be a baby, pulled the child's underwear off and used tissue to wipe the child's penis. The "therapist" justified this behavior on the basis that she was following the child's lead, as was recommended in play therapy literature. Obviously, this "play therapist" did not understand the concept of following the child's lead and had limited understanding of boundary issues and ethical behavior. The therapist's participation in the child's play can facilitate the therapeutic relationship only if the therapist's participation facilitates and promotes independence and not dependence in the child.

Even when following the child's directions for play, an ever-present possibility is that of influencing or inhibiting the child's play. When Susie tells the therapist to draw a picture of birds, sits watching, and then tries to copy the therapist's drawing, the needs of the therapist seem to be being met, rather than the therapist facilitating opportunities for the child's positive growth. Confirmation for this conclusion comes from Susie's statement later in the waiting room, "She (the therapist) draws better pictures than I can."

The potential influence of the therapist's participation in the child's play is a subtle but powerful force, and the therapist should be ever mindful of this fact. Five-year-old Carmen is playing with the doctor kit in her third session:

Carmen: Take off your shirt. I'm going to give you a shot.
Therapist: My shirt is not for taking off. You can pretend the doll is me and take the doll's shirt off.
Carmen: Okay. (Takes the female doll's shirt off, then completely undresses the doll, uses the syringe to act out on the doll very explicit sexual activity.)

Children can act out behaviors and express feelings on inanimate objects that could never be expressed on the person of the therapist. Therefore, the presence of the therapist in the play can be a structuring or inhibiting factor, regardless of the therapist's intent. Following Carmen's activity with the doll, the therapist learned she had been sexually abused. Would the therapist have discovered that if she had removed the jacket which covered her shirt? Possibly not, but one cannot be sure.

The therapist must be sensitive to her own potential feelings that may be aroused as a result of playing. Chasing and retrieving darts for 20 minutes may result in the therapist feeling irritated, frustrated, or even angry toward the child. Therefore, the skilled therapist would stop long before negative feelings emerged or would refuse participation in such a game altogether. Attempting to respond with understanding while running around the room can be very difficult. Participation in a child's play may be most effective when the therapist's participation is limited in a controlled manner—allowing herself to be handcuffed, for example, but not to be led endlessly around the room.

The skilled therapist who is ever mindful of the risks of influencing the child or of being manipulated is not likely to compromise therapeutic effectiveness by limited participation in the child's play. However, reservations about the subtle influence of the presence of the therapist in the play still hold.

The question of whether or not to participate in a child's play depends on the child, the situation, and the therapist. A nonplaying or limited play relationship may be the most effective way to assure nonstructuring and that the time together belongs to the child. If the therapist chooses not to play, the suggestion can be made for the child to act out the therapist's part.

Accepting Gifts From Children in Play Therapy

What an awkward situation this can be. In many homes, children have been taught by their parents' behavior that love, affection, and appreciation are expressed by giving presents. Parents returning from a trip bring gifts home for the children. Special toys are purchased by parents as a way of asking forgiveness or to try to restore a damaged relationship. Consequently, children learn to express feelings through gift giving. The natural result is that they may sometimes bring the therapist a gift to express their liking for this special person in their life or to try to win the therapist back after giving him a particularly difficult time in the playroom. **Timing of the gift, then, is an important consideration in determining whether or not to accept a gift.** Did the child break several limits in the previous session and is now using a gift to make amends for giving the therapist a hard time? If that is the case, acceptance of the gift sends the wrong message about how to appropriately restore a relationship.

Cost of the gift is also a factor. Acceptance of expensive gifts can obligate the therapist or cause the therapist to lose his objectivity. Additionally, the code of ethics of some professional organizations sets a dollar limit on receiving gifts. This factor is generally a lesser concern because the dollar amount is often much higher than a child's gift might typically be.

When a child appears with a present in hand, the therapist will very likely experience an emotional tug to accept the present. After all, the therapist does not want to disappoint the child. But what are the potential consequences of accepting a gift? "If I do this, what will the child learn? Will this help to strengthen our relationship? Will this facilitate the child's inner growth as a person? Will this help the child to become more independent?" These are important questions the therapist examines in relation to his own behavior. Accepting gifts may help perpetuate a kind of external giving that is separate from self. The play therapy relationship is an emotional relationship, and what is shared emotionally is more significant than what could be shared in some tangible way. In play therapy children learn to share themselves emotionally. Sharing a gift may blur the significance of emotional sharing. **Emotional gifts are more powerful and more satisfying than tangible gifts.**

An important factor affecting the decision to accept a gift is the kind of gift presented by the child. Artwork or something created by the child is an extension of the child and therefore can be viewed as an extension of emotional giving because it is a part of the child, what the child has created. Accepting nonpurchased items would be acceptable in most cases, such as a flower picked by the child or a drawing. The therapist receives such gifts with warm appreciation, prizing with tone of voice, commenting on details, but, as in the playroom, avoiding overt expressions of praise. "Oh, what a beautiful picture," would be unacceptable. Prizing and appreciation can be shown by reaching out and gently, tenderly taking the object, commenting on it, and carefully placing the object on a nearby table or shelf.

Gifts that are accepted should not be displayed, because this might foster competition or encourage other children to bring gifts. These special items should be kept in a special place until termination of play therapy. They can be a great source of satisfaction if the child asks to see the item later. Some children will hand the therapist a painting and state, "You can hang this on your wall," to which the therapist can respond. "I have a place in my office where I keep special things like this so they will be safe."

Accepting purchased items, even though they may be inexpensive such as a candy bar, can restrict the possibility of emotional sharing by the child and may subtly obligate the therapist in some unconscious way. A determining factor is whether or not the purchased item is given as a preplanned present or is spontaneously shared, as in the case of unwrapping a stick of gum, breaking it in two pieces, and sharing one-half. Among my prized possessions are two tiny, little, round pieces of pink and yellow candy spontaneously shared in the waiting room by a 3-year-old child from a batch clutched in her fist just before she popped the rest into her mouth.

The issue of accepting a gift could perhaps most easily be dealt with by a blanket rule of no gifts that were purchased, regardless of cost. However, I feel very awkward about that. So much depends on the child's intent and the spontaneity of the moment. Declining a gift can be a very awkward and trying moment for the therapist, but it is so important for children to learn they can give of themselves and that presents are not necessary to express emotional meanings. At such moments, the therapist will want to convey sensitive understanding and appreciation. In declining the gift, the therapist can respond with, "You bought this just for me. That says you were thinking about me. I really appreciate that, but here you don't have to give a gift to say you like me. I would like for you to have this." Or, if the item is a present purchased at the store just for the therapist, "I would like for you to take this and get something for yourself." In elementary schools where giving gifts to teachers at Christmas time is a common practice, declining a Christmas gift might be confusing to a child.

No hard and fast rule prevails in regard to the issue of gift giving. A sensitive, empathic therapist should be able to handle the situation with a minimum of frustration by using the best judgment in considering (a) the timing of the gift giving, (b) the nature of the gift, (c) the cost of the gift, and (d) the implications of accepting or not accepting the gift.

Giving the Child a Reward at the End of Sessions or a Memento at Termination

The practice of giving a child a piece of candy, a happy face sticker, stamping a picture on the back of the child's hand, and so on at the end of each play therapy session is not conducive to therapeutic growth and is inconsistent with the rationale for using play therapy. Children have already learned in other experiences that the purpose of such gifts is to reward "good" behavior, and they know how to obtain them. Therefore, such rewards inhibit children's behaviors in the play therapy experience. Children who receive such rewards are not as likely to express aggressive behaviors in the playroom, try to shoot the play therapist with the dart gun, make a mess, tell the play therapist they hate her, or reveal personal issues. **Play experiences for children are intrinsically rewarding. They do not need a reward for playing.** Therefore, whose needs are being met by the giving of a gift?

A related issue is that of giving the child a memento at termination of the play therapy relationship, "so the child will have something by which to remember the therapist and the experience." This has been an emotional relationship, and cannot possibly be adequately represented by a tangible item. What a child carries away in his heart is infinitely more important than anything the child can hold in his hand. What is held in the hand can be lost. **What is held in the heart can never be lost.** Does the therapist need to be remembered? If so, why? The therapist must be willing to turn loose of the child, to no longer be needed by the child. This turning loose process begins in the first encounter with the child and is a continual process of returning responsibility to the child, a continual process of empowering the child. If the therapist is never remembered by the child, that should be okay. The therapist's job is to help the child to grow strong enough to no longer need him.

Asking the Child to Clean Up

Some children seem to need to be messy to fully express themselves. They play with toys and quickly move on to other toys without putting the first items back on the shelf. Some children may be like Carlos, whose home situation was chaotic; his play expressed what his life was like, disorganized and messy. At the end of the sessions, toys were all over the floor. Should these children be asked to clean up? What are the implications of such a request? Whose needs are being met by asking the child to clean up? Some play therapists feel they are "letting a child get away with something" if the child walks out of the playroom leaving a mess. Some therapists may ask the child to clean up because they are irritated or angry at the child for being so messy, and they personalize the child's behavior, feeling the behavior is an act against them.

Some therapists rationalize that if the child is to be helped to function outside the playroom, then the child must learn there are consequences associated with her behavior in the playroom. Therefore, the child must be made to clean up. If the therapist is doing an adequate job of setting therapeutic limits when they are appropriate in other areas of play, then the question of learning to control self should not be an issue. In examining this issue, the therapist should reexamine the rationale for placing children in play therapy. Children need the toys and materials to fully express themselves and the totality of their life experiences. *Toys are children's words, and play is their language.* If that is the case, then a request that the child clean up is a request to clean up what has been expressed. Would a therapist with adult clients ever ask them to clean up their language or talk less graphically about a topic? Probably not. What therapist would ever ask an adult client to dispose of the Styrofoam coffee container or sweep up the mud tracked on the carpet, or ask an emotional client to gather up the tear-soiled tissues before leaving? When this kind of comparison is made with adults, it becomes clear we are saying children are less respected than adults if we ask them to clean up. After all, if learning the consequences of one's behavior really is the issue, is it not also important that adults learn the consequences of their behavior?

After observing a play therapy session, a graduate student wrote,

> I wonder at what point it becomes appropriate to help James recognize the consequences of his messy behavior. Granted, he didn't break things, but the room was in total disarray when he left. Is there a point in the therapy where this freedom and release of energy needs to be modified? Perhaps the play therapist should say, "James, you can decide what you want to do in here, but at the end of our time we will put everything back the way it was."

Would such a statement ever be made to an adult who was being verbally aggressive, distraught, and loud? If play is the child's language, why can't the play language be accepted?

Another graduate student wrote, "I have made a few attempts at involving the child in the clean-up process. Twice this has been with a very messy child. I suspect my motive was more for punishment than therapy." This student's honesty is a good reminder of the importance of asking whose needs are being met by asking the child to clean up.

In the play therapy relationship, what is expressed and experienced in play is much more significant in the therapeutic process than learning how to clean up. Requiring a child to clean up or beginning to clean up in an effort to model for the child will inhibit the child's expression in the next session, because the message most likely to be internalized by the child is that making a mess really is not permissible. Also the child may feel punished for having made a mess.

The therapist also is faced with a dilemma if the child refuses to clean up. What is the therapist to do now, engage in a physical battle to make the child clean up or allow the request to be ignored? Neither option is acceptable. What choice can be presented to the child: no session next week, or place all the toys that are left on the floor off limits for the next session? What if *all* of the toys in the room are left in the middle of the floor? These options are just not acceptable. Trying to get the child to clean up takes the therapist out of the role of acceptance and understanding she has worked hard to try to communicate throughout the session. The therapist also should avoid trying to encourage a child to clean up with responses such as, "Boy, you remembered just where to put that back on the shelf," or "You do such a good job of cleaning up."

Because cleaning up is not the responsibility of the child, that leaves the therapist or some other adult to do the job. The proposed solution by some authors of having a neutral third party or a maid clean up is financially unrealistic. I know of no play therapy room anywhere in the United States that has a maid or neutral third party who cleans up after each session. That leaves the therapist to clean up, and although not ideal, that is workable. A child who is being messy can severely test the limits of the therapist's acceptance as the therapist watches Tinker Toys being spilled all over the floor, the dollhouse furniture dumped, and all the toy soldiers left scattered in and around the sandbox.

As the therapist will need time to put the room in order for the next child, the 15 minutes following a 45-minute session is generally sufficient. If a child is especially messy and additional time is needed to return the room to order, the session can be shortened by a few minutes without announcing the time change to the child. To announce the change would cause the child to feel punished for being messy.

Informing Children of the Reason They Are in Play Therapy

Some therapists inform children of the specific reason they are in play therapy, believing the child's knowing is necessary for behavior change to occur. The child then is expected to work on the identified problem, and the therapist assists by structuring to keep the session content focused on the problem. This poses the problem of placing the therapist in the lead and the sessions becoming problem focused rather than child focused. This approach also assumes that the identified problem is indeed the dynamic to be dealt with and overlooks the possibility of other or deeper issues that may concern the child.

Because the child-centered approach is nonprescriptive and is not based on diagnostic information, the therapist often may not know a great deal about the specifics of an individual referral, especially in terms of diagnostic testing. Therefore, the therapist may not have specific reasons to relay to the child.

The child-centered position is that informing children of the specific reason they are coming to the playroom is not necessary. Such information is not necessary for change and growth to occur. Children's behavior can and does change without them knowing what they are working on or, indeed, without working on trying to change anything. If an understanding of the reason for referral was necessary before change could occur, how could a depressed 4-year-old or a manipulative 3-year-old or a 2-year-old who tries to injure her baby brother ever be helped to change? What would 7-year-old Ryan, who had terminal cancer, have been told he needed to work on? Should he have been told, "You are coming to the playroom because you are dying, and you need to accept death?" Certainly not! Ryan focused on issues of living, just like the rest of us. Impending death was only a part of his living. What therapist is omnipotent enough to know what a dying child should work on in therapy? This may be viewed as an extreme example, but perhaps an extreme example is necessary to force us to examine the essence of an issue. If a requirement for behavioral change is really necessary for change, then it should be necessary in all cases, irrespective of age or presenting problem.

To volunteer a reason why children are coming to the playroom is to imply that something about them is unacceptable. The child-centered therapist avoids any implication that something is wrong with children or that they need to correct or change their behavior or themselves. Acceptance by the therapist promotes self-acceptance by children, and both are prerequisites to change and growth.

The specifics of some reasons for referral would be much too punishing to a child. Providing a general reason is best when a child is curious. If a child asks, "Why am I coming to the playroom?" the therapist can respond, "Your parents are concerned because sometimes things don't seem to go very well for you at home, and they thought you would like to have a special time in the playroom each Tuesday just for you."

Bringing a Friend to the Playroom

Prohibiting the bringing of a friend to the playroom is practiced by play therapists, although not universally, from all theoretical approaches (Ginott & Lebo, 1961). Within the child-centered approach, differences in approach to this question range from Ginott's (1994) serious reservations about allowing children to select their own group members for play therapy to Axline's (1969) conclusion that, "If the therapy is truly child-centered, the child-chosen group should be more valuable to the child choosing the group than a group chosen by the therapist" (p. 41).

According to Dorfman (1951),

> If therapy can be effective when it is not solely a relationship between two people, as in group therapy, then perhaps allowing a child to bring a friend to an individual therapy session need not hinder the process.... Surely, it cannot always be a mere accident that a child brings one person rather than another to his play contact. Sometimes a child may bring in, one by one, those people who represent his areas of difficulty, and then dismiss each one as his need disappears. (p. 263)

Allowing a child to bring a friend to the playroom would be contraindicated for children who need the therapist's total attention and acceptance, and for those who are sensitive to comparisons with other children. Children who have been sexually abused or those who are overly aggressive may perpetrate sexual or aggressive behaviors on other children in the playroom in the early stages of therapy. Traumatized children usually are very needy and require all of the therapist's attention.

When another child is present, the therapist must be extra careful not to imply by his response that what one child is doing or has accomplished is better. If a cautious child brings a friend who is more active, the therapist may unintentionally respond verbally more to the active child simply because more observable activity is present. Responding to one child more than another also can be perceived as comparative and critical. "Jennifer, you stacked those blocks just like you wanted them to be" is a natural tracking response, but what kind of response is likely to be made to a child who is sitting holding a doll or sitting in the sandbox sifting sand through her fingers? Will the absence of a similar response imply that what the active child is doing is better? Perhaps it would be best for this kind of child to bring a friend at a later date, when the relationship with the therapist is well-established and can weather some storms.

Consideration also must be given to the timing of the child's request to bring a friend. Does the request follow a particularly difficult session in which numerous limits were set? Does the child fear he is no longer liked? Will the presence of another child interfere with the rebuilding of the relationship? Has the child just revealed something he feels awkward about, is embarrassed over, or is afraid should not have been revealed?

The presence of another child changes the dynamics of the relationship rather dramatically. Some children may be reluctant to share very personal material about themselves or their family with an invited friend present who has not been a part of the developing relationship, as in group play therapy. Children may compete with one another for the therapist's attention, or one child may spend most of the session showing toys to the therapist, piling things in the therapist's lap to capture attention, or standing near the therapist trying to keep attention through conversation.

The skill of the therapist is a major consideration in determining whether or not to allow a child to invite friends, because the dynamics of the interaction increase geometrically with the addition of another child. Everything is potentially intensified. The situation is not simply the addition of one more child. Children stimulate each other, challenge each other, and activities requiring limit setting are exacerbated. Unique skills and training are required to be effective in group play therapy.

Inviting friends is not a typical request and, when allowed after consideration of the needs of the child and the therapist, can be beneficial to children. If group play therapy is determined to be the most effective way to meet a child's needs, then compassionate concern for all children who hurt would dictate that those children in need of therapy should be given priority in the forming of a group. For nonsexually abused children and children who are not overly aggressive, the therapist must consider that there may be a valid reason for a child's request to bring a friend. The child's lead may need to be followed here.

Inviting Parents or Siblings to the Playroom

The playroom usually is such an exciting place to children that they may want to show their parents or siblings this special place. However, the request to do so may come in the middle of a session. Just what the child has in mind should be determined before allowing a parent or sibling to join the session. Generally, parents are not allowed in sessions. Usually, allowing a child to show parents and siblings the playroom after a session has ended is sufficient. If the child requests again at a later time and the request is not associated with wanting to show something that has been made or manipulation to get Mom into the playroom, then the child may want to communicate some important message to the parent. The concerns related to inviting a friend also hold true for inviting parents. The presence of a parent in the playroom can severely restrict the development of the relationship between the therapist and the child. The presence of a parent in a play therapy session should be a rare occasion. Once in the playroom, an anxious child's request to go get a parent would be denied with careful attention to responding to feelings. On the other hand, an overly anxious child's request for Mother would be allowed, lest the child's anxiety level become debilitating.

If siblings are invited in at the end of a session to see the room, care must be taken to see that they do not use this as a play time. The playroom is a special place for building relationships, and what goes on in the playroom is always consistent. If at a later time the sibling needed play therapy, a new kind of relationship would have to be established.

References

Axline, V. (1969). *Play therapy.* New York: Ballantine.

Dorfman, E. (1951). Play therapy. In C. R. Rogers (Ed.), *Client-centered therapy* (pp. 235–277). Boston: Houghton Mifflin.

Ginott, H. (1994). *Group psychotherapy with children: The theory and practice of play therapy.* New York: McGraw-Hill.

Ginott, H., & Lebo, D. (1961). Play therapy limits and theoretical orientation. *Journal of Consulting Psychology, 25,* 337–340.

Chapter 14

Children in Play Therapy

Cases described in this chapter were selected to present a cross-sectional view of the child-centered approach to play therapy. The sentence structure and language used in the sessions has been left exactly as the children expressed themselves to provide a realistic picture of what the sessions were like. Before presenting these three cases, a summary review of the child-centered approach to play therapy seems to be in order to make clear the purpose of the therapist's behavior in facilitating an accepting emotional climate.

The child-centered play therapist's objective is to relate to the child in ways that will release the child's inner-directional, constructive, forward-moving, creative, self-healing power. The play therapist consistently conveys a deep and abiding belief in the child's ability to make appropriate decisions in the playroom and allows the child to do so. The play therapist listens actively with tenderness and concern and returns responsibility for decision making to the child. The child's capacity for self-direction is respected. No attempt is made to direct the child's activities or to change the child to meet preconceived expectations or standards of behavior. The child is given freedom, within minimal boundaries, to express and explore himself in an accepting climate of faith and trust.

Although actively involved emotionally in experiencing with the child the child's world at the moment, the play therapist is not a playmate; this would potentially interfere with the child's freedom of expression. Children are allowed to lead the way, to determine their own direction, and to fully express feelings, interests, and experiences within acceptable limits. Although a feeling of permissiveness exists, all behaviors are not permissible. For example, a child's attempts to pour sand in the middle of the floor would be responded to with a statement such as, "The sand is for staying in the sandbox."

In the safety of the emotionally accepting climate of the playroom, the child is free to express confusion, insecurity, hostility, or aggression without feeling guilty about having done so. As children feel more secure, they feel more adequate in coping with their own attitudes and feelings. In the therapeutic process, positive feelings and attitudes are expressed gradually, and children come to view themselves as neither completely good nor bad but, rather, as a balanced, acceptable whole. This enables children to feel adequate and to express themselves in terms of their unique, positive potentials and abilities. This seems to be an accurate description of the process for the children described in this chapter.

Nancy—From Baldness to Curls*

Nancy stood in the middle of the waiting room, in the midst of a new and strange environment known as the Center for Play Therapy on the University of North Texas campus. The fingers of her left hand made small circling movements over her head, as if entwining strands of hair, while two fingers of her right hand completely filled her mouth. For the most part, Nancy looked like any other 4-year-old. There was one distinguishing characteristic, though, that could not be overlooked. She was completely bald. The circling movement of the fingers of her left hand left little doubt that she once had hair.

Nancy's parents reported that as a 3-year-old, Nancy had curly blonde hair, but during the past year she had begun to suck her thumb, pull her hair out, and eat it. Nancy's parents had decided

---

* The case of "Nancy—From baldness to curls" is the from Barlow, Strother, & Landreth (1985) and is reprinted with permission of the American Association for Counseling and Development.

that she needed counseling. After diagnostic interviews with her mother, the counseling staff concurred and determined that play therapy, accompanied by periodic parent interviews, would be the most efficient therapeutic procedure.

Family Background

Although family background is not essential information for the play therapist at the onset of play therapy, Moustakas (1982) suggested that a parallel exists between early emotional development in the family and emotional growth in play therapy. "Childhood emotions develop and grow in and through family relationships, reflecting the variety and intensity of interpersonal attitudes within the family. During the first five years of life, the most dramatic and formative emotional learning takes place" (p. 217).

To better understand Nancy, her play, and the changes she exhibited in play therapy, a description of her family and their interaction is important.

Nancy, age 4, lives with her mother, father, and sister, age 4 months. Nancy was adopted when she was a few days old. Her sister is the biological child of the two parents. Both parents are college graduates; the father is a technician for a major corporation, and the mother is a homemaker. There are several complicating factors in Nancy's family background that are directly related to the themes of Nancy's play.

Nancy and her parents had lived with Nancy's maternal grandparents for the first 2 years of her life. The family then moved into their own household. The mother's relationship with the new baby was one of overprotectiveness and little mother–child separation. Nancy seldom had her mother to herself, even for short periods of time. Nancy may have seen herself as "dethroned" from her position as the center of attention.

Nancy's father has a son from a previous marriage who visits and then returns to his mother. This situation may validate Nancy's fear of the lack of anything permanent in her life. Adding to this possible fear is the fact that Nancy's mother suffers from an illness that results in frequent hospitalization for periods of several days. The mother also must receive daily injections at home for her illness.

Nancy's mother and grandmother take an instructional approach with Nancy, which results in restrictive limits being placed on almost all of her behavior. Areas that are stressed constantly are neatness, manners, learning, and performing what she has learned for others. The environment is loving. Nancy's mother tries diligently to be a good mother, even though many limits are set for Nancy. The results manifest themselves in Nancy's fear of separation from her mother, competition with her younger sister, and rebellion against the overwhelming number of limits and demands placed on her.

Nancy in Play Therapy
A Cautious Beginning Turns Messy

In the waiting room before the first session, Nancy sucked her thumb and called for her mother to pick her up. As her mother was already holding Nancy's baby sister Mary, Nancy contented herself with sucking her thumb and standing to one side, warily eyeing the play therapist. The family was invited to walk down the hall together to the playroom. At the door, Mary and her mother were asked to return to the waiting room, and Nancy began her play therapy experience. She turned slowly around and looked at all the toys, much like a china doll revolving in a department store window. After carefully exploring the room with her eyes, she began to tentatively touch and examine the toys in the room. Making contact with most of the toys seemed important to her.

By the middle of the second session, off came the shoes and Nancy daintily put a little sand between all her toes. The water faucet caught her eye. Sand and water trips became the order of the day, with each trip adding water and sand to the floor. The play therapist said, "The sandbox can hold 2 more cups of water, Nancy, or the sink can hold 20 cups of water." She laughed and chose to continue playing in the sand without additional water. The play therapist sensed that Nancy felt more trusting in this session.

Being Free and Accepted

During the third session, Nancy shoved two baby dolls into the stove and doused them with water. She then proceeded to take their place in the baby bed and suck on their water-filled bottle.

Baby play continued as the primary act in the next three sessions. For the first time, Nancy felt free to push back the restrictive boundaries set for her by her mother and grandmother. The therapist was always given at least one and sometimes two babies to hold in her lap while Nancy played with other babies and surreptitiously sucked on the baby bottle. She climbed inside the dollhouse and the refrigerator to spend more time sucking on her bottle.

She further released her emotions by crumbling playdough and walking in it and spilling paint. When Nancy spilled the paint, she said, "I'm going to tell my mommy, and she will be so mad," verbalizing her awareness of her boundaries. Whereas her paintings formerly were straight lines and structured, now her paintings became free, flowing, and expressive. This movement to be more free carried over to the playdough. At first, she would only touch it; now she willingly stuck her fingers in it.

Whatever Nancy produced or felt was accepted by the therapist. No value statements were made. Nancy's reactions to her own behaviors were supported. The play therapist conveyed acceptance of Nancy's thoughts and decisions in the playroom. This kind of unconditional acceptance seemed to be freeing to Nancy and to help her trust herself.

In the fifth session, Nancy threw clay, painted the riding car, and then carefully dumped the brand new shoes that her grandmother had just bought her into the water-filled sink. After this outburst of anger, she threw the babies out of their bed, got into their bed, covered up, sucked the bottle, and said, "You come get me when I cry." The therapist responded, "You want to be held and loved." Nancy got up out of the baby bed, walked over, and climbed onto the therapist's lap with the baby bottle. They rocked and crooned for about 3 minutes. Nancy's eyes glazed over as she got back into the baby bed and acted out the baby role.

Nancy more or less staggered out to her car that day. She could not quite shake the intensity of her role as the baby. She angrily said, "No!" to instructions given her by her mother.

Although Nancy had never attempted to pull her hair during the play therapy sessions, this was the first day that she did not pull her hair in the waiting room in the presence of her mother. The play therapist noticed wisps of fine baby hair covering her head.

Even though she continued to suck on the bottle for short amounts of time in later sessions, Nancy never returned to her baby role with the intense emotion that was displayed this day. Being the mother of the babies was a new and rewarding role for Nancy. Painting, cutting up playdough, sticking her hands into the paint, and using lots of glue and paper began to develop as the primary activities. Babies were a thing of the past.

Nancy With Curls

When Nancy came bouncing in for the seventh session, her head was covered with short, naturally curly, blonde hair. She continued to play with a wide variety of toys, especially the expressive arts and crafts materials. She began to play "Mother and Nancy" with the play therapist. Nancy, who was the mother, said "No, no, no, this is mine. You can't have it. Play with your toys." The therapist, who was asked to play the role of Nancy, whispered, "Tell me what Nancy does when Mother says no, no, no." She said, "You suck your thumb and pull your hair and eat it." The therapist demonstrated to make sure the procedure was correct and asked, "Now what?" Nancy, in a mother's voice, said, "Don't do that," and laughed. She was aware of her habit.

In the waiting room, her grandmother was trying to manage Nancy and wanted her to put on her coat. Nancy said, "No," instead of retreating to her former behavior of sucking her thumb and pulling her hair. This ability to resist was short-lived. Grandmother's attempt to control Nancy was to recite a poem, "I'll tell you of cabbages and kings." Nancy's response was to freeze and stare into space as she began to suck her thumb and pull her hair. With both of them shuffling out the door, the grandmother took Nancy's thumb out of her mouth and stated, "Wet thumbs get chapped in the cold air." Even though Nancy occasionally succumbed to this instructional pressure, her hair continued to grow.

In the eighth session, Nancy was reminded that this would be the final session. She did not respond verbally, but began her usual play, which no longer included crawling into holes, sucking on the bottle, acting like a baby, or asking the therapist to hold the babies. Nancy's play with the babies during the last three sessions was characterized by assigning the role of "Mommy" to herself. With the paints, playdough, and sand, her play was free but not so messy. Knowing this was her last session, Nancy's usual goodbye to the toys was given an added dimension; she took the bottle of water and poured just a little bit on each of her favorite toys. She smiled again and sauntered out of the playroom.

In the waiting room, dialogue about this being her last session, with an invitation to her to visit any time, met with silence and a basic refusal to acknowledge the conversation. There was, however, no anger, thumb sucking, or hair pulling.

Parent Consultation

Consulting with parents in conjunction with the child's play therapy experience can enhance the therapeutic process by facilitating communication in the home. When consulting with parents, the play therapist must explain to parents that the child's play therapy sessions are confidential. Therefore, the consultation sessions will not revolve around the specifics of the child's play. In Nancy's case, the play therapist met with her parents every other week for approximately a half-hour and, on two occasions, full 1-hour sessions were conducted. During these consultation sessions, the therapist's goals were to provide insight for the parents with respect to Nancy's feelings and perception of her world and to develop communication skills, which would enhance the parents' relationship with Nancy, and parenting skills, which, if adopted, would benefit both Nancy and her parents.

Discussion

Nancy's play can be described in the following observable stages outlined by Guerney (1983):

1. Children begin by acclimating themselves to the playroom situation and the play therapist.
2. Children begin to test limits, express anger, and experience freedom.
3. Children deal with the independence/dependence relationship.
4. Children begin to express positive feelings about themselves and the world. Children also begin to make decisions about how they will deal with their world.

The play therapy experience provided Nancy a way to organize her experiences, express her feelings, and explore relationships. The development of the relationship between Nancy and the play therapist grew from one of caution to one of trust and acceptance. As a result of Nancy's environment and her perceptions of it, she began her play as she would any other new experience. She was guarded to protect herself from *dos* and *don'ts*. Nancy had never experienced an atmosphere in which she could decide, without fear or disapproval, what she wanted to do. This atmosphere created by the play therapist, the single most important factor, enabled Nancy to feel what she had never felt before: the freedom to express herself.

Axline (1982) believed that "the intensity of the feelings that some children hold at very early ages, as these are revealed through a series of play therapy contacts, are often surprising" (p. 49). Through her play, Nancy acted out her feelings of frustration and anger. These became apparent in relation to her apparent confusion concerning her place in the family and her mother's attachment to her younger sister. Nancy's play with babies, bottles, and the baby bed provided her a unique experience through which she experimented and began to resolve this inner conflict. Nancy's anxiety related to separation from her mother, and her anger toward sharing her mother with her sister seemed to be resolved as the play therapy progressed. She began to accept and live the role of older sister, not baby. This change was evident in the play-room and at home.

The second apparent frustration with which Nancy was strug-gling was her constant anger at the vast array of limits placed on her by her mother and grandmother. In trying to fulfill the role of the good mother and the good grandmother, Nancy's elders had discouraged her from learning to set her own limits. One symp-tom of this anxiety was Nancy's baldness. Nancy chose to experi-ment with limit setting through water play, paints, and getting her shoes and clothes wet or dirty. After some time, she found a nice balance for herself. She enjoyed the water play and the paints, but she no longer needed to go to extremes.

More intense emotional behaviors often seemed to be preceded by a well-planned testing of limits by Nancy. Reflections of her feelings, accompanied by the ACT model of limit setting in a matter-of-fact way, allowed Nancy to work through the intensity of her feelings.

Sometimes important actual events in children's lives fail to enter either into their play or into their associations, and the whole emphasis, at times, lies on apparently minor happenings. But these minor happenings are of great importance to children, because they have stirred up their emotions and fantasies. Nancy never sucked her thumb or pulled out her hair in the playroom. Only once did she express an interest in the wig, which was one of the toys in the playroom. When she was in the waiting room outside the playroom, she occasionally did suck her thumb, and once or twice pulled her hair when she was overwhelmed with parental instructions.

Finally, the playroom atmosphere provided Nancy with a rela-tionship other than the usual teaching relationship she had with her mother and grandmother. The play therapist had no precon-ceived expectations of Nancy and did not direct her play. Nancy soon learned that the therapist believed that she could make her own decisions. Nancy's newfound courage to make her own deci-sions became apparent in play therapy and also in Nancy's world outside the playroom.

Nancy was able to use her experiences in the play therapy ses-sions to reorient herself to her world. This process can take place only in an atmosphere where the child feels unconditionally accepted, encouraged to make choices, and emotionally safe. The regrowth of Nancy's hair seemed to be dramatic evidence that these conditions were met.

Cindy—A Manipulative Child

Mrs. M described her 5-year-old daughter Cindy as, "She is careful to take care of her toys and things, always puts things back, and cleans up her room when I ask her to. She's a good child, but I don't know … (long pause). I'm always angry at her, and I don't know why. I know it's not good for me to be so angry at her, but I am. (Pause.) That's hard for me to admit, but it's true. I don't know what could be wrong. I'm just angry at her a lot. She's not a problem or anything at home. We do have a conflict when I have to discipline her. She tells me I'm stupid. She seems to say that a lot. She wants her way all the time."

An exploratory play therapy session with Cindy seemed warranted to formulate a picture of Cindy on her own terms and to decide whether or not play therapy was needed, so an appointment was scheduled for the next week in a play therapy room in the Center for Play Therapy. During the session, Cindy attempted to manipulate and control me (Landreth), insisting that I get items for her even though they were within her reach, asking me questions and then making decisions for me. She was not able to tolerate even the slightest mistake in her paintings, and kept saying, "I can do one better" as she wadded the paintings up and threw them into the trash can.

When I announced the 5-minute caution, Cindy said, "I don't care. I'm not leaving." At the end of the session, I indicated the time was up as I stood up, and Cindy said, "I told you I'm not leaving. I'm going to do some, uh, art." She moved over to the art materials and began painting. I responded, "You would like to be the one who decides just how long you stay, but our time is up. It's time to go to the waiting room where your mother is." I took a couple of steps toward the door. Cindy continued to paint and to verbalize her resistance. I continued to reflect her wants and to set the limit on ending the session. My patience paid off when Cindy voluntarily walked out under her own steam after 5 minutes.

Cindy exhibited so much manipulative behavior that it was strongly suspected this was typical of her behavior at home. An interview with Mom confirmed that Cindy was doing a lot of subtle manipulative things of which Mom was unaware, and that this was the basic reason for her anger toward Cindy. Additional sessions were scheduled with Cindy. Her second play therapy session was very revealing of manipulative behavior and her efforts to build a relationship with me.

Second Play Therapy Session

Cindy: (Cindy enters the playroom, goes directly to the sand-box, and begins playing. Sitting on the side of the sand-box, sifting sand, Cindy talks about the new house her family has moved into.) I know how long…a, uh, long time…more weeks…uh, I just don't know how many days that has been.

Therapist: You can remember how long you've been there. You just don't know how many weeks that makes.

Cindy: (Continues playing with the sand.) I kind of like you better today.

Therapist: You like me better than last time.

Cindy: Yes. (Moves from the sandbox to the table where the paints are.) Come on let's paint…. You may help me if you want, or you may watch if you like. What do you want to do, watch?

Therapist: I'll watch.

Cindy: (Goes into the bathroom, begins washing brushes and the paint jar in the sink.) A black sink.

Therapist: You made the sink black?

Cindy: Yes, with black water.

Therapist: Oh.

Cindy: (Continues mixing water with paints.) You hear that water?

Therapist: Uhhmm. I can hear it all the way in here.

Cindy:	Well, here it goes again. Better watch out. (Turns the water on full force. Stays in the bathroom running the water for several minutes. Comes from the bathroom and gets a large piece of paper.) Watch what I'm going to put on this.
Therapist:	You're really going to work on that.
Cindy:	First thing I was going to do was paint. I did, right?
Therapist:	You decided that before you came.
Cindy:	Yes, I did. It was yesterday. My birthday was day before yesterday. (Selects playdough can.) Is it alright to put.... I'm going to put water in this so I can rinse this out. (Goes into the bathroom. Her sandals slip on sand on the floor and make a scraping noise.) These are slippery sandals.
Therapist:	They look slippery.
Cindy:	They are slippery. (Comes back and starts painting. I am sitting directly across the table from Cindy.) Are you interested in art?
Therapist:	I like art, and it looks like you like art.
Cindy:	I like to make it. Yesterday, I think I made...uh, yeah, I made a tree with some flowers with a kitten in it and, uh, a fountain in it by the kitten.
Therapist:	So you put lots of things in that picture.
Cindy:	And some birds and a sky...some white birds and a blue sky and some leaves...and...grass and then I hung it on the bulletin board I got for my birthday. It was on the fourth of July.
Therapist:	So that made it a real special birthday.
Cindy:	When the people celebrated. I was a firecracker.
Therapist:	Lots of things happened on your birthday.
Cindy:	Uhhmmm,... and the reason was the police were out and they were looking for people who were doing firecrackers.
Therapist:	Hmmm. (Cindy continued before I could respond.)
Cindy:	Maybe they were after people, because you aren't supposed to do that. You get hurt.
Therapist:	So they were trying to keep people from getting hurt.

Cindy:	Uhhmmm. (Continues to paint. As she moves the brush from the painting to dip into a paint jar, I turned my head to follow the brush.) Without moving your head you can watch me paint at the same time.
Therapist:	Sometimes some of the things I do bother you.
Cindy:	Yes. (Moves the paintbrush back and forth rapidly in front of the therapist's face, with a taunting look on her face. Giggles.)
Therapist:	I guess you were wondering then if I would play a game with you.
Cindy:	Uhhmmm.
Therapist:	And I just decided I would watch you.
Cindy:	(Sticks the paintbrush toward my face and giggles.) I fooled you didn't I? You thought I was going to paint on you.
Therapist:	You like to fool me sometimes.
Cindy:	Yes, I just like to fool you.
Therapist:	Oh, you just like to fool me.
Cindy:	Right. I can't fool Debbie. She's my cousin, because she don't like it.
Therapist:	She doesn't like for you to play games with her.
Cindy:	No. Uh, see, she don't like me playing tricks on her.
Therapist:	Uhhmmm.
Cindy:	But Robin don't mind.
Therapist:	So with some people it's okay, and with some other people it's not.
Cindy:	Uhhmmm. Robin's my favorite because Janie won't let me do that.
Therapist:	You really like the people who will let you play tricks on them.
Cindy:	Uhhmmm. Robin's my best one because anyway she was…. (Continues to paint.) Blue and red (as she draws house with blue and red windows).
Therapist:	A blue window and a red window.
Cindy:	And a purple house with a black door.
Therapist:	You used lots of colors.
Cindy:	Is time almost up?

Therapist: We have 30 more minutes today. (She is painting a black door on the house and the black runs into the other colors.)

Cindy: Good. I can mess my picture up. Next time I won't splash it. I can make something better. I can make…a little something…better. (Said thoughtfully.)

Therapist: You think you can make one better than that.

Cindy: I can! I just… I can. (Wads the wet picture up into a ball and throws it into the trash can.)

Therapist: You just know you can.

Cindy: (She discovers finger paints and decides to finger paint.) These smell like finger paints don't they?

Therapist: You've played with finger paints before.

Cindy: Yes, in Sunday school. Do you water finger paints?

Therapist: In here you can choose what you want to do.

Cindy: (Goes into the bathroom, puts water into the finger paints, returns, and begins to paint carefully with a brush. It is obvious she doesn't want to get paint on her hands. She uses the brush to paint with the finger paints for awhile, then dips the brush into the finger paints and starts to transfer the brush to her other hand, but notices paint on the brush handle just as her fingers are about to close around the brush and quickly moves her hand away.)

Therapist: Just not sure whether or not to put your fingers into that.

Cindy: Yes I can. It's finger paints. (She goes into the bathroom and washes the brush, comes out, and continues to use a brush to paint finger paints, using all the colors to paint circles. She goes back to the bathroom, washes the brush, and comes out, leaving the water running. Then she mixes several colors of fingerpaint on her painting.)

Therapist: Now it has lots of colors all mixed up.

Cindy: Would you be quiet so I can do this?

Therapist: When I talk that bothers you.

Cindy: Yeah.

Therapist: You just don't like for people to bother you when you are doing things.

Cindy:　　It's all right except for the talking, because I don't want, like to be bothered when I'm doing art. Rhonda's all right because she's just a baby, and she don't know better, but you do! And you better be quiet!

Therapist:　I should know better.

Cindy:　　Yes.

Therapist:　And I should do what you tell me to do.

Cindy:　　Right. (She continues painting and then goes into the bathroom, washes her hands, comes out, and begins to paint with just the tip of one finger; draws a tree.) There. A tree. I can do a better tree than that.

Therapist:　A lot of times it just seems to you like you could do it better.

Cindy:　　Well, I can.

Therapist:　You keep telling yourself, "I can do one better."

Cindy:　　Well, I can.

Therapist:　Uh hmm, and you just know you can.

Cindy:　　That's right. I know. Now would you please be quiet? Remember what I said?

Therapist:　And you'd like for me to do what you tell me to.

Cindy:　　Well. I sure do. (Continues painting, hums a tune while painting vigorously using both hands—really leans into the activity of swirling her hands around on the paper.) I'm going to put a little glue in there. Okay? ... Okay?

Therapist:　You're wondering, "Can I use that glue?"

Cindy:　　Uh huh. May I?

Therapist:　You're just not sure whether you should or not.

Cindy:　　Can I? (Talks about Bobo the punching toy and goes into the bathroom, washes her hands. Returns and begins mixing paste with her finger painting. Gets double handfuls of paste from the quart jar.)

Therapist:　You got just as much as you wanted.

Cindy:　　(Gets a huge handful of paste.) It looks like ice cream.

Therapist:　Just reminds you of ice cream.

Cindy:　　Yes. It's going to be purple ice cream.

Therapist:　So you know just how you want it to look.

Cindy:　　Purple is a pretty color.

Therapist: That's a color you really like.

Cindy: Uh huh, it's my favorite. (Gets more large scoops of paste and mixes with finger paint on the paper.)

Cindy: Are you Mister Rogers? (Giggles.)

Therapist: I guess I remind you of somebody else.

Cindy: Yes, you do.... He likes art. I like him, too.

Therapist: So you like both of us.

Cindy: Yes, I do.

Cindy: Now I've got purple hands.

Therapist: Uh Humm.

Cindy: (Goes to the bathroom, washes her hands for a long time, comes out, and says) One more time of it and then I will be through. But first I'm going to use a little teensy bit of sand in it.

Therapist: So you know just how you want it to look, and you know just what you want in it.

Cindy: (Gets a little bit of sand, adds it to her painting, and announces) That's not enough. (Goes back to the sand-box and gets two huge handfuls of sand and dumps it onto the picture, glances up at the therapist to check his reaction.)

Therapist: You got just as much as you wanted.

Cindy: (Smooths the sand out, adds more paste to the sand, mixes it up, and says) This will stick on.

Therapist: You kind of know how that will turn out.

Cindy: Yeah. (Mixes more paste; has paste and sand all over her hands and arms.) It's some kind of an art ... that I made up ... just for you. (Adds more sand.)

Therapist: So you made it up just for me.

Cindy: And you may have it if you want it. Do you want it?

Therapist: If you want to leave it for me, that will be fine. You made it just for me. (Shows prizing in tone of voice.)

Cindy: You can take it home with you.

Therapist: You would just like for me to have it.

Cindy: Uh hmmm. (Goes to the bathroom and washes her hands.)

Therapist: Cindy, we have 5 more minutes in the playroom today and then it will be time to go to the waiting room where your mother is.

Cindy: (Gets a pan full of sand from the sandbox and adds it to her art project, pats it down, begins to add finger paint to the sand-and-paste art project, and says) I'll have to use all of the blue. Okay?

Therapist: You just decided you are going to use every bit of it.

Cindy: I'll need to. (Empties all the blue finger paint and mixes with sand. Throws the empty paint container in the trash, goes to the bathroom and washes her hands, leaves the water running, comes out, and says) I've been painting all day haven't I?

Therapist: Seems to you you've been painting a long time.

Cindy: (Continues to stir and mix all the colors of finger paints into the sand project, then announces) I'm finally through.

Therapist: Finished.

Cindy: For the day. (She goes to the bathroom, washes her hands, and turns the water off.) Now it's going to be a taco. (Folds the sheet of newsprint over smears paste on the edge of the paper to stick the edges together.)

Therapist: Just like a big taco.

Cindy: (Tries to lift the "taco" up by holding the edges of the paper. The sand-paste-paint mixture is too heavy, and the paper tears.) Oops! I thought I needed a lot. Looks like we're gonna have to do it like this. (Folds the ends of the paper over.)

Therapist: Have to do it a different way.

Cindy: Yes. It's like a sandwich. (Looked like one.)

Therapist: Uh humm. A big sandwich.

Cindy: Uh huh. Finished for the day. There we go. There's your ... art. (Hands "art" to the therapist.) You may have it.

Therapist: You made it just for me. (Shows prizing and appreciation in the tone of voice. Gently takes the "art" and carefully places it on the table.) Cindy, our time is up for today.

In this second session, Cindy made an immediate move to make amends for the difficult time she had given me in the first session by saying, "I like you better today." Her motivation seems obvious in view of the fact that this statement was made in the first couple of minutes of the session, hardly enough time for me to demonstrate I was different in any way. Cindy continued, however, to test my patience and acceptance of her by insisting that I not move my head and that I stop talking. Her anxiety and need to do things just right were expressed in her destruction of her first painting. Cindy's increasing inner freedom was evident as she became more involved, free, and expressive with the finger paints and then was able to cope and adjust when her taco art project ripped apart. The making of an art project for me was Cindy's way of building the relationship. By the end of this second session, Cindy was more self-assured, able to tolerate a mess, expressed herself more creatively, and no longer needed to try to manipulate me.

Amy—A Selective Mute Child*

Brown and Lloyd (cited in Kolvin & Fundudis, 1981) reported that for every 1,000 children, there may be as many as 7.2 who do not speak at school at the age of 5. Kolvin and Fundudis (1981) defined this phenomenon, selective mutism, as "a strange condition where talking is confined to a familiar situation and a small group of intimates" (p. 219). They further reported that parents of selective mute children observed normal speech development when the children began to talk, but as they were placed in more social situations, shyness became prevalent.

Selective Mutism and Enuresis

In this section, the case study of Amy, a 5-year-old selective mute child, is described. Her mother referred her to the center because she was concerned about Amy's refusal to talk at school or in any situation away from the home. Amy also exhibited excessive shyness and suffered from enuresis (nighttime bed wetting). Amy was the middle child in her nuclear family. She had two brothers. She

---

* "Amy–A selective mute child" is from Barlow, Strother, & Landreth (1986) and is reprinted with permission of the American Association for Counseling and Development.

seemed especially close to and dependent on her mother, which is common among selective mute children (Kolvin & Fundudis, 1981).

Selective mute children seem to be very dependent on their parents, especially their mothers. This seemed to be true in Amy's case. Her mother initiated the process of play therapy and was the parent who followed through during the entire treatment period. Amy's father was never involved, but he was reported to be cooperative in the process at home. When counseling children, it is ideal for counselors to have both parents involved and informed. This case, however, demonstrates that play therapy can have positive results even though both parents are not involved in the parent consultation process.

In addition to being concerned with the selective mutism, Amy's mother reported a concern over Amy's nighttime bedwetting. Amy's brothers also suffered from this condition. In a study of 24 selective mute children, Kolvin and Fundudis (1981) reported a significantly high level of enuresis among the participants. They also found that these children had a higher ratio of behavioral problems, suffered from excessive shyness, exhibited more immaturity (especially in speech development), that more girls than boys were selective mutes, and that selective mutism proved to be rather intractable. The American Psychiatric Association (2000), in *The Diagnostic and Statistical Manual of Mental Disorders* (fourth edition), also described selective mute children as suffering from excessive shyness, social isolation, behavioral difficulties, and possibly enuresis.

Behaviors Exhibited

Amy's behavior and development paralleled that of children in the Kolvin and Fundudis (1981) study. According to Amy's teacher, she did seem to be developmentally behind and still suffered from enuresis at age 5. She was extremely shy and, according to her mother and teachers, exhibited some behaviors that were not normal for a child of her age. No distinguishable clues were identified as to the events that led to Amy's selective mutism. In their review of the literature, Kolvin and Fundudis (1981) found no specific or conclusive causes for selective mutism.

Amy did not speak one word during the first 5 months she was enrolled in the early childhood program at her school. She passed all the nonverbal items at the appropriate age level on an early childhood screening test and was put in a special education transition class. Amy's teachers observed her to be a passive little girl, who sat and observed activity around her. Her social skills were virtually nonexistent. She did not play with groups of children, but preferred to play alone or with an adult. When a new quiet girl took a special interest in her, Amy did accept her. Initially the new girl talked to Amy, but later she just followed Amy's gesturing. As the school year progressed, Amy became more active and her facial expressions became more animated. She even smiled and laughed occasionally.

Outside, Amy would linger on the playground and trail her classmates. She did not interact with the other children. When the teacher would take her hand to lead her to the sandbox or swings, Amy would pull away.

Amy displayed some additional unusual behaviors. She grasped the teacher aide's neck with her hands in a stronghold, smiling while she did it. She repeatedly stabbed the playhouse doll with a fork. She would wet her pants if the teachers forgot to ask her if she needed to go to the bathroom, although she had been told that she could go to the bathroom any time.

Her mother reported that Amy did not show pain. She once sat in a tub of very hot water and just looked at her grandmother blankly when she asked Amy why she was still in the water. Amy had her pierced earrings pulled through her ears while playing and did not complain to the teacher, although her ears were bleeding. She fell in the gymnasium at school, which caused her mouth to bleed, and when the teacher asked her if it hurt, she shook her head from side to side. She did not show excitement or happiness on field trips or party days.

Teacher's Efforts

Amy's teachers used several techniques to try to elicit some type of verbal response. She was accepted as a nonverbal participant. On other occasions she was ignored when she would not respond verbally. When this failed, she was required to sit in a "time out" chair if she did not speak, but Amy seemed to take pleasure in sitting in the chair. According to her teacher, she was as sassy as anyone could be without saying a word. She did respond to being touched and on several occasions initiated sitting on the teacher's lap, following the lead of other children in the class. Amy was described by her teachers as passive, resistant, voluntarily nonverbal, occasionally hostile, compulsive, controlling, and emotionally unexpressive, as well as accepting of some people, responsive to affection, and willing to copy other children's behavior.

Play Therapy

For a child exhibiting selective mutism, it is imperative that therapeutic communication be based on a means of expression with which the child feels comfortable. The therapist who relies exclusively on verbal means of communication with such children often is defeated in efforts to establish an effective relationship. The selective mute child easily controls the interaction with silence, thus also controlling development of the relationship with the counselor. Efforts to entice, encourage, cajole, or trick such children into a verbal exchange typically result in continued silence and a frustrated therapist.

The selective mute child has discovered from previous experiences what adults want—verbalization—and how to easily thwart their efforts by resisting through silence. Therefore, because play is the natural medium of self-expression for children, play therapy was selected as the preferred therapeutic approach with Amy. Her therapist believed Amy needed a therapeutic setting in which she could feel comfortable, a place where she could be in charge, within limits, of the relationship with an adult, and could communicate on her own terms without using words, as expected of her by other adults.

Regarding the value of play, Conn (1951) stated, "Every therapeutic play method is a form of learning process during which the child learns to accept and to utilize constructively that degree of personal responsibility and self-discipline necessary for effective self-expression and social living" (p. 753).

A Silent Beginning

During the initial session in play therapy, Amy was totally non-verbal. She hid under the paint easel and gestured for 45 minutes. The therapist responded with similar gestures and verbal comments, hoping to communicate understanding of her feelings. If the therapist remained motionless and silent for even a short time, Amy would look out from under the easel to make sure she still had the therapist's undivided attention. At the end of the session, Amy readily emerged from under the easel.

Amy's cousin Susan accompanied her to the center for the second session. When Amy resisted returning to the playroom, the therapist invited Susan to come into the playroom, too. Susan began talking as soon as the playroom door opened, and Amy returned to her hiding place under the easel. Susan played with many of the toys and, after about 10 minutes, Amy joined her. They chatted back and forth and played contentedly for the 45 minutes. One would not have believed there was anything unusual about Amy at this time.

This was such an unexpected turn of events that the therapist decided to add Amy's 9-year-old brother, Ben, to the third session to better understand the dynamics of Amy's interpersonal interactions. In this session, Susan and Ben played together and ignored Amy, who finally retreated into her hiding place under the easel. After the third session, Susan returned to her home in another town. The therapist had to decide whether to see Amy by herself or to include her older brother in the session. Amy also had a younger brother, Ned, who was very eager to come into the playroom.

Sibling Group Play Therapy

The question of placing siblings together in group play therapy has received little attention in existing literature on play therapy. Ginott (1994) has been one of the few authors to even mention the issue of siblings; however, he has done so only in the context of recommending that children experiencing intense sibling rivalries be excluded from group play therapy. Consideration of placing siblings together is not mentioned.

The possibility of placing siblings together in group play therapy often is ruled out by requiring children selected for group play therapy to be the same age. According to Gazda (1989) and Ginott (1994), children in group play therapy should not differ in age by more than 1 year. Ginott (1994) did suggest that other considerations may take precedence over age, such as when aggressive children are placed in older age groups or immature children are placed in groups with children younger than themselves. Ginott further restricted the possibility of having siblings together in play therapy by recommending that school-age children be separated by sexes. We have found little need to separate children by sex until approximately the age of 8 or 9.

It seems reasonable to assume that the basic reasons for placing children in group play therapy may be equally as important for sibling group play therapy. If the presence of several children in the playroom helps to anchor the experience to the world of reality (Ginott, 1994), this would seem to be even truer for siblings together in group play therapy (Figure 14.1). If, as Ginott (1994) proposed, children help each other assume responsibility in interpersonal relationships, the impact on siblings would be even more significant because of the opportunity to naturally and immediately extend those interactions with siblings outside the setting of group play therapy.

Searching for the Right Combination

In Amy's case, a combination of sibling group play therapy, individual play therapy, and brief family consultation was found to be the most appropriate approach. When Amy played in the playroom with Ben, he was the responsible one—for himself and for Amy. She did not have to do anything; Ben talked and played for both of them. When Amy played in the playroom with Ned, she was the teacher and helper, although Ned was independent. When both boys came into the playroom, they played together and ignored Amy. When the children came into the room with their mother, they all tended to act out somewhat but behaved with fairly equal exchanges.

FIGURE 14.1 Sibling group play therapy facilitates the development and exploration of issues and interactions that are not possible in individual play therapy.

When Amy played alone in the playroom, she remained shy, yet verbal. She would hide in her usual place under the easel for 10 or 15 minutes, until she felt safe enough to emerge. Her play often was inappropriate, in the sense of periodic bursts of hostility or lengthy laughter or destructiveness. Modeling play behaviors that she had experienced with her brothers did generalize, however, to her individual play.

Amy's Need to Control

One theme continued for most of the play sessions. Amy wanted to be in total control and used silence to accomplish it. When the therapist continued to reflect her feelings verbally, Amy resented the loss of control. She repeatedly said, "Don't look at me. Don't talk to me." The therapist used a compromising approach on this issue. Amy was given control of "looks" and the therapist was given control of "talk." Amy seemed satisfied to have a well-defined area of control and was willing to let the therapist have one, too. Gradually, Amy began to accept partial control in other areas. Ben and Amy divided the room into two parts. Each had to obtain verbal permission from the other to play in their respective control zones. Practicing, even in a structured way, the give-and-take that occurs naturally with many children seemed to give Amy the confidence she needed to develop her social skills, rather than to turn inward.

As Amy became more independent, Ben dropped his role as protector and responsible member of the family. He acted out to the extent that his mother had to discipline him publicly—a first in this family. Ben gradually was able to let Amy be her own person and retain his significant position of being one of several responsible members of the family. The mother encouraged this shift in communication at home by giving Amy more responsibility and not allowing Ben to take over her tasks, even when he could do them better and faster. Ned also maintained a balanced independence, rather than adopting Amy's role of being helpless and in total control or Ben's role of being responsible and in total control. Amy began to express her feelings more frequently. Raising her closed fist was her way of saying, "Don't come close to me," or "This will keep me safe when I have to walk close to you."

A Different Amy

Amy's new confidence extended into the classroom. Talking, singing, and participating in class became fun for her. Her play sessions shifted to depict the school setting. She loved to be the teacher. When Amy forgot some mathematical fact or how to spell a new word she had learned, she would report what this word would be in Spanish. The therapist reflected the idea that sometimes only Amy would be able to tell what the word really meant. Amy's love of learning became evident in the safe environment of the playroom. She had initially concentrated on receiving information and not expressing.

In later sessions, Amy actively participated in expressing each new learning situation. The pace of Amy's progress was like a door bursting open. She even read a Christmas story over the loudspeaker at school. After 9 months and 36 sessions of combining sibling and individual play therapy, the final reward was Amy's assignment to a regular first-grade classroom in the spring of the year. As Amy became more verbal and more actively participated in her world, the enuresis occurred less frequently.

Significance of Sibling Group Play Therapy

What was gained by having Amy's brothers in play therapy with her? As in family therapy, ideally, the focus shifts from intrapersonal to interpersonal patterns of communication. In this particular case, lack of verbal communication skills and underdeveloped social skills were paralyzing Amy's efforts to function in society beyond her immediate family.

It was obvious in sessions with Amy and her younger brother, Ned, that Amy had some basic social and communication skills. Observation of Ben and Amy in the playroom revealed that Ben had assumed responsibility for both himself and Amy. By helping Ben and Amy shift their ways of communicating, the therapist helped Amy to gain confidence to try a new way of entering the world of people instead of having someone take responsibility for her. Although individual play therapy eventually might have produced similar results, the sibling group play therapy approach in this case seemed to bring faster results, because the issues could be defined immediately, and work in sessions and at home could begin on the shift in communication patterns.

We are not suggesting that sibling group play therapy be used exclusively in every situation, or that it is the answer to cases in which the child has experienced trauma, but it can add a dimension to play therapy that previously has not been seriously considered. In fact, Amy definitely needed some time by herself to try out new behaviors learned in the setting that included her brothers, but the sibling setting served as a diagnostic tool for the therapist and as an intimate environment in which Amy could interact safely.

Summary

Kolvin and Fundudis (1981) stated that selective mutism is rather intractable. This case study of Amy demonstrates that play therapy was a viable treatment for a selective mute child.

Because selective mute children have a purpose for their behavior, verbal prodding by adults usually reaps few benefits. It only widens the gap between themselves and the child. The selective mute child has chosen not to communicate verbally with those outside the immediate family for reasons that may revolve around fear of social situations in which the child is expected to interact verbally with others. It seems valuable, consequently, to provide an alternative for the child. With group and sibling group play therapy, the therapist can provide an atmosphere in which the child feels safe and where there is no pressure to talk.

References

American Psychiatric Association. (2000). *Diagnostic and statistical manual of mental disorders* (4th ed.). Washington, DC: Author.

Axline, V. (1982). Entering the child's world via play experience. In G. L. Landreth (Ed.), *Play therapy: Dynamics of the process of counseling with children* (pp. 47–57). Springfield, IL: Thomas.

Barlow, K., Strother, J., & Landreth, G. (1985). Child-centered play therapy: Nancy from baldness to curls. *The School Counselor, 32*(5), 347–356.

Barlow, K., Strother, J., & Landreth, G. (1986). Sibling group play therapy: An effective alternative with an elective mute child. *The School Counselor, 34*, 44–50.

Conn, J. (1951). Play interview therapy of castration fears. *American Journal of Orthopsychiatry, 25*, 747–754.

Gazda, G. (1989). *Group counseling: A developmental approach*. Boston: Allyn & Bacon.

Ginott, H. (1994). *Group psychotherapy with children: The theory and practice of play therapy*. Northvale, NJ: Aronson.

Guerney, L. (1983, April). Play therapy conference. Conference held at North Texas State University, Denton.

Kolvin, I., & Fundudis, T. (1981). Elective mute children: Psychological development and background factors. *Journal of Child Psychology and Psychiatry and Allied Disciplines, 22*, 219–232.

Moustakas, C. (1982). Emotional adjustment and the play therapy process. In G. L. Landreth (Ed.), *Play therapy: Dynamics of the process of counseling with children* (pp. 217–230). Springfield, IL: Thomas.

Chapter 15

Determining Therapeutic Process and Termination

The therapeutic process of growth in play therapy sessions and assessing children's readiness for ending play therapy sessions have received little attention in the literature. Perhaps these topics have not been dealt with because the answers are not easily determined. The void also may exist because therapists have difficulty dealing with the ending of relationships. Typically therapists do not enter into relationships with a conscious goal to move toward ending them. After all, we are in the business of building and facilitating relationships. The ending of the therapeutic relationship, however, is just as important as the beginning of the relationship and should be dealt with openly.

The issue of ongoing change or progress is actually more significant to the therapist than to the child and is a result of the therapist's need to know rather than a prerequisite for the child's growth. Seldom do children wonder if they are making progress. They are simply and completely engaged in the continual process of the unfolding of the wonder of living. The child-centered play therapist appreciates this process with children. But, at the same time, practical issues must be dealt with, such as the therapist's own feelings about needing to know change is indeed occurring and the reality of not keeping children in therapy forever. At some point in time, decisions must be made. It is hoped that children will always be a part of these decisions.

Determining Therapeutic Movement Within Sessions

During the process of play therapy, changes within children are not always easily determined or observable in the context of their expressions in the playroom. Children may demonstrate similar kinds of play behavior session after session, with no immediately observable change in pattern or content of play. At the same time, changes in children's behavior outside the playroom may indeed be observable. This can be accounted for by recognizing that, as children's needs to express themselves in negative ways are met in the playroom, they have less need to express those needs in inappropriate ways outside the playroom. These negative behaviors can be discarded and creative energy focused on more positive behaviors. At the same time, children may continue to express similar previously exhibited behaviors in the playroom, because this is a safe place to do so, and also because the need to express and examine those feelings has not been completely met.

When children continue to demonstrate the same behaviors session after session, the therapist may begin to experience some anxiety because of her need to have things happen more quickly and the need to see observable change. The therapist may begin to experience some doubt about her own adequacy and the adequacy of the approach. We all want to know we are doing well, that we are being helpful to children. When there is a lack of concrete observable change in children's playroom behavior, the therapist may experience doubt about herself as a therapist, begin to lose faith in the process, and decide that a more directive approach is needed. Therapists need to be aware that this is usually a move to meet their own needs to feel more adequate and is not really an attempt to meet children's needs. The responsibility of children in play therapy does not include satisfying the therapist's schedule for change in behavior. Children have their own inner-developed schedules, and the therapist must wait patiently for each child's self to emerge.

Seldom do children make gigantic, insightful breakthroughs in play therapy. Growth is a slow process and so is change in behavior. The therapist must be patient with the process. The therapist who expects momentous and dramatic changes by children will probably be disappointed and, if unaware of this need, very likely will become inconsistent in his approach by trying first one technique and then another in an effort to bring about more rapid change. **When the therapist is feeling the greatest urge to do something different, may well be the time when the therapist needs to be most consistent, patient, and understanding.** To do otherwise may result in the child feeling rejected and wanting to please the therapist.

Children's nonverbal behavior can provide significant cues to understanding the totality of their way of behaving or functioning and useful information in understanding the therapeutic process in play therapy. Change is occurring in hundreds of little ways, and the therapist just has to look for those indications of the process of change.

Dimensions of Change

Firsts (First-Time Behaviors)

That movement in the therapeutic process is occurring can be determined by carefully noting in each session those behaviors that the therapist can recall as having occurred for the first time in the relationship with the child. For example, this may be the first time in the initial five sessions that Jason has played near the therapist, or perhaps Jason played very near the therapist and this is the first time he has ventured to play in another part of the room away from the therapist.

Perhaps Kathy has painted pictures at the easel every session, and in this session she does not paint. The therapist needs to recognize that a reason does exist for Kathy's not painting in this session. Something is different. An emotional change has occurred. This may be the first session in which the therapist has had to set a limit on Kathy's behavior, or the first session in which limits have not had to be set. Such changes in behavior signal emotional changes within the child.

RULE OF THUMB:

Look for firsts.

A dramatic first in one of my experiences with 5-year-old Scott—an extremely withdrawn, cautious child ("shy" is avoided in references to children because it carries a negative connotation)— occurred in our fourth session together, when he handed me the alligator puppet to hold for him while he went looking for something else. For some observers, the significance of this behavior might go unnoticed. For Scott to approach me in this way for the first time indicated an emotional change in how he felt about our relationship. This happening seemed to indicate he now felt more comfortable in the relationship and safe enough to approach me directly.

Handing me the alligator puppet was also his way of including me in his play for the first time. To approach me in this way required courage on his part and a feeling that he could direct his own play. Could this be the beginning of becoming self-directing, of taking care of himself? Change for children begins in little ways like this, not with some magnificently insightful, verbalized pronouncement of a decision to forevermore be independent and self-directing.

Perhaps such meaningful change begins with Ali going through an entire sixth session without once asking the therapist for help or trying to get the therapist to make a decision for her, as she had done in the previous five sessions. Could significant meaning be associated with the fact that Brent plays out elaborate scenes of cooking food and feeding every single doll in every session, and now he does not cook or feed any dolls in this session? I think so, just as there is significance in the fact that this is the first time Tammy has played in the sandbox in the first six sessions. A careful examination of such firsts across sessions can help the therapist become aware of significant movement in the therapeutic process.

Themes in Play Behavior

A second dimension that can provide insight into the inner emotional dynamics of the child is the development of themes that occur in the child's play. Emotional experiences and happenings that are important or have in some way significantly impacted children will often show up as repeated behaviors in their play. A theme is the recurrence of certain events or topics in a child's play, either within a session or across several sessions. A key point here is the recurrence of the play after some lapse of time or an intervening period of play in which the theme is not played out. For several minutes, Haley repeatedly buries a dinosaur in the sandbox, digs it up, and buries the dinosaur again. Then she goes over to the easel and paints pictures, returns to the sandbox and repeats the burying behavior. She then plays with the medical kit for a few minutes and returns to the sandbox to continue burying the dinosaur. This repeated play behavior during one play therapy session, with breaks between the repeated play, may indicate the development of a theme.

Shawn's play with the rubber snake for 20 minutes in our first play therapy session would not be considered a theme, even though that would be considered an unusually long time for a 4-year-old to engage in such play. Although the play may be significant and an important occurrence in the developing relationship, the expression must occur more than once or twice to be considered a theme. When Shawn came to the playroom for his second session and again played out the same scene of the rubber snake crawling around the dollhouse, sticking its head into each window and door, and then slowly and deliberately crawling around the top of the dollhouse, I suspected a theme. This suspicion was confirmed when Shawn repeated the same play in the third session. At this point, I learned that Shawn's home had been burglarized twice just a few weeks prior to his first play therapy session.

In play therapy sessions 3 through 8, 8-year-old Jacob played out a scene involving the horses, corral, and barn. He pretended to put a bridle on the horse and commented, "It doesn't hurt his mouth." Then he took the horse to the barn and said, "When the horse kicks the stall, a light comes on over here in the house where the man stays who takes care of the horses so he will know the horse needs help." The significance of this play is evident when it is known that Jacob was receiving electrical stimulation twice a week to strengthen the muscles in his jaws as a part of his speech therapy program. Small electrodes were placed inside his mouth and the procedure was generally painless. However, sometimes the muscles got tense from the stimulation, and Jacob would let the speech therapist know he was experiencing some discomfort by pressing a button to make a light come on.

The theme may not always be readily recognizable, because what is being played, the activity, or the toys being played with may be different each time, but the theme of the play or the underlying meaning of the play is the same. This was the case with Paul, as described in Chapter 10. A theme of reluctance to leave the security of home was evident in the scenes he played out involving the airplane trip in which he announced, "They're going on a trip to New York," loaded the doll family into the airplane, and then promptly announced, "They're back!" without the people ever having flown away from the dollhouse. A second scene involved a family trip in which Paul loaded the family into a truck, drove the truck within inches around the dollhouse, and quickly announced, "They're back." The third scene consisted of him announcing, "They're going to move," loading all the dollhouse furniture and fixtures into a truck, and then quickly saying "They decided to live here again," as he unloaded and replaced the furniture in the dollhouse. Paul experienced tremendous fear of abandonment. Such repeated play behaviors can indicate emotional issues the child is playing out.

Frequency of *repetition of play behaviors* can indicate emotional issues the child is playing out. The *intensity and emotional energy*, not physical energy but emotional energy expended by a child when repeating play behaviors, is another factor that may identify a theme. When the play therapist is experiencing being with a child, this intensity is sensed and felt by the therapist. There is a feeling of knowing something important is being experienced. When the theme is no longer observable that can be an indication the child has been able to emotionally move toward resolution and adjustment.

The purpose for clarifying themes is to help the therapist understand what a child is exploring, experiencing, and working on in the play therapy process. This increased awareness and understanding can help the therapist to be more sensitive and more fully in tune with a child's internal struggle. The purpose is not to provide information for the child or to facilitate insight to meet an objective of promoting change in a child. Determining what a child's symbolic play behavior means is a challenge and often at best an educated guess on the part of the therapist and could be wrong. There is also the factor of perception and the possibility that the therapist is seeing in the child's play only what the therapist is looking for. (You may want to read again about the child in the section on Background Information in Chapter 7.) The play therapist who is well aware of these cautions can have some assurance of accuracy when the play behaviors or events closely approximate a known significant event in a child's life as in the case of the child's home that had been burglarized or the child in speech therapy.

Understanding themes can help the therapist better understand a child's internal process. Emotional growth, resolution of specific problems, or working through and being able to leave an issue can sometimes be observed in changes in the way a child plays out a theme. Changes might be observed in frequency of theme play or changes in the sequencing of events that are played out. The therapist may note a decrease in the child's intensity or perhaps there is now an absence of intensity. While playing out the theme, there may be a change in the child's physical activity, less agitated, less rushed, the play or verbalization of the theme no longer seems pushed from deep inside the child. After several sessions of theme play, playing out the theme may stop completely indicating the child has achieved resolution, played out what was inside, set that problem aside, and moved on to adjustment.

Calling attention to or identifying themes in a child's play for the benefit of the child is interpretative, structuring, distracting to a child, interferes with the process of the child's play, and places the therapist in the lead in the relationship. The therapist's need to educate or inform a child or stimulate insight in the child places the focus on the therapist, and the therapist is no longer being with the child. Pointing out themes is a cognitive process. It is not possible to work on informing a child about themes and at the same time to be in touch with the emotional person of the child. The relationship with the child is more important than what the therapist knows about the meaning of the child's play.

The Meaning of Termination

Termination is a harsh-sounding term and seems so final that it does not at all convey what I would like to communicate about discontinuing regular contacts with children. The words "concluding" or "ending" could be used, but again these seem so final, as though the relationship is completely severed and will in no way continue to exist. Nothing could be further from the truth. Child and therapist have shared—sometimes tentatively, sometimes painfully, sometimes eagerly, and sometimes in rocky ways—in developing and building a meaningful, sensitively caring relationship. Tender moments have occurred, times of great excitement, joy that could almost not be contained, periods of anger and frustration screamed out at the world, points of grand discovery, intervals of quiet being together when words or sounds were not necessary, and a season of shared understanding and acceptance. Such a relationship can never be terminated, for it goes on and on as a part of those persons who have shared in it. Such important experiences live on in the persons who have experienced them and do not end just because someone decides not to meet on a regular basis again.

> The leaving of the old and the beginning of the new constitute the ever-recurring shifting of the scenes in human development. The old is terminated with full regard for the values and satisfactions that have accrued from it. If these values must, however, be measured and felt only in the circumstances in which they were experienced originally, then they cease to be growth-inducing influences and lose their positive meaning. Values from any life experience retain their positive meaning only as the individual is free to use them in the ever-recurring newness of living. This is not forgetting and repressing the old, but it is using the old to provide the structure of the new. (Allen, 1942, p. 293)

A single word seems so inadequate in attempting to describe accurately this part of the process, which the therapist has been moving toward since the initial contact with the child. The therapist's purpose in being in the relationship has been to contribute to the child's development of self-responsibility, enhancement of self, and unfolding of self-directed change. That the child would no longer need the immediacy of this kind of relationship then is a natural development in the process of growth—not an ending, but rather an extending. If the therapist has been successful in truly making contact with the child on a significant emotional level leading to the sharing of the inner self of the child and the therapist, then a significant relationship has been established—and the ending of personal relationships can be difficult.

Reference Points for Determining Termination

Because the child-centered play therapist has no predetermined, individually tailored, specific goals for children in play therapy, the question of when to terminate is not always easily answered, as might be the case when in the judgment of the therapist a specific behavioral problem has been ameliorated. No specific goals have been established to point to as having been achieved, thus indicating readiness for termination. The therapeutic relationship has focused on the child rather than on a specific problem. Therefore, no empirical checkpoints exist to use as reference points of success. Haworth (1994) suggested the following questions as guides for determining a child's readiness for termination:

1. Is there less dependence on the therapist?
2. Is there less concern about other children using the room or seeing his therapist?
3. Can the child now see and accept both good and bad in the same person?
4. Have there been changes in the child's attitude toward time, in terms of awareness, interest, or acceptance?
5. Has there been a change in his reactions to cleaning up the room: less concern if he formerly had been meticulous or interest in cleaning up as contrasted to earlier messiness?

6. Does the child now accept self?
7. Are there evidences of insight and self-evaluation; does the child compare her former actions or feelings with those of the present?
8. Is there a change in the quality or amount of verbalization?
9. Is there less aggression toward, or with, toys?
10. Does the child accept limits more readily?
11. Have his forms of art expression changed?
12. Is there less need to engage in infantile (e.g., bottle) or regressive (e.g., water) play?
13 Is there less fantasy and symbolic play and more creative constructive play?
14. Has there been a diminution in the number and intensity of fears? (p. 416)

Change is best viewed in terms of a global nature, and these questions help the therapist to focus on the process of change rather than on the attainment of some specific objective that has been predetermined. Any attempt to determine whether or not sufficient change has taken place to merit consideration of discontinuing play therapy should focus primarily on examining changes in children. The play therapist can give consideration to the following areas of self-initiated change within children as a basis for possible discontinuation of play therapy.

1. Child is less dependent.
2. Child is less confused.
3. Child expresses needs openly.
4. Child is able to focus on self.
5. Child accepts responsibility for his own actions and feelings.
6. Child limits her own behavior appropriately.
7. Child is more inner-directed.
8. Child is more flexible.
9. Child is more tolerant of happenings.
10. Child initiates activities with assurance.
11. Child is cooperative but not conforming.
12. Child expresses anger appropriately.
13. Child has moved from negative–sad affect to happy–pleased.

14. Child is more accepting of himself.
15. Child is able to play out story sequences; her play has direction.

Children will give cues in a general way about their readiness to bring the relationship to a close. Some children may begin to stand around in the playroom, no longer as interested in the toys. They may seem listless, uninvolved, and almost as though they are playing in slow motion. Children often express a general complaint of having nothing to do; they seem bored and wander around the room. At such times, some children will announce, "I don't think I need to come anymore." Such a statement is a declaration of the child's wholeness and ability to separate from the therapist and to rely fully upon self. This is a very positive affirmation of self. Sometimes children will compare present behaviors or reactions with their earlier, different reactions, thus noting the changes in self. The therapist may note a general change in the feeling-tone of the time together in the playroom. The time together just doesn't "feel" the same. Changes described by parents and teachers also should be considered as part of the whole in a decision to end the play therapy relationship.

Procedures for Ending the Relationship

The age of the child and thus the child's developmental concept of the future, as well as the child's ability to comprehend and effectively participate in the verbal pursuit of abstractions imposed by words, will determine to a considerable degree the approach taken by the therapist to initiate the process of concluding the play therapy experience. In keeping with the child-centered philosophy, the child should be included in the planning necessary for ending this significant relationship. When the therapist determines the child no longer needs the play therapy experience or becomes aware of the child's readiness to discontinue the relationship, this should be responded to in the session with the same degree of sensitivity as would any other feeling or decision by the child. Sometimes the child can be included in the decision regarding bringing the relationship to a close and the date for the last session by the therapist asking how many more times the child feels she needs to come to the playroom. In school settings and some agencies, the end of the school year will dictate the ending of the relationship, at least for a 3-month period, even though the child may not be ready to terminate. With the exception of deciding how many more sessions are needed, the other termination procedures would still be utilized.

Discontinuing the relationship should be a smooth process, not abrupt, and should be accomplished with great sensitivity to the feelings of children. If termination of the play therapy experience is not handled properly, children may feel rejected, punished, or a sense of loss. Actually, no guarantee can be given that the child will not experience some of these feelings, no matter how well the ending is handled. That children may feel anxious about separation from this meaningful relationship and this now significant person in their life is understandable. These feelings are accepted, and no effort is made to try to make a child "feel better" about leaving. To do so would discount the child's feelings of anxiety, hurt, anger, or whatever else the child experiences about leaving the relationship. Leaving the door open for children to return if they feel the need to do so, by informing them that they can come back, sometimes helps children with the turning loose process.

Children will need time in the playroom to live out the ending of this important relationship, just as they have lived out other significant parts of their lives. Therefore, the process for actual termination will need to be started two or three sessions prior to the final session. In the beginning of this relationship, the child needed time to discover and develop a way of being in the relationship. Now the child will need time to work through emerging feelings about ending this meaningful part of life and to explore feelings about no longer having this area of support. Through participating in the planning for ending the relationship, the child has the opportunity to discover what the ending of a meaningful relationship feels like.

During the process of preparing for ending, some children may regress temporarily for part of a session and demonstrate behaviors observed in earlier sessions. This may be the child's way of revisiting old behaviors and experiencing the satisfaction of being able to compare the present with the past. A child may mess up a picture being painted and then say, "Used to, that would have made me mad." One could speculate that the child's playing out of earlier behaviors could be a belated attempt to say, "I don't want to leave. Please let me continue to come here."

With some children, the therapist may want to consider a tapering off process for termination by moving from a once-a-week schedule to once every other week for the final two sessions. Another variation would be to schedule one last follow-up session a month after the last regular weekly contact. This determination should be based on the child's needs, not the therapist's need to know how things are going or the therapist's reluctance to turn loose. Once the process for ending the relationship has begun, children need to be reminded of how many more times they will have in the playroom at the beginning and at the end of the remaining two or three sessions. For some children, a week is a long time to remember how many more times they will get to come to the playroom. At the beginning of the third to last play therapy session, the therapist might say, "Kara, I want to remind you that you will be in the playroom today and two more times after today, and that will be all for now." The "for now" leaves the door open if the child should need to return at some later date. This statement is repeated at the end of the session, and the process is repeated in the next session and at the beginning of the last session.

Children's Reactions to the Last Session

Trying to predict how a child will react in the final session usually is not possible. Some children approach the final session in a rather matter-of-fact way. They may not even make a comment about this being the last time they will be in the playroom. The therapist should suppress any urge to make a big deal out of the last session, either through conversation or through lingering goodbye hugs. If initiated by the child, that would be appropriate.

Otherwise, such activity should be recognized as the therapist's need and dealt with accordingly. The therapist avoids such comments as, "I'm going to miss you," or, "I have really enjoyed our time together," because these comments could cause the child to feel guilty if she had not already had such a thought. Even the last minute is still the child's time, a time for the child's needs to be expressed and responded to by the therapist. Some children may indicate their reluctance to end the relationship by lingering at the door on their way out, commenting about the room, or thinking of a variety of things they want to tell the therapist.

Some children may be very angry about ending the relationship, as was the case with 7-year-old Brad. We had experienced 12 wonderful times together, during which Brad had never been overly messy or aggressive. He had played very actively but in careful ways. In our last session, Brad entered the playroom, made a comment about, "Yeah, this is our last one," and began to pull toys off the shelves and dump them in the middle of the floor. Although he said not one word during this process, he was obviously angry. He did not stop until he had emptied all the shelves. What a mess! With hardly a glance to take in the mess he had made, Brad began to replace the toys on the shelves and did not stop until the job was completed. That was quite a task and occupied most of the time left in the session. With 10 minutes remaining, he prepared the most delightful and elaborate meal for both of us, commenting about what he was cooking and foods he liked. Time was then up, and he walked out of the playroom without a goodbye or any verbal reference to that being the last time together in the playroom. Brad had eloquently communicated his mixed feelings about the ending of our relationship.

Some children are very open in sharing their feelings about ending the relationship, as was the case with 7-year-old Lori, who graphically expressed the importance of the relationship with the therapist in the following conversation, which occurred in the final session:

Lori: (While filling pots and pans with sand.) I have lots of friends. They'll be my friends forever! (Looking sideways at the counselor.) You're one of my friends.

Therapist: Sounds like you think we'll always be friends.

Lori: (With an intense, affirmative head nod.) Uh, huh! Even when you're not here.

Therapist: So, we'll still be friends even when I'm gone.

Lori: You can just talk to Jesus about me.

Therapist: Seems like it's real important for me to always remember you.

Lori: We'll have a secret code. (Writes her phone number on a piece of paper, and puts four stickers on another paper.) Here. This is my number if you have an emergency. And, you can look at these pictures and say "Jesus" or "God," whatever you want, and we'll be connected.

Therapist: So, you figured out a way for us to always be connected—and friends.

Lori: Yup (affirmative head nod), always connected.

Premature Termination

Sometimes a parent will stop bringing a child to play therapy without notifying the therapist; so there is no opportunity for the therapist to prepare the child for termination. This process is usually abrupt and disconcerting to the child and often occurs at the most inopportune time (i.e., the child has just shared something dramatic or personal with the therapist, tested or broke limits for the first time, or in the last session made a significant change in assuming responsibility). If the child does not get to come back to the playroom, the child may internalize the experience as punishment for what occurred in the last session. When a parent unexpectedly discontinues therapy, the therapist should contact the parent and explain the importance of a termination session.

A final session allows children to experience a positive end to a relationship that has been important to them.

References

Allen, F. (1942). *Psychotherapy with children.* New York: Norton.

Haworth, M. (1994). *Child psychotherapy: Practice and theory.* Northvale, NJ: Aronson.

Chapter 16

Intensive and Short-Term Play Therapy

We live in a world driven by the need for instant gratification, immediate success, and the quick fix. Precooked, premixed, ready-to-use is a way of life that permeates society, molds attitudes, affects relationships, and, unfortunately, has even shaped and molded some areas of the field of mental health. Quick solutions to life's problems are insisted on rather than focusing on the process of learning how to live life. Play therapists are encouraged to resist the pressures for quick solutions, to trust what they believe about the process of the child-centered play therapy relationship, and to be diligent in educating managed care providers and agency administrators about the emotional and developmental needs of children and the efficiency of the play therapy process.

Play therapy is not necessarily a long-term process requiring many months or even years of therapy. Many behavioral problems and experiences of children can be dealt with effectively in a relatively short period of time, when the inner dynamic natural creative resources of a child emerge in the facilitative safety of the child-centered play therapy relationship. A child's natural developmental state consists of a continual process of movement toward the solution of problems. Therefore, there is no need for the therapist to impose predetermined solutions on the child in order to hurry up the process of growth.

Intensive Play Therapy

Child-centered play therapy provides the relationship necessary for children to develop adaptive coping mechanisms on their own terms and at their own emotional pace. We do not look at a developing toddler and say, "You aren't changing fast enough." We are patient and trust the natural process of development. This same logic can be applied to children in play therapy. When provided with the kind of relationship described in this book, children are capable of changing at a remarkable pace. I do not mean to imply, however, that all children's problems can be dealt with in a few sessions of play therapy.

Rather than focusing on the number of play therapy sessions, perhaps what is more important is that the scheduled frequency of sessions be examined. The traditional concept of scheduling play therapy sessions once a week does not always match the dynamic developmental growth of children. A week between sessions can be a very long time in the life of a child, especially when the child has been sexually abused, is experiencing the trauma of divorce, or is facing some equally debilitating crisis.

Play therapists are encouraged to consider the possibility of condensing the time between sessions for some children. We simply do not know what the human organism is capable of assimilating, nor the amount of time needed by children between play therapy sessions to process changes facilitated during the play therapy sessions. The traditional scheduling of sessions once a week is designed to meet the needs of the therapist and may not necessarily meet the emotional needs of the child.

When a child has experienced a crisis or trauma, the play therapist should consider intensive play therapy in which the child is scheduled for play therapy sessions two or three times a week for the first 2 weeks in order to speed up the therapeutic process. Intensive play therapy also is recommended for a child who is already being seen in play therapy and has such an experience. If there has been a death in the family, major car accident, sexual or physical abuse, domestic violence, attack by an animal, bombing, or other stressful life event, a week between sessions can be an eternity for a child. In some cases of psychic trauma, a child may need to be scheduled for play therapy 5 or 6 days a week for the first week or two.

The natural response of children is to reenact or play out traumatic happenings in an unconscious effort to comprehend, overcome, develop a sense of control, or assimilate the experience. Because children's significant emotional experiences are expressed symbolically as they play out happenings in their lives, there is an emotional distancing from the actual event that protects children from feeling overwhelmed. It is the dynamic of this distancing from the actual experience through play that enables children to deal with and assimilate intense emotional experiences when sessions are scheduled more closely together. This process allows children to work through traumatic experiences without having to identify and label the events as their own or deal with them directly, as is required when children must identify and label frightening or painful experiences at the direction of the therapist. The child-centered play therapist establishes the kind of child-paced therapeutic environment in which children feel accepted, understood, respected, and safe enough to deal with threatening feelings.

The play therapist does not push, encourage, or direct the child's play in any way. Therefore, the child explores areas she feels safe enough to express and at a pace she feels adequate to cope with at any given time. When sessions are not structured by the therapist, the child is allowed to pace her exploration as fast or as slow as needed to accommodate her level of functioning. The trusting of this intuitive knowing on the part of the child is crucial in intensive play therapy experiences, which reduce the time between sessions. Directing or structuring a child to play out traumatic experiences could retraumatize a child if he is not emotionally ready to confront the event. *The child-centered play therapist trusts the child's inner direction, allows the child to lead in all areas of the relationship, and resists any urge to direct the child's play or conversation. The child leads the relationship and the direction of the play.*

Several variations of intensive play therapy have been used in the Center for Play Therapy at the University of North Texas. One unique model has been the scheduling of some carefully selected children for three 30-minute play therapy sessions each day for

3 days, with 30-minute breaks between sessions for bathroom breaks, snacks, and time in the waiting room. An interesting observation is that the play therapy process for each of these sessions appears to be similar to the process that occurs in once-a-week sessions. For example, the process of exploration described by play therapists for a typical third session is similar to what occurs in session 3 of three sessions scheduled in a single day. Parents have reported positive behavioral changes for children in these experiences.

Research on Intensive Play Therapy

Kot, Landreth, and Giordano (1998) used an intensive model of short-term child-centered play therapy in working with children who had witnessed domestic violence and were residing in a domestic violence shelter with their mothers. The 11 children in the experimental group received 12 45-minute individual play therapy sessions, 1 each day, in a 2-week period in addition to shelter services. Eleven children in the control group received only the shelter services. Child witnesses in the experimental group demonstrated a significant increase in self-concept, significant reduction in their externalizing behavior problems, and significant reduction in their total behavior problems, as compared to the control group. The short-term intensive model fits particularly well with the unstable and transient life situations of families residing in domestic violence shelters.

Tyndall-Lind, Landreth, and Giordano (2001) conducted a comparative analysis of intensive short-term child-centered individual play therapy and intensive short-term child-centered sibling group play therapy with child witnesses of domestic violence residing in a domestic violence shelter with their mothers. The 10 children in the group play therapy group received 12 45-minute sibling group play therapy sessions, 1 each day in a 2-week period in addition to shelter services. The comparison group of individual play therapy and the control group were obtained from the Kot et al. (1998) study. Child witnesses in the sibling group play therapy group

FIGURE 16.1   The presence of several children in the playroom facilitates the reluctant child's discovery that the therapist is a safe person by observing other children.

(Figure 16.1) demonstrated a significant increase in self-concept; a significant decrease in externalizing and internalizing behavior problems; a significant decrease in overall behavior problems; and significant decreases in aggression, anxiety, and depression, as compared to the control group. Intensive short-term sibling group play therapy and intensive short-term individual play therapy were found to be equally effective with children who witnessed family violence.

Jones and Landreth (2002) studied the effects of child-centered play therapy on chronically ill children with insulin-dependent diabetes mellitus. Children were randomly assigned to an experimental or nonintervention control group. Children in the experimental group received a total of 12 30-minute child-centered play therapy sessions and regularly scheduled camp therapeutic interventions during a 3-week summer camp for diabetic children. Children in the control group participated in the therapeutic camping experiences provided. Both groups demonstrated improved anxiety scores. Children in the experimental group showed a statistically significant increase in diabetes adaptation over the control group.

Shen (2002) randomly assigned child earthquake victims from a rural elementary school in Taiwan to a child-centered play therapy group or a control group. All children were scored at high risk for maladjustment. The child-centered play therapy groups received 10 40-minute group play therapy sessions over 4 weeks. Results indicated that the child-centered play therapy group demonstrated a significant decrease in overall anxiety, physiological anxiety, worry/oversensitivity, and suicide risk. The results also indicated a large overall treatment effect on anxiety and a small to medium treatment effect on reducing children's suicide risk.

Smith and Landreth (2003) investigated the effects of an intensive format of the Landreth Child–Parent Relationship Therapy (CPRT) 10-week filial therapy model (12 sessions in 3 weeks), with child witnesses of domestic violence residing in a domestic violence shelter with their mothers. Children in the filial therapy group demonstrated a significant increase in self-concept; a significant decrease in overall behavior problems; a significant decrease in internalizing and externalizing behavior problems; and significant decreases in aggression, anxiety, and depression, as compared to the control group.

Baggerly (2004) conducted a pretest/posttest single-group design for children living in a homeless shelter. Children participated in 9 to 12, 30-minute child-centered play therapy sessions once or twice a week. Results revealed significant improvement in self-concept, significance, competence, negative mood and negative self-esteem related to depression, and anxiety.

Short-Term Play Therapy

For the purposes of this discussion, short-term play therapy is considered to be 10 to 12 sessions or fewer. Short-term play therapy would not be appropriate for all children needing play therapy. Children who have experienced prolonged sexual or physical abuse or trauma and those who have severe emotional problems would certainly need longer-term therapy. Short-term child-centered play therapy has been found to be effective with developmental issues;

with a wide variety of childhood problems, such as chronic illness, school-related learning problems, behavioral problems, emotional adjustment, and self-concept problems; and with child victims of domestic violence. Remarkable progress is possible when children experience a warm, caring, empathic, understanding, and accepting relationship characteristic of child-centered play therapy and are allowed to set the direction and pace of the experience.

Research on Short-Term Play Therapy

Although the literature contains many reports of successful short-term play therapy using a variety of theoretical approaches, this review will focus on the effectiveness of short-term child-centered play therapy as reported in the literature.

Fleming and Snyder (1947) found that after 12 nondirective group play therapy sessions, the girls' group showed significant improvement in personality adjustment as compared to the control group.

Axline (1948) reported significant progress using child-centered play therapy with a selective mute 5-year-old boy who would not interact with other children, would not speak to anyone, and rolled up into a ball and hid his face when approached by another child. He had developed normally until age 3, when he ceased talking and walking, and reverted to infantile behaviors. By the fifth play therapy session, his mother reported noticeable improvements in his behavior at home, including less regressive behavior and increased verbalization. The school also reported positive changes in his behavior.

Bills (1950) studied the effectiveness of child-centered play therapy as an intervention for third-grade children experiencing reading difficulties. Eight children received six weekly individual play therapy sessions and three weekly group play therapy sessions. A control group received no treatment. On the posttesting, each of the children in play therapy demonstrated increased reading skills, and their total reading skills group score was statistically significant.

Cox (1953) found that after 10 weeks of individual play therapy and a 13-week follow-up period, young children (3 years old) showed significant improvement in social adjustment as compared to a control group. Older children (13 years old) showed significant improvement on the sociometric measure as compared to the control group.

Irwin (1971) conducted six sessions of child-centered play therapy with a 16-year-old girl hospitalized for schizophrenia. She would not make eye contact, remained in bed throughout the day, displayed no affect, lacked bladder and bowel control, presented an expressionless stare, and spoke only the word "yellow." Significant behavioral changes were reported by hospital staff after only two play therapy sessions, and at the conclusion of six sessions, she was consistently leaving her room voluntarily during the day, was reading aloud in front of other hospital patients, was communicating verbally, made eye contact, displayed affect, and had bladder and bowel control. A 2-month follow-up report noted that she was attending school and continuing to display remarkable progress.

Pelham (1972) conducted a comparative analysis of individual nondirective play therapy and nondirective group play therapy with socially immature kindergarten children. Children in both groups received six to eight sessions. Children in both treatment groups made positive gains in social maturity when compared to a control group. Teacher ratings indicated that children participating in both treatment groups improved significantly in classroom behavior when compared to a control group.

Oualline (1975) studied the effectiveness of child-centered play therapy with 12 hearing-impaired children, ages 4 to 6, who were described as having behavioral problems. The treatment group received 10 weekly 50-minute play therapy sessions and scored significantly higher on a scale measuring social maturity than a matched control group. Oualline noted that child-centered play therapy is especially appropriate for hearing-impaired children because of the lack of emphasis on verbalization.

Barlow, Strother, and Landreth (1985) reported eight weekly sessions of child-centered play therapy to be effective with a 4-year-old child experiencing trichotillomania (pulling out and then eating her own hair). The authors concluded that the atmosphere created by the play therapist was the single most important factor of the therapeutic procedure and enabled the child to feel a freedom to express herself that she had never felt before. By the seventh session, new hair growth covered the child's head, providing significant visual evidence of the effectiveness of short-term child-centered play therapy.

Perez (1987) conducted a comparative analysis of child-centered individual play therapy and child-centered group play therapy with sexually abused children. Children in both groups received 12 sessions. The self-concepts of children in both treatment groups increased at a significant level while those in the control group scored lower at posttest. The self-mastery scores of children in both treatment groups increased significantly while those in the control group dropped. There were no differences between individual and group play therapy.

Trostle (1988) found after 10 sessions of nondirective group play therapy that bilingual Puerto Rican children showed significant improvement compared to the control group on self-control, and the higher developmental level play behaviors of make-believe and reality. Boys who received child-centered play therapy became more accepting of others than boys or girls in the control group.

Rae, Worchel, Upchurch, Sanner, and Daniel (1989) found that hospitalized children receiving two child-centered play therapy sessions showed a significant reduction in hospital fears as compared to a verbally oriented support condition, diversionary play condition (allowed to play with toys), and a control group. A reduction in fears was not evidenced in any other group.

Crow (1990) reported significant changes in self-concept using 10 weekly 30-minute individual child-centered play therapy sessions conducted in an elementary school with 12 first-grade students who had been retained because of poor reading performance. The treatment group also demonstrated an improvement in locus of control, as compared to the control group.

LeVieux (1994) used a child-centered play therapy approach with a 5-year-old girl who was grieving the loss of her father. At the onset of therapy, the child was described as stubborn, uncooperative, moody, and depressed. By the seventh session, the child's mother reported notable changes, including her daughter's ability to more easily discuss the father's death and to express her sadness and anger.

Johnson, McLeod, and Fall (1997) examined the effects of six child-centered play therapy sessions on children identified as having an emotional or physical disorder that affected learning in the school setting. Researcher observations, teacher reports, and parent reports confirmed a reduction in the children's impulsive behavior, increased control of their environment, and increased ability to express emotions.

Post (1999) found that at-risk children who participated in four child-centered play therapy sessions maintained the same level of self-esteem and internal locus of control, while children in the control group dropped at a statistically significant level.

Brandt (2001) found that young children with behavioral adjustment difficulties who participated in 7 to 10 child-centered play therapy sessions improved significantly on internalizing behaviors (withdrawn behavior, somatic complaints, and anxiety/depression) in comparison to a matched control group. Although not significant, parents of children who received play therapy reported a remarkably larger decrease in parenting stress, as compared to the control group over time.

Webb (2001) reported the effective use of one to three play therapy sessions as a part of a crisis team response to the Oklahoma City bombing. Using her tote bag of play materials, Webb converted space in a small storage room in an elementary school near the bomb site and had 30-minute play therapy sessions with children referred by teachers in the building.

Short-Term Child Parent Relationship Therapy (CPRT)

The 10-session Child Parent Relationship Therapy (CPRT) model I developed is by the very nature of the structure of the model a short-term child-centered play therapy intervention. Parents receive 10 sessions of training in basic child-centered play therapy principles and skills and the actual number of play sessions children have with their parents is 7, due to the fact that parents do not start play sessions with their children until after the third filial training session.

CPRT is a well-researched modality with more than 40 controlled-outcome research studies involving over 1,000 paraprofessionals (primarily parents). Collectively, the body of research on the effectiveness of CPRT is compelling. That improvements have been achieved in both parents and children demonstrates the robustness of this approach. The efficacy of this model in so few sessions is especially noteworthy. Bratton, Landreth, and Lin (2010) further analyzed the meta-analytic data gathered by Bratton, Ray, Rhine, and Jones (2005) to determine the overall treatment effect of CPRT methodology. Statistical analysis yielded an overall ES of 1.25 for CPRT studies and an even stronger ES of 1.30 for parent-only CPRT (omitting teachers and student mentors). Only those CPRT studies in which the individual researchers were trained and supervised directly by Bratton or Landreth were included in the analysis to ensure adherence to the treatment protocol.

CPRT research studies have demonstrated significantly positive results with a variety of issues and populations, including sexually abused children, children living in domestic violence shelters, children whose mothers or fathers were incarcerated, children experiencing adjustment difficulties at home and school, and children diagnosed with learning differences, pervasive developmental disorders, chronic illness, and a broad range of internalized and externalized behavior problems.

CPRT has been conducted in a variety of settings, including hospitals, churches, shelters, a Native American reservation, prison, county jail, Head Start programs, public and private schools, and community agencies with significantly positive results. The effects of CPRT have also been investigated with diverse populations of parents, including German, Hispanic, immigrant Latino, African American, Native American, Israeli, immigrant Chinese, Korean, and immigrant Korean with significantly positive results in the areas of parental stress, parental empathy, parental acceptance, and family environment.

The reader is referred to Chapter 17 that provides specific research data on the CPRT research studies referred to in this section.

Summary

Although many adults typically require sufficient time between appointments to process information or insights obtained during a therapy session, children do not appear to have the same need. The objective of experimenting with the play therapy schedule is to provide an opportunity for children to make sense of their world through play as quickly and efficiently as possible. Some children apparently can benefit from several play therapy sessions clustered together. Positive results from a variety of studies support deviating from the traditional one session per week and consideration of the condensing of the time between sessions. The use of 12 or fewer play therapy sessions and a format of scheduling play therapy sessions every day for selected populations of children have proven to be effective. The results of research studies suggest that even as few as two or three sessions of play therapy can help children to cope and to develop skills that will enable them to work through emotions and to move on to more adjusted behavior. That children can begin sorting through issues and resolving them when provided with just a few sessions of play therapy is a tribute to the power of the play therapy relationship in the lives of children.

References

Axline, V. M. (1948). Some observations on play therapy. *Journal of Consulting Psychology, 11,* 61–69.

Baggerly, J. (2004). The effects of child-centered group play therapy on self-concept, depression, and anxiety of children who are homeless. *International Journal of Play Therapy, 13,* 31–51.

Barlow, K., Strother, J., & Landreth, G. (1985). Child-centered play therapy: Nancy from baldness to curls. *The School Counselor, 32*(5), 347–356.

Bills, R. E. (1950). Nondirective play therapy with retarded readers. *Journal of Consulting Psychology, 14,* 140–149.

Brandt, M. A. (2001). An investigation of the efficacy of play therapy with young children. *Dissertation Abstracts International: Section A. Humanities and Social Science, 61*(07), 2603.

Bratton, S., Landreth, G., & Lin, Y. (2010). Child parent relationship therapy: A review of controlled-outcome research. In J. Baggerly, D. Ray, & S. Bratton (Eds.), *Child-centered play therapy research: Evidence base for effective practice* (pp. 267–293). New York: Wiley.

Bratton, S., Ray, D., Rhine, T., & Jones, L. (2005). The efficacy of play therapy with children: A meta-analytic review of treatment outcomes. *Professional Psychology: Research and Practice, 36*(4), 376–390.

Cox, F. (1953). Sociometric status and individual adjustment before and after play therapy. *Journal of Abnormal Social Psychology, 48,* 354–356.

Crow, J. (1990). Play therapy with low achievers in reading (Doctoral dissertation, University of North Texas). *Dissertation Abstracts International,* 50(09), B2789.

Fleming, L., & Snyder, W. (1947). Social and personal changes following nondirective group play therapy. *American Journal of Orthopsychiatry, 17,* 101–116.

Irwin, B. L. (1971). Play therapy for a regressed schizophrenic patient. *JPN and Mental Health Services, 9,* 30–32.

Johnson, L., McLeod, E., & Fall, M. (1997). Play therapy with labeled children in the schools. *Professional School Counseling, 1*(1), 31–34.

Jones, E., & Landreth, G. (2002). The efficacy of intensive individual play therapy for chronically ill children. *International Journal of Play Therapy, 11,* 117–140.

Kot, S., Landreth, G. L., & Giordano, M. (1998). Intensive child-centered play therapy with child witnesses of domestic violence. *International Journal of Play Therapy, 7*(2), 17–36.

LeVieux, J. (1994). Terminal illness and death of father: Case of Celeste, age 5½. In N. B. Webb (Ed.). *Helping bereaved children: A handbook for practitioners* (pp. 81–95). New York: Guilford.

Oualline, V. J. (1975). Behavioral outcomes of short-term nondirective play therapy with preschool deaf children (Unpublished doctoral dissertation, North Texas State University, Denton).

Pelham, L. (1972). Self-directive play therapy with socially immature kindergarten students (Doctoral dissertation, University of Northern Colorado, 1971). *Dissertation Abstracts International, 32,* 3798.

Perez, C. (1987). A comparison of group play therapy and individual play therapy for sexually abused children (Doctoral dissertation, University of Northern Colorado, 1987). *Dissertation Abstracts International, 48,* 3079.

Post, P. (1999). Impact of child-centered play therapy on the self-esteem, locus of control, and anxiety of at-risk 4th, 5th, and 6th grade students. *International Journal of Play Therapy, 8*(2), 53–74.

Rae, W., Worchel, E., Upchurch, J., Sanner, J., & Daniel, C. (1989). The psychosocial impact of play on hospitalized children. *Journal of Pediatric Psychology, 14,* 617–627.

Shen, Y. (2002). Short-term group play therapy with Chinese earthquake victims: Effects on anxiety, depression, and adjustment. *International Journal of Play Therapy, 11*(1), 43–63.

Smith, N., & Landreth, G. (2003). Intensive filial therapy with child witnesses of domestic violence. A comparison with individual and sibling group play therapy. *International Journal of Play Therapy, 12*(1), 67–88.

Trostle, S. (1988). The effects of child-centered group play sessions on social-emotional growth of three- to six-year-old bilingual Puerto Rican children. *Journal of Research in Childhood Education, 3,* 93–106.

Tyndall-Lind, A., Landreth, G., & Giordano, M. (2001). Intensive group play therapy with child witnesses of domestic violence. *International Journal of Play Therapy, 10*(1), 53–83.

Webb, P. (2001). Play therapy with traumatized children. In G. Landreth (Ed.), *Innovations in play therapy: Issues, process, and special populations* (pp. 289–302). Philadelphia: Brunner-Routledge.

Chapter **17**

Research in
Play Therapy

Although research on child-centered play therapy (CCPT) spans over 60 years and provides evidence of effectiveness in a multitude of settings and across a wide variety of presenting problems, the focus of this chapter is on research conducted on CCPT from 1995 to 2010, with the exception of two of the meta-analytic studies reviewed. CCPT is the most thoroughly researched theoretical approach in the field of play therapy. Baggerly, in *Child Centered Play Therapy Research* (Baggerly, Ray, & Bratton, 2010), pointed out,

> You will notice that all the research studies described (in this book) are based on the child-centered play therapy (CCPT) theoretical orientation and filial therapy approach. This focus is because virtually all play therapy research studies that were published in a professional journal since the year 2000 (2000 to 2010) were CCPT or filial therapy. (pp. xiii–xiv)

Ray (2008) conducted the largest published research study of CCPT on record involving 202 children ages 2 to 13. She statistically analyzed archival data on children referred over a 9-year period to a university counseling clinic who received weekly individual CCPT. Children were assigned to data groups according to presenting problem and length of therapy as the independent variable and parent–child relationship stress as the dependent variable. CCPT demonstrated statistically significant effects for externalizing problems, combined externalizing/internalizing problems, and nonclinical problems (parent relationship). Results also indicated that CCPT effects increased with number of sessions specifically reaching statistical significance at 11 to 18 sessions with large effect sizes.

The large number of participants in Ray's study is atypical in not only play therapy research but also in the field of psychotherapy in general. Consistent with most outcome research in the field of psychotherapy, CCPT research is limited by generally small sample sizes that restrict the generalization of research findings. Meta-analysis makes it possible to overcome the limitations associated with small sample sizes by combining research findings across studies to determine an overall treatment effect.

Meta-Analytic Research Studies

Studies by LeBlanc and Ritchie (2001) and Bratton, Ray, Rhine, and Jones (2005) were the first meta-analytic studies to focus exclusively on the efficacy of play therapy. Both studies demonstrated the effectiveness of play therapy and have contributed to the acceptance of play therapy and filial therapy in the broader field of child psychotherapy. The findings of both studies supported the use of play therapy as a viable modality for use with children.

LeBlanc and Ritchie's (2001) meta-analysis reviewed 42 controlled play therapy studies dated 1950 to 1996 and found a moderate treatment effect size of 0.66 standard deviations for the 42 studies. Twenty of the 42 studies utilized child-centered play therapy without caregiver involvement. These studies were found to have an overall average effect size of 0.43, considered a moderate treatment effect.

Bratton et al. (2005) conducted a more comprehensive meta-analysis of 93 controlled-outcome studies of play therapy research dated 1942 to 2000 that met the following criteria: use of a controlled research design, sufficient data for computing effect size, and the identification by the author of a labeled *play therapy* intervention. A play therapy intervention was further defined to include studies that examined the use of paraprofessionals (primarily parents) as well as professionals as the direct provider of the intervention. The majority of studies that fell into the paraprofessional category used filial therapy methodology.

Bratton et al. used Cohen's d (1988) guidelines (0.20 = small; 0.50 = medium; 0.80 = large) to interpret treatment effect size (ES). They found that play therapy demonstrated an overall large treatment effect (ES 0.80); meaning that, on average, children receiving play therapy performed 0.80 standard deviations above children who did not receive play therapy on specified outcome measures. The average age of study participants was 7.

Additionally, Bratton et al. found that play therapy had a moderate to large beneficial effect for internalizing (ES = 0.81), externalizing (ES = 0.79), and combined problem types (ES = 0.93). Treatment effects on outcomes for measures of self-concept, social adjustment, personality, anxiety, adaptive functioning, and family functioning, including quality of the parent–child relationship, were also reported in the moderate to large range. Age and gender were not found to be significant factors in predicting play therapy outcomes. Play therapy appeared to be equally effective across age and gender.

Of the 93 outcome studies, 26 measured the effects of play therapy conducted by paraprofessionals, defined as a parent, teacher, or peer mentor who was trained in play therapy procedures and supervised by a mental health professional. All studies coded to this group used CPRT (Child–Parent Relationship Therapy, a 10-session filial therapy model) or another filial therapy training methodology; thus all studies included were theoretically consistent in the use of child-centered play therapy principles and skills. Bratton et al. further analyzed this group of studies in order to explore the effect of filial therapy conducted by parents as a treatment modality apart from play therapy conducted by a mental health professional. The authors found that filial therapy showed stronger evidence of treatment effectiveness (ES = 1.15; a large effect size) compared to traditional play therapy (ES = 0.72; a moderate-to-large effect size). Bratton, Landreth, and Lin (2010) further analyzed the meta-analytic data to determine the overall treatment effect for filial therapy studies that employed only CPRT methodology (generally referred to in early studies as the

10-session filial therapy model developed by Landreth). Statistical analysis yielded an overall ES of 1.25 for CPRT studies and an even stronger ES of 1.30 for parent-only CPRT studies (omitting teachers and student mentors) in which the individual researchers were trained and supervised directly by Bratton or Landreth. This requirement ensured adherence to the treatment protocol.

The effect size (ES = 0.92) reported by Bratton et al. for humanistic play therapy interventions, primarily defined as child-centered and nondirective in the reviewed studies, was in the large effect category. It should be noted that humanistic studies included studies with caregiver involvement (filial therapy, etc.) as well as studies with professionally delivered treatment. The findings for humanistic play therapy interventions are encouraging in light of the most recent survey of Association for Play Therapy members that indicated the majority of its members subscribed to the child-centered play therapy (CCPT) approach (Lambert et al., 2005).

Although meta-analytic research studies have investigated the effects of CCPT as part of larger reviews of play therapy research (Bratton et al., 2005; Leblanc & Ritchie, 2001), Lin (2011) was the first researcher to conduct a meta-analytic study focused exclusively on CCPT's effectiveness. He reviewed studies conducted from 1995 to 2010 and selected 52 controlled-outcome studies that met the following criteria: use of CCPT methodology, use of control or comparison repeated measure design, use of standardized psychometric assessment, and clear reporting of effect size or sufficient information for conducting an effect size calculation.

Following the suggestion of Bratton et al. that researchers use more stringent research methods, Lin's meta-analytic study incorporated a high level of methodological rigor including meticulous coding procedures, multiple strategies for accessing publication bias, adoption of the hierarchical linear modeling (HLM) technique, and the use of stringent effect size calculations. In light of this more rigorous approach, Lin cautioned that although some of his findings appear discrepant with results from previous meta-analyses, the results must be interpreted in light of differences in the effect size calculation formula and statistical analysis method used in his study.

The mean age of all child participants in Lin's collected studies was 6.7. Thirty-three of the 52 collected studies had a majority of boys, 11 studies had a majority of girls, and 8 studies did not identify gender. The treatment format utilized in the studies included individual play therapy, individual activity therapy, group play therapy, group activity therapy, and CPRT/filial therapy. The mean number of treatment sessions was 11.87 with a standard deviation of 4.20.

HLM analysis estimated a statistically significant overall effect size of 0.47 for the 52 collected studies ($p < 0.001$). This result indicated that children who received CCPT interventions improved from pretreatment to posttreatment by approximately ½ standard deviation more than children who did not receive CCPT treatment. CCPT had a moderate positive effect for caregiver/child relationship stress (ES = 0.60), self-efficacy (ES = 0.53), and total behavior problem types (ES = 0.53), and a small positive effect for internalizing (ES = 0.37) and externalizing problems (ES = 0.34). Lin concluded that CCPT should be considered to be an effective mental health intervention for children. It had the greatest impact on broad spectrum behavioral problems, child self-esteem, and caregiver/child relationship stress.

Child ethnicity was found to be a factor in treatment outcome. In 15 of the selected studies, the majority of children were Caucasian. Non-Caucasian children (3 studies with majority African American, 4 with majority Hispanic/Latino children, 5 with majority Asian/Asian American children, and 3 with other ethnic populations) made up the majority in 15 other studies, and 16 of the studies were mixed groups. Non-Caucasian children demonstrated substantially greater improvement as a result of CCPT than Caucasian children. Lin concluded that this finding strongly suggests that practitioners can confidently consider CCPT as a culturally responsive intervention.

Cross-Cultural Child-Centered Play Therapy Research

Child-centered play therapy (CCPT) has been demonstrated to have broad cross-cultural applications. Numerous research studies have shown CCPT to be effective across diverse cultures: school-based CCPT with Hispanic children (Garza & Bratton, 2005), short-term CCPT training with Israeli school counselors and teachers (Kagan & Landreth, 2009), group play therapy with Chinese earthquake victims (Shen, 2002), group play therapy with Puerto Rican children (Trostle, 1988), brief CCPT with African American children (Post, 1999), brief CCPT with Japanese children (Ogawa, 2006), brief CCPT training for professionals working with vulnerable children in Kenya (Hunt, 2006), and CCPT with Iranian children with internalized problems (Bayat, 2008).

Multiple studies have also demonstrated the benefits of Child–Parent Relationship Therapy (CPRT), a 10-session model of filial therapy, with diverse parent populations: Chinese parents (Chau & Landreth, 1997; Yuen, Landreth, & Baggerly, 2002), Korean parents (Jang, 2000; Lee & Landreth, 2003), German parents (Grskovic & Goetze, 2008), Israeli parents (Kidron & Landreth, 2010), Native American parents (Glover & Landreth, 2000), African American parents (Sheely-Moore & Bratton, 2010), and Hispanic parents (Villarreal, 2008; Ceballos & Bratton, 2010).

Review of Experimental and Quasi-Experimental CCPT Research

The following review is limited to CCPT controlled-outcome studies published from 1995 to 2010 that met the following criteria: use of CCPT methodology, use of control or comparison repeated measure design, and use of standardized psychometrics.

CHILD-CENTERED PLAY THERAPY (CCPT) CONTROLLED OUTCOME RESEARCH 1995–2010

Authors	Participants/Methods	Findings
Beckloff, D. R. (1998). Filial therapy with children with spectrum pervasive development disorders. *Dissertation Abstracts International: Section B. Sciences and Engineering,* 58(11), 6224.	N = 23 parents of 3- to 10-year-olds identified with Pervasive Developmental Disorder; assigned to treatment groups based on parents' schedules C = 11 no-treatment wait-list E = 12 CPRT CPRT group received 10 sessions of CPRT training (1/wk, 2 hr) and conducted 7 play sessions with their children (1/wk, 30 min) *quasi-experimental design*	Compared to the control group, CPRT-trained parents made statistically significant gains from pre- to posttesting in their ability to recognize and accept their child's need for autonomy and independence. Although not statistically significant, parents reported a greater increase in their overall acceptance of their child, compared to the control group.
Blanco, P., & Ray, D. (2011). Play therapy in the schools: A best practice for improving academic achievement. *Journal of Counseling and Development,* 89, 235–242.	N = 43, academically at-risk first-graders; randomly assigned by school site to two groups C = 20 no-treatment wait-list E = 21 children received 16 sessions of CCPT (2/wk, 30 min) *experimental design*	Compared to the control group, children in the experimental group demonstrated a statistically significant greater improvement on academic achievement composite scores, which indicated children's overall academic abilities increased.
Brandt, M. A. (2001). An investigation of the efficacy of play therapy with young children. *Dissertation Abstracts International: Section A. Humanities and Social Science,* 61(07), 2603.	N = 26 children referred by parents or teachers as having adjustment difficulties, ages 4 to 6 E = 13 CCPT (randomly selected from two university clinics) C = 13 no-treatment control (randomly selected from an elementary school) CCPT group received 7 to 10 CCPT sessions (1/wk, 45 min) *quasi-experimental design*	According to parent reports, children in CCPT group demonstrated a statistically significant decrease in internalizing behavior problems, as compared to control group over time. Although not statistically significant, parents of children in CCPT group reported a remarkably larger decrease in parenting stress, as compared to control group over time.

continued

CHILD-CENTERED PLAY THERAPY (CCPT) CONTROLLED OUTCOME RESEARCH 1995–2010

Authors	Participants/Methods	Findings
Bratton, S. C., & Landreth, G. L. (1995). Filial therapy with single parents: Effects on parental acceptance, empathy, and stress. *International Journal of Play Therapy, 4*(1), 61–80.	N = 43 single parents of 3- to 7-year-olds identified with behavioral concerns; random drawing to treatment groups C = 21 no-treatment wait-list E = 22 CPRT CPRT group received 10 sessions of CPRT training (1/wk, 2 hr) and conducted 7 play sessions with their children (1/wk, 30 min) *experimental design*	Between-group differences over time revealed that parents in the CPRT group demonstrated a statistically significant increase in empathic interactions with their children as directly observed by independent raters. CPRT parents also reported a statistically significant gain in parental acceptance, as well as statistically significant reductions in parent–child relationship stress and in their children's behavior problems, compared to the control group over time.
Bratton, S. C., Ceballos, P., Sheely, A., Meany-Walen, K., & Prochenko, Y. (in review). An early mental health intervention on disruptive behaviors of at-risk prekindergarten children enrolled in head start.	N = 54 preschool children, ages 3 to 4, identified with disruptive behaviors; random drawing to treatment groups C = 27 active control E = 27 CCPT Experimental group received 16 to 20 sessions of individual CCPT (2/wk, 30 min) Active control group received 16 to 20 sessions of bibliomentoring (2/wk, 30 min) *experimental design*	Between-group differences over time revealed that children in CCPT group demonstrated a statistically significant improvement in their externalizing behaviors, aggressive behaviors, attention deficit-hyperactivity disorder (ADHD) behaviors, oppositional defiant behaviors as reported by their teachers.
Ceballos, P., & Bratton, S. C. (2010). School-based child-parent relationship therapy (CPRT) with low-income first-generation immigrant Latino parents: Effects on children's behaviors and parent-child relationship stress. *Psychology in the Schools, 47*(8), 761–775.	N = 48 immigrant Hispanic parents of Head Start children identified with behavioral problems; random drawing to treatment groups C = 24 no-treatment wait-list E = 24 CPRT CPRT group received 11 sessions of culturally adapted CPRT training (1/wk, 2 hr) and conducted 7 play sessions with their children (1/wk, 30 min); CPRT curriculum translated and sessions conducted in Spanish *experimental design*	Compared to the control group over time, CPRT-trained parents reported statistically significant improvement in: (a) their children's externalizing and internalizing behavior problems, and (b) parent-child relationship stress. CPRT showed a large treatment effect on all dependent variables. 85% of children in the CPRT group moved from clinical or borderline behavior problems to normal levels; 62% of parents reported a reduction from clinical levels of parenting stress to normative functioning. Findings were discussed in light of culturally relevant observations.

Chau, I., & Landreth, G. (1997). Filial therapy with Chinese parents: Effects on parental empathic interactions, parental acceptance of child and parental stress. *International Journal of Play Therapy, 6*(2), 75–92.	N = 34 immigrant Chinese parents of 2- to 10-year-olds; parents assigned to treatment groups based on random drawing and parents' schedules C = 16 no-treatment wait-list E = 18 CPRT CPRT group received 10 sessions of CPRT training (1/wk, 2 hr) and conducted 7 play sessions with their children (1/wk, 30 min) *quasi-experimental design*	Compared to the control group over time, parents in the CPRT group demonstrated a statistically significant increase in empathic interactions with their children as directly observed in play sessions by independent raters. From pre to post, parents in the CPRT group also reported a statistically significant increase in parental acceptance and a statistically significant decrease in parent–child relationship stress, compared to the control group.
Costas, M., & Landreth, G. (1999). Filial therapy with nonoffending parents of children who have been sexually abused. *International Journal of Play Therapy, 8*(1), 43–66.	N = 26 nonoffending parents of sexually abused 5- to 9-year-olds; assigned to treatment groups based on random drawing and location C = 12 no-treatment wait-list E = 14 CPRT CPRT group received 10 sessions of CPRT training (1/wk, 2 hr) and conducted 7 play sessions with their children (1/wk, 30 min) *quasi-experimental design*	Between-group differences over time revealed that parents receiving CPRT training (1) demonstrated statistically significant gains in their empathic interactions with their children as rated by independent raters, (2) reported a statistically significant increase in acceptance of their children, and (3) reported a statistically significant reduction in parent–child relationship stress. Although not statistically significant, CPRT-trained parents reported a marked improvement from pre- to posttesting in their children's behavior problems, anxiety, emotional adjustment, and self-concept.
Danger, S., & Landreth, G. (2005). Child-centered group play therapy with children with speech difficulties. *International Journal of Play Therapy, 14*(1), 81–102.	N = 21 Pre-K to K children referred for speech problems, ages 4 to 6 Random drawing to two groups C = 10 no-treatment wait-list with regular speech therapy only E = 11 child-centered group play therapy concurrent with regularly speech therapy; 25 sessions (1/wk, 30 min, per dyad). Because of 11 children in the experimental group, one group consisted of three children *experimental design*	Children in experimental group demonstrated a large treatment effect on improving young, speech-delayed children's expressive language skills and a moderate treatment effect on their receptive skills when compared to children in control group, although between-group differences across time were not statistically significant.

continued

CHILD-CENTERED PLAY THERAPY (CCPT) CONTROLLED OUTCOME RESEARCH 1995–2010

Authors	Participants/Methods	Findings
Doubrava, D. A. (2005). The effects of child-centered group play therapy on emotional intelligence, behavior, and parenting stress. *Dissertation Abstracts International: Section B. The Sciences and Engineering, 66*(03), 1714.	N = 19 children with at least one *Diagnostic and Statistical Manual of Mental Disorders*, fourth edition (DSM-IV) Axis I diagnosis, ages 7 to 10 Random drawing to two groups C = 10 no-treatment wait-list E = 9 child-centered group play therapy; 10 sessions (2/wk, 40 min) *experimental design*	No statistically significant findings were found between groups across time on children's emotional intelligence based on child self-reports and their problem behavior according to parent reports. Compared to control group over time, parents of children in experimental group did not report a statistically significant decrease on parenting stress.
Fall, M., Balvanz, J., Johnson, L., & Nelson, L. (1999). A play therapy intervention and its relationship to self-efficacy and learning behaviors. *Professional School Counseling, 2*(3), 194–204.	N = 62 5- to 9-year-old children whose coping mechanisms did not facilitate learning behaviors C = 31 no-treatment control E = 31 CCPT Random drawing to groups 6 sessions (1/wk, 30 min) *experimental design*	Although no statistically significant between-group differences across time were found, children in experimental group demonstrated improvement in self-efficacy, but children in control group slightly worsened. Teachers reported improvement in classroom behavior behaviors for both groups, especially greater improvement in experimental group, although the classroom observations by research assistants did not support teachers' report.
Flahive, M. W., & Ray, D. (2007). Effect of group sandtray therapy with preadolescents. *The Journal for Specialists in Group Work, 32*(4), 362–382.	N = 56 fourth and fifth graders C = 28 no-treatment control E = 28 group sandtray with preadolescents identified with behavioral difficulties Random drawing to groups 10 sessions (1/wk, 45 min) *experimental design*	According to teacher reports, experimental group demonstrated statistically significant improvements on children's total, externalizing, and internalizing behavioral problems, as compared to control group over time. The parents of the children in the experimental group reported a statistically significant improvement on their children's externalizing behavioral problems, when compared to the reports from the parents of children in control group across time.

Reference	Sample/Method	Results
Garza, Y., & Bratton, S. C. (2005). School-based child-centered play therapy with Hispanic children: Outcomes and cultural considerations. *International Journal of Play Therapy, 14*, 51–79.	N = 29 K to fifth grade Hispanic children, identified at-risk, ages 5 to 11 C = 14 small group guidance curriculum E = 15 CCPT Random drawing to groups 15 sessions (1/wk, 30 min) Both groups were facilitated by bilingual counselors *experimental design*	According to parent report, from pre- to posttesting, Hispanic children receiving CCPT from a bilingual counselor showed statistically significant decreases in externalizing behavior problems with a large treatment effect as compared to the curriculum-based treatment group across time. Although the results revealed no statistically significant between group differences, the CCPT demonstrated a medium treatment effect on children's internalizing behavioral problems.
Glover, G., & Landreth, G. (2000). Filial therapy with Native Americans on the Flathead Reservation. *International Journal of Play Therapy, 9*(2), 57–80.	N = 21 Native American parents of 3- to 10-year-olds, living on a reservation in western United States; parents assigned to treatment groups based on location they lived on the reservation C = 10 no-treatment wait-list E = 11 CPRT CPRT group received 10 sessions of CPRT training (1/wk, 2 hr) and conducted 7 play sessions with their children (1/wk, 30 min) *quasi-experimental design*	Compared to the control group over time, parents in CPRT group demonstrated a statistically significant increase in their empathic interactions with their children as directly observed in play sessions by independent raters, and their children also demonstrated a statistically significant increase in desirable play behaviors with their parents (independent raters). CPRT-trained parents also reported an increase in parental acceptance and a decrease in parent–child relationship, and their children reported increased self-concept, although these results were not statistically significant.
Grskovic, J., & Goetze, H. (2008). Short-term filial therapy with German mothers: Findings from a controlled study. *International Journal of Play Therapy, 17*(1), 39–51.	N = 33 German mothers in a 2-week residential treatment facility; children's ages ranged from 4 to 12 years C = 18 in control group E = 15 in filial group, entire training program lasted 2 weeks, pretraining consisted of two 90-min sessions, mothers were encouraged to have at least five play sessions with their children throughout the 2 weeks *quasi-experimental*	According to parent reports, children of the parents in filial therapy group demonstrated statistically significant improvements on the total behavior and internalizing problems, as compared to the control group over time. Also, parents in filial therapy group showed a statistically significant increase on their positive attention toward their children, as compared to parents in the control group.
Hacker, C. C. (2009). *Child parent relationship therapy: Hope for disrupted attachment*. (Unpublished doctoral dissertation.) University of Tennessee, Knoxville.	N = 30 foster children (2- to 8-year-olds); 30 foster parents C = 15 children/8 parents (Parent Support Group) E = 15 children/15 parents CPRT CPRT group received five sessions of CPRT training (1/wk, 3 hr) and conducted six play sessions with their children (2/wk, 30 min) *quasi-experimental design*	Although the results showed no statistically significant differences of changes across time between children in CPRT and comparison groups, foster children in both groups demonstrated improvement on their attachment difficulties according to parent reports.

continued

CHILD-CENTERED PLAY THERAPY (CCPT) CONTROLLED OUTCOME RESEARCH 1995–2010

Authors	Participants/Methods	Findings
Harris, Z. L., & Landreth, G. (1997). Filial therapy with incarcerated mothers: A five week model. *International Journal of Play Therapy*, *6*(2), 53–73.	N = 22 incarcerated mothers of 3- to 10-year-olds; assigned to treatment groups in cycles (based on number of mothers entering the county jail at a given point) through a combination of random drawing and selection of parents to groups to maintain equal number of subjects in each group C = 10 no-treatment wait-list E = 12 CPRT CPRT group received 10 sessions of CPRT (2/wk, 2 hrs) and conducted 7 play sessions with their children at the jail during visitation (2/wk, 30 min) *quasi-experimental design*	Compared to the control group over time, mothers in the CPRT group demonstrated a statistically significant increase in their empathic interaction with their children as directly observed by independent raters, and reported statistically significant gains in their parental acceptance and a statistically significant decrease in their children's behavior problems.
Helker, W. P., & Ray, D. (2009). The impact child–teacher relationship training on teachers' and aides' use of relationship-building skills and the effect on student classroom behavior. *International Journal of Play Therapy, 18*(2), 70–83.	N = 24 Head Start teachers (12 teacher-aide pairs) of at-risk preschoolers identified with behavior problems; teachers assigned to treatment groups based on random drawing and teachers' schedules; children (n = 32) assigned to treatment group based on teachers' group assignment C = 12 (6 pairs) active control E = 12 (6 pairs) child–teacher relationship training (CTRT) CTRT group received teacher adapted 10-session CPRT protocol, followed by 8 weeks (3/wk, 15 min) in-class coaching Companion study with Morrison (2007) *quasi-experimental design*	Between group differences over time revealed that CTRT-trained teachers and aides demonstrated a statistically significant greater use of relationship-building skills in the classroom. Results showed a statistically significant relationship between CTRT-trained teachers' and aides' higher use of relationship-building skills in the classroom and students' decrease in externalizing behaviors as compared to the active control group. Experimental group children demonstrated a statistically significant decrease in externalizing problems from pre to mid to post when compared to the children in the active control group.

Citation	Study details	Results
Holt, K. (2011). Child–parent relationship therapy with adoptive children and their parents: Effects in child behavior, parent–child relationship stress, and parental empathy. *Dissertation Abstracts International: Section B. Sciences and Engineering, 71*(8).	N = 61 adoptive or foster-to-adopt parents of 2- to 10-year-olds C = 29 no-treatment wait-list E = 32 CPRT CPRT group received 10 sessions of CPRT training (1/wk, 2 hr) and conducted 7 play sessions with their children (1/wk, 30 min) *experimental design*	Adoptive parents reported statistically significant greater improvement demonstrated by CPRT children across time on their total behavioral problem and externalizing behavior problem in comparison with children in no treatment control group. In addition, adoptive parents in CPRT group also reported a statistically significant greater reduction from pre- to posttreatment on parent–child relationship stress as compared to adoptive parents in no treatment control group.
Jang, M. (2000). Effectiveness of filial therapy for Korean parents. *International Journal of Play Therapy, 9*(2), 39–56.	N = 30 Korean mothers of 3- to 9-year-olds C = 16 no-treatment wait-list E = 14 adapted CPRT CPRT group received 8 sessions of CPRT (2/wk, 2 hr) and conducted 7 play sessions with their children *quasi-experimental design*	Compared to the control group, CPRT-trained parents demonstrated a statistically significant increase in empathic interactions with their children as directly observed in play sessions. CPRT-trained parents also reported a statistically significant decrease in their children's behavior problems compared to control group.
Johnson-Clark, K. A. (1996). The effect of filial therapy on child conduct behavior problems and the quality of the parent–child relationship. *Dissertation Abstracts International: Section B. Sciences and Engineering, 57*(4), 2868.	N = 52 mother–child pairs (children's ages 3 to 5) E1 = 17 filial therapy group (mothers received ten 2-hr weekly filial training sessions and conducted seven 30-min weekly play sessions with their children) E2 = 18 play-only group (mothers conducted seven 30-min weekly play sessions with their children, without receiving any training) C = 17 nontreatment control group *experimental design*	Compared to play-only comparison group and no-treatment control group across time, parents in filial therapy group reported a statistically significant difference in their children's conduct behavior problems, in which parents in filial therapy group reported statistically significant lower concerns for their children's conduct behavior problems, as compared to play-only comparison group and no-treatment control group at the follow-up.
Jones, E. M., & Landreth, G. (2002). The efficacy of intensive individual play therapy for chronically ill children. *International Journal of Play Therapy, 11*(1), 117–140.	N = 30 7- to 11-year-old children diagnosed with insulin-dependent diabetes mellitus (IDDM) C = 15 no treatment E = 15 CCPT (14 children received 12 sessions during the 3-week, one child received 10 sessions) random drawing to groups *experimental design*	Compared to control group, children in CCPT group demonstrated a statistically significant improvement in diabetes adaptation from pretest to posttest, according to parent reports. However, both CCPT and control groups demonstrated minimal change in diabetes adaption at follow-up. Although the between group difference over time was not statistically significant, parents of children in CCPT group reported a marked improvement in their behavior problems.

continued

CHILD-CENTERED PLAY THERAPY (CCPT) CONTROLLED OUTCOME RESEARCH 1995–2010

Authors	Participants/Methods	Findings
Jones, L., Rhine, T., & Bratton, S. (2002). High school students as therapeutic agents with young children experiencing school adjustment difficulties: The effectiveness of filial therapy training model. *International Journal of Play Therapy, 11*(2), 43–62.	N = 31 junior and senior high school students enrolled in year-long peer mentoring courses; one class randomly drawn to receive CPRT protocol; other class assigned to traditional PALS curriculum (children randomly drawn to treatment groups) C = 15 PALS curriculum E = 16 adapted CPRT (to fit year-long course structure) 26 children (ages 4 to 6) randomly assigned to experimental group (e = 14) or control group (c = 12) Both groups of mentors received training during regular class time and conducted approximately 20 play sessions with children (ages 4 to 6) identified at-risk for achieving academic success by teachers. CPRT mentors' weekly 20-min. play sessions were directly supervised by professionals trained in play therapy and CPRT protocol. Data from both Jones (2002) and Rhine (2002), *experimental design*	Compared to PALS group over time, parents of children in the CPRT group reported statistically significant decreases in their children's internalizing and total behavior problems. Although not statistically significant, parents of children in CPRT group also reported a marked improvement in their children's externalizing behavior, as compared to PALS group over time. According to teacher reports, children in CPRT group also demonstrated a marked increase in desirable behaviors over time but children in PALS group only showed a slight increase, although no statistically significant differences were found between CPRT and PALS groups.
Kale, A. L., & Landreth, G. (1999). Filial therapy with parents of children experiencing learning difficulties. *International Journal of Play Therapy, 8*(2), 35–56.	N = 22 parents of 5- to 10-year-olds with learning difficulties; random drawing to treatment groups C = 11 no-treatment wait-list E = 11 CPRT CPRT group received 10 sessions of CPRT training (1/wk, 2 hr) and conducted 7 play sessions with their children (1/wk, 30 min) *experimental design*	Results indicated statistically significant improvement in parental acceptance and reduction in parent–child relationship stress from pre- to posttesting for the CPRT-trained group compared to the no treatment control. While not statistically significant, parents trained in CPRT reported greater improvement in child behavior problems compared to the control group.

Citation	Study details	Findings
Kaplewicz, N. L. (2000). Effects of group play therapy on reading achievement and emotional symptoms among remedial readers. *Dissertation Abstracts International: Section B. Sciences and Engineering, 61*(01), 535.	N = 40 third and fourth graders ages from 8 to 10 identified for remedial reading; random drawing to treatment groups using a random numbers table C1 = 13 no-treatment control C2 = 13 placebo/active control E = 14 Group CCPT All child participants continued receiving remedial reading CCPT group received 10 30-min play therapy sessions in a period of 10 weeks Placebo/active control group received 10 30-min nontherapeutic sessions over 10-week period *quasi-experimental design*	According to parent reports, no statistically significant differences of changes on behavioral symptoms across time between children in these three groups. Teachers also reported no statistically significant differences of changes on children's behavioral symptoms as well as reading performance across time between children in these three groups. The results of child self-reports indicated no statistically significant differences of changes on emotional symptoms as well as school adjustment across time between these three groups. However, according to group leader reports, children in CCPT and placebo groups demonstrated statistically significant increases on engagement over the intervention period.
Kellam, T. L. (2004). The effectiveness of modified filial therapy training in comparison to a parent education class on acceptance, stress, and child behavior. *Dissertation Abstracts International: Section B. Sciences and Engineering, 64*(08), 4043.	N = 37 parent-child pairs referred by CPS; random drawing to treatment groups C = 17 parent education class E = 20 modified CPRT protocol Both groups attended 8 weekly sessions for 1.5 hr/wk *experimental design*	Results of this study showed no statistically significant between- or within-group differences over time for stress related to parenting and child behavior problems. CPRT-trained parents reported a greater increase in parental acceptance over the comparison group, although the finding was not statistically significant.
Kidron, M., & Landreth, G. (2010). Intensive child parent relationship therapy with Israeli parents in Israel. *International Journal of Play Therapy, 19*(2), 64–78.	N = 27 Israeli parents of 4- to 11-year-olds; assigned to treatment groups based on parents' schedules C = 13 no-treatment wait-list E = 14 CPRT CPRT group received 10 sessions of CPRT training (1/wk, 2 hr) and conducted 7 play sessions with their children (1/wk, 30 min) *quasi-experimental design*	Compared to control parents, the CPRT group demonstrated a statistically significant increase pre to post in empathic interactions with their children as rated by observers blind to study, and reported a statistically significant reduction in parent–child relationship stress. Compared to the control group over time, CPRT parents also reported a statistically significant reduction in their children's externalized behavior problems.

continued

CHILD-CENTERED PLAY THERAPY (CCPT) CONTROLLED OUTCOME RESEARCH 1995–2010

Authors	Participants/Methods	Findings
Kot, S., Landreth, G., & Giordano, M. (1998). Intensive child-centered play therapy with child witnesses of domestic violence. *International Journal of Play Therapy, 7(2),* 17–36.	N = 22 child residents aged from 4 to 10 in domestic violence shelters, assigned to groups depending on the time period they stayed in the shelter. C = 11 no-treatment control E = 11 CCPT CCPT group received 12, 45-min play therapy sessions in a period of 12 days to 3 weeks Control group only received a 45-min play session for each pretest and posttest period. *quasi-experimental design*	Compared to control group over time, parents of children in CCPT group reported statistically significant improvements in children's total behavior and externalizing behavior problems. Children in CCPT group also demonstrated a statistically significant increase in their self-concept, as compared to children in control group across time. According to ratings from independent raters, children in CCPT group also demonstrated statistically significant increases in the physical proximity between the child and the therapist and in positive play themes, as compared to control group over time.
Landreth, G., & Lobaugh, A. (1998). Filial therapy with incarcerated fathers: Effects on parental acceptance of child, parental stress, and child adjustment. *Journal of Counseling & Development, 76,* 157–165.	N = 32 incarcerated fathers of 4- to 9-year-olds; random drawing to treatment groups C = 16 no-treatment wait-list E = 16 CPRT CPRT group received 10 sessions of CPRT training (1/wk, 1.5 hr) and conducted 8 to 10 play sessions with their children during weekly family visitation at the prison *experimental design*	Compared to the control group over time, fathers in the CPRT group reported a statistically significant increase in their parental acceptance toward their children, and a statistically significant reduction in parent–child relationship stress. In addition, children whose fathers were in the CPRT group reported a statistically significant increase in their self-esteem from pre- to posttesting.
Lee, M., & Landreth, G. (2003). Filial therapy with immigrant Korean parents in the United States. *International Journal of Play Therapy, 12(2),* 67–85.	N = 32 immigrant Korean parents of 2- to 10-year-olds; random drawing to treatment groups C = 15 no-treatment wait-list E = 17 CPRT CPRT group received 10 sessions of CPRT training (1/wk, 2 hr) and conducted 7 play sessions with their children (1/wk, 30 min) *experimental design*	Between-group differences over time revealed that parents in the CPRT group (1) demonstrated a statistically significant increase in their empathic interactions with their children as directly observed by independent raters, and (2) reported a statistically significant increase in their parental acceptance toward their children as well as a statistically significant reduction in parent–child relationship stress.

McGuire, D. E. (2001). Child-centered group play therapy with children experiencing adjustment difficulties. *Dissertation Abstracts International: Section A. The Humanities and Social Sciences*, 61(10), 3908.	N = 29 kindergartners identified with adjustment difficulties, ages 5 and 6 C = 14 no-treatment wait-list E = 15 group CCPT Children in experimental group received 12 sessions of child-centered group play therapy (1/wk, 40 min) Control group data from Baggerly (1999) *quasi-experimental design*	Although no statistically significant differences between control and experimental group over time, positive trends were found in children's behavior for children in experimental group. In addition, parents of children in experimental group also reported a decrease in parent–child relationship stress, although no statistically significant differences were found between two groups over time.
Morrison, M., & Bratton, S. (2010). An early mental health intervention for Head Start programs: The effectiveness of child-teacher relationship training (CTRT) on children's behavior problems. *Psychology in the Schools*, 47(10), 1003–1017.	N = 24 Head Start teachers (12 teacher-aide pairs) of at-risk preschoolers identified with significant behavior problems; teachers assigned to treatment groups based on random drawing and teachers' schedule; children (n = 52) were assigned to treatment group based on teachers' group assignment C = 12 (6 pairs) active control E = 12 (6 pairs) CTRT CTRT group received teacher adapted 10-session CPRT protocol, followed by 8 weeks (3/wk, 15 min) in-class coaching *quasi-experimental design*	According to teacher reports, children whose teachers received CTRT demonstrated statistically significant reductions in externalizing and total behavior problems, compared to the active control group across three points of measure. Treatment effects were determined to be large. CTRT also showed a moderate treatment effect on reducing children's internalizing problem behaviors, as compared to the active control group. Eighty-four percent of the children receiving CTRT moved from clinical or borderline behavior problems to normal levels of functioning.
Packman, J., & Bratton, S. C. (2003). A school-based group play/activity therapy intervention with learning disabled preadolescents exhibiting behavior problems. *International Journal of Play Therapy*, 12, 7–29.	N = 24 fourth and fifth graders ages 10 to 12 identified with behavioral difficulties; random drawing to treatment groups C = 12 no-treatment control E = 12 Group CCPT/Activity Therapy CCPT group received 1-hour/wk play therapy sessions in a period of 12 weeks *experimental design*	In comparison with children in control group, children in experimental group demonstrated statistically significant improvement across time on their total behavior and internalizing problems, according to parent reports. Although statistically significant differences were not found between children in two groups on the improvement of externalizing problems across time, children in experimental group demonstrated noteworthy improvement on their delinquent and aggressive behaviors.

continued

CHILD-CENTERED PLAY THERAPY (CCPT) CONTROLLED OUTCOME RESEARCH 1995–2010

Authors	Participants/Methods	Findings
Post, P. (1999). Impact of child-centered play therapy on the self-esteem, locus of control, and anxiety of at-risk 4th, 5th, and 6th grade students. *International Journal of Play Therapy, 8*(2), 1–18.	N = 168 at-risk fourth to sixth graders, ages 9 to 12 years old C = 91 no-treatment control E = 77 CCPT CCPT group received play therapy, 1–25 (mean = 4) sessions (1/wk) No random drawing *quasi-experimental design*	Found a statistically significant difference between CCPT and control groups over time on children's self-esteem. More precisely, the overall self-esteem in children in CCPT group remained approximately the same, but children in control group showed deterioration in overall self-esteem. Although no statistical significance between group differences was found over time, the locus of control of children in CCPT group remained approximately the same, but children in control group showed remarkable deterioration in their locus of control.
Post, P., McAllister, M., Sheely, A., Hess, B., & Flowers, C. (2004). Child centered kinder training for teachers of pre-school children deemed at risk. *International Journal of Play Therapy, 13*(2), 53–74.	N = 17 teachers of at-risk preschoolers with behavioral concerns; study logistics did not allow for random assignment of teachers or children to treatment groups C = 8 no treatment; E = 9 adapted CPRT CPRT teachers got a total of 23 wk of intervention: 10 wk of adapted CPRT group sessions (1/wk, 2 hr) in which they conducted 7 weekly 30-minute play sessions with an identified student and received 45 min. of individual supervision; the next 13 wk of group intervention focused on helping teachers to generalize CPRT skills to classroom (1/wk, 2 hr) *quasi-experimental design*	According to teacher reports children in the experimental group, compared to the control group over time, demonstrated a statistically significant improvement in adaptive, internalized, and overall behavior. CPRT-trained teachers demonstrated a statistically significant increase in empathic interactions and use of target play therapy skills in 1-on-1 play sessions with children and in the classroom (assessed through direct observation by raters blinded to study).
Ray, D. C. (2007). Two counseling interventions to reduce teacher–child relationship stress. *Professional School Counseling, 10*(4), 428–440.	N = 93 at-risk pre-K to fifth graders, ages 4 to 11 (n = 59 teachers) E1 = 32 CCPT children received 16 CCPT sessions (2/wk, 30 min) E2 = 29 teacher consult (TC) Teachers received 8 TC sessions (1/wk, 10 min) E3 = 32 CCPT + TC children received 16 CCPT sessions (2/wk, 30 min); teachers received 8 TC sessions (1/wk, 10 min) Random drawing to groups *experimental design*	Although no statistically significant between group differences across time were found, teachers in all three groups reported statistically significant improvement over time in teacher–child relationship stress. According to teacher reports, among 22 children identified at or above the clinical levels on ADHD domain at pretest, 11 children were identified below clinical levels at posttest; 7 out of 13 children who were identified at or above the clinical levels at pretest on Student Characteristics domain were identified with below clinical levels at posttest.

Ray, D. C., Blanco, P. J., Sullivan, J. M., & Holliman, R. (2009). An exploratory study of child-centered play therapy with aggressive children. *International Journal of Play Therapy*, 18(3), 162–175.	N = 41 aggressive children, ages 4 to 11 C = 22 no-treatment wait-list E = 19 CCPT Children first referred to PT were assigned in CCPT group and received 14 sessions over 7 weeks (2/wk, 30min) Only 32 parents completed pretest and posttest (E = 15, C = 17) Teachers completed pretest and posttest for all 41 children. *quasi-experimental design*	Although between-group differences over time were not statistically significant, teachers of children in CCPT group reported a remarkably larger decrease in children's aggressive behaviors as compared to children in control group.
Ray, D. C., Schottelkorb, A., & Tsai, M., (2007). Play therapy with children exhibiting symptoms of attention deficit hyperactivity disorder. *International Journal of Play Therapy*, 16(2), 95–111.	N = 60 K to fifth graders identified with attention problems and hyperactivity, ages 5 to 11 C = 29 Reading Mentoring (RM); E = 31 CCPT Children in CCPT group received 16 CCPT sessions (1/wk, 30 min) Children in RM group received 16 sessions individual reading mentoring (1/wk, 30 min) Randomly drawing to groups *experimental design*	No statistically significant between group differences were found on children's ADHD symptoms. Compared to RM group over time, teachers of children in CCPT group reported statistically significant improvements on children's stress toward teachers in personal characteristics, which also indicated moderate treatment effect of CCPT on reducing children's emotional distress, anxiety, and withdrawal difficulties.
Ray, D. E. (2003). The effect of filial therapy on parental acceptance and child adjustment (*Unpublished masters' thesis*). Emporia State University, Kansas.	N = 50 parents of 3- to 10-year-olds identified with attachment problems C = 25 no-treatment wait-list E = 25 CPRT CPRT group followed 10 session outline for CPRT training (1/wk, 2 hr) and conducted play sessions with their children *quasi-experimental design*	Compared to the control group, CPRT parents reported a statistically significant increase pre to post in parental acceptance. While not statistically significant, CPRT trained parents reported a reduction in parent–child relationship stress as well as their children's behavioral problems, compared to control group parents.

continued

CHILD-CENTERED PLAY THERAPY (CCPT) CONTROLLED OUTCOME RESEARCH 1995–2010

Authors	Participants/Methods	Findings
Rennie, R. L. (2003). A comparison study of the effectiveness of individual and group play therapy in treating kindergarten children with adjustment problems. *Dissertation Abstracts International: Section A. The Humanities and Social Sciences, 63*(09), 3117.	N = 42 kindergartners identified with adjustment problems C = 13 no treatment E1 = 1 individual CCPT E2 = 15 group CCPT Individual CCPT group received 10 to 12 30-min weekly sessions in 12 wk Group CCPT group received 12 to 14 45-min weekly sessions in 14 weeks Random drawing to E1 and C; E2 data from McGuire (1999) *quasi-experimental design*	Compared to no-treatment control group over time, parents of children in individual CCPT group reported statistically significant improvements on children's total behavior and externalizing behavior problems. No statistically significant differences were found between individual and group CCPT treatment interventions.
Rhine, T. J. (2002). The effects of a play therapy intervention conducted by trained high school students on the behavior of maladjusted young children: Implications for school counselor. *Dissertation Abstracts International: Section A. The Humanities and Social Sciences, 62*(10), 3304.	Companion study with Jones (2002), and published in Jones, Rhine, & Bratton (2002).	

Citation	Description	Findings
Schumann, B. (2010). Effectiveness of child-centered play therapy for children referred for aggression. In J. Baggerly, D. Ray, & S. Bratton (Eds.), *Child-centered play therapy research: The evidence base for effective practice* (pp. 193–208). Hoboken, NJ: Wiley.	N = 37 aggressive K to fourth graders, ages 5 to 12 E = 20 CCPT C = 17 curriculum-based small-group guidance group CCPT group received 12 to 15 CCPT sessions (1/wk, 30 min) Small-group guidance group received 8 to 15 group sessions Randomly drawing to groups *experimental design*	No statistically significant differences between CCPT group and small-group guidance group were found. However, more children in CCPT group demonstrated improvement in aggressive behaviors than in small-group guidance group, according to parent reports.
Shashi, K., Kapur, M., & Subbakrishna, D. K., (1999). Evaluation of play therapy in emotionally disturbed children. *NIMHANS Journal, 17*(2), 99–111.	N = 10 children identified with emotional disorder, ages 5 to 10 E = 5 nondirective PT C = 5 no treatment PT group received 10 nondirective PT sessions, and the caretakers received 2 to 3 family counseling sessions Caretakers in control group only received one family counseling session *experimental design*	Statistically significant differences were not found at pretest between no treatment control group and nondirective PT group, but parents and teachers of children in PT group reported statistically significant lower concerns on children's overall behaviors and emotional as well as behavioral problems as compared to control group at posttest.
Sheely-Moore, A., & Bratton, S. (2010). A strengths-based parenting intervention with low-income African American families. *Professional School Counseling, 13*(3), 175–183.	N = 23 low-income African American parents of Head Start children identified with behavioral problems; random drawing to treatment groups C = 10 no-treatment wait-list E = 13 CPRT CPRT group received 10 sessions of CPRT training (1/wk, 2 hr) and conducted 7 play sessions with their children (1/wk, 30 min) *experimental design*	Findings indicated that when compared to the no-treatment control group, the CPRT group demonstrated statistically significant improvements over time in children's overall behavior problems and parent–child relationship stress. Treatment effects were large. Cultural considerations were discussed in light of the findings.

continued

CHILD-CENTERED PLAY THERAPY (CCPT) CONTROLLED OUTCOME RESEARCH 1995–2010

Authors	Participants/Methods	Findings
Shen, Y. (2002). Short-term group play therapy with Chinese earthquake victims: Effects on anxiety, depression, and adjustment. *International Journal of Play Therapy, 11*(1), 43–63.	N = 30 third to sixth graders identified with high-risk maladjustment, ages 8 to 12 years C = 15 no-treatment control E = 15 child-centered group PT Random drawing to groups CCPT group received group play therapy for 4 weeks (2 to 3/wk, 40 min) *experimental design*	Compared to control group over time, children in experimental group demonstrated statistically significant decreases in their overall anxiety, physiological anxiety, worry/oversensitivity, and suicide risk. The results also indicated large overall treatment effects of child-centered group play therapy on reducing children's anxiety, worry, and oversensitivity, and small to medium treatment effect on reducing children's suicide risk.
Smith, D. M., & Landreth, G. L. (2004). Filial therapy with teachers of deaf and hard of hearing preschool children. *International Journal of Play Therapy, 13*(1), 13–33.	N = 24 teachers of deaf and hard of hearing 2- to 6-year-olds; classrooms assigned to treatment groups based on stratified random drawing to ensure groups were equal on children's age C = 12 no-treatment wait-list E = 12 CPRT CPRT teachers received 10 training sessions (1/wk, 2 hr) and conducted 7 play sessions with identified students (1/wk, 30 min) *experimental design*	Between-group differences over time revealed that children in the CPRT group made statistically significant improvement in behavior problems and social-emotional functioning. Compared to control teachers, CPRT-trained teachers demonstrated statistically significant gains in their empathic interactions with students (direct observation by blinded raters) and also reported statistically significant increases in acceptance of their students.
Smith, N., & Landreth, G. (2003). Intensive filial therapy with child witnesses of domestic violence: A comparison with individual and sibling group play therapy. *International Journal of Play Therapy, 12*(1), 67–88.	N = 44 4- to 10-year-olds who had witnessed domestic violence C = 11 children in no-treatment comparison (from Kot et al., 1998) E1 = 11 children of mothers receiving CPRT E2 = 11 children in individual play therapy (from Kot et al., 1998) E3 = 11 children in sibling group play therapy (from Tyndall-Lind et al., 2001) CPRT group received 12 sessions (1.5 hrs) of CPRT training over 2–3 weeks and conducted an average of 7 play sessions (30 min) with their children *quasi-experimental design*	Compared to no-treatment control over time: (1) CPRT-trained parents reported statistically significant decreases in their children's behavior problems, and (2) children in CPRT group reported a statistically significant increase in self-esteem. Additionally, CPRT parents demonstrated a statistically significant increase from pre to post in their empathic interactions with their children (direct observation by blinded raters). Results across treatment groups revealed no statistically significant differences between interventions.

Swanson, R. C. (2008). The effect of child-centered play therapy on reading achievement in 2nd graders reading below grade level. *Master Abstracts International: Section A: Humanities and Social Sciences, 46*(5).	N = 19 second graders reading below grade level C = 11 no-treatment control E = 8 CCPT Random drawing to groups Children in CCPT group received 14 individual CCPT sessions (1/wk, 30 min) *experimental design*	Although no statistically significant between-group differences over time were found, the mean scores of both experimental and control groups on DRA revealed improvements in reading ability across three testing periods. The mean scores of both groups on RR also revealed improvements over the treatment period although no statistical analyses were conducted on the assessment results.
Tew, K., Landreth, G., Joiner, K. D., & Solt, M. D. (2002). Filial therapy with parents of chronically ill children. *International Journal of Play Therapy, 11*(1), 79–100.	N = 23 parents of hospitalized, chronically ill 3- to 10-year-olds; parents assigned to treatment groups based on parents' schedule C = 11 no-treatment wait-list E = 12 CPRT CPRT group received 10 sessions of CPRT training (1/wk, 2 hr) and conducted 7 play sessions with their children (1/wk, 30 min) *quasi-experimental design*	Compared to control group, CPRT-trained parents reported a statistically significant reduction in parent–child relationship stress and in their children's behavior problems. CPRT parents also reported a statistically significant increase in parental acceptance, compared to control parents over time.
Tyndall-Lind, A., Landreth, G., & Giordano, M. (2001). Intensive group play therapy with child witnesses of domestic violence. *International Journal of Play Therapy, 10*(1), 53–83.	N = 32 child residents of domestic violence shelters, ages 4 to 10 C = 11 no-treatment wait list E1 = 10 sibling group CCPT E2 = 11 individual CCPT E1 (experimental group) received 12 sibling group CCPT sessions (45 min) within 12 days E2 (comparison group) received 12 individual CCPT sessions (45 min) within 12 days Children were assigned to E1 and control groups according to the time periods of their residence in shelters *quasi-experimental design*	Compared to control group over time, children in experimental group demonstrated statistically significant enhancement on their self-concept according to self-reports, and statistically significant improvements on their total behavior problems, externalizing behavior problems, aggressive behaviors, and anxious and depressed behaviors according to parent reports. However, no statistically significant differences over time were found between experimental and comparison groups, which revealed similar treatment effects on two treatment interventions.

continued

CHILD-CENTERED PLAY THERAPY (CCPT) CONTROLLED OUTCOME RESEARCH 1995–2010

Authors	Participants/Methods	Findings
Villarreal, C. E. (2008). School-based child parent relationship therapy (CPRT) with Hispanic parents. *Dissertation Abstracts International: Section A. The Humanities and Social Sciences*, 69(2).	N = 13 Hispanic parents of 4- to 10-year-olds; random drawing to treatment groups C = 7 no-treatment wait-list E = 6 CPRT CPRT group received 10 sessions of CPRT training (1/wk, 1.5 hrs) and conducted 7 play sessions with their children (1/wk, 30 min) *experimental design*	CPRT-trained parents reported a statistically significant decrease in their children's internalizing problems from pre- to posttesting as compared to parents in control group. While not statistically significant, CPRT-trained parents also reported a greater decrease in their children's externalizing problems over the control group.
Watson, D. (2007). An early intervention approach for students displaying negative externalizing behaviors associated with childhood depression: A study of efficacy of play therapy in the school. *Dissertation Abstracts International Section A: Humanities and Social Sciences*, 68(5), 1820.	N = 30 pre-K to first graders identified with externalizing behavior problems, ages 4 to 7 random drawing to groups C = 15 no treatment control (treatment as usual) E = 15 Group PT Experimental group received 16 group play therapy sessions (2/wk, 30 min) *experimental design*	Paired sample *t* tests were conducted individually for both control and experimental groups. The results indicated no statistically significant differences over time for control group on children's social skills and problem behaviors. The experimental group demonstrated statistically significant improvements over time on social skills, but not on problem behaviors. However, no between-group differences were analyzed in this study.
Yuen, T., Landreth, G., & Baggerly, J. (2002). Filial therapy with immigrant Chinese families. *International Journal of Play Therapy*, 11(2), 63–90.	N = 35 immigrant Chinese parents of 3- to 10-year-olds; random drawing to treatment groups C = 17 no-treatment wait-list E = 18 CPRT CPRT group received 10 sessions of CPRT training (1/wk, 2 hr) and conducted 7 play sessions with their children (1/wk, 30 min) *experimental design*	Between-group differences over time revealed that parents in the CPRT group demonstrated a statistically significant increase in empathic interactions with their children as directly observed in play sessions by independent raters. Statistically significant between-group results in favor of CPRT were also found for increased parental acceptance, a reduction in parent–child relationship stress, and reduced child behavior problems.

Note: Treatment groups are denoted by E = Experimental, C = Control or Comparison. The format and majority of information in this chart are from Bratton (2010); Bratton, Landreth, and Lin (2010); Lin (2011); and Ray and Bratton (2010).

Final Summing Up

Child-centered play therapy is a dynamic process of relating to children on their own terms in developmentally appropriate ways that allows children to express themselves through their natural medium of communication play. The play therapy relationship is a continual process of discovery of self for the child facilitated by the therapist's unwavering belief in the child and commitment to understanding and acceptance of the child, which create a relationship of safety and are internalized by the child in ways that free the child to express and explore dimensions of self that have typically not been shared with other adults.

The child-centered play therapist is focused fully upon the child, as opposed to the child's "problem." Therefore, the content and direction of the child's play are determined by the child. The child-centered approach is not a prescriptive approach dependent on the identified problem of the child. A key concept is that behavior is a function of the child's perception of his or her world and how the child feels about self. Therefore, the therapist works hard to understand the child's perceptual view. The child's behavior must always be understood by looking through the child's eyes.

Child-centered play therapy is the most thoroughly researched theoretical model in the field of play therapy, and the results are unequivocal in demonstrating the effectiveness of this approach with a wide variety of children's problems and in time-limited settings involving intensive and short-term play therapy. Child-centered play therapy has and will continue to focus on the process of being and becoming.

References

Baggerly, J., Ray, D., & Bratton, S. (2010). *Child-centered play therapy research: The evidence base for effective practice.* Hoboken, NJ: Wiley.

Bayat, M. (2008). Nondirective play therapy for children with internalizing problems. *Journal of Iranian Psychology,* 4(15), 267–276.

Beckloff, D. R. (1998). Filial therapy with children with spectrum pervasive development disorders. *Dissertation Abstracts International: Section B. Sciences and Engineering,* 58(11), 6224.

Blanco, P., & Ray, D. (2011). Play therapy in the schools: A best practice for improving academic achievement. *Journal of Counseling and Development, 89*, 235–242.

Brandt, M. A. (2001). An investigation of the efficacy of play therapy with young children. *Dissertation Abstracts International: Section A. Humanities and Social Science, 61*(07), 2603.

Bratton, S. C., Ceballos, P., Shelly, A., Meany-Walen, K., & Prochenko, Y. (in review) An early mental health intervention on disruptive behaviors of at-risk prekindergarten children enrolled in head start.

Bratton, S. C., & Landreth, G. L. (1995). Filial therapy with single parents: Effects on parental acceptance, empathy and stress. *International Journal of Play Therapy, 4*(1), 61–80.

Bratton, S. C., Landreth, G. L., & Lin, Y. W. (2010). Child parent relationship therapy: A review of controlled-outcome research. In J. Baggerly, D. Ray, & S. Bratton (Eds.), *Child-Centered Play Therapy Research: Evidence Base for Effective Practice* (pp. 267–293). Hoboken, NJ: Wiley.

Bratton, S., Ray, D., Rhine, T., & Jones, L. (2005). The efficacy of play therapy with children: A meta-analytic review of treatment outcomes. *Professional Psychology: Research and Practice, 36*(4), 376–390.

Ceballos, P., & Bratton, S. C. (2010). School-based child-parent relationship therapy (CPRT) with low-income first-generation immigrant Latino parents: Effects on children's behaviors and parent-child relationship stress. *Psychology in the Schools, 47*(8), 761–775.

Chau, I., & Landreth, G. (1997). Filial therapy with Chinese parents: Effects on parental empathic interactions, parental acceptance of child and parental stress. *International Journal of Play Therapy, 6*(2), 75–92.

Cohen, J. (1988). *Statistical power analysis for the behavioral sciences* (2nd ed.). Hillside, NJ: Erlbaum.

Costas, M., & Landreth, G. (1999). Filial therapy with nonoffending parents of children who have been sexually abused. *International Journal of Play Therapy, 8*(1), 43–66.

Danger, S., & Landreth, G. (2005). Child-centered group play therapy with children with speech difficulties. *International Journal of Play Therapy, 14*(1), 81–102.

Doubrava, D. A. (2005). The effects of child-centered group play therapy on emotional intelligence, behavior, and parenting stress. *Dissertation Abstracts International: Section B. The Sciences and Engineering, 66*(03), 1714.

Fall, M., Balvanz, J., Johnson, L., & Nelson, L. (1999). A play therapy intervention and its relationship to self-efficacy and learning behaviors. *Professional School Counseling, 2*(3), 194–204.

Flahive, M. W., & Ray, D. (2007). Effect of group sandtray therapy with pre-adolescents. *Journal for Specialists in Group Work, 32*(4), 362–382.

Garza, Y., & Bratton, S. C. (2005). School-based child-centered play therapy with Hispanic children: Outcomes and cultural considerations. *International Journal of Play Therapy, 14*(1), 51–79.

Glover, G., & Landreth, G. (2000). Filial therapy with Native Americans on the Flathead Reservation. *International Journal of Play Therapy, 9*(2), 57–80.

Grskovic, J., & Goetze, H. (2008). Short-term filial therapy with German mothers: Findings from a controlled study. *International Journal of Play Therapy, 17*(1), 39–51.

Hacker, C. C. (2009). Child parent relationship therapy: Hope for disrupted attachment (Unpublished doctoral dissertation, University of Tennessee, Knoxville).

Harris, Z. L., & Landreth, G. (1997). Filial therapy with incarcerated mothers: A five week model. *International Journal of Play Therapy, 6*(2), 53–73.

Helker, W. P., & Ray, D. (2009). The impact child-teacher relationship training on teachers' and aides' use of relationship-building skills and the effect on student classroom behavior. *International Journal of Play Therapy, 18*(2), 70–83.

Holt, K. (2011). Child-parent relationship therapy with adoptive children and their parents: Effects in child behavior, parent-child relationship stress, and parental empathy. *Dissertation Abstracts International: Section B. Sciences and Engineering, 71*(8).

Hunt, K. (2006). Can professionals offering support to vulnerable children in Kenya benefit from brief play therapy training? *Journal of Psychology in Africa, 16*(2), 215–221.

Jang, M. (2000). Effectiveness of filial therapy for Korean parents. *International Journal of Play Therapy, 9*(2), 39–56.

Johnson-Clark, K. A. (1996). The effect of filial therapy on child conduct behavior problems and the quality of the parent-child relationship. *Dissertation Abstracts International: Section B. Sciences and Engineering, 57*(4), 2868.

Jones, E. M., & Landreth, G. (2002). The efficacy of intensive individual play therapy for chronically ill children. *International Journal of Play Therapy, 11*(1), 117–140.

Jones, L., Rhine, T., & Bratton, S. (2002). High school students as therapeutic agents with young children experiencing school adjustment difficulties: The effectiveness of filial therapy training model. *International Journal of Play Therapy, 11*(2), 43–62.

Kagan, S., & Landreth, G. (2009). Short-term child-centered play therapy training with Israeli school counselors and teachers. *International Journal of Play Therapy, 18*(4), 207–216.

Kale, A. L., & Landreth, G. (1999). Filial therapy with parents of children experiencing learning difficulties. *International Journal of Play Therapy, 8*(2), 35–56.

Kaplewicz, N. L. (2000). Effects of group play therapy on reading achievement and emotional symptoms among remedial readers. *Dissertation Abstracts International: Section B. Sciences and Engineering, 61*(01), 535.

Kellam, T. L. (2004). The effectiveness of modified filial therapy training in comparison to a parent education class on acceptance, stress, and child behavior. *Dissertation Abstracts International: Section B. Sciences and Engineering, 64*(08).

Kidron, M., & Landreth, G. (2010). Intensive child parent relationship therapy with Israeli parents in Israel. *International Journal of Play Therapy, 19*(2), 64–78.

Kot, S., Landreth, G., & Giordano, M. (1998). Intensive child-centered play therapy with child witnesses of domestic violence. *International Journal of Play Therapy, 7*(2), 17–36.

Lambert, S., LeBlanc, M., Mullen, J., Ray, D., Baggerly, J., White, J., et al. (2005). Learning more about those who play in session: The national play therapy in counseling practice project (Phase I). *International Journal of Play Therapy, 14*(2), 7–23.

Landreth, G., & Lobaugh, A. (1998). Filial therapy with incarcerated fathers: Effects on parental acceptance of child, parental stress, and child adjustment. *Journal of Counseling & Development, 76*, 157–165.

LeBlanc, M., & Ritchie, M. (2001). A meta-analysis of play therapy outcomes. *Counseling Psychology Quarterly, 14*(2), 149–163.

Lee, M., & Landreth, G. (2003). Filial therapy with immigrant Korean parents in the United States. *International Journal of Play Therapy, 12*(2), 67–85.

Lin, Y. (2011). Contemporary research of child-centered play therapy (CCPT) modalities: A meta analytic review of controlled outcome studies (Unpublished doctoral dissertation, University of North Texas, Denton).

McGuire, D. E. (2001). Child-centered group play therapy with children experiencing adjustment difficulties. *Dissertation Abstracts International: Section A. Humanities and Social Sciences, 61*(10), 3908.

Morrison, M., & Bratton, S. (2010). An early mental health intervention for Head Start programs: The effectiveness of child-teacher relationship training (CTRT) on children's behavior problems. *Psychology in the Schools, 47*(10), 1003–1017.

Ogawa, Y. (2006). Effectiveness of child-centered play therapy with Japanese children in the United States. *Dissertation Abstracts International, 68*(026), 0158.

Packman, J., & Bratton, S. C. (2003). A school-based group play/activity therapy intervention with learning disabled preadolescents exhibiting behavior problems. *International Journal of Play Therapy, 12*(2), 7–29.

Post, P. (1999). Impact of child-centered play therapy on the self-esteem, locus of control, and anxiety of at-risk 4th, 5th, and 6th grade students. *International Journal of Play Therapy, 8*(2), 1–18.

Post, P., McAllister, M., Sheely, A., Hess, B., & Flowers, C. (2004). Child centered kinder training for teachers of pre-school children deemed at risk. *International Journal of Play Therapy, 13*(2), 53–74.

Ray, D. C. (2007). Two counseling interventions to reduce teacher-child relationship stress. *Professional School Counseling, 10*(4), 428–440.

Ray, D. C. (2008). Impact of play therapy on parent-child relationship stress at a mental health training setting. *British Journal of Guidance and Counselling, 36,* 165–187.

Ray, D. C., Blanco, P. J., Sullivan, J. M., & Holliman, R. (2009). An exploratory study of child-centered play therapy with aggressive children. *International Journal of Play Therapy, 18*(3), 162–175.

Ray, D. C., Schottelkorb, A., & Tsai, M. (2007). Play therapy with children exhibiting symptoms of attention deficit hyperactivity disorder. *International Journal of Play Therapy, 16*(2), 95–111.

Ray, D. E. (2003). The effect of filial therapy on parental acceptance and child adjustment (Unpublished masters' thesis, Emporia State University, Kansas).

Rennie, R. L. (2003). A comparison study of the effectiveness of individual and group play therapy in treating kindergarten children with adjustment problems. *Dissertation Abstracts International: Section A. Humanities and Social Sciences, 63*(09).

Rhine, T. J. (2002). The effects of a play therapy intervention conducted by trained high school students on the behavior of maladjusted young children: Implications for school counselor. *Dissertation Abstracts International: Section A. Humanities and Social Sciences, 62*(10), 3304.

Schumann, B. R. (2010). Effectiveness of child-centered play therapy for children referred for aggression. In J. Baggerly, D. Ray, & S. Bratton (Eds.), *Child–centered play therapy research: The evidence base for effective practice* (pp. 143–208). Hoboken, NJ: Wiley.

Shashi, K., Kapur, M., & Subbakrishna, D. K. (1999). Evaluation of play therapy in emotionally disturbed children. *NIMHANS Journal, 17*(2), 99–111.

Sheely-Moore, A., & Bratton, S. (2010). A strengths-based parenting intervention with low-income African American families. *Professional School Counseling, 13*(3), 175–183.

Shen, Y. (2002). Short-term group play therapy with Chinese earthquake victims: Effects on anxiety, depression, and adjustment. *International Journal of Play Therapy, 11*(1), 43–63.

Smith, D. M., & Landreth, G. L. (2004). Filial therapy with teachers of deaf and hard of hearing preschool children. *International Journal of Play Therapy, 13*(1), 13–33.

Smith, N., & Landreth, G. (2003). Intensive filial therapy with child witnesses of domestic violence: A comparison with individual and sibling group play therapy. *International Journal of Play Therapy, 12*(1), 67–88.

Swanson, R. C. (2008). The effect of child centered play therapy on reading achievement in 2nd graders reading below grade level. *Master Abstracts International: Section A: Humanities and Social Sciences, 46*(5).

Tew, K., Landreth, G., Joiner, K. D., & Solt, M. D. (2002). Filial therapy with parents of chronically ill children. *International Journal of Play Therapy, 11*(1), 79–100.

Trostle, S. (1988). The effects of child-centered group play sessions on social-emotional growth of three- to six-year-old bilingual Puerto Rican children. *Journal of Research in Childhood Education, 3*, 93–106.

Tyndall-Lind, A., Landreth, G., & Giordano, M., (2001). Intensive group play therapy with child witnesses of domestic violence. *International Journal of Play Therapy, 10*(1), 53–83.

Villarreal, C. E. (2008). School-based child parent relationship therapy (CPRT) with Hispanic parents. *Dissertation Abstracts International: Section A. Humanities and Social Sciences, 69*(2).

Watson, D. (2007). An early intervention approach for students displaying negative externalizing behaviors associated with childhood depression: A study of efficacy of play therapy in the school. *Dissertation Abstracts International: Section A. Humanities and Social Sciences, 68*(5).

Yuen, T., Landreth, G., & Baggerly, J. (2002). Filial therapy with immigrant Chinese families. *International Journal of Play Therapy, 11*(2), 63–90.

Index

The Author

Garry L. Landreth, Ed.D., LPC, RPT-S, internationally known for his writings and work in promoting the development of child-centered play therapy, is a Regents Professor in the Department of Counseling, Development, and Higher Education at the University of North Texas. He is the founder of the Center for Play Therapy, the largest play therapy training program in the world and definitive leader in process and outcome research on Child-Centered Play Therapy and Child Parent Relationship Therapy (CPRT): A 10-Session Filial Therapy Model. Landreth has published more than 150 journal articles, books, and DVDs and is a frequent speaker at play therapy conferences around the world.

His award-winning book *Play Therapy: The Art of the Relationship* has been translated into several languages. Landreth's latest books *Child Parent Relationship Therapy (CPRT): A 10-Session Filial Therapy Model* and an accompanying *Child Parent Relationship Therapy (CPRT) Treatment Manual* received the 2010 Association for Parent Education Best Practices Award.

Landreth is a licensed professional counselor and Registered Play Therapy Supervisor. He is a founding member and Director Emeritus of the Association for Play Therapy (APT) and received the

APT Lifetime Achievement Award and the APT Research Award, the Meadows Honor Professor Award, the President's Outstanding Teacher Award, the Shelton Excellence in Teaching Award, the Toulouse Scholar Award, and the American Counseling Association Humanitarian and Caring Person Award. He is also the recipient of the Association for Humanistic Counseling Humanistic Impact Award, the Distinguished Service to International Education Award, and the Virginia Axline Distinguished Professional Award for his work in conceptualizing and advancing the child-centered approach to play therapy.